MADE IN AMERICA

MADE

—IN—

AMERICA

An Informal History of the English
Language in the United States

★ ★ ★

BILL BRYSON

WILLIAM MORROW AND COMPANY, INC.

New York

Library of Congress Cataloging-in-Publication Data
Bryson, Bill.
Made in America : an informal history of the English language in the
United States / Bill Bryson.
p.   cm.
Includes bibliographical references and index.
ISBN 0-688-10312-X
1. English language—United States—History.   2. Americanisms—
History.   I. Title.
PE 2809.B79 1995
420'.973—dc20   94-46451
                                                                          CIP

Printed in the United States of America

4   5   6   7   8   9   10

BOOK DESIGN BY SUSAN HOOD

To David, Felicity, Catherine, and Sam

CONTENTS

CONTENTS

INTRODUCTION

In the 1940s, a British traveler to Anholt, a small island fifty miles out in the Kattegat strait between Denmark and Sweden, noticed that the island children sang a piece of doggerel that was clearly nonsense to them. It went:

> *Jeck og Jill*
> *Vent op de hill . . .*
> *Og Jell kom tombling after*

The ditty, it turned out, had been brought to the island by occupying British soldiers during the Napoleonic Wars, and had been handed down from generation to generation of children for 130 years, even though the words meant nothing to them.

In London, this small discovery was received with interest by a couple named Peter and Iona Opie. The Opies had dedicated their lives to the scholarly pursuit of nursery rhymes. No one had put more effort into investigating the history and distribution of these durable but largely uncelebrated components of childhood life. Something that had long puzzled the Opies was the curious fate of a rhyme called "Brow Bender." Once as popular as "Humpty Dumpty" and "Hickory Dickory Dock," it was routinely included in children's nursery books up until the late eighteenth century, when it quietly and mysteriously vanished. It had not been recorded in print anywhere since 1788. Then one night as the Opies' nanny was tucking their children into bed, they overheard her reciting a nursery rhyme to them. It was, as you will have guessed, "Brow Bender," exactly as set down in the 1788 version but with five lines never before recorded.

Now what, you may reasonably ask, does any of this have to do with a book on the history and development of the English language in America? I bring it up for two reasons. First, to make the point that it is often the little, unnoticed things that are most revealing about the history and nature of language. Nursery rhymes, for example, are fastidiously resistant to change. Even when they make no sense, as in the case of "Jack and Jill" with children on an isolated Danish isle, they are generally passed from generation to generation with solemn precision, like treasured incantations. Because of this, they are sometimes among the longest-surviving features of any language. "Eenie, meenie, minie, mo" is based on a counting system that predates the Roman occupation of Britain, that may even be pre-Celtic. If so, it is a rare surviving link with the very distant past. It not only gives us a fragmentary image of how children were being amused at the time Stonehenge was built, but tells us something about how their elders counted and thought and ordered their speech. Little things, in short, are worth looking at.

The second point is that songs, words, phrases, ditties—any feature of language at all—can survive for long periods without anyone particularly noticing, as the Opies discovered with "Brow Bender." That a word or phrase hasn't been recorded tells us only that it hasn't been recorded, not that it hasn't existed. The inhabitants of England in the age of Chaucer commonly used an expression, *to be in hide and hair,* meaning to be lost or beyond discovery. But in about 1400 the expression vanished from the written record. For four hundred years there was no sign of it. Then, suddenly and unexpectedly, it resurfaced in America in 1857 as *neither hide nor hair.* So what exactly happened to this useful expression during those four long centuries, and what prompted its abrupt return to prominence in the sixth decade of the nineteenth century in a country two thousand miles away?

Why, come to that, did we in America save such good old English words as *skedaddle, chitterlings,* and *chore,* but not *fortnight* or *heath?* Why did we keep the irregular British pronunciations in words like *colonel* and *hearth,* but go our own way with *lieutenant* and *schedule* and *clerk?* Why, in short, is American English the way it is?

This is, it seems to me, a profoundly worthwhile and fascinating question, and yet until relatively recent times it is one that hardly anyone thought to ask. Until well into this century, serious studies of American speech were left almost entirely to amateurs—people like the heroic Richard Harwood Thornton, an English-born lawyer who devoted years of his spare time to poring through books, journals, and manuscripts from the earliest colonial period in search of the first appearances of hundreds of American terms. In 1912 he produced the two-volume

American Glossary. It was a work of invaluable scholarship, and he could not find a single American publisher prepared to take it on. Eventually, to the shame of American scholarship, it was published in London.

Not until the 1920s and 1930s, with the successive publications of H. L. Mencken's incomparable *The American Language*, George Philip Krapp's *The English Language in America*, and Sir William Craigie and James R. Hulbert's *Dictionary of American English on Historical Principles*, did America at last get books that seriously addressed the nature of its language. But by then the inspiration behind many American expressions had passed into the realms of the unknowable, so that now no one can say with any certainty why we *paint the town red, talk turkey, take a powder,* or hit practice flies with a *fungo bat.*

This book is a modest attempt to examine how and why American speech came to be the way it is, and in particular where our words come from. It is not, I hope, a conventional history of the American language. Much of it is unashamedly discursive. You could be excused for wondering what Mrs. Stuyvesant Fish's running over her servant three times in succession with her car has to do with the history and development of the English language in the United States, or how James Gordon Bennett's lifelong habit of yanking the cloths off every table he passed in restaurants connects to the linguistic development of the American people. I would argue that unless we understand the social context in which words were formed—unless we can appreciate what a bewildering novelty the car was to those who first encountered it, or how dangerously extravagant and out of touch with the masses a turn-of-the-century businessperson could be—we cannot begin to appreciate the richness and vitality of the words that make up our speech.

Oh, and I've included these incidental anecdotes for a third reason: because I thought they were interesting and hoped you might enjoy them. One of the small agonies of researching a book like this is that you come across stories that have no pressing relevance to the topic and must be passed over. I call them Ray Buduick stories.

I came across Ray Buduick when I was thumbing through a 1941 volume of *Time* magazines looking for something else altogether. It happened that one day in that year Buduick decided, as he often did, to take his light aircraft up for an early-Sunday-morning spin. Nothing remarkable in that, except that Buduick lived in Honolulu and that this particular morning happened to be December 7, 1941. As he headed out over Pearl Harbor and Mamala Bay, Buduick was taken aback, to say the least, to find the western skies dark with Japanese Zeroes, all bearing down on him. The Japanese raked his plane with fire, and Buduick, presumably issuing utterances along the lines of "Golly Moses," banked sharply and cleared off. Miraculously, he managed to land his plane safely in the midst of one of the greatest airborne attacks in history, and lived to tell the tale. In so doing he became the first American to engage the Japanese in combat, however inadvertently.

Of course, this has nothing at all to do with the American language. But everything else that follows does. Honestly.

I would like to express my gratitude to the following for generously sharing with me their time, knowledge, or research materials: Lawrence P. Ashmead, Samuel H. Beamesderfer, Bonita Lousie Billman, Bruce Corson, Heidi Du Belt, Andrew Franklin, Gary Galyean, Maria Guarnaschelli, James Mansley, Hobie and Lois Morris, Geoff Mulligan, Eric P. Newman, Robert M. Poole, Oliver Salzmann, Allan M. Siegal, Dr. John L. Sommer, Karen Voelkening, Erla Zwingle, and the staffs of the Drake University Library in Des Moines, the University of Massachusetts Library in Amherst, and the National Geographic Society Library in Washington. I am especially indebted to my mother, Mary Bryson, for feeding and accommodating me for long periods, and to Tom Engelhardt for his scrupulous copy editing, though any mistakes that remain are, of course, my own. Above all, and as ever, my infinite, heartfelt thanks to my wife, Cynthia.

MADE IN AMERICA

Chapter 1

THE *MAYFLOWER* AND BEFORE

I

The image of the spiritual founding of America that generations of Americans have grown up with was created, oddly enough, by a poet of limited talents (to put it in the most magnanimous possible way) who lived two centuries after the event in a country three thousand miles away. Her name was Felicia Dorothea Hemans and she was not American but Welsh. Indeed, she had never been to America and appears to have known next to nothing about the country. It just happened that one day in 1826 her local grocer in Rhyllon, Wales, wrapped her purchases in a sheet of two-year-old newspaper from Boston, and her eye was caught by a small article about a founders' day celebration in Plymouth. It was very probably the first she had heard of the *Mayflower* or the Pilgrims. But inspired as only a mediocre poet can be, she dashed off a poem, "The Landing of the Pilgrim Fathers (in New England)," which begins

> *The breaking waves dashed high*
> *On a stern and rock-bound coast,*
> *And the woods, against a stormy sky,*
> *Their giant branches toss'd*
>
> *And the heavy night hung dark*
> *The hills and water o'er,*
> *When a band of exiles moor'd their bark*
> *On the wild New England shore*

and carries on in a vigorously grandiloquent, indeterminately rhyming vein for a further eight stanzas. Although the poem was replete with errors—the *Mayflower* was not a bark, it was not night when they moored, Plymouth was not "where first they trod" but in fact marked their fourth visit ashore—it became an instant classic, and formed the essential image of the *Mayflower* landing that most Americans carry with them to this day.★

The one thing the Pilgrims certainly didn't do was step ashore on Plymouth Rock. Quite apart from the consideration that it may have stood well above the high-water mark in 1620, no prudent mariner would try to bring a ship alongside a boulder in a heaving December sea when a sheltered inlet beckoned nearby. If the Pilgrims even noticed Plymouth Rock, there is no sign of it. No mention of the rock is found among any of the surviving documents and letters of the age, and indeed it doesn't make its first recorded appearance until 1715, almost a century later.[1] Not until about the time Ms. Hemans wrote her swooping epic did Plymouth Rock become indelibly associated with the landing of the Pilgrims.

Wherever they landed, we can assume that the 102 Pilgrims stepped from their storm-tossed little ship with unsteady legs and huge relief. They had just spent nine and a half damp and perilous weeks at sea, crammed together on a creaking vessel small enough to be parked on a modern tennis court. The crew, with the customary graciousness of sailors, referred to them as *puke stockings,* on account of their apparently boundless ability to spatter the latter with the former, though in fact they had handled the experience reasonably well.[2] Only one passenger had died en route, and two had been added through births (one of whom ever after reveled in the exuberant name of Oceanus Hopkins).

They called themselves *Saints.* Those members of the party who were not Saints they called *Strangers. Pilgrims* in reference to these early voyagers would not become common for another two hundred years. Even later was *Founding Fathers.* It isn't found until the twentieth century, in a speech by Warren G. Harding. Nor, strictly speaking, is it correct to call them *Puritans.* They were *Separatists,* so called because they had left the Church of England. *Puritans* were those who remained in the Anglican Church but wished to purify it. They wouldn't arrive in America for another decade, but when they did they would quickly eclipse, and eventually absorb, this little original colony.

It would be difficult to imagine a group of people more ill-suited to a life in the wilderness. They packed as if they had misunderstood the purpose of the trip. They found room for sundials and candle snuffers,

---

★Mrs. Hemans's other contribution to posterity was the poem "Casabianca," now remembered for its opening line: "The boy stood on the burning deck."

a drum, a trumpet, and a complete history of Turkey. One William Mullins packed 126 pairs of shoes and thirteen pairs of boots. Yet they failed to bring a single cow or horse, plow or fishing line. Among the professions represented on the *Mayflower's* manifest were two tailors, a printer, several merchants, a silk worker, a shopkeeper, and a hatter—occupations whose indispensability is not immediately evident when one thinks of surviving in a hostile environment.[3] Their military commander, Miles Standish, was so diminutive of stature that he was known to all as "Captain Shrimpe"[4]—hardly a figure to inspire awe in the savage natives, whom they confidently expected to encounter. With the uncertain exception of the little captain, probably none in the party had ever tried to bring down a wild animal. Hunting in seventeenth-century Europe was a sport reserved for the aristocracy. Even those who labeled themselves farmers generally had scant practical knowledge of husbandry, since *farmer* in the 1600s, and for some time afterward, signified an owner of land rather than one who worked it.

They were, in short, dangerously unprepared for the rigors ahead, and they demonstrated their incompetence in the most dramatic possible way: by dying in droves. Six expired in the first two weeks, eight the next month, seventeen more in February, a further thirteen in March. By April, when the *Mayflower* set sail back to England,* just fifty-four people, nearly half of them children, were left to begin the long work of turning this tenuous toehold into a self-sustaining colony.[5]

At this remove, it is difficult to imagine just how alone this small, hapless band of adventurers was. Their nearest kindred neighbors—at Jamestown in Virginia and at a small and now all but forgotten colony at Cupers (now Cupids) Cove in Newfoundland†—were five hundred

---

*The *Mayflower*, like Plymouth Rock, appears to have made no sentimental impression on the colonists. Not once in *History of Plimouth Plantation*, William Bradford's history of the colony, did he mention the ship by name. Just three years after its epochal crossing, the *Mayflower* was unceremoniously broken up and sold for salvage. According to several accounts, it ended up being made into a barn that still stands in the village of Jordans, Buckinghamshire, about twenty miles from London, on the grounds of the British headquarters of the British Society of Friends, or Quakers. Coincidentally, almost in its shadow is the grave of William Penn, the founder of Pennsylvania. He almost certainly had no idea that the barn beside his eventual final resting place had once been the ship that carried Pilgrims to the land he himself did so much to promote.

†Founded in 1610, this small colony was abandoned in the 1630s, though it was soon replaced by other British settlements on the island. Because of their isolation, Newfoundlanders created a peculiarly colorful patois blending new coinages and old English dialectal words that now exist nowhere else: *diddies* for a nightmare,

miles off in opposite directions. At their back stood a hostile ocean, and before them lay an inconceivably vast and unknown continent of "wild and savage hue," in William Bradford's uneasy words. They were about as far from the comforts of civilization as anyone had ever been (certainly as far as anyone had ever been without a fishing line).

For two months they tried to make contact with the natives, but every time they spotted any, the Indians ran off. Then one day in February a young brave of friendly mien approached a party of Pilgrims on a beach. His name was Samoset and he was a stranger in the region himself. But he had a friend named Tisquantum from the local Wampanoag tribe, to whom he introduced them. Samoset and Tisquantum became the Pilgrims' fast friends. They showed them how to plant corn and catch wildfowl and helped them to establish friendly relations with the local *sachem,* or chief. Before long, as every schoolchild knows, the Pilgrims were thriving, and Indians and settlers were sitting down to a cordial Thanksgiving feast. Life was grand.

A question that naturally arises is *how* they managed this. Algonquian, the language of the eastern tribes, is an extraordinarily complex and agglomerative tongue (or more accurately family of tongues), full of formidable consonant clusters that are all but unpronounceable by the untutored, as we can see from the first primer of Algonquian speech prepared some twenty years later by Roger Williams in Connecticut (a feat of scholarship deserving of far wider fame, incidentally). Try saying the following and you may get some idea of the challenge:

> *Nquitpausuckowashâwmen*—There are a hundred of us.
> *Chénock wonck cuppee-yeâumen?*—When will you return?
> *Tashúckqunne cummauchenaûmisz?*—How long have you been sick?
> *Ntannetéimmin*—I will be going.[6]

Clearly this was not a language you could pick up in a weekend, and the Pilgrims were hardly gifted linguists. They weren't even comfortable with Tisquantum's name; they called him Squanto. The answer, surprisingly glossed over by most history books, is that the Pilgrims didn't have to learn Algonquian for the happy and convenient reason that Samoset and Squanto spoke English—Samoset only a little, but Squanto with total assurance (and some Spanish into the bargain).

---

nunny-bag for a kind of knapsack, *cocksiddle* for a somersault, *rushing the waddock* for the game of rugby. They continue to employ many odd pronunciations. *Chitterlings,* for instance, is pronounced "chistlings." The one word that Newfoundland has given the world is *penguin.* No one has any idea what inspired it.

That a straggly band of English settlers could in 1620 cross a vast ocean and find a pair of Indians able to welcome them in their own tongue seems little short of miraculous. It was certainly lucky—the Pilgrims would very probably have perished or been slaughtered without them—but not as wildly improbable as it at first seems. The fact is that by 1620 the New World wasn't really so new at all.

II

No one knows who the first European visitors to the New World were. Credit generally goes to the Vikings, who reached the New World in about A.D. 1000, but others *could* have been there earlier. An ancient Latin text, the *Navigatio Sancti Brendani Abbatis*, or *The Voyage of St. Brendan the Abbot*, recounts with persuasive detail a seven-year trip to a land across the sea claimed to have been made by this Irish saint and a band of acolytes some four centuries before the Vikings—and this, it was said, on the advice of another Irishman who claimed to have been there earlier still.

Even the Vikings didn't think themselves the first. Their sagas record that when they first arrived in the New World they were chased from the beach by a group of wild white people. They subsequently heard stories from natives of a settlement of Caucasians who "wore white garments and . . . carried poles before them to which rags were attached"[7]—precisely how an Irish religious procession might have looked to the uninitiated. Whether by Irish or Vikings—or Italians or Welsh or Bretons or any of the other many groups for whom credit has been sought—crossing the Atlantic in the Middle Ages was not quite as daring a feat as it would at first appear, even allowing for the fact that it was done in small, open boats. The North Atlantic is conveniently scattered with islands that could serve as stepping-stones—the Shetland Islands, the Faroes, Iceland, Greenland, and Baffin Island. It would be possible to sail from Scandinavia to Canada without once crossing more than 250 miles of open sea.

We know beyond doubt that Greenland—and thus, technically, North America—was discovered in 982 by one Eric the Red (Eirík Rauei), father of Leif Ericson (or Leif Eiríksson), and that he and his followers began settling it in 986. Anyone who has ever flown over the frozen wastes of Greenland could be excused for wondering what they saw in the place. In fact, Greenland's southern fringes are farther south than Oslo and offer an area of grassy lowlands as big as the whole of Britain.[8] Certainly it suited the Vikings. For nearly five hundred years they kept a thriving colony there, which at its peak boasted sixteen churches, two churches, two monasteries, some three hundred farms, and a population of four thousand. The one thing Greenland lacked was wood with which to build new ships and repair old ones—a somewhat vital consideration for a seagoing people. Iceland, the nearest landmass to the east, was barren. The most natural thing would be to head west to see what was out there. In about 1000, according to the sagas, Leif Ericson did just that. His expedition discovered a new landmass, probably Baffin Island, far up in northern Canada, over a thousand miles north of the present-day United States, and many other places, most notably the region they called Vinland.

Vinland's location is a tantalizing historical puzzle. Through careful readings of the sagas and calculations of Viking sailing times, various scholars have put Vinland all over the place—on Newfoundland or Nova Scotia, in Massachusetts, even as far south as Virginia. A Norwegian scholar named Helge Ingstad claimed in 1964 to have found Vinland at a place called L'Anse au Meadow in Newfoundland. Others suggest that the artifacts Ingstad unearthed were not of Viking origin at all, but merely the detritus of later French colonists.[9] The name is no help. According to the sagas, the Vikings called it Vinland because of the grapevines they found growing in profusion there. The problem is that no place within a thousand miles of where they might have been is likely to have supported wild grapes in abundance. One possible explanation is that Vinland was a mistranslation. *Vinber,* the Viking word for grapes, could be used to describe many other fruits—cranberries, gooseberries, and red currants, among them—that might have been found at these northern latitudes. Another possibility is that Vinland was merely a bit of deft propaganda, designed to encourage settlement. These were, after all, the people who thought up the name *Greenland.*

The Vikings made at least three attempts to build permanent settlements in Vinland, the last in 1013, before finally giving up. Or possibly not. What is known beyond doubt is that sometime after 1408 the Vikings abruptly disappeared from Greenland. Where they went and what became of them is a mystery.[10] The tempting presumption is that they found a more congenial life in North America.

There is certainly an abundance of inexplicable clues. Consider the matter of lacrosse, a game long popular with Indians across wide tracts of North America. Interestingly, the rules of lacrosse are uncannily like those of a game played by the Vikings, including one feature—the use of paired teammates who may not be helped or impeded by other players—so unusual, in the words of one anthropologist, "as to make the probability of independent origin vanishingly small." Then there were the Haneragmiuts, a tribe of Inuits living high above the Arctic Circle on Victoria Island in northern Canada, a place so remote that its inhabitants were not known to the outside world until early in this century. Yet several members of the tribe not only looked distinctly European but were found to be carrying indubitably European genes.[11] No one has ever provided a remotely satisfactory explanation of how this could be. Or consider the case of Olof and Edward Ohman, father and son, who in 1888 were digging up tree stumps on their farm near Kensington, Minnesota, when they came upon a large stone slab covered with runic inscriptions, which appear to describe how a party of thirty Vikings had returned to that spot after an exploratory survey to find the ten men they had left behind "red with blood and dead." The inscriptions have been dated to 1363. The one problem is how to explain why a party of weary explorers, facing the likelihood of renewed attack by hostile natives, would take the time to make elaborate carvings on a rock deep in the American wilderness, thousands of miles from where anyone they knew would be able to read it. Still, if a hoax, it was executed with unusual skill and verisimilitude.

All this is by way of making the point that word of the existence of a land beyond the Ocean Sea, as the Atlantic was then known, was filtering back to Europeans long before Columbus made his celebrated voyage. The Vikings did not operate in isolation. They settled all over Europe, and their exploits were widely known. They even left a map— the famous Vinland map—which is known to have been circulating in Europe by the fourteenth century. We don't positively know that Columbus was aware of this map, but we do know that the course he set appeared to be making a beeline for the mythical island of Antilla, which was featured on it.

Columbus never found Antilla or anything else he was looking for. His epochal voyage of 1492 was almost the last thing—indeed almost the only thing—that went right in his life. Within eight years, he would find himself summarily relieved of his post as Admiral of the Ocean Sea, returned to Spain in chains, and allowed to sink into such profound obscurity that we don't know for sure where he is buried. To achieve such a precipitous fall in less than a decade required an unusual measure of incompetence and arrogance. Columbus had both.

He spent most of those eight years bouncing around the islands of the Caribbean and coast of South America without ever having any real idea of where he was or what he was doing. He always thought that *Cipangu,* or Japan, was somewhere nearby and never divined that Cuba was an island. To his dying day he insisted that it was part of the Asian mainland (though there is some indication that he had his own doubts, since he made his men swear under oath that it was Asia or have their tongues cut out). His geographic imprecision is most enduringly preserved in the name he gave to the natives: *Indios,* which of course has come down to us as *Indians.* He cost the Spanish crown a fortune and gave in return little but broken promises. And throughout he behaved with the kind of impudence—demanding to be made hereditary Admiral of the Ocean Sea, as well as viceroy and governor of the lands that he conquered, and to be granted one-tenth of whatever wealth his enterprises generated—that all but invited his eventual downfall.

In this he was not alone. Many other New World explorers came seriously a cropper in one way or another. Juan Díaz de Solís and Giovanni da Verrazano were eaten by natives. Balboa, after discovering the Pacific, was betrayed by his colleague Francisco Pizarro and executed on trumped-up charges. Pizarro in his turn was murdered by rivals. Hernando de Soto marched an army pointlessly all over what is now the southeastern United States for four years until he caught a fever and died. Scores of adventurers, drawn on by tales of fabulous cities—*Quivira, Bimini,* the *City of the Caesars,* and *Eldorado* ("the gilded one")—went looking for wealth, eternal youth, or a shortcut to the Orient and mostly found misery. Their fruitless searches live on, sometimes unexpectedly, in the names on the landscape. *California* commemorates a Queen Califía, unspeakably rich but unfortunately nonexistent. *Amazon* denotes a mythical tribe of one-breasted women. *Brazil* and the *Antilles* recall fabulous, but also fictitious, islands.

Farther north the English fared little better. Sir Humphrey Gilbert perished in a storm off the Azores in 1583 after trying unsuccessfully to found a colony on Newfoundland. His half brother Sir Walter Raleigh, attempting to establish a settlement in Virginia, lost a fortune, and eventually his head, in the effort. Henry Hudson pushed his crew a little too far while looking for a northwest passage and found himself, Bligh-like, put to sea in a little boat, never to be seen again. The endearingly hopeless Martin Frobisher explored the Arctic region of Canada, found what he thought was gold, and carried fifteen hundred tons of it home on a dangerously overloaded boat only to be informed that it was worthless iron pyrites. Undaunted, Frobisher returned to Canada, found another source of gold, carted thirteen hundred tons of it back, and was informed, with presumed weariness on the part of the royal assayer, that it was the same stuff. After that, we hear no more of Martin Frobisher.

It is interesting to speculate what these daring adventurers would think if they knew how whimsically we commemorate them today. Would Giovanni da Verrazano think being eaten by cannibals a reasonable price to pay for having his name attached to a toll bridge between Brooklyn and Staten Island? I suspect not. De Soto found transient fame in the name of an automobile, Frobisher in a distant icy bay, Raleigh in a city in North Carolina, a brand of cigarettes, and a make of bicycle. On balance, Columbus, with a university, two state capitals, a country in South America, a province in Canada, and high schools almost without number, among a great deal else, came out of it pretty well. But in terms of linguistic immortality no one got more mileage from less activity than a shadowy Italian-born businessman named Amerigo Vespucci.

A Florentine who had moved to Seville, where he ran a ship supply business (one of his customers was his compatriot Christopher Columbus), Vespucci seemed destined for obscurity. How two continents came to be named in his honor involved an unlikely measure of coincidence and error. Vespucci did make some voyages to the New World (authorities differ on whether it was three or four), but always as a passenger or lowly officer. He was not, by any means, an accomplished seaman. Yet in 1504–1505, letters of unknown authorship began circulating in Florence, collected under the title *Nuovo Mundo* (New World), which stated that Vespucci had not only been captain of these voyages but had discovered the New World.

The mistake would probably have gone no further except that an instructor at a small college in eastern France named Martin Waldseemüller was working on a revised edition of the works of Ptolemy and decided to freshen it up with a new map of the world. In the course of his research he came upon the Florentine letters and, impressed with their spurious account of Vespucci's exploits, named the continent in his honor. (It wasn't quite as straightforward as that: first he translated *Amerigo* into the Latin *Americus,* then transformed that into its feminine form, *America,* on the ground that Asia and Europe were feminine. He also considered, and rejected, the name *Amerige.*) Even so it wasn't until forty years later that people began to refer to the New World as America, and then they meant only South America.

Vespucci did have one possible, if slightly marginal, claim to fame. He is thought to have been the brother of Simonetta Vespucci, the model for Venus in the famous painting by Botticelli.[12]

III

Since neither Columbus nor Vespucci ever set foot on the landmass that became the United States, it might have been more aptly named for Giovanni Caboto, an Italian mariner better known to history by his anglicized name of John Cabot. Sailing from Bristol in 1495, Cabot "discovered" Newfoundland and possibly Nova Scotia and a number of smaller islands, and in the process became the first known European since the Vikings to visit North America, though in fact he probably was merely following fishing fleets already trawling the Grand Banks. What is certain is that in 1475, because of a war in Europe, British fisherman lost access to their traditional fishing grounds off Iceland. Yet British cod stocks did not fall, and in 1490 (two years before Columbus sailed), when Iceland offered the British fishermen the chance to come back, they declined. The presumption is that they had discovered the cod-rich waters off Newfoundland and didn't want anyone else to know about them.[13]

Whether Cabot inspired the fishermen or they him, by the early 1500s the Atlantic was thick with English vessels. A few came to prey on Spanish treasure ships, made sluggish and vulnerable by the weight of gold and silver they were carrying back to the Old World. Remarkably good money could be made from this.* From a single voyage Sir Francis Drake returned to England with booty worth, at today's values, $60 million.[14] On the same voyage, Drake briefly put ashore in what is now Virginia, claimed it for the crown, and called it *New Albion*.[15]

To give the claim weight, and to provide a supply base for privateers, Queen Elizabeth I decided it might be a good idea to establish a colony there. She gave the task to Sir Walter Raleigh. The result was the ill-fated "lost colony" of Roanoke, whose 114 members were put ashore just south of Albemarle Sound in what is now North Carolina in 1587. From that original colony sprang seven names that still feature on the landscape: *Roanoke* (which has the distinction of being the first Indian word borrowed by English settlers), *Cape Fear, Cape Hatteras,* the *Chowan* and *Neuse* rivers, *Chesapeake,* and *Virginia.*[16] (Previously Virginia had been called *Windgancon,* meaning "what gay clothes you wear"—apparently what the locals had replied when an early reconnoitering party had asked the place's name.) But that, alas, was about all the colony achieved. Because of war with Spain, no English ship was able to return for three years. When at last a relief ship called, it found the colony deserted. Although the neighboring Croatoan tribe was eventually discovered to have incorporated several words of Elizabethan English into its own tongue, no firm evidence of the colony's fate was ever found.

Mostly what drew the English to the New World was the fishing, es-

---

*Spain was preyed on not only by sailors from rival nations, but also by mutineer sailors of her own. These latter were called *buccaneers* because after fleeing their Spanish masters they would sustain themselves on the preserved flesh of wild hogs, smoked on a wooden frame called a *boucan,* until they could capture a becalmed ship and make it their own.

pecially along the almost unimaginably bounteous waters off the northeast coast of North America. For at least 120 years before the *Mayflower* set sail, European fishing fleets had been an increasingly common sight along the eastern seaboard. The fleets would put ashore to dry fish, replenish stocks of food and water, or occasionally wait out a harsh winter. As many as a thousand fishermen at a time would gather on the beaches. It was from such groups that Samoset had learned his few words of English.

As a result, by 1620 there was scarcely a bay in New England or eastern Canada that didn't bear some relic of their passing. The Pilgrims themselves within their first days came upon an old cast-iron cooking pot, obviously of European origin, and while plundering some Indian graves they uncovered the body of a blond-haired man—"possibly a Frenchman who had died in captivity."[17]

New England may have been a new world to the Pilgrims, but it was hardly *terra incognita*. Much of the land around them had already been mapped. Eighteen years earlier, Bartholomew Gosnold and a party described as "24 gentlemen and eight sailors" had camped for a few months on nearby Cuttyhunk Island and left behind many names, two of which endure: *Cape Cod* and the romantically mysterious *Martha's Vineyard* (mysterious because we don't know who Martha was).

Seven years before, John Smith, passing by on a whaling expedition, had remapped the region, diligently taking heed of the names the Indians themselves used. He added just one name of his own devising: *New England*. (Previously the region had been called *Norumbega* on most maps. No one now has any clear idea why.) But in a consummate display of brownnosing, upon his return to England Smith presented his map to Charles Stuart, the sixteen-year-old heir apparent to the throne, along with a note "humbly intreating" His Highness "to change their barbarous names for such English, as posterity might say Prince Charles was their Godfather." The young prince fell to the task with relish. He struck out most of the Indian names that Smith had so carefully transcribed and replaced them with a whimsical mix that honored himself and his family, or that simply took his fancy. Among his creations were *Cape Elizabeth, Cape Anne,* the *Charles River,* and *Plymouth.* Consequently, when the Pilgrims landed at Plymouth one of the few tasks they didn't have to manage was thinking up names for many of the landmarks around them.

Sometimes the early explorers took Indians back to Europe with them. Such was the fate of the heroic Squanto, whose life story reads like an implausible picaresque novel. He had been picked up by a seafarer named George Weymouth in 1605 and carried off—whether voluntarily or not is unknown—to England. There he spent nine years working at various jobs before returning to the New World as an interpreter for John Smith on his voyage of 1613. In reward for his help, Smith gave Squanto his liberty. But no sooner had Squanto been reunited with his tribe than he and nineteen of his fellows were kidnapped by another Englishman, who carried them off to Málaga, Spain, and sold them as slaves. Squanto worked as a house servant in Spain before somehow managing to escape to England, where he worked briefly for a merchant in the City of London before finally, in 1619, joining yet another exploratory expedition along the New England coast.[18] Altogether he had been away for nearly fifteen years, and he returned to find that only a short while before his tribe had been wiped out by a plague—almost certainly smallpox introduced by visiting sailors.

Thus Squanto had certain grounds to be disgruntled. Europeans not only had inadvertently exterminated his tribe, but twice had carried him off and once sold him into slavery. Fortunately for the Pilgrims, Squanto was of a forgiving nature. He settled with them and for the next year, until he died of a sudden fever, served as their teacher, interpreter, ambassador, and friend. Thanks to him, the future of English in New England was assured.

The question of what kind of English it was, and would become, lies at the heart of what follows.

Chapter 2

BECOMING AMERICANS

We who*f*e names are underwritten, the loyal *f*ubjects of our dread *f*overeigne Lord, King James, by ye grace of God, of Great Britaine, France and Ireland, King, defender of ye faith, etc., haveing undertaken for ye glory of God and advancement of ye Christian faith, and honour of our King and countrie, a voyage to plant ye fir*f*t Colonie in ye Northerne parts of Virginia, doe by the*f*e pre*f*ents *f*olemnly, and mutualy . . . covenant and combine our*f*elves togeather into a civil body politick for our better ordering and pre*f*ervation and furtherance of ye end afore*f*aid . . .

So begins the Mayflower Compact, written in 1620 shortly before the *Mayflower* Pilgrims stepped ashore. The passage, I need hardly point out, contains some differences from modern English. We no longer use *f* for *s,* or *ye* for *the.** A few spellings—*Britaine, togeather, Northerne*—clearly vary from modern practice, but generally only slightly and not enough to confuse us, whereas only a generation before we would have found far greater irregularities (e.g., *gelousie, conseil, audacite, wiche, loware* for *jealousy, council, audacity, which,* and *lower*). We would not nowadays refer to a "dread sovereign," and if we did we would not mean by it one to be held in awe. But allowing for these few anachronisms, the passage is clear, recognizable, wholly accessible English.

Were we, however, somehow to be transported to the Plymouth Colony of 1620 and allowed to eavesdrop on the conversations of those who drew up and signed the Mayflower Compact, we would almost certainly be astonished at how different—how frequently incomprehensible—

---

*And that, incidentally, is all *ye* ever was—another way of writing *the*. It was a convenience for scribes and printers, a device that made it easier to justify lines. It was not pronounced "yee."

much of their spoken language would be to us. Though it would be clearly identifiable as English, it would be a variety of English unlike any we had heard before. Among the differences that would most immediately strike us:

• *Kn-*, which was always sounded in Middle English, was at the time of the Pilgrims going through a transitional phase in which it was commonly pronounced *tn*. Where the Pilgrims' parents or grandparents would have pronounced *knee* as "kuh-nee," they themselves would have been more likely to say "t'nee."

• The interior *gh* in words like *night* and *light* had been silent for about a generation, but on or near the end of words—in *laugh, nought, enough, plough*—it was still sometimes pronounced, sometimes left silent, and sometimes given an *f* sound.

• There was no sound equivalent to the *ah* in the modern *father* and *calm*. *Father* would have rhymed with the present-day *lather* and *calm* with *ram*.

• *Was* was pronounced not "wuz" but "wass," and remained so, in some circles at least, long enough for Byron to rhyme it with *pass* in "To Lucasta." Conversely, *kiss* was often rhymed with *is*.

• *War* rhymed with *car* or *care*. It didn't gain its modern pronunciation until about the turn of the nineteenth century.[1]

• *Home* was commonly spelled *whome* and pronounced, by at least some speakers, as it was spelled, with a distinct *wh-* sound.

• The various *o* and *u* sounds were, to put it mildly, confused and unsettled. Many people rhymed *cut* with *put, plough* with *screw, book* with *moon, blood* with *load*. As late as the second half of the seventeenth century, the poet John Dryden made no distinction between *flood, mood* and *good*, though quite how he intended them to be pronounced is anybody's guess. The vicissitudes of the wandering *oo* are still evident both in its multiplicity of modern pronunciations (e.g., *flood, mood, good*) and the number of such words in which the pronunciation is not fixed even now, notably *roof, soot*, and *hoof*.

• *Oi* was sounded with a long *i*, so that *coin'd* sounded like *kind* and *voice* like *vice*. The modern *oi* sound was sometimes heard, but was considered a mark of vulgarity until about the time of the American Revolution.

• Words that now have a short *e* were often pronounced and sometimes spelled with a short *i*. Shakespeare commonly wrote *bin* for *been*, and as late as the tail end of the eighteenth century Benjamin Franklin was defending a short *i* pronunciation for *get, yet, steady, chest, kettle*, and the second syllable of *instead*[2]—though by this time he was fighting a losing battle.

• Speech was in general much broader, with more emphatic stresses and a greater rounding of *r*'s. A word like *never* would have been pronounced more like "nev-*arr.*"[3] Interior vowels and consonants were more frequently suppressed, so that *nimbly* became "nimly," *fault* and *salt* became "faut" and "saut," *somewhat* was "summat." Other letter combinations were pronounced in ways strikingly at variance with their modern forms. In his *Special Help to Orthographie or the True-writing of English* (1643), a popular book of the day, Richard Hodges listed the following pairs of words as being "so neer alike in sound . . . that they are sometimes taken one for another": *ream* and *realm, shoot* and *suit, room* and *Rome, were* and *wear, poles* and *Paul's, flea* and *flay, eat* and *ate, copies* and *coppice, person* and *parson, Easter* and *Hester, Pierce* and *parse, least* and *lest.* The spellings—and misspellings—of names in the earliest records of towns like Plymouth and Dedham give us some idea of how much more fluid early colonial pronunciation was. These show a man named Parson sometimes referred to as Passon and sometimes as Passen; a Barsham as Barsum or Bassum; a Garfield as Garfill; a Parkhurst as Parkis; a Holmes as Holums; a Pickering as Pickram; a St. John as Senchion; a Seymour as Seamer; and many others.[4]

• Differences in idiom abounded, notably with the use of definite and indefinite articles. As Albert C. Baugh and Thomas Cable note in their classic *History of the English Language,* Shakespeare commonly discarded articles where we would think them necessary—"creeping like snail," "with as big heart as thou" and so on—but at the same time he employed them where we would not, so that where we say "at length" and "at last," he wrote "at the length" and "at the last." The preposition *of* was also much more freely employed. Shakespeare used it in many places where we would require another: "it was well done of [by] you," "I brought him up of [from] a puppy," "I have no mind of [for] feasting," "That did but show thee of [as] a fool."[5] One relic of this practice survives in American English in the way we tell time. Where we commonly say that it is "ten of three" or "twenty of four," the British only ever say "ten to" or "twenty to."

• *Er* and *ear* combinations were frequently, if not invariably, pronounced "ar," so that *convert* became "convart," *heard* was "hard" (though also "heerd"), and *serve* was "sarve." *Merchant* was pronounced and often spelled "marchant." The British preserve the practice in several words, saying "clark" and "darby" for *clerk* and *derby.* In America the custom was long ago abandoned but for a few well-established exceptions like *heart, hearth* and *sergeant,* or else the spelling was amended, so that *sherds* became *shards* and *Hertford,* Connecticut, was transformed to *Hartford.*

• Generally, words containing *ea* combinations—*tea, meat, deal* and so on—were pronounced with a long *a* sound (and of course many still are), so that, for example, *meal* and *mail* were homonyms. The modern *ee* pronunciation in such words was just emerging, so that Shakespeare could, as his whim took him, rhyme *please* with either *grace* or *knees.* Among more conservative users the old style persisted well into the eighteenth century, as in the well-known lines by the poet William Cowper

> *I am monarch of all I survey . . .*
> *From the centre all round to the sea.*

Different as this English was from modern English, it was nearly as different again from the English spoken only a generation or two before in the mid-1500s. In countless ways, the language of the Pilgrims was strikingly more advanced, less visibly rooted in the conventions and inflections of Middle English, than that of their grandparents or even parents.

The old practice of making plurals by adding *-n* was rapidly giving way to the newer convention of adding *-s,* so that by 1620 most people were saying *knees* instead of *kneen, houses* instead of *housen, fleas* instead of *flean.* The transition was by no means complete at the time of the Pilgrims—we can find *eyen* for *eyes* and *shoon* for *shoes* in Shakespeare—and indeed survives yet in a few words, notably *children, brethren* and *oxen.*

A similar transformation was happening with the terminal *-th* on verbs like *maketh, leadeth,* and *runneth,* which also were increasingly being given an *-s* ending. Shakespeare used *-s* terminations almost exclusively except for *hath* and *doth.* Only the most conservative works, such as the King James Bible of 1611, which contains no *-s* forms, stayed faithful to the old pattern. Interestingly, it appears that by the early seventeenth century even when the word was spelled with a *-th* termination it was pronounced as if spelled with an *-s.* In other words, people wrote *hath* but said "has," saw *doth* (pronounced "duth," incidentally, and not to rhyme with *moth*) but thought "does," read *goeth* as "goes." The practice is well illustrated in Hodges's *Special Help to Orthographie,* which lists as homophones such seemingly odd bedfellows as *weights* and *waiteth, cox* and *cocketh, rights* and *righteth, rose* and *roweth.*

At the same time, endings in *-ed* were beginning to blur. Before the Elizabethan age, an *-ed* termination was accorded its full phonetic value, as it still frequently is in *beloved* and *blessed* and a very few other words. But by the time of the Pilgrims the modern habit of eliding the ending (except after *t* and *d*) was taking over. For nearly two hundred years, this truncated pronunciation would be indicated in writing with an apostrophe: *drown'd, frown'd, weav'd,* and so on. Not until the end of the eighteenth century would the elided pronunciation become so general as to render this spelling distinction unnecessary.

The median *t* sound in *Christmas, soften, hasten,* and other such words was beginning to disappear. Just coming into vogue, too, was the *sh* sound of *ocean, creation, passion* and *sugar.* Previously such words had been pronounced with an *s* sound, as many Britons still say "tiss-you" and "iss-you" for *tissue* and *issue.*

The early colonists were among the first to use the new word *goodbye,* contracted from *God be with you* and still at that time often spelled *Godbwye,* and were among the first to employ the more democratic forms *ye* and *you* in preference to the traditional *thee, thy,* and *thou,* though many drifted uncertainly between the forms, as Shakespeare himself did, even sometimes in adjoining sentences as in *Henry IV, Part I:* "I love thee infinitely. But hark you, Kate."

They were also among the first to make use of the newly minted letter *j.* Previously *i* had served this purpose, so that Chaucer, for instance, wrote *ientyl* and *ioye* for *gentle* and *joy.* At first, *j* was employed simply as a variant of *i,* as *f* was a variant for *s.* Gradually *j* took on its modern *juh* sound, a role previously filled by *g* (and hence the occasional freedom in English to choose between the two letters, as with *jibe* and *gibe*).

Perhaps no period in history has been more accommodating to verbal innovation, more alive with neologisms, more kissed with genius, than that into which the Pilgrims were privileged to be born. Just in the century or so that preceded the Pilgrims' arrival in the New World, English gained ten thousand additional words, about half of them sufficiently useful as to be with us still. Shakespeare alone has been credited with some two thousand—*reclusive, gloomy, barefaced, radiance, dwindle, countless, gust, leapfrog, frugal, summit*—but he was by no means alone in this unparalleled outpouring.

A bare sampling of words that entered English around the time of the Pilgrims gives some *hint* (another Shakespeare coinage, incidentally) of the lexical vitality of the age: *alternative* (1590); *incapable* (1591); *noose* (1600); *nomination* (1601); *fairy, surrogate,* and *sophisticated* (1603); *option* (1604); *creak* in the sense of a noise and *susceptible* (1605); *coarse* in the sense of being rough (as opposed to natural) and *castigate* (1607); *obscenity* (1608); *tact* (1609); *commitment, slope, recrimination,* and *gothic* (1611); *co-*

alition (1612); *freeze* in a metaphoric sense (1613); *nonsense* (1614); *cult, boulder,* and *crazy* in the sense of insanity (1617); *customer* (1621); *inexperienced* (1626).

If the Pilgrims were aware of this linguistic ferment into which they had been born, they gave little sign of it. Nowhere in any surviving colonial writings of the seventeenth century is there a single reference to Shakespeare or even to the Puritans' own revered Milton. And in some significant ways their language is curiously unlike that of Shakespeare. They did not, for instance, show any particular inclination to engage in the new fashion of turning nouns into verbs, a practice that gave the age such perennially useful innovations as *to gossip* (1590), *to fuel* (1592), *to attest* (1596), *to inch* (1599), *to preside* (1611), *to surround* (1616), *to hurt* (1662), and several score others, many of which (*to happy, to property, to malice*) didn't last.

Yet the peculiar circumstances in which they found themselves forced the colonists to begin tinkering with their vocabulary almost from the first day. As early as 1622, they were using *pond,* which in England designated a small artificial pool, to describe large and wholly natural bodies of water. *Creek* in England described an inlet of the sea; in America it came to signify a stream. For reasons that have never, so far as I can tell, been properly investigated, the colonials quickly discarded many seemingly useful English topographic words—*hurst, mere, mead, heath, moor, marsh,* and (except in New England) *brook*—and began coming up with new ones, like *swamp* (first recorded in John Smith's *Generall Historie of Virginia* in 1626),[6] *ravine, hollow, range* (for an open piece of ground), and *bluff.* Often these were borrowed from other languages. *Bluff,* which has the distinction of being the first word attacked by the British as a misguided and obviously unnecessary Americanism, was probably borrowed from the Dutch *blaf,* meaning a flat board. *Swamp* appears to come from the German *zwamp,* and *ravine,* first recorded in 1781 in the diaries of George Washington though almost certainly used much earlier, is from the French.

Oddly, considering the extremities of the American climate, weather words were slow to arise. *Snowstorm,* the first meteorological Americanism, isn't recorded until 1771, and no one appears to have described a *tornado* in print before 1804. In between came *cold snap* in 1776, and that about exhausts America's contribution to the world of weather terms in the first two hundred years of European settlement. *Blizzard,* a word without which any description of a northern winter would seem incomplete, did not come to describe a heavy snowstorm until 1870, when a newspaper editor in Estherville, Iowa, applied it to a particularly fierce spring snow. The word, of unknown origin, had been coined in

America some fifty years earlier, but previously had denoted a blow or series of blows, as from fists or guns.

Where they could, however, the first colonists stuck doggedly to the words of the Old World. They preserved words with the diligence of archivists. Scores, perhaps hundreds, of English terms that would later perish from neglect in their homeland live on in America thanks to the essentially conservative nature of the early colonists.

Fall for *autumn* is perhaps the best known. It was a relatively new word at the time of the Pilgrims—its first use in England was recorded in 1545—but it remained in common use in England until the second half of the nineteenth century. Why it died out there when it did is unknown. The list of words preserved in America is practically endless. Among them: *cabin* in the sense of a humble dwelling, *bug* for any kind of insect, *hog* for a pig, *deck* as in a pack of cards and *jack* for a knave within the deck, *raise* for rear, *junk* for rubbish, *mad* in the sense of angry rather than unhinged, *bushel* as a common unit of measurement, *closet* for cupboard, *adze, attic, jeer, hatchet, stocks* as in stocks and bonds (the British have a stock market, but it deals in *shares*), *cross-purposes, livestock, gap* and (principally in New England) *notch* for a pass through hills, *gully* for a ditch or channel, *rooster* for the male fowl, *attic* for the topmost story of a house (the British say *loft*), *slick* as a variant of *sleek*, *zero* for nought, *back and forth* (instead of *backwards and forwards*), *plumb* in the sense of utter or complete, *noon★* for *midday*, *molasses* for *treacle*, *cesspool, homespun, din, trash, talented, chore, mayhem, maybe, copious*—and that is just a bare sampling.

The first colonists also brought with them many regional terms, little known outside their private corners of Britain, which prospered on American soil and have often since spread to the wider English-speaking world: *drool, teeter, hub, swamp, squirt* (as a term descriptive of a person), *spool* (for thread), *to wilt, catercornered, skedaddle* (a north British dialect word meaning to spill something noisy, like a bag of coal), *gumption, chump* (an Essex word meaning a lump of wood),[7] *scalawag, dander* (as in *to get one's dander up*), *chitterlings, chipper, chisel* in the sense of to cheat, and *skulduggery*. The last named has nothing to do with skulls—which is why it is spelled with one *l*—but comes from the Scottish *sculdudrie*, a word denoting fornication. *Chitterlings*, or *chitlins*, for the small intestines

---

★*Noon* is something of a curiosity. It comes from the Old English *nones*, meaning the ninth hour of daylight, or 3 P.M., when prayers were commonly said. It changed to 12 P.M. in the Middle Ages when the time of prayers changed to midday. But in Britain for a time it represented either of the twelfth hours, which explains references in older texts to "the noon of midnight" and the like.

of the pig, was unknown outside Hampshire until nourished to wider glory in the New World.[8] That it evolved in some quarters in America into *kettlings* suggests that the *ch-* may have been pronounced, by at least some people, with the hard *k* sound of *chaos* or *chorus.*

And of course they brought many words with them that have not survived in either America or Britain, to the lexical impoverishment of both—*flight* for a dusting of snow, *fribble* for a frivolous person, *bossloper* for a hermit, *spong* for a parcel of land, *bantling* for an infant, *sooterkin* for a sweetheart, *gurnet* for a protective sandbar, and the much-missed *slobberchops* for a messy eater, among many hundreds of others.

Everywhere they turned in their newfound land, the early colonists were confronted with objects that they had never seen before, from the mosquito (at first spelled *mosketoe* or *musketto*) to the persimmon to poison ivy, or "poysoned weed" as they called it. At first, no doubt overwhelmed by the wealth of unfamiliar life in their new Eden, they made no distinction between pumpkins and squashes or between the walnut and pecan trees. They misnamed plants and animals. *Bay, laurel, beech, walnut, hemlock, robin* (actually a thrush), *blackbird, hedgehog, lark, swallow* and *marsh hen* all signify different species in America from those of England.[9] The American rabbit is actually a hare. (That the first colonists couldn't tell the difference offers some testimony to their incompetence in the wild.) Often they took the simplest route and gave the new creatures names imitative of the sounds they made—*bobwhite, whippoorwill, katydid*—and when that proved impractical they fell back on the useful, and eventually distinctively American, expedient of forming a new compound from two older words.

Early American English positively teems with such constructions: *jointworm, eggplant, canvasback, copperhead, rattlesnake, bluegrass, backtrack, bobcat, catfish, bluejay, bullfrog, sapsucker, timberland, underbrush, cookbook, frostbite,* and *hillside* (at first sometimes called a *sidehill*), plus such vital later additions as *tightwad, sidewalk, cheapskate, sharecropper, skyscraper, rubberneck, drugstore, barbershop, hangover, rubdown, blowout,* and others almost without number. These new terms had the virtues of directness and instant comprehensibility—useful qualities in a land whose populace would increasingly include large numbers of nonnative speakers of English. *Frostbite* is clearly more descriptive than *chilblains, sidewalk* than *pavement, eggplant* than *aubergine, doghouse* than *kennel, bedspread* than *counterpane.*

One creature that very much featured in the lives of the earliest colonists was the passenger pigeon. The name comes from an earlier sense of *passenger* as one that passes by, and passenger pigeons certainly did that in almost inconceivably vast numbers. One early observer estimated a passing flock as being a mile wide and 240 miles long. They literally darkened the sky. At the time of the *Mayflower* landing there were perhaps nine billion passenger pigeons in North America, more than twice the number of all the birds found on the continent today. With such numbers they were absurdly easy to hunt. One account from 1770 reported that a hunter brought down 125 with a single shot from a blunderbuss. Some people ate them, but most were fed to pigs. Millions more were slaughtered for the sheer sport of it. By 1800 their numbers had been roughly halved, and by 1900 they were all but gone. On September 1, 1914, the last one died at the Cincinnati Zoo.

The first colonists were not, however, troubled by several other creatures that would one day plague the New World. One was the common house rat. It wouldn't reach western Europe for another century (emigrating there abruptly and in huge numbers from Siberia for reasons that have never been explained) and did not make its first recorded appearance in America until 1775, in Boston. Many other now-common animals, among them the house mouse and the common pigeon, were also yet to make their first trip across the ocean.

We know with some precision, however, when some species arrived, most notoriously that airborne irritant the starling, which was brought to America by one Eugene Schieffelin, a wealthy German emigrant who had the odd, and in the case of starlings regrettable, idea that he should introduce to the American landscape all the birds mentioned in the writings of Shakespeare. Most of the species he introduced failed to prosper, but the forty pairs of starlings he released in New York's Central Park in the spring of 1890, augmented by twenty more pairs the following spring, so thrived that within less than a century they had become the most abundant bird species in North America, and one of its greatest pests. Many thanks, Herr Schieffelin. The common house sparrow (actually not a sparrow at all but an African weaverbird) was in similar fashion introduced to the New World in 1851 or 1852 by the president of the Natural History Society of Brooklyn, and the carp by the secretary of the Smithsonian Institution in the 1870s.[10] That there were not greater ecological disasters from such well-meaning but often misguided introductions is a wonder.

Partly from lack of daily contact with England, partly from conditions peculiar to American life, and partly perhaps from whim, American English soon began wandering off in new directions. As early as 1682, Americans were calling folding money *bills* rather than *notes*. By 1751, *bureau* had lost its British meaning of a writing desk and come to mean a chest of drawers. *Barn,* in Britain a storehouse for grain, in America took on the wider sense of being a general-purpose farm building. *Av-*

enue by 1780 was being used to designate any wide street in America; in Britain it implied a line of trees—indeed, still does to the extent that many British towns have streets called Avenue Road. Other words of which Americans gradually enlarged the meanings include *apartment, pie, store, closet, pavement,* and *block. Block* in late-eighteenth-century America described a group of buildings having a similar appearance—what the British call a *terrace*—then came to mean a collection of adjoining lots, and finally, by 1823, was being used in its modern sense to designate an urban rectangle bounded by streets.[11]

But the handiest, if not always the simplest, way of filling voids in the American lexicon was to ask the local Indians what words they used. At the time of the first colonists there were perhaps fifty million Indians in the New World (though other estimates have put the figure as high as one hundred million and as low as eight million). Most lived in Mexico and the Andes. The whole of North America had perhaps no more than two million inhabitants. The Indians of North America are generally broken down into six geographic, rather than linguistic or cultural, families: Plains (among them the Blackfoot, Cheyenne, and Pawnee), Eastern Woodlands (the Algonquian family and Iroquois Confederacy), Southwest (Apache, Navajo, Pueblo), Northwest Coast (Haida, Modoc, Tsimshian), Plateau (Paiute, Nez Percé), and Northern (Kutchin, Naskapi). Within these groups, considerable variety was to be found. Among the Plains Indians, the Omaha and Pawnee were settled farmers, while the Cheyenne and Comanche were nomadic hunters. There was also considerable movement: the Blackfoot and Cheyenne, for example, began as eastern seaboard Indians, members of the Algonquian family, before pushing west into the Great Plains.

Despite, or perhaps because of, the relative paucity of inhabitants in North America, the variety of languages spoken on the continent was particularly rich, with perhaps as many as five hundred altogether. Put another way, the Indians of North America accounted for roughly one-twentieth of the population of the New World, but perhaps as much as a quarter of its tongues. Many of these languages—Puyallup, Tupi, Assiniboin, Hidatsa, Bella Coola—were spoken by only a handful of people. Even among related tribes the linguistic chasm could be considerable. The historian Charlton Laird has pointed out: "The known native languages of California alone show greater linguistic variety than all the known languages of the continent of Europe."[12]

Almost all the Indian terms taken directly into English by the first colonists come from the two eastern groups: the Iroquois Confederacy, whose members included the Mohawk, Cherokee, Oneida, Seneca, Delaware, and Huron tribes, and the even larger Algonquian group, which included Algonquin, Arapaho, Cree, Delaware, Illinois, Kicka-poo, Narragansett, Ojibwa, Penobscot, Pequot, Sac, and Fox, among many others. But here, too, there was considerable variability, so that to the Delaware Indians the river was the *Susquehanna*, while to the neigh-boring Hurons it was the *Kanastoge* (or *Conestoga*).

The early colonists began borrowing words almost from the moment of first contact. *Moose* and *papoose* were taken into English as early as 1603. *Raccoon* is first recorded in 1608, *caribou* and *opossum* in 1610, *moc-casin* and *tomahawk* in 1612, *hickory* in 1618, *powwow* in 1624, *wigwam* in 1628.[13] Altogether, the Indians provided some 150 terms to the early colonists. Another 150 came later, often after being filtered through in-termediate sources. *Toboggan,* for instance, entered English by way of Canadian French. *Hammock, maize,* and *barbecue* reached us via Spanish from the Caribbean.

Occasionally Indian terms could be adapted fairly simply. The Algon-quian *seganku* became without too much difficulty *skunk.* The *wuchak* settled into English almost inevitably as the *woodchuck.* (Despite the tongue twister, no woodchuck ever chucked wood.) *Wampumpeag* be-came *wampum.* The use of *neck* in the northern colonies was clearly in-fluenced by the Algonquian *naiack,* meaning a point or corner, from which comes the expression *that neck of the woods.* Similarly the prepon-derance of *capes* in New England is at least partly due to the existence of an Algonquian word, *kepan,* meaning a closed-up passage.[14]

Most Indian terms, however, were not so amenable to simple translit-eration. Many had to be brusquely and repeatedly pummeled into shape before any English speaker could feel comfortable with them. John Smith's first attempt at transcribing the Algonquian word for a tribal leader came out as *cawcawwassoughes.* Realizing that this was not re-motely satisfactory, he modified it to a still somewhat hopeful *coucorouse.* It took a later generation to simplify it further to the form we know to-day: *caucus.*[15] *Raccoon* was no less challenging. Smith tried *raugroughcum* and *rahaugcum* in the same volume, then later made it *rarowcun,* and sub-sequent chroniclers attempted many other forms—*aracoune* and *rockoon,* among them—before finally finding phonetic comfort with *rackoone.*[16] *Misickquatash* evolved into *sacatash* and eventually *succotash.* *Askutasquash* became *isquontersquash* and finally *squash.* *Pawcohiccora* became *pohickery* became *hickory.*

Tribal names, too, required modification. *Cherokee* was really *Tsalaki.* *Algonquin* emerged from *Algoumequins.* *Choctaw* was variously rendered as *Chaqueta, Shacktau,* and *Choktah* before settling into its modern angli-cized form. Even the seemingly straightforward *Mohawk* has no fewer than 142 recorded spellings.

Occasionally the colonists gave up. For a time they referred to an edible cactus by its Indian name, *metaquesunauk*, but eventually abandoned the fight and called it a *prickly pear.*[17] Success depended largely on the phonetic accessibility of the nearest contact tribe. Those who encountered the Ojibwa Indians found their dialect so deeply impenetrable that they couldn't even agree on the tribe's name. Some said *Ojibwa,* others *Chippewa.* By whatever name, the tribe employed consonant clusters of such a confounding density—*mtik, pskikye, kchimkwa,* to name but three[18]—as to convince the new colonists to leave their tongue in peace.

Often, as might be expected, the colonists misunderstood the Indian terms and misapplied them. To the natives, *pawcohiccora* signified not the tree but the food made from its nuts. *Pakan* or *paccan* was an Algonquian word for any hard-shelled nut. The colonists made it *pecan* (after toying with such variants as *pekaun* and *pecaun*) and with uncharacteristic specificity reserved it for the produce of the tree known to science as *Carya illinoensis.* ★

Despite the difficulties, the first colonists were perennially fascinated by the Indian tongues, partly no doubt because they were exotic, but also because they had a beauty that was irresistible. William Penn wrote: "I know not a language spoken in Europe, that hath words of more sweetness or greatness, in accent or emphasis, than theirs."[19] And he was right. You have only to list a handful of Indian place-names—*Mississippi, Susquehanna, Rappahannock*—to see that the Indians found a poetry in the American landscape that has all too often eluded those who displaced them.

If the early American colonists treated the Indians' languages with respect, they didn't always show such scruples with the Indians themselves. When circumstances were deemed to warrant it, they did not hesitate to impose a quite shocking severity, as a note from soldiers to the governor of the Massachusetts Bay Colony during King Philip's War reminds us: "This aforesaid Indian was ordered to be tourne to peeces by dogs, and she was so dealt with."[20] Indeed, early accounts of American encoun-

---

★At least the English colonists generally made some attempt to honor the Indian names. The French and Spanish appeared scarcely to notice what names the tribes used. The French ignored the name *Chopunnish,* the name used by a tribe of the Pacific Northwest, and instead called the people the *Nez Percé,* "pierced nose," for their habit of wearing seashells in their nostrils. They performed a similar disservice with *Siwash,* which is actually just a modified form of the French *sauvage,* "savage," and with *Gros Ventre* (French for "big belly"). The Spanish, meanwhile, ignored the comely, lilting name *Ha-no-o-shatch* ("children of the sun") and called this southwestern tribe *Pueblos,* "people."

ters with Indians tell us as much about colonial violence as about seventeenth-century orthography. Here, for instance, is William Bradford writing in his *History of Plimouth Plantation* describing a surprise attack on a Pequot village. The victims, it may be noted, were mostly women and children: "Those that scaped the fire were slaine with the sword; some hewed to peeces, others rune throw with rapiers, so as they were quickly dispatchte. . . . It was a fearful sight to see them thus frying in the fyre . . . and horrible was the styncke and sente there of, but the victory seemed a sweete sacrifice. . . ."[21] In 1675 in Virginia, John Washington, an ancestor of George, was involved in a not untypical incident in which the Indians were invited to settle a dispute by sending their leaders to a *powwow* (first recorded in 1624). The Indians sent five chiefs to parley, and when things did not go to the European settlers' satisfaction, they had the chiefs taken away and killed. Even the most faithful Indians were treated as expendable. When John Smith was confronted by hostile natives in Virginia in 1608, his first action was to shield himself behind his Indian guide.

In the circumstances, it is little wonder that the Native Americans began to view their new rivals for the land with a certain suspicion and to withdraw their goodwill. This was a particular blow to the Virginia colonists—or "planters," as they were somewhat hopefully called—who were as helpless at fending for themselves as the *Mayflower* Pilgrims would prove to be a decade later. In the winter of 1609–1610, they underwent what came to be known as the "starving time," during which brief period the number of Virginia colonists fell from five hundred to about sixty. When Sir Thomas Gates arrived to take over as the new governor the following spring, he found "the portes open, the gates from the hinges, the church ruined and unfrequented, empty howses (whose owners untimely death had taken newly from them) rent up and burnt, the living not able, as they pretended, to step into the woodes to gather other fire-wood; and, it is true, the Indian as fast killing without as the famine and pestilence within."[22]

Fresh colonists were constantly dispatched from England, but they perished almost as fast as they could be replaced. Between December 1606 and February 1625, Virginia received 7,289 immigrants and buried 6,040 of them. Most barely had time to settle in. All but 500 of the 3,500 immigrants who arrived in the three years 1619–1621 were dead by the end of the period. To go to Virginia was effectively to commit suicide.

For those who survived, life was a succession of terrors and discomforts, from hunger and homesickness to the dread possibility of being tomahawked in one's bed. The colonist Richard Frethorne wrote with a touch of forgivable histrionics: "I thought no head had been able to hold so much water as hath and doth dailie flow from mine eyes." He, too, was dead within the year.[23]

At least he was spared the messy end that awaited many of those who survived him. On Good Friday 1622, during a period of amity between the colonists and Native Americans, the Indian chief Opechancanough sent delegations of his tribes to the newly planted Virginia settlements of Kecoughtan, Henricus (also called Henrico or Henricopolis), and Charles City and their neighboring farms. It was presented as a goodwill visit—some of the Indians even "sate down at Breakfast," as one appalled colonial wrote afterward—but upon a given signal, the Indians seized whatever implements happened to come to hand and murdered every man, woman, and child they could catch, 350 in all, or about a third of Virginia's total English population.[24]

Twenty-two years later, in 1644, the same chief did the same thing, killing about the same number of people. But by this time the 350 deaths represented less than a twentieth of Virginia's English inhabitants, and Opechancanough's incursion was more a brutal annoyance than a catastrophe. Something clearly had changed in the interim. What it was can be summed up in a single word: *tobacco*. To the Indians of Virginia this agreeable plant was not tobacco, but *uppówoc*. *Tobacco* was a Spanish word, taken from the Arabic *tabāq*, signifying any euphoria-inducing herb. The first mention of tobacco in English was in 1565 after a visit by John Hawkins to a short-lived French outpost in Florida. With a trace of bemusement, and an uncertain mastery of the expository sentence, Hawkins reported that the French had "a kind of herb dried, who with a cane and an earthen cup on the end, with fire,—doe suck through the cane the smoke thereof."[25] Despite Hawkins's apparent dubiousness about just how much pleasure this sort of thing could bring, he carried some tobacco back to England with him, where it quickly caught on in a big way. At first the practice of partaking of tobacco was called "drinking" it, before it occurred to anyone that "smoking" might be a more apt term. Wonderful powers were ascribed to the plant. Tobacco was believed to be both a potent aphrodisiac and a marvelously versatile medicine, which "purgeth superfluous phlegm and other gross humours, and openeth all the pores and passages of the body."[26] Before long, it was all the rage and people simply couldn't get enough of it.

The Jamestown colonists began planting it in the second decade of the seventeenth century and found to their joy that it grew nearly as well as poison ivy. Suddenly fortunes were to be made in Virginia. People began to flock to the colony in numbers the Indians couldn't cope with. Virginia's future was secure, and almost entirely because of an addictive plant.

In the meantime, the persecution of Puritans in Britain made New England a much less lonely spot. During the years 1629–1640, eighty thousand Puritans fled the Old World for the New. Only some twenty thousand went to New England. As many more settled in the Caribbean, in places like Barbados and St. Kitts. Some formed a new, and now almost wholly forgotten, colony on Old Providence Island along Nicaragua's Mosquito Coast. The West Indies for a long time were in fact the most populous part of the New World. By 1700, Barbados had almost a third more English-speaking inhabitants than Virginia and more than twice as many as New York. Nonetheless, enough Britons settled in Massachusetts to secure its future beyond doubt. By the beginning of the eighteenth century it had a population of eighty thousand. Its wealth, too, had an unseemly side. As early as 1643, just twenty-two years after the Pilgrim Fathers first planted their feet on American soil with a view to creating a good and godly place, New England entrepreneurs were busily engaged in an enterprise that would make them very rich indeed: the slave trade.

Such was the outflow of immigrants in the seventeenth century that by 1700 the British government had grown considerably alarmed by the exodus of sturdy, industrious people and effectively cut off the supply, apart from regular boatloads of transported felons.★ Convicts apart, very few true English men or women emigrated to America after 1700. Nonetheless, in the first half of the century the population of the colonies quadrupled. It achieved this apparent paradox by drawing large numbers of people from other New World colonies—Carolina, for instance, was founded in 1669 by only about a hundred people from England; the rest were planters from Barbados[27]—and from an influx of non-English peoples: Germans, French, and most especially Scotch-Irish from Ulster, of whom possibly as many as 250,000 arrived just in the middle fifty years of the eighteenth century.[28] All of this contributed significantly to America's long, slow drift away from the standard, London-based branch of English.

★Not all of them made it. In the late seventeenth century a Thomas Benson secured a contract to transport convicts from Britain to the southern colonies of America, but quickly realized it was simpler to dump them on the isle of Lundy, a lump of granite within sight of the Devon coast. When he was at last caught, he claimed to have fulfilled his contract because he had taken them "overseas." The magistrates were unpersuaded and fined him £7,872. The fate of the stranded convicts is unknown.

Sprinkled among the new arrivals were a small number of involuntary immigrants from West Africa. The first twenty black Africans, or "Negars" as they were described on the ship's manifest, were sold in Virginia as early as 1619, though not until late in the century did blacks begin to arrive in substantial numbers. At first, Africans were regarded as servants, with the same rights of eventual earned freedom as indentured whites. White and black servants alike were called *slaves,* the term having temporarily lost its sense of permanent involuntary servitude. Servants were termed *indentured* because their contract was indented, or folded, along an irregular line and torn in two, master and servant each keeping one half.[29]

For most blacks, the prospect of eventual earned freedom did not last long. By the 1650s, an estimated 70 percent of Africans in Virginia were regarded by their masters as chattel, and sometimes used as collateral for loans or passed on in wills, actions unthinkable for white servants.[30] In 1705, Virginia made the matter official by enacting a law decreeing that "all servants imported and brought into this country, by sea or land, who were not christians in their native country" could be held in permanent involuntary servitude ("notwithstanding a conversion to christianity afterwards," the law added in a tone of afterthought).[31] The *peculiar institution,* as it would become euphemistically known, was born.

Against this complex background of movement and social change, a country began to emerge—loosely structured, governed from abroad, populated by an unlikely mix of refugees, idealists, slaves and convicts, but a country nonetheless. By the fourth decade of the eighteenth century the British were feeling sufficiently confident of their standing in the New World to begin looking for an excuse to throw their weight around a little. In 1739, the Spanish gave it to them when they made manifest their long and wholly understandable exasperation with British privateers by cutting off the ear of an English smuggler named Edward Jenkins. Never mind that Jenkins was little more than a common criminal. The British responded by launching possibly the only interesting sounding conflict in history, the War of Jenkins' Ear.

The war was in fact pretty dull, but it did have a couple of interesting linguistic spinoffs. One came with the introduction of a daily ration of rum and water for the sailors of the British fleet on the instructions of Admiral Edward Vernon. Vernon's nickname was Old Grog—no one seems to know why—and the drink, as you will doubtless have guessed, was soon called *grog.* (And those who drank too much of it would perforce become *groggy.*) Vernon was by all accounts an inspiring figure, and was greatly loved by his men. One of his colonial officers, Lawrence

Washington, half brother of George, was so taken with the admiral that he named his Virginia plantation Mount Vernon in his honor.

But—and here we come to the point of all this—the euphonious if largely forgotten War of Jenkins' Ear marked a telling semantic transition. It was then for the first time that the British began to refer to their colonial cousins as *Americans,* rather than as *provincials* or *colonials.* *American* had been recorded as early as 1578, but previously had been applied only to the native Indians. No one realized it yet, but a new nation had begun.

Chapter 3

A "DEMOCRATICAL PHRENZY": AMERICA IN THE AGE OF REVOLUTION

I

When dawn broke on that epochal year 1776—a year that would also see the publication of Adam Smith's *Wealth of Nations* and the first volume of Edward Gibbon's *Decline and Fall of the Roman Empire*—America's war with her British masters was already, in a sense, several years old.

The much-despised Stamp Act was eleven years in the past. It was nearly three years since the Boston Tea Party (which wouldn't in fact generally be called that for another half century) and six since the infamous Boston Massacre. It had been nine months since some unknown soul had stood on Concord green and fired, in Emerson's memorable phrase, "the shot heard round the world," and not much less since the bloody, curiously misnamed Battle of Bunker Hill, which did not take place on Bunker Hill at all (or Bunker's Hill, as it was then more commonly called). Though the battle was intended to take place on Bunker Hill (these matters being rather more formally arranged in the eighteenth century), for reasons unknown colonial troops under Colonel William Prescott fortified neighboring Breed's Hill instead, and it was there that the first pitched battle of America's war for independence was fought. To complicate matters, Breed's Hill was often thereafter referred to as Bunker Hill.

At any rate, and by any measure, in January 1776, Britain and a significant portion of her American colonies were at war.

We might reasonably ask why. In 1776, Americans already were "the freest people in the world," as Samuel Eliot Morison has noted.[1] Most Americans enjoyed economic mobility, the right to vote for their own local representatives, a free press, and the benefits of what one English contemporary tellingly called a "most disgusting equality." They ate better, were more comfortably housed, and on the whole were probably better educated than their British cousins. (In Massachusetts, for instance, the literacy rate was at least double that of Britain.)[2] The Revolution when it came would not be to secure America's freedom, but to preserve it.

What they did lack was seats in Parliament. They resented—not unreasonably, it seems to us today—being required to pay taxes to the mother country when they were denied a voice in the House of Commons. To the British, such a notion was overambitious, if not actually preposterous, since most Britons did not themselves enjoy such a lavish franchise. Only about one Briton in twenty had the right to vote, and even some large thriving cities such as Liverpool and Manchester had no directly elected member of Parliament. Why should mere colonists, the semi-British, be accorded greater electoral privilege than those reared on British soil?

Nor, it should be noted, were the taxes levied on the colonists by any stretch onerous. The principal aim of the stamp duties and other revenue-raising measures was to fund the protection of the colonies. It was hardly beyond the bounds of reason to expect the colonists to make a contribution toward the cost of their own defense. Even so, Americans were lightly taxed. In the 1760s, it was estimated, the average American paid about sixpence a year in tax. The average Briton paid twenty-five shillings—fifty times as much. And in any case, Americans seldom actually paid their taxes. The hated Townshend duties cost £170,000 to implement and raised just £295 in revenue in their first year. The equally reviled Stamp Act duties were never collected at all.

Nonetheless, as every schoolchild knows, throughout the 1770s America rang with the cry "Taxation without representation is tyranny." Actually, not. James Otis, to whom the phrase is commonly attributed, appears never to have said any such thing—or at least if he did no one at the time noticed. The famous words weren't ascribed to him until 1820, nearly forty years after he died.[3]

In fact, many of the expressions traditionally associated with the struggle for independence were never uttered. Patrick Henry, for example, almost certainly didn't issue the defiant cry "If this be treason, make the most of it" or any of the other deathless remarks confidently attributed to him in the Virginia House of Burgesses in May 1765. The clerk of the convention made no notes of Henry's speech, and none of those present gave any hint in their correspondence that Henry's remarks had been particularly electrifying that day. According to the one surviving eyewitness account—written by a French hydrologist who just happened to be present, and found quite by chance in the archives of the

National Hydrological Institute of France in 1921—Henry *did* make some intemperate remarks, but, far from being defiant, he immediately apologized to the House of Burgesses if "the heat of passion might have lead [*sic*] him to have said something more than he intended" and timidly professed undying loyalty to the king—not quite the show of thrust-jawed challenge portrayed in countless schoolbooks.[4]

If Henry did engage in a little nervous backpedaling, we should not be altogether surprised. He was the junior member of the house, having taken his seat only nine days earlier. His brave and eloquent challenge to monarchy appears to have been invented from whole cloth forty-one years later, seventeen years after Henry died, by a priggish biographer named William Wirt, who had never met, seen, or heard him. Thomas Jefferson, who *was* there, made no comment about the accuracy or otherwise of Wirt's account of events on that day, but he did freely offer the opinion that Wirt's effort was "a poor book, written in bad taste, and gives an imperfect idea of Patrick Henry." Nor, while we are at it, is there any evidence that Henry ever uttered the other famous remark attributed to him: "I know not what course others may take; but as for me, give me liberty or give me death." Indeed, there is no evidence that Henry ever said *anything* of substance or found space in his head for a single original thought. He was a country bumpkin, unread, poorly educated, and famously indolent. His turn of phrase was comically provincial and frequently ungrammatical. He did, it is true, have certain oratorical powers, but these appeared to owe more to a gift for hypnotic sonorosity than to any command of thought or language. His style of speech was a kind of verbal sleight of hand that, in the words of one contemporary, "baffled all description." Jefferson once bemusedly recalled: "When he had spoken in opposition to my opinion, had produced a great effect, and I myself been highly delighted and moved, I have asked myself when it ceased, 'What the Devil has he said,' and could never answer the enquiry."[5]

Even those events that did unquestionably take place were often selectively reinterpreted to show the colonials in a more favorable light. Take, for example, the Boston Massacre, or the "Bloody Massacre Perpetrated in King Street, Boston," as it was provocatively called in Paul Revere's famous engraving. Revere's rendition shows the British Redcoats, or *lobsterbacks* as they were dismissively known, taking careful aim in broad daylight at a small, startled gathering of colonials, as if impulsively executing midday shoppers. It wasn't like that. Five colonials did lose their lives in the incident, but at night, amid great confusion, and after twenty British soldiers were repeatedly taunted, jostled, pelted with stones and other missiles, and generally menaced by a drunken mob. By the standards of the day, the British troops were eminently justified in replying with fire. John Adams, at any rate, had no hesitation in defending the soldiers in court (and securing the acquittal of all but two, who had their thumbs branded, a light punishment indeed in a murder trial). It was his more hotheaded cousin, Sam Adams, who with the help of Paul Revere's artwork turned the incident into effective propaganda and popularized the expression *Boston Massacre*.★

Two hundred years of mythmaking have left us with the impression that by early 1776 most patriotic Americans were aching to break free of their British shackles. In point of fact, in early 1776 most Americans were not merely reluctant to part with Britain, they had never even *dreamed* of such a thing. Until well after the Revolution had started, Washington and his officers were continuing the nightly tradition of toasting the mother country (if not the monarch himself) and the Continental Congress was professing an earnest—we might almost say slavish—loyalty, insisting, even as it was taking up arms, that "we mean not to dissolve the union which has so long and happily subsisted between us" and professing a readiness to "cheerfully bleed in defense of our Sovereign in a righteous cause." Their argument, they repeatedly assured themselves, was not with Britain but with George III. (The Declaration of Independence, it is worth noting, indicted only "the present King of Great Britain.") As the historian Bernard Bailyn has put it: "It is not much of an exaggeration to say that one had to be a fool or a fanatic in early January 1776 to advocate American independence."[6]

Fortunately there existed a man who was a little of both. He had been born Thomas Pain, though upon arrival in America he whimsically changed the spelling to Paine, and he was about as unlikely a figure to change the course of history as you could imagine. A tumbledown drunk, coarse of manner, blotchy-faced and almost wholly lacking in acquaintance with the virtues of soap and water—"so neglectful in his person that he is generally the most abominably dirty being upon the face of the earth," in the words of one contemporary—he had been a

---

★For almost a century afterward, Paul Revere was known in America, insofar as he was known at all, not for his midnight ride but as the maker of that engraving. It wasn't until Henry Wadsworth Longfellow wrote his romantic and widely inaccurate poem "Paul Revere's Ride" (from *Tales of a Wayside Inn*) in 1863 that Revere became known as anything other than an engraver and silversmith. Among the inaccuracies, Revere didn't hang the lanterns in the old North Church, because it wasn't called that until later, and at the time of the Revolution it was Christchurch; he made two rides, not one; and he never made it to Concord, as Longfellow has it, but in fact was arrested along the way.

failure at every trade he had ever attempted, and he had attempted many, from corset making to tax collecting, before finally, at the age of thirty-eight, abandoning his native shores and his second wife and coming to America.

But he could write with extraordinary grace and power, and at a time of immense emotional confusion in America, he was possessed of an unusually clear and burning sense of America's destiny. In January 1776, less than two years after he had arrived in the colonies, Paine anonymously published a slender pamphlet that he called (at the suggestion of his friend and mentor Benjamin Rush) *Common Sense.*

To say that it was a sensation merely hints at its impact. Sales were like nothing that had been seen before in the New World. A hundred thousand copies were sold in the first two months, 400,000 copies overall—this in a country with just three million inhabitants. It was the greatest best-seller America has ever seen, and it didn't make Paine a penny. He assigned the copyright to the Continental Congress, and thus not only galvanized America into revolution but materially helped to fund it.

It was a breathtakingly pugnacious tract. Writers did not normally refer to the king as "a sottish, stupid, stubborn, worthless, brutish man" and "the royal brute of England" or accuse him of sleeping with "blood upon his soul."[7] Above all, Paine argued forcefully and unequivocally for independence: "Everything that is right or reasonable pleads for separation. The blood of the slain, the weeping voice of nature cries, 'Tis time to part.' " He was one of the first writers to employ *republic* with a positive connotation and helped to give *revolution* its modern sense, rather than merely to describe the movements of celestial spheres. And he did it all in language that anyone who could read could understand.

Jefferson freely acknowledged that his prose in the Declaration of Independence was indebted to Paine, whose "ease and familiarity of style" he thought unrivaled. Others were less convinced. Benjamin Franklin believed Paine's writing lacked dignity. Gouverneur Morris dismissed him as "a mere adventurer." John Adams, never short of an acid comment, called *Common Sense* "a poor, ignorant, malicious, short-sighted, crapulous mass," and likened Paine to a common criminal. But it had the desired effect.

Paine's value was not as an originator of ideas, but as a communicator of them. He was a consummate sloganeer. In *Common Sense* and a flurry of following works, he showered the world with ringing phrases that live on yet: "the Age of Reason"; "the Rights of Man"; "That government is best which governs least"; "These are the times that try men's souls"; "The summer soldier and the sunshine patriot." Less poetically but no less memorably, he was the first to refer to the "the United States of America." Previously even the boldest patriot had spoken of the "United Colonies." Under Paine's influence, Americans became seized with what one British onlooker uneasily termed "a Democratical phrenzy."[8]

It is easy to forget that those who started the Revolution did not think of themselves as Americans in anything like the way we do today. They were British and proud of it. To them, *American* was more a descriptive term than an emotional one. Their primary attachments were to their colonies. When Jefferson wrote to a friend that he longed "to return to my own country," he meant Virginia.[9] In 1765, Christopher Gadsden of South Carolina lamented: "There ought to be no New England men, no New York, etc., known on the Continent, but all of us Americans."[10] That he felt it necessary to articulate the sentiment is revealing.

Their exposure to other colonies was often strikingly limited. John Adams, for one, had never been out of his home colony. In 1776, Philadelphia was the second-largest city in the English-speaking world, but more of the delegates to the Second Continental Congress had been to London than to Pennsylvania. Despite the interposition of three thousand miles of ocean, London remained the effective center of American culture and politics. Garry Wills has noted: "Till almost the eve of the Revolution, resistance to imperial policy was better schemed at in London than in the colonies. . . . London [was] where policy was made and colonial protests directed, where colonial agents were located and a community of Americans from the whole continent resided."[11]

In Philadelphia, they convened in a spirit of excitement mixed with high caution. Though they came from similar backgrounds—nine of Virginia's twelve delegates were related by blood or marriage[12]—they were wary of one another, and not without reason. They were engaged in treason, and anyone who betrayed them would have much to gain. The step they were taking was radical and irreversible, and the consequences terrifying. The penalty for treason was to be hanged, cut down while still alive, disemboweled and forced to watch your organs burned before your eyes, then beheaded and quartered.[13] The widows of such traitors would be deprived of their estates and their children subjected to a life of opprobrium. Benjamin Franklin was no more than half jesting when he quipped to his fellow delegates—and here at last we have a famous remark that appears actually to have been uttered—"We must all hang together or assuredly we shall all hang separately." (Yet Franklin, thanks to his close ties with England and his initial support for the

Stamp Act, was held by many of his fellows to be one of the most suspect of the lot.)

So what did they sound like, these new Americans? Had they by 1776 adopted a distinctive American accent? Did Jefferson speak with a southern drawl and Adams with the pinched nasal tones of a New Englander, or did they sound like the Englishmen they still loosely felt themselves to be? The evidence is tantalizingly ambiguous. Certainly regional differences had been evident in America for some time. As early as 1720, visitors to New England spoke of a "New England twang," which bore a noticeable resemblance to the "Norfolk whine" of England. In much the same way, visitors to the South sometimes remarked on the resemblance of speech there to the Sussex accent. Some detected quite specific differences. One observer in 1780 claimed that natives of the neighboring towns of Easthampton and Southampton on Long Island could be distinguished in an instant by their peculiarities of speech. Much the same claim was sometimes made for proximate communities in Virginia.

The evidence suggests that in 1776, Southerners would have been struck by the New England habit of saying "kee-yow" and "nee-yow" for *cow* and *now,* for saying "marcy" for *mercy,* "crap" for *crop,* and "drap" for *drop.* (This last variation, incidentally, accounts for our pair of words *strap* and *strop.*) Northerners would have regarded as curious the Southerners' habit of saying "holp" for *help,* for rhyming *wound* in the sense of an injury with *swooned*—New Englanders rhymed it with *crowned*—and for using *y'all* for a collective sense of *you* (a practice that had been a distinguishing feature of southern speech since the 1600s).

In his much-praised book *Albion's Seed,* David Hackett Fischer argues that regional accents—indeed, discrete regional cultures—were in place in America by the time of the Revolution. He points out that American colonists came in four distinct waves: Puritans from eastern England to New England, 1629–1640; a mix of elite royalists and indentured servants to Virginia, 1642–1675; groups from the north Midlands and Wales to the Delaware Valley, beginning in about 1675; and a great mass from the Scottish borders and Northern Ireland to Appalachia, 1718–1775. "By the year 1775," he writes, "these four cultures were fully established in British America. They spoke distinctive dialects of English, built their houses in diverse ways, and had different methods of doing much of the ordinary business of life."[14]

By assembling in America in enclaves that reflected their geographic origins, the four main waves of immigrants thus managed to preserve distinctive regional identities. That is why, for instance, horses in New

England (as in East Anglia) *neigh,* while those in the middle states of America (and the Midlands of England) *whinny.*[15] Noting that many words became associated early on with the speech of Virginia—*afeared, howdy, catercorner, innards, traipse, woebegone, bide* and *tarry* for stay awhile, *tote* for carry, *disremember* for forget, *pekid* for being pale or unwell—Fischer says: "Virtually all peculiarities of grammar, syntax, vocabulary and pronunciation which have been noted as typical of Virginia were recorded in the [southern England] counties of Sussex, Surrey, Hampshire, Dorset, Wiltshire, Somerset, Oxford, Gloucester, Warwick or Worcester."[16] They may indeed have been recorded there—it would be surprising if they were not—but at least some of the words he uses to support his thesis (for instance, *poorly* for being unwell and *right good* for something meritorious or agreeable) were primarily northern English expressions.

Neat though it is, Fischer's argument presents two problems. First, with the exception of the final wave of immigrants from the Scottish borders and Ulster, the geographic background of colonial immigrants was nothing like as uniform as Fischer implies. The Puritan movement may have had its base in East Anglia—and this clearly accounts for the preponderance of East Anglian place-names in Massachusetts and Connecticut—but its followers came from every corner of England. The *Mayflower* manifest alone shows passengers hailing from Yorkshire, Devon, Lincolnshire, Westmorland, and many other counties linguistically distinct from East Anglia. Equally, an indentured servant was as likely to come from Lanarkshire or Wales or Cornwall as from London. George Washington's forebears emigrated to America from Northumbria and settled in Virginia. Benjamin Franklin's came from a town just a dozen miles away, but settled in Boston. Throughout the colonial period, immigrants came from all over and settled all over. And once settled in the New World, significant numbers of them moved on—as, for example, Franklin transplanted himself from Boston to Philadelphia or Alexander Hamilton from the West Indies to New York.

The second problem with Fischer's thesis is that many contemporary accounts do not bear it out. Surprise at the uniformity of American speech is found again and again in letters and journals throughout the eighteenth century and into the nineteenth. In 1770 a William Eddis found it a cause of wonder that "the language of the immediate descendants of such a promiscuous ancestry is perfectly uniform and unadulterated; nor has it borrowed any provincial, or national accent, from its British or foreign parentage."[17] Another observer stated flatly: "There is no dialect in all North America."[18] John Pickering, president of the American Academy of Arts and Sciences and arguably the leading authority on American speech of his day, thought America was marked not by the variety of its speech but by its consistency. One could find "a greater difference in dialect between one county and another in Britain than there is between one state and another in America," he contended, and attributed this to "the frequent removal of people from one part of our country to another." He cited his own New Jersey as an example: "People from all the other states are constantly moving into and out of this state so that there is little peculiarity of manner."[19]

This isn't to say that there *weren't* distinctive regional varieties of speech in America by the time of the Revolution, merely that they appear not to have been as fixed, evident, and susceptible to generalization as we might sometimes be led to believe. Even less certain is the degree to which American speech had by 1776 become noticeably distinctive. As early as 1720, according to Flexner, Americans were aware that their language "differed seriously" from that of England.[20] In 1756, Samuel Johnson referred without hesitation to an "American dialect," and a popular American play of the day, *The Politician Out-Witted*, instructed the actors to render British speech as "effeminate cries,"[21] suggesting that differences in cadence and resonance, if not necessarily in pronunciation, were already evident. On the other hand, as Krapp notes, visitors to Boston at the time of the Revolution commonly remarked that the accent of the people there was almost indistinguishable from the English of England.[22]

What is certain is that Britons and Americans alike sounded quite different from Britons and Americans of today, and in a multitude of ways. Both would have dropped the *w* sound in *backward, Edward,* and *somewhat,* but preserved it in *sword.* They would not have pronounced the *c* in *verdict* or *predict* or the *l* in *vault, fault* and *soldier.* Words like *author* and *anthem* would have been pronounced with a hard *t,* as in *orator,* or even sometimes a *d. Fathoms,* for instance, was often spelled *fadams. Banquet* would have been pronounced "banket." *Balcony* rhymed with *baloney* (Byron would soon rhyme it with *Giorgione*). *Barrage* was pronounced "bair-idge" and apparently remained so up to the time of the First World War. Words that we now pronounce with an interior *ew* sound frequently lacked it then, so that *mute, volume,* and *figure* would have been "moot," "voloom," and "figger." Vowel sounds in general were much less settled and specific. Combinations that are now enunciated were then glossed over, so that many speakers said "partickly" (or "puhtickly") for *particularly,* "actilly" for *actually,* "poplar" for *popular* and so on.

Eighteenth-century users had a greater choice of contractions than now. As well as *can't, don't, isn't,* and the like, there was *han't* (sometimes *hain't*) for "have not" and *an't* for "are not" and "am not." *An't,* first recorded in 1723 in print in America though probably older, evolved in two directions. Rhymed with *taunt,* it took on the spelling *aren't* (the *r* being silent, as it still is in British English). Rhymed with *taint,* it took on the spelling *ain't.* There was nothing intrinsically superior in one form or the other, but critics gradually developed a distaste for *ain't.* By the nineteenth century it was widely, if unreasonably, condemned as vulgar, a position from which it shows no sign of advancing.[23]

Contemporary writings, particularly by the indifferently educated, offer good clues to pronunciation. Paul Revere wrote *git* (for *get*), *imeaditly,* and *prittie* and referred to blankets as being *woren out.* Elsewhere we can find *libity* for *liberty, patchis* for *purchase, ort* for *ought,*[24] *weamin* for *women, through* for *throw, nater* for *nature,*[25] *keer* for *care, jest* for *just, ole* for *old, pizen* for *poison, darter* (or even *dafter*) for *daughter.* The pronunciations "chaw" for *chew,* "varmint" for *vermin,* "stomp" for *stamp,* "heist" for *hoist,* "rile" for *roil,* "hoss" for *horse,* and "tetchy" for *touchy* were commonly, if not invariably, heard among educated speakers on both sides of the Atlantic. All of this suggests that if we wished to find a modern-day model for British and American speech of the late eighteenth century, we could probably do no better than Yosemite Sam.

To this day it remains a commonplace in England that American English is a corrupted form of British speech, that we in the New World display a kind of helpless, chronic "want of refinement" (in the words of Frances Trollope) every time we open our mouths and attempt to issue sounds. In fact, in several significant ways it is British speech that has become corrupted—or, to put it in less reactionary terms, has quietly evolved. The tendency to pronounce *fertile, mobile,* and other such words as if spelled *fertle* and *moble,* to give a *ŭ* sound to *hover, grovel,* and *Coventry* rather than the rounded *o* of *hot,* and to pronounce *schedule* with an initial *sk-* rather than a *sh-* reflects British speech patterns up to the close of the eighteenth century.* Even the feature that Americans most closely associate with modern British speech, the practice of saying "bahth," "cahn't," and "banahna" for *bath, can't,* and *banana,* appears to have been unknown among educated British speakers at the time of the American Revolution. Pronunciation guides until as late as 1809 give no hint of the existence of such a pronunciation in British speech, although there is some evidence to suggest that it was used by London's cockneys (which would make it one of the few instances in modern linguistics in which a manner of utterance traveled upward from the lower classes). Not only did English speakers of the day, Britons and Ameri-

---

*It is, of course, no more than a tendency. Many Americans rhyme *grovel* with *novel* and say *mercantīle, infantīle* and *servīle* in contradiction of the usual pattern.

cans alike, say *bath* and *path* with a flat *a,* but even apparently such words as *jaunt, hardly, palm,* and *father.* Two incidental relics of this old pattern of pronunciation are the general American pronunciation of *aunt* (i.e., "ant") and *sassy,* which is simply how people once said *saucy.*

II

In the summer of 1776, when it occurred to the delegates assembled in Philadelphia that they needed a document to spell out the grounds of their dissatisfaction with Britain, the task was handed to Thomas Jefferson. To us, he seems the obvious choice. He was not.

In 1776, Thomas Jefferson was a fairly obscure figure, even in his own Virginia. Aged just thirty-three, he was the second-youngest of the delegates in Philadelphia and one of the least experienced. The Second Continental Congress was in fact his first exposure to a wider world of affairs beyond those of his native colony. He had not been selected to attend the First Continental Congress and was called to the second only as a late replacement for Peyton Randolph, who had been summoned home at short notice. Jefferson's reputation rested almost entirely on his *Summary View of the Rights of British America,* written two years earlier. An aggressive and youthfully impudent essay advising the British on how they ought to conduct themselves in their principal overseas possession, it had gained him some attention as a writer. To his fellow Virginia delegates he was known as a dilettante (a word that did not yet have any pejorative overtones; taken from the Italian *dilettare,* it simply described one who found pleasure in the richness of human possibility) and admired for the breadth of his reading in an age when that truly meant something. (He was adept at seven languages.)

But by no means did he have what we might call a national standing. Nor did he display any evidence of desiring one. He showed a distinct lack of keenness to get to Philadelphia, dawdling en route to shop for books and to buy a horse, and once there he said almost nothing. "During the whole time I sat with him I never heard him utter three sentences together," John Adams later marveled. Moreover, for reasons that are unclear, he went home to Virginia in December 1775, in the midst of debates, and did not return for nearly five months. Had he been able, he would gladly have abandoned the Congress altogether, leaving the drafting of the Declaration of Independence to someone else, to take part in the drawing up a new constitution for Virginia, a matter much closer to his heart.[26]

Nonetheless, because he showed a "peculiar felicity for expression," as John Adams put it, he was chosen with John Adams, Benjamin

Franklin, Roger Sherman, and Robert R. Livingston to compose a Declaration of Independence, and this Committee of Five selected him to come up with a working draft. The purpose, as Jefferson saw it, was "not to find out new principles, or new arguments, never before thought of, not merely to say things which had never been said before; but to place before mankind the common sense of the subject, in terms so plain and firm as to command their assent."[27]

Of course, the Declaration of Independence is much more than that. As Garry Wills has put it, it stands as "perhaps the only piece of practical politics that is also theoretical politics and also great literature."[28] Consider the opening sentence:

> When in the Course of human events, it becomes necessary for one people to dissolve the political bands which have connected them with another, and to assume, among the powers of the earth, the separate and equal station to which the Laws of Nature and of Nature's God entitle them, a decent respect to the opinions of mankind requires that they should declare the causes which impel them to the separation.

In a single sentence, in clear, simple language that anyone can understand, Jefferson has not only encapsulated the philosophy of what is to follow, but set in motion a cadence that gradually becomes hypnotic. You can read the preamble to the Declaration of Independence for its rhythms alone. As Stephen E. Lucas notes, it captures in just 202 words "what it took John Locke thousands of words to explain in his Second Treatise of Government. In its ability to compress complex ideas into a brief, clear statement, the preamble is a paradigm of eighteenth-century prose style."[29]

What is less well known is that the words aren't entirely Jefferson's. George Mason's recently published draft of the Virginia Declaration of Rights provided what might most charitably be called liberal inspiration. Consider perhaps the most famous sentence in the Declaration of Independence—

> We hold these truths to be self-evident, that all men are created equal, that they are endowed by their Creator with certain unalienable Rights, that among these are Life, Liberty and the pursuit of happiness.

—and compare that with Mason's Virginia Declaration:

> All men are born equally free and independent, and have certain inherent natural rights, of which . . . they cannot, by any compact, de-

prive or divest their posterity; among which are the enjoyment of life and liberty, with the means of acquiring and possessing property, and pursuing and obtaining happiness and safety.

"Pursuit of happiness" may be argued to be a succinct improvement on "pursuing and obtaining happiness and safety," but even that compelling phrase wasn't original with Jefferson. "Pursuit of happiness" had been coined by John Locke almost a century before and had appeared frequently in political writings ever since.

Nor are the words in that famous, inspiring sentence the ones that Jefferson penned. His original version shows considerably less grace and rather more verbosity:

> We hold these truths to be sacred & undeniable; that all men are created equal and independant, that from that equal creation they derive rights inherent and inalienable, among which are the preservation of life, & liberty, & the pursuit of happiness.[30]

The sentence took on its final resonance only after it had been through the hands of the Committee of Five and then subjected to active debate in Congress itself. Congress did not hesitate to alter Jefferson's painstakingly crafted words. Altogether it ordered forty changes to the original text. It deleted 630 words, about a quarter of the total, and added 146. Like most writers who have been subjected to the editing process, Jefferson thought the final text depressingly inferior to his original, and, like most writers, he was wrong. Indeed, seldom has a writer been better served. Congress had the wisdom to leave untouched those sections that were unimprovable—notably the opening paragraph—and excised much that was irrelevant or otiose.

Though now one of the most famous passages in English political prose, the preamble attracted far less attention then than later. At the time the listing of grievances against the king, which takes up some 60 percent of the entire text of the Declaration, was far more daring and arresting.

The twenty-seven charges against the king were mostly—sometimes recklessly—overstated. Charge four, for instance, accused him of compelling colonial assemblies to meet in locales that were "unusual, uncomfortable and distant . . . for the sole purpose of fatiguing them into compliance with his measures." In fact, in only three of the thirteen colonies were the assemblies ever compelled to move, and in two of those it happened only once. Only Massachusetts suffered it for an extended period, and there the assembly was moved just four miles to Cambridge—hardly an odious imposition.

Or consider charge ten: "He has erected a multitude of New Offices, and sent hither swarms of Officers to harass our people, and eat out their substance." In fact, the swarms numbered no more than about fifty, and much of their activity, such as trying to stop smuggling (which, incidentally, had helped to make John Hancock one of the richest men in New England), was legitimate by any standards.[31]

In Britain, the Declaration was received by many as arrant hogwash. The *Gentleman's Magazine* mocked the assertion that all men are created equal. "In what are they created equal?" it asked. "Is it in size, strength, understanding, figure, moral or civil accomplishments, or situation of life? Every plough-man knows that they are not created equal in any of these. All men, it is true, are equally created, but what is this to the purpose? It certainly is no reason why the Americans should turn rebels."[32] Though the writer of that passage appears to have had perhaps one glass of Madeira too many at lunch, there was something in his argument. No one in America truly believed that all men were created equal. Samuel Johnson touched on the incontestable hypocrisy of the American position when he asked, "How is it that we hear the loudest yelps for liberty among the drivers of Negroes?"[33]

Jefferson's draft of the Declaration contains several spellings and usages that strike us today—and indeed appear to have struck at least some of his contemporaries—as irregular. For one thing, Jefferson always wrote *it's* for the possessive form of *it,* a practice that now looks decidedly illiterate. In fact, there was some logic to it. As a possessive form, the argument went, *its* required an apostrophe in precisely the same way as did words like *children's* or *men's.* Others contended, however, that on certain common words like *ours* and *yours* it was customary to dispense with the apostrophe, and that *its* belonged in this camp. By about 1815, the non-apostrophists had their way almost everywhere, but in 1776, it was a fine point, and one to which Jefferson clearly did not subscribe.[34]

Jefferson also favored some unusual spellings, notably *independant* (which Thomas Paine likewise preferred), *paiment,* and *unacknoleged,* all of which were subsequently changed in the published version to their more conventional forms. He veered with apparent indecisiveness between the two forms for the third person singular present indicative of *have,* sometimes using the literary *hath* ("experience hath shown") and sometimes the more modern *has* ("he has kept among us"). Two further orthographic uncertainties of the age are reflected in Jefferson's text—whether to write *-or* or *-our* in words like *honor* and whether to use -*ise* or -*ize* in words like *naturalize*. Jefferson was inconsistent on both counts.

Much is sometimes made of the irregularity of spelling among writers of English in the eighteenth century. Noting that Adam Smith's *Wealth of Nations* varied in its spellings between *public* and *publick, complete* and *compleat,* and *independent* and *independant,* David Simpson observes in *The Politics of American English*: "Except for Samuel Johnson, no one in 1776, on either side of the ocean, seems to show much concern for a standard spelling practice."[35]

This is almost certainly overstating matters. Although Thomas Jefferson did have some spelling quirks—among many others, he persistently addressed his letters to "Doctr. Franklyn" when he must *surely* have realized that the good doctor spelled his name otherwise[36]—to suggest that he or any other accomplished writer of his age was cavalier with his spelling does him an injustice. To begin with, such a statement contains the implied conceit that modern English is today somehow uniform in its spellings. It is anything but. In 1972, a scholar named Lee C. Deighton undertook the considerable task of comparing the spellings of every word in four leading American dictionaries and found that there are no fewer than 1,770 common words in modern English for which there is no general agreement on the preferred spelling. To take one example, the *Random House Dictionary* gives *innuendos* as the preferred plural of *innuendo,* the *American Heritage* opts for *innuendoes, Webster's New World* prefers *innuendoes* but recognizes *innuendos,* and *Webster's Seventh Collegiate* gives equal merit to both. The dictionaries are equally—we might fairly say hopelessly—split on whether to write *discussible* or *discussable; eyeopener, eye opener,* or *eye-opener; dumfound* or *dumbfound; gladiolus* (for the plural), *gladioli,* or *gladioluses; gobbledegook* or *gobbledygook;* and many hundreds of others. (The champion of orthographic uncertainty appears to be *panatela,* which can also pass muster as *panatella, panetela,* or *panetella.*) The principal difference between irregular spellings now and in Jefferson's day is that in Jefferson's day the number was very much larger—as you would expect in an age that was only just becoming acquainted with dictionaries. So just as we seldom note whether a particular writer uses *big-hearted* or *bighearted, omelette* or *omelet, O.K.* or *okay,* so I suspect Jefferson and Paine would think it singular that we had even noticed that they sometimes wrote *honour* and sometimes *honor.*

That isn't to say that spelling or any other issue of usage in this period was considered inconsequential. In fact, the opposite. The Second Continental Congress contained within it many men—Jefferson, Adams, John Jay, Benjamin Franklin, John Witherspoon (first president of

Princeton University and the first authority on American English)—who constantly displayed a passionate interest in language and its consistent, careful application. They argued at length over whether the Declaration should use *independent* or *independant, inalienable* or *unalienable,* whether the principal nouns were to be capitalized as Franklin wished or presented lowercase as Jefferson desired (and as was the rather racy new fashion among the younger set).* Anything to do with language exercised their interests greatly—we might almost say disproportionately. Just a month after the completion of the Declaration of Independence, at a time when the delegates might have been expected to occupy themselves with more pressing concerns—like how they were going to win the war and escape hanging—Congress quite extraordinarily found time to debate the business of a motto for the new nation. (Their choice, *E Pluribus Unum,* "One from Many," was taken from, of all places, a recipe for salad in an early poem by Virgil.) Four years later, while the war still raged, John Adams was urging Congress to establish an American Academy along the lines of the Académie Française in France with the express purpose of setting national standards of usage. To suggest that these men showed not much concern for matters of usage and spelling is to misread them utterly.

Where there was evident uncertainty was in what to call the new nation. The Declaration referred in a single sentence to "the united States of America" and "these United Colonies." The first adopted form of the Declaration was given the title *A Declaration by the Representatives of the United States of America, in General Congress Assembled,* though this was improved in the final published version to the rather more robust and assertive *The Unanimous Declaration of the 13 United States of America.* (It wasn't really unanimous at all. At least a quarter of the delegates were against it, but voting was done by delegation rather than by individuals, and each delegation carried a majority for.) It was the first time the country had been officially designated the United States of America, though in fact until 1778 the formal title was the United States of *North* America.[38] Even after the Declaration, "united" was often left lowercased, as if to emphasize that it was merely descriptive, and the country was variously referred to throughout the war as "the colonies," "the united Colonies," the "United Colonies of America," and "the United Colonies of North America." (The last two are the forms under which officers were commissioned into the army.)

That we celebrate the signing of the Declaration of Independence on

---

*Among the words Jefferson lowercased were *nature, creator,* and even *God.* Most were later uppercased by the printer.[37]

the Fourth of July is a small historical curiosity. America did *not* declare independence on July 4, 1776. That had happened two days earlier, when the proposal was adopted. The proceedings on July 4 were a mere formality endorsing the form of words that were to be used to announce this breach. Most people had no doubt that July 2 was the day that would ring through the ages. "The second day of July, 1776 will be the most memorable Epocha in the History of America," John Adams wrote to his wife Abigail on July 3. Still less was the Declaration signed on July 4, except by the president of the proceedings, John Hancock, and the secretary, Charles Thomson.★ It was not signed on July 4 because it had first to be transcribed onto parchment. The official signing didn't begin until August 2 and wasn't concluded until 1781 when Thomas McKean of Delaware, the last of the fifty-six signatories, finally put his name to it. Such was the fear of reprisal that the names of the signers were not released until January 1777, six months after the Declaration's adoption.

Equally mistaken is the idea that the adoption of the Declaration of Independence was announced to a breathless Philadelphia on July 4 by the ringing of the Liberty Bell. For one thing, the Declaration was not read out in Philadelphia until July 8, and there is no record of any bells being rung. Indeed, though the Liberty Bell was there, it was not so called until 1847, when the whole inspiring episode was recounted in a book titled *Washington and His Generals*, written by one George Lippard, whose previous literary efforts had been confined almost exclusively to producing mildly pornographic novels.[40] He made the whole thing up.

John Dunlap, a Philadelphia printer, hastily ran off an apparently unknown number of copies. (Until recently only twenty-four were thought to survive—two in private hands and the rest lodged with institutions. But in 1992, a shopper at a flea market in Philadelphia found a copy, later estimated to be worth up to $3 million, folded into the back of a picture frame, apparently as padding.) Dunlap's version was dated July 4, and it was this, evidently, that persuaded the nation to make that the day of revelry. The next year, at any rate, the great event was being celebrated on July 4 "with Pomp and Parade, with Shews, Games, Sports, Guns, Bells, Bonfires, and Illuminations from one End of this Continent to the other," in John Adams's words, and so it has stayed ever since. The first anniversary, incidentally, saw the entrance of a new word into the language: *fireworks*. Fireworks themselves weren't new, but previously they had been called *rockets*.

★Though John Hancock became immediately famous for his cockily outsized signature on the Declaration, the expression "Put your John Hancock here" for a signature didn't apparently occur to anyone until 1903.[39]

America wasn't yet a nation, but more a loose confederation of thirteen independent sovereignties—what the Articles of Confederation would later call "a firm league of friendship." True nationhood would have to wait a further twelve perilous, unstable years for the adoption of the Constitution. But before we turn to that uneasy period, let us pause for a moment to consider the fate of poor Tom Paine, the man who set the whole process of revolution in motion.

Despite the huge success of *Common Sense*, the publication brought him no official position. By the end of 1776, he was a common foot soldier. After the war, Paine traveled to France, where he performed a similar catalytic role in the revolution there with his pamphlet *The Rights of Man* before falling foul of the erratic Robespierre, who had him clapped into prison for daring to suggest a merciful exile for King Louis XVI (on the grounds that Louis had supported the American rebels). Unappreciated in France and a pariah in his own country, he returned to America and sank almost at once into dereliction and obscurity.

Not long before he died, Paine was found by an old friend in a tavern in New Rochelle, New York, passed out, dressed in tatters, and bearing "the most disagreeable smell possible." The friend hauled him to a tub of hot, soapy water and scrubbed him from head to foot three times before the odor was pacified. His nails had not been cut for years. Soon afterward, this great man, who had once dined with Washington, Jay, and Jefferson, who had been a central figure in the two great revolutions of the modern age, died broken and forgotten. William Cobbett, the essayist, stole his bones and took them back to England with him, but likewise died before he could find a suitable resting place for them.

And so the remains of one of the great polemicists of his or any other age were unceremoniously carted off by a rag and bone merchant and vanished forever.

Chapter 4

MAKING A NATION

It began with a dispute between oyster fishermen.

In 1632, Charles I placed the border between Virginia and Maryland not in the middle of the Potomac River, as was normal practice, but instead gave his chum Lord Baltimore the whole of the river up to the Virginia bank, to the dismay and frustration of Virginia fishermen, who were thus deprived of their right to gather the river's delicious and lucrative bivalves. Over time, the dispute also caught up Pennsylvania and Delaware, led to occasional skirmishes known collectively and somewhat grandly as the Oyster War, and eventually led to the calling of a gathering to try to sort out this and other matters involving trade and interstate affairs.

Thus in May 1787, representatives from across America began to assemble at the old State House in Philadelphia in what would come to be known as the Constitutional Convention. Though America had declared its independence eleven years earlier, it was not yet in any real sense a nation, but rather an uneasy alliance of states bound by a document known formally as the Articles of Confederation and Perpetual Union. Enacted in 1781, the Articles had established a central government of sorts, but had left it subordinate to the states and embarrassingly lacking in clout. In consequence, as the historian Charles L. Mee, Jr., has put it, in 1787 the government of the United States "could not reliably levy taxes, could not ensure that its laws would be obeyed, could not repay its debts, could not ensure that it would honor its treaty obligations. It was not clear, in fact, that it could be called a government at all."[1]

Since the conclusion of the war with Britain, the States had increasingly fallen to squabbling. Connecticut boldly claimed almost a third of the territory of Pennsylvania after many of its residents settled there. Pennsylvania was so fearful of New York's imposing tariffs on its man- ufactures that it insisted on having its own access to the Great Lakes. (If you have ever wondered why Pennsylvania's border takes an abrupt up- ward jag at its northwestern end to give it an odd umbilicus to Lake Erie, that is why.) New York bickered over patches of land with little Rhode Island, and Vermont constantly threatened to leave the union. Clearly something needed to be done. The obvious solution would be a new agreement superseding the Articles of Confederation and creating a more powerful central government: in a word, a constitution. Without it, America could never hope to be a nation. As Page Smith has put it: "The Revolution had created the possibility, not the reality, of a new nation. It is the Constitution that for all practical purposes is synony- mous with our nationhood."[2]

But there were problems. To begin with, the delegates had no authority to form a constitution. Their assignment was to amend the Articles of Confederation, not replace them. (Which is why it wasn't called the Constitutional Convention until afterward.)[3] Then, too, the scale of the American continent and the diversity of its parts seemed fated to thwart any hope of meaningful unification. With fifteen hun- dred miles of coastline and a vast inland wilderness, the United States was already one of the largest countries in the world—ten times larger than any previous federation in history—and the disparities in popula- tion, wealth, and political outlook among the states presented seemingly insurmountable obstacles to finding a common purpose. If proportional representation was instituted, Virginia and Pennsylvania between them would possess one-third of the nation's political power, while Delaware would be entitled to a mere one-ninetieth. Little states thus feared big ones. Slave-owning states feared non-slave-owning states. Eastern states with fixed borders feared those of the West with an untapped continent on their doorsteps, suspecting that one day these western upstarts would overtake them in population and they would find their destinies in the hands of rude frontiersmen in tasseled buckskins—an unthinkable pros- pect. All the states, large and small, had proud, distinct histories, often going back nearly two centuries, and were reluctant to relinquish even the smallest measure of autonomy to an unproven central authority. The challenge of the Constitutional Convention was not to give powers to the states, but to take powers away from them, and to do it in a way they would find palatable.

Some states refused even to entertain the notion. Rhode Island, which had declared independence from Britain two months before the rest of America, now refused to send delegates to Philadelphia (and rather sulkily declined to join the union until 1790). Vermont likewise snubbed the convention and made it clear from the outset that it was disinclined to abide by its decisions. Others, like Maryland, could barely find people willing to go. The first five men selected as representatives all declined to attend, and at the opening of the convention the legislature was still trying to find willing delegates. New Hampshire was prepared to send two delegates, but refused to underwrite their expenses and as a result had no representatives at the convention for the first crucial weeks. Many delegates attended only fitfully, and six never came at all. Altogether only about thirty of the sixty-one elected delegates attended from start to finish.[4]

Fortunately for us, those who attended included some of the most steady, reflective, and brilliant intellects any young nation has ever produced: Benjamin Franklin, Alexander Hamilton, James Mason, Roger Sherman, Gouverneur Morris, John Dickinson, Edmund Randolph, and, of course, the regal, rocklike George Washington, whose benign presence as president of the convention lent the proceedings an authority and respectability they could not otherwise have claimed.

In many ways the most interesting of the delegates was Benjamin Franklin. Aged eighty-one, he was coming to the end of his long life— and in the view of many of his fellow delegates had long since passed the useful part of it. But what a life it had been. One of seventeen children of a Boston soap and candle maker, he had left home as a boy after receiving barely two years of schooling and established himself as a printer in Philadelphia. By dint of hard work and steady application he had made himself into one of the most respected thinkers and wealthiest businessmen in the colonies. His experiments with electricity, unfairly diminished in the popular mind to inventing the lightning rod and nearly killing himself by foolishly flying a kite in a thunderstorm, were among the most exciting scientific achievements of the eighteenth century and made him one of the celebrated scientists of the day (though he was never called a *scientist* in his lifetime, the word not being coined until 1840; in the 1700s, scientists were *natural philosophers*). The terms he created in the course of his experiments—*battery, armature, positive, negative,* and *condenser,* among others[5]—show that he was a good deal more than a mildly quizzical fellow who just wanted to see what would happen if he nudged a kite into some storm clouds.

His life was one of relentless industry. He invented countless useful objects, and helped to found America's first volunteer fire department, its first fire insurance company (the Hand-in-Hand), one of Philadelphia's first libraries, and the respected if somewhat overnamed American Philosophical Society for the Promotion of Useful Knowledge to be

Held at Philadelphia.[6] He created an eternal literary character, the Richard of *Poor Richard's Almanack*, filled the world with maxims and bons mots, corresponded endlessly with the leading minds of Europe and America, wrote essays on everything from how to select a mistress (take an older woman) to how to avoid flatulence (drink perfume), and in 1737 drew up the first list of American slang terms for drunkenness. (He came up with 228.) He represented America overseas with intelligence and skill and, of course, was one of the shapers of the Declaration of Independence. He dabbled in property speculation and ran a printing business with holdings as far afield as Jamaica and Antigua. He became the largest dealer in paper in the colonies and made *Poor Richard's Almanack* such an indispensable part of almost every American household that it was for twenty-five years the country's second-best-selling publication. (The Bible was first.) Such was his commercial acumen that he was able to retire from active business in 1748, aged just forty-two, and devote himself to gentlemanly pursuits like politics, science, and writing.

And in between all this he somehow managed to find time—quite a lot of time—to pursue what was his greatest, if least celebrated, passion: namely, trying *to roger* (to use the argot of the day) just about any woman who passed before him. From earliest adulthood, Franklin showed an unwavering inclination to engage in "foolish intrigues with low Women," as he himself somewhat sheepishly put it.[7] One such encounter resulted in an illegitimate son, William, born in 1730 or 1731 and raised in Franklin's house by his long-suffering common-law wife, Deborah. Throughout his long life, Franklin's hyperactive libido was a matter of wonder to his contemporaries. The artist Charles Willson Peale, calling on the great man in London, found him with a young woman on his knee[8]—or at least was discreet enough to say it was his knee—and others commonly arrived for appointments to find him *in flagrante* with a parlor maid or other yielding creature.

During his years in England he became close friends with Sir Francis Dashwood, who presided over a notorious den called the Order of St. Francis, but more popularly known as the Hellfire Club, at his country house at West Wycombe in Buckinghamshire. Members took part in black masses and other wildly blasphemous ceremonies that invariably culminated in drunken orgies involving pliant women garbed as nuns. In his quieter moments, Dashwood was joint postmaster general of England and coauthor with Franklin of a revised version of the Book of Common Prayer. There is no certain evidence that Franklin took part in these debauches, but it would have been a wrenching break with his character had he not. It is certainly known that he was a frequent, not to say eager, visitor to Dashwood's house, and it would take a generous spirit indeed to suppose that he ventured there repeatedly just to discuss postal regulations and the semantic nuances of the Book of Common Prayer.

But then the eighteenth century, it must be remembered, was a decidedly earthier and more free-spirited age. It was a period that teemed with indelicate locutions—*pisspot* for a doctor, *shit-sack* for a nonconformist, *groper* for a blind person, *fartcatcher* for a footman (because he followed behind), to name just four. Words and metaphors that would bring blushes to a later age were used without hesitation or embarrassment. At the Constitutional Convention, Elbridge Gerry would make a famous remark (curiously absent from modern high school textbooks) in which he compared a standing army to an erect penis—"an excellent assurance of domestic tranquility, but a dangerous temptation to foreign adventure"[9]—and no one thought it inapt or unseemly, at least in the company of men. Franklin himself peppered his almanacs with maxims that were, to modern ears, coarse to the point of witlessness: "The greatest monarch on the proudest throne is obliged to sit upon his own arse," "He that lives upon hope, dies farting," "Relation without friendship, friendship without power, power without will . . . are not worth a farto."

It is worth noting that few of his aphorisms, coarse or otherwise, were of his own devising. Though a few cannot be traced to earlier sources—e.g., "An empty bag cannot stand upright" and "Experience keeps a dear school, yet fools will learn in no other"—most were plundered without hesitation or scruple from other similar publications of the day, such as James Howell's *Lexicon Tetraglotton*, Thomas Fuller's *Gnomologia* and other writings, George Herbert's *Outlandish Proverbs*, and, especially, Jonathan Swift's *Bickerstaff Papers*. It was from Swift that Franklin took the droll idea of predicting in the almanac's annual forecasts the imminent death of his leading competitor.[10] "Why should I give my Readers bad lines of my own when good ones of other People's are so plenty?" he quipped.[11] (Nor, while we are at it, did he hesitate to make up stories for his newspapers when the real news was thin and unarresting.)

He did, it must be said, often improve on others' maxims. He took the proverb "God restoreth health and the physician hath the thanks" and made it into the pithier "God heals and the doctor takes the fee."[12] But more often than not he merely embellished them with a reference to flatulence, incontinence, sexual intercourse, or some other frailty. James Howell's "A Fort which begins to parley is half gotten," for example, he made into "Neither a Fortress nor a Maidenhead will hold out long after they begin to parly."[13]

No discussion of Franklin and language would be complete without a mention of his *Proposal for a Reformed Alphabet* of 1768. Though much is sometimes made of Franklin's tinkering with English spelling, and though he did offer occasional statements sympathetic to the cause of reform (e.g., "If Amendments are never attempted and things continue to grow worse and worse they must come to be in a wretched Condition at last"), it is not clear whether he regarded his modified alphabet as a serious attempt at orthographic reform or merely as an amusing way of writing mildly flirtatious letters to a pretty young correspondent.

Certainly there is no persuasive evidence that he worked very hard at it. His new alphabet was surprisingly clumsy and illogical. It contained six additional letters, so it offered no improvements in terms of simplicity. Moreover, it was arbitrary, whimsical, and hopelessly bewildering to the untutored, and it routinely resulted in spellings that were far longer and more complex than those they were intended to replace. Under Franklin's reforms, for example, *changes* became *tseendsez* and *Chinese* became *Tsuiniiz*. His first letter in the new alphabet, dated July 20, 1768, is replete with spellings that suggest Franklin either had a peculiar sense of pronunciation or, more likely, carelessly applied his own pronunciation guide. *Has,* according to his letter, would be pronounced "haze"; *people* would be "pee-peel"; *Richmond* would be "Reechmund."[14]

So used are we to regarding Franklin as a sage and mentor that it can come as a small shock to realize that he was not much venerated in his own day. John Adams, for one, detested him.[15] After Franklin's death in 1790, so little was his loss felt that the first edition of his collected writings didn't appear until twenty-eight years later. His *Autobiography* aroused less interest still and did not appear in a complete form in America until 1868—seventy-eight years after he died and long after it had been published elsewhere.[16] At the time of the Constitutional Convention, Franklin was generally held to be at best of no real account, at worst little more than a doddering old fool. His infrequent proposals to the convention—that the President of the United States not be paid a salary, that each session be started with a prayer—were always roundly defeated. (His prayer motion failed to carry not because the delegates were ungodly but, as they patiently explained to him, because they had no funds to pay a chaplain.)

Franklin was merely a visible, wheezing reminder that the business of America had passed in large part to a new generation. With the principal exception of the fifty-five-year-old General Washington (who in any case didn't take part in the debates), the delegates were strikingly youthful. Five were in their twenties, and most of the rest were in their thirties or forties. James Madison was thirty-five, Alexander Hamilton just thirty-two. South Carolina's baby-faced Charles Pinckney, twenty-nine, enhanced his air of extreme youthfulness by vociferously insisting he was but twenty-four.[17] The oddest and least prepossessing figure of all was perhaps the most important: James Madison. Nothing about the young Virginian bespoke greatness. He was almost ridiculously short—no more than "half a bar of soap" in the words of one contemporary—squeaky-voiced, pale, shy, and neurotically obsessed with his health. But he had a towering intellect, and he tirelessly shunted between rival factions squeezing and cajoling compromise out of often obdurate delegates. No one else did more in that long, hot summer to make the Constitution a reality.

In not quite four months these thirty or so men created a framework for government that has lasted us to this day and was like nothing seen before. From May 25 to September 17 they worked in session five hours a day, six days a week, and often for long hours outside of that. It was, as Page Smith has put it with perhaps no more than a blush of hyperbole, "the most remarkable example of sustained intellectual discourse in history."[18] It is certainly no exaggeration to say that never before or since has any gathering of Americans shown a more dazzling array of talent and of preparedness. Madison's background reading included the histories of Polybius, the orations of Demosthenes, Plutarch's *Lives*, Fortune Barthélemy de Felice's thirteen-volume *Code de l'Humanité* in the original French, and much, much else. Alexander Hamilton in a single speech bandied about references to the Amphyctionic Councils of ancient Greece and the Delian Confederacy. These were men who knew their stuff.

And they were great enough to put aside their differences. In the space of a single uncomfortable summer they created the foundations of government: the legislature, the presidency, the courts, the system of checks and balances, the whole intricate framework of American democracy—a legacy that is all the more arresting when you consider that almost to a man they were against democracy in anything like the modern sense.

For a time they actually considered creating a monarchy, albeit one elected by the legislature. So real did this prospect seem that a rumor—quite without foundation—swept the colonies that the position was to be offered to the Duke of York, George III's second son. In fact, the idea of a monarch was quickly deemed incompatible with a republic. Alexander Hamilton suggested as an alternative a president and senate elected for life from men of property, with absolute power over the states.[19] Edmund Randolph preferred that the presidency be shared among three men, to give the executive office greater collective wisdom and less scope for despotism, sectionalism, and corruption.[20] (The prospect of corruption worried them mightily.) Almost all envisioned an America ruled by a kind of informal aristocracy of propertied gentlemen—men much like themselves. So distant from their thinking was the idea of an open democracy that when James Wilson of Pennsylvania moved that the executive be chosen by popular vote, the delegates "were entirely dumbfounded." In the end, they threw the matter of electing a president to the states, creating an electoral college and leaving each state to decide whether its collegial delegates would be chosen by the people or by the legislature (which is why to this day when you vote for the President you are, strictly speaking, voting not for a person but for a block of delegates who have promised to give their vote to your candidate).

In a spirit of compromise, they decreed that the House of Representatives would be chosen by the people and the Senate by the state legislatures, an arrangement that remained in force until 1912, when senators were at last popularly elected. In the matter of the vice-presidency they decided—unwisely with the benefit of hindsight—that the job should fall to whoever came second in the presidential poll. It seemed the fair thing to do, but it failed to take into account the distinct possibility that the Vice-President might represent a rival faction from that of the President. In 1804 the practice was abandoned and the custom of electing a two-man slate was adopted.

When most of the rudiments were agreed upon, the delegates appointed a Committee of Detail to put their proposals on paper. One of the committee members, John Rutledge, was an admirer of the Iroquois and recommended that the committee familiarize itself with the treaty of 1520 that had created the Iroquois Confederacy. It begins: "We, the people, to form a union . . ." These were, of course, essentially the very words they chose. There is something profoundly pleasing and appropriate in the thought that the calmly elegant phrase that begins this most important document was first uttered by Native Americans.[21] The preamble reads:

We, the people of the United States, in Order to form a more perfect Union, establish Justice, insure domestic Tranquility, provide for the common defence, promote the general Welfare, and secure the Blessings of Liberty to ourselves and our Posterity, do ordain and establish this Constitution for the United States of America.

After this simple statement of intent, there follow six articles that set out—sometimes sketchily, sometimes with fastidious detail—the mechanisms of government, with a seventh announcing that the document would take effect once it had been ratified by nine states. (A number not chosen lightly; the delegates thought it doubtful that more than nine states would ratify.)

At just twenty-five pages, the Constitution is a model of concision. (The state constitution of Oklahoma, by contrast, is 158 pages long.)[22] On some matters it was explicit and forthright—on the age and citizenship requirements for senators, representatives, and the President, and especially on the matter of impeachment. The framers seemed intent almost to the point of paranoia on providing instructions for how to depose those found to be disloyal or corrupt. But on other matters they were curiously vague. There was no mention of a cabinet, for instance. They mandated the setting up of a Supreme Court, independent from the other branches, but then rather airily decreed that the rest of the judiciary should consist of "such inferior courts as the Congress may from time to time ordain and establish." Sometimes this vagueness was a consequence of oversight and sometimes of an inability to arrive at a more specific compromise. Where the document was specific, it almost always left room for later change. After decreeing that Congress should assemble at least once a year, beginning on the first Monday in December, it thoughtfully added "unless they shall by law appoint a different day." The upshot is that the Constitution is an extraordinarily adaptable set of ground rules.

In terms of its composition, surprisingly few oddities of spelling and syntax stand out. Three words are spelled in the British style, *behaviour, labour,* and *defence,* but not *tranquility,* which even in 1787 was sometimes being given a single *l* in America. Only once is there an inconsistency of spelling—*empeachments* in one paragraph and *impeachment* in the next—and only two other words are spelled in an archaic way: *chuse* and *encreased.* The opening sentence contains a double superlative ("more perfect"), which might not survive the editing process today, though it was unexceptionable enough at the time. The occasional appearance of a discordant article and noun combination ("an uniform"), a rather more fastidious use of the subjunctive ("before it become a law," "if he approve he shall sign it"), the occasional capitalization of nouns that would now be lowercased ("our Posterity"), and the treating of "the United States" as a plural (it would remain so treated until about the time of the Civil War)[23] more or less exhaust the list of distinctions.

The Constitution is more notable for what it does not include. Nowhere does it mention *slaves* or *slavery.* Slaves are referred to only as "all other persons," by which was meant those who were neither free nor Indian. For purposes of determining representation and taxation, each slave was counted as three-fifths of a person, an absurdity that was not lost on many of the delegates. "Upon what principle is it that slaves shall be computed in the representation?" Gouverneur Morris of Pennsylvania asked sarcastically during the debates. "Are they Men? Then make them Citizens and let them vote. Are they property? Why then is there no other property included? The Houses in this City are worth more than all the wretched slaves which cover the rice swamps of South Carolina." The arrangement, he noted angrily, meant that "the inhabitant of Georgia and South Carolina who goes to the Coast of Africa, and in defiance of the most sacred laws of humanity tears away his fellow creatures from their dearest connections and damns them to the most cruel bondages shall have more votes in a Government instituted for protection of the rights of mankind than the citizen of Pennsylvania or New Jersey who views with a laudable horror so nefarious a practice."[24] Nonetheless, the compromise carried, as did a proposal by Roger Sherman of Connecticut to remove the words *slave* and *slavery* wherever they appeared.

The words *nation* and *national* also appear nowhere in the document, and again not by accident or oversight. Fearing that *national* smacked of a system in which power was dangerously centralized, the delegates instead used the more neutral and less emotive *federal,* derived from the Latin *fides,* "faith," and in the eighteenth century still carrying the sense of a relationship resting on trust.[25]

The ten amendments known as the Bill of Rights came later. They were not adopted until 1791 (and in the case of Massachusetts not until 150 years later, when it was discovered that their ratification had been accidentally overlooked). These guarantees of basic freedoms were as radical and prescient as anything that preceded them, but it is worth bearing in mind that the framers often meant by them something quite different from what they are taken to mean today. Consider the wording of the First Amendment: "Congress shall make no law respecting an establishment of religion, or prohibiting the free exercise thereof; or abridging the freedom of speech, or of the press, or of the right of the people peaceably to assemble . . ."* Note in particular those first five words: "Congress shall make no law . . ." The founders were not trying to free America from such restrictions, but merely endeavoring to en-

---

Peaceably to assemble is an interesting and early example of the ginger avoidance of a split infinitive. The curious conviction that infinitives should not be split had only recently come into fashion.

sure that matters of censorship and personal liberty be left to the states.[26] Nor, it should be noted, was the much-vaunted right of the people to keep and bear arms ever intended as a carte blanche, semidivine injunction to invest in a private arsenal for purposes of sport and personal defense, as the full sentence makes clear: "A well regulated militia being necessary to the security of a free State, the right of the people to keep and bear Arms shall not be infringed." The framers had in mind only the necessity of raising a defense force at short notice. If they did favor the idea of keeping guns for shooting animals and household intruders, they never said so.

At the time of its adoption, almost no one saw the Constitution as a great document. Most of the delegates left Philadelphia feeling that they had created an agreement so riddled with compromise as to be valueless—"a weak and worthless fabric," as Alexander Hamilton dispiritedly described it. Fifteen of the convention delegates refused to sign it, among them George Mason, Elbridge Gerry, and even two of the five men who had written it, Edmund Randolph and Oliver Ellsworth. (Randolph soon showed an even more breathtaking measure of hypocrisy by accepting the post as the nation's first Attorney General, thus becoming the man most directly in charge of upholding the document he had lately disowned.) Even its heartiest proponents hoped only that the Constitution might somehow hold the fragile nation together for a few years until something better could be devised.[27]

Nonetheless, the document was duly ratified, Washington was selected as the first President, and March 4, 1789, was chosen as the day to begin the new government. Unfortunately, only eight senators and thirteen representatives troubled to show up on the first day. Another twenty-six days would have to pass before the House of Representatives could muster a quorum and even longer before the Senate could find enough willing participants to begin productive work.[28]

One of the first orders of business was what to call the new Chief Executive. The Constitution had referred to "the President of the United States," but such had been the pomp and costly splendor of Washington's inauguration and so stately the demeanor of the new officeholder that Congress was inclined to consider a title with a grander ring to it. Among the suggestions were *His Highness, His Mightiness, His Magistracy, His Supremacy,* and *His Highness the President of the United States and Protector of their Liberties.* This last was the title very nearly chosen before the congressmen returned to their senses, and the original wording of the Constitution, and settled for the respectful but republican *President of the United States.* Even so, Martha was often referred to as "Lady Washington." The vice-presidency seems to have caused no such difficulty, though some among the droller elements of Congress joked that the first incumbent, the portly John Adams, should be referred to as "His Rotundity."

Washington was a firm believer in the dignity of his office. Visitors were expected to remain standing in his presence, and even his closest associates found him aloof and disquietingly kingly in his deportment (leading one to wonder if America had exchanged George III for George I). To be fair to Washington, he had to establish from the outset that the President should be treated with the utmost respect. In the early days of his presidency, people would actually wander in off the street to wish him luck or ask how things were going. (Eventually, he hit on a system whereby twice a week he set aside time during which any "respectably dressed person" could come and see him.) He was acutely aware that he was setting patterns of executive behavior that would live beyond him. "There is scarcely any part of my conduct which may not hereafter be drawn into precedent," he wrote a trifle gloomily. After sitting through hours of inconclusive debates in the Senate, he fled, muttering that he "would be damned" if he ever subjected himself to such unproductive tedium again, and since that time no American President has taken part in legislative debates, a striking departure from British practice, though there is nothing in the Constitution to forbid it.[29]

One of the more intractable myths of this period is that an early Congress considered abandoning English, as a kind of snub to the British, and adopting German or some other language as the national speech of the United States. The story has been repeated so often, sometimes even by eminent authorities,* that it is worth pointing out that it is without foundation. In 1789, 90 percent of America's four million white inhabitants were of English descent. The idea that they would in an act of petulance impose on themselves a foreign tongue is risible. The only known occasion on which German was ever an issue was in 1795 when the House of Representatives briefly considered a proposal to publish federal laws in German as well as in English as a convenience to recent immigrants, and that proposal was defeated.[30] Indeed, as early as 1778, the Continental Congress decreed that messages to foreign emissaries be issued "in the language of the United States."[31]

However, considerable thought *was* given in early Congresses to the

---

*"At the time when the United States split off from Britain, for example, there were proposals that independence should be linguistically acknowledged by the use of a different language from that of Britain" (Professor Randolph Quirk, *The Use of English,* p. 3).

possibility of renaming the country. From the start, many people recognized that *United States of America* was unsatisfactory. For one thing, it allowed of no convenient adjectival form. A citizen would have to be either a *United Statesian* or some other such clumsy locution, or an *American,* thereby arrogating to ourselves a title that belonged equally to the inhabitants of some three dozen other nations on two continents. Several alternatives to *America* were actively considered—*Columbia, Appalachia, Alleghania, Freedonia* or *Fredonia* (whose denizens would be called *Freeds* or *Fredes*)—but none mustered sufficient support to displace the existing name.[32]

United States of Columbia was a somewhat unexpected suggestion, since for most of the previous 250 years Christopher Columbus had been virtually forgotten in America. His Spanish associations had made him suspect to the British, who preferred to see the glory of North American discovery go to John Cabot. Not until after the Revolutionary War, when Americans began casting around for heroes unconnected with the British monarchy, was the name *Columbus* resurrected, generally in the more elegant Latinized form *Columbia,* and his memory generously imbued with a spirit of grit and independent fortitude that wasn't altogether merited.

The semi-deification of Columbus began with a few references in epic poems, and soon communities and institutions were falling over themselves to create new names in his honor. In 1784, King's College in New York became Columbia College, and two years later, South Carolina chose Columbia as the name for its capital. In 1791, an American captain on a ship named *Columbia* claimed a vast tract of the Northwest for the young country and dubbed it Columbia. (It later became the states of Washington, Oregon, and Idaho, though the original name lives on north of the border in British Columbia.) Journals, clubs, and institutes (among them the Columbian Institute for the Promotion of the Arts and Sciences, better known to us today as the Smithsonian Institution*) were named for the great explorer. The song "Hail Columbia" dates from 1798.[33]

After this encouraging start, Columbus's life was given a kick into the higher realms of myth by Washington Irving's ambitious, if resplendently inaccurate, *History of the Life and Voyages of Christopher Columbus,*

---

*It was renamed the Smithsonian in honor of a shadowy Englishman named James Smithson. The bastard son of a Duke of Northumberland, Smithson had never been to America and had no known American friends or connections, but he left his fortune of £100,000 to the government of the United States with the sole stipulation that it name an institution of learning after him.[34]

which came out in 1828 and was a phenomenal best-seller in America, Europe, and Latin America throughout the nineteenth century.

Irving later wrote a life of George Washington that was just as successful and no less indebted to his fictive powers. But it is to Mason Locke Weems—or Parson Weems as history knows him—that we must turn for many of our most treasured misconceptions about the Father of Our Country. His hugely successful *Life of George Washington: With Curious Anecdotes, Equally Honourable to Himself and Exemplary to His Young Countrymen*, first printed in book form in 1806, proved Weems to be not just a fictionalizer of rare gifts but a consummate liar. Even for the time, the style was more than a little saccharine. Consider the well-known story of Washington cutting down the cherry tree. We join the action at the point where George's father has asked him if by any chance he can explain how a productive fruit tree has come to be horizontal, and whether the hatchet in his hand might have something to do with it.

> "I can't tell a lie, Pa; you know I can't tell a lie. I did cut it with my hatchet."
> "Run to my arms, you dearest boy," cried his father in transports, "run to my arms; glad am I, George, that you killed my tree; for you have paid me for it a thousand fold. Such an act of heroism in my son, is more worth than a thousand trees. . . ."[35]

Weems of course made the whole thing up. Almost everything in the book beyond the hero's name and place of residence was made up or lavishly embellished. Even the title page included a brazen falsehood. Weems advertised himself as the former "Rector of Mount-Vernon Parish." There was no such parish and never had been. Nonetheless, the work went through some twenty editions and was one of the great sellers of its age.

Washington was in fact more flawed and human than Weems or many subsequent chroniclers would have us believe. He was moody, remote, and vain (he encouraged his fellow officers in the Revolutionary War to address him as "Your Excellency"), he detested being touched by strangers, and had an embarrassing proclivity to weep like a babe in public, as when things weren't going well during the Revolution or when offering his final farewells to his officers at Fraunces Tavern in New York at the war's conclusion. He was not a gifted military commander. Far from being a hero of the French and Indian Wars, as Weems and others have suggested, he actually helped to provoke them. In 1754, while an inexperienced lieutenant colonel with the Virginia Regiment, he led an unnecessary and essentially irrational attack on a party of Frenchman encamped in the Ohio Valley, killing ten of them. This and other such incidents so outraged the French that they went to war with the British. To compound his haplessness, Washington soon after was routed in battle and naively signed a document in which he apologized for the "assassination" of the Frenchmen, thereby outraging his own masters.[36]

But there was about him an incontestable greatness. He was brave, resolute, and absolutely incorruptible. No one gave more time or endured greater risks or hardships to secure America's independence and democracy. For eight years he doggedly prosecuted a war in which neither the Continental Congress nor the people gave him anything like the support his valor deserved. During one long march across New Jersey, he watched in dismay as his army evaporated from 30,000 men to barely 3,400. To add to his problems, he often discovered he was being served by traitors. Benedict Arnold is the best-known example, but there were others, such as Major General Charles Lee, who while serving as one of Washington's aides-de-camp was simultaneously supplying the British with advice on how to beat the Americans.[37] It is no wonder that he sometimes wept.

He genuinely and nobly wanted only what was best for his country. Such was the delirium of joy that greeted his triumph over the British that he could have had any tribute he cared to ask for—a kingship, a lavish life pension, his own Blenheim Palace on the Potomac. He asked only to be allowed to return to a quiet life at Mount Vernon. When elected President he requested Congress not to pay him a salary, but only to meet his expenses—a position all the more honorable when you consider that he was chronically hard up. "My estate for the last 11 years has not been able to make both ends meet," he wrote in despair to his cousin shortly before becoming President, and when he made the trip from Mount Vernon to New York to be sworn in, he had to borrow £100 to pay his costs.[38]

(Financial hardship was a common problem for Virginia planters. Jefferson was so chronically pressed for money that in 1815 he sold his beloved private library to Congress for a much-needed $23,950, though he rather undid this achievement by almost immediately beginning to acquire another just as splendid. By the time of his death, he was over $100,000 in debt, and most of the contents of Monticello had to be auctioned off.)

Congress refused to heed Washington's request and insisted he take a salary of $25,000 a year. It also did him the honor of allowing him to choose the site of the nation's permanent capital—in part because it couldn't decide on a location itself. At least forty sites had been considered and argued over, from Germantown, Pennsylvania, to Kingston, New York, before Washington was authorized to make his choice. He selected a ten-mile square flanking the Potomac River. (In 1846, Virginia reclaimed the portion on its side of the river, which explains why the modern District of Columbia has ruler-straight boundaries on three sides but an irregular wriggle on the fourth.) In 1791, the city-to-be was named *Washington;* the 6,100-acre tract within which it was situated was called the *Territory of Columbia* (eventually, of course, changed to *District of Columbia*), thus neatly enshrining in one place the two great mythic names of the age.

Two years later, Washington laid the cornerstone for the Capitol, and in 1800 the city of Washington opened for business. America was on its way.

Chapter 5

By the Dawn's Early Light: Forging a National Identity

Bombardments in the early nineteenth century provided a spectacle that must have been quite thrilling to anyone not on the receiving end. The art of the matter was to cut fuses to just the right length so that they would detonate at or near the moment of impact. In practice, they went off all over the place. Hence the "bombs bursting in air" of the American national anthem. As most people know, the words to the anthem were inspired by the bombardment of Fort McHenry in Baltimore Harbor during the War of 1812. Francis Scott Key, a young lawyer, had been sent to try to negotiate the release of an American prisoner, and found himself detained aboard a British man-of-war.

Through the night, Key watched as the British fleet ranged around the harbor threw a colorful fusillade of explosives at the embattled fort. When dawn broke and Key saw the American flag still flying, tattered but defiant, he was sufficiently moved to dash off a poem. The poem was frankly terrible, but it bore an emotional impact easily forgotten at this remove. Published under the title "Defence of Fort M'Henry," and set to the decidedly funereal tune of an English song called "To Anacreon in Heaven" (the beat has since been considerably enlivened), it became a sensation. Soon almost everyone had forgotten its original title and was calling it "The Star-Spangled Banner," by which name it has been known ever since.

The flag that Key saw flying over Fort McHenry had fifteen stars and fifteen stripes. In the early years of independence, the custom was to add a star and a stripe to the flag each time a state joined the Union. By 1818, Congress was flying a flag with no fewer than eighteen stripes and it was becoming evident that the practice would soon become unsustainable. Deciding enough was enough, Congress officially decreed that henceforth flags should have thirteen stripes (one for each of the original colonies) and as many stars as there were states.

The War of 1812 also saw the birth of another American icon: Uncle Sam. He appears to have arisen in 1813 in Troy, New York, but little more than that is known.[1] Previously the United States had been personified by a character of no less obscure origins called Brother Jonathan, who usually appeared in opposition to the English John Bull. The inspiration for Uncle Sam is sometimes traced to one Samuel Wilson, an army inspector in Troy, but it seems more probable that the name was merely derived from the initials *U.S.* The top-hatted, striped-trousered figure we associate with the name was popularized in the 1860s in the cartoons of Thomas Nast, and later reinforced by the famous I WANT YOU recruiting posters of the artist James Montgomery Flagg, in which Uncle Sam lost his genial sparkle and took on a severe, almost demonic look.

Thus by the end of the second decade of the nineteenth century, America had a national anthem (though it would not be officially recognized as such until 1931), a more or less fixed flag, and a national symbol in the form of Uncle Sam. It was, in short, beginning to accumulate the rudiments of a national identity.

But in other ways America remained a collection of disparate parts, each following its own course. This was most arrestingly seen in the absence of uniform times. Until as late as 1883, there were no fixed times in America. When it was midnight in New York, it was 11:47 in Washington and 11:55 in Philadelphia. In 1869, when the railroad tycoon Leland Stanford struck the golden spike that marked the completion of America's first transcontinental railroad (in fact, he couldn't manage to drive the spike in; the work had to be completed by someone more adept with a manual implement), the news was instantly telegraphed to a breathlessly waiting nation. In Promontory, Utah, the great event happened at 12:45, but in nearby Virginia City it was deemed to be 12:30. In San Francisco it was 11:46 or 11:44, depending on whose authority you accepted, and in Pittsburgh the information was simultaneously received at six places and logged in at six different official times.

In an age when most information arrived by horseback, a few minutes here or there hardly mattered. But as the world became more technologically sophisticated, the problem of variable timekeeping did begin to matter. It was a particular headache for the railroads and those who traveled on them. In an effort to arrive at some measure of conformity, most railroad companies synchronized the clocks along their own lines, but often these bore no relationship to the times used either locally or by competing railroads. Stations would often have a multiplicity of clocks—one showing the station time, another the local time, and the rest showing the times on each of the lines serving that station. Passengers unfamiliar with local discrepancies often arrived to catch a train only to find that it had already departed. Making connections in a place like Chicago, where fifteen lines met, required the careful study of fat books of algorithms showing all the possible permutations.

Clearly something needed to be done. The first person to push for uniform time for the country at large was the rather unlikely figure Charles F. Dowd, head of the Temple Grove Ladies' Seminary in Saratoga Springs, New York. In 1860, Dowd began agitating for the adoption of four time zones very much along the lines of those we use today. The idea met with surprisingly heated objections. Many thought it somehow ungodly to tinker with something as elemental as time. Some communities saw it as an impudence to expect them to change their clocks for the benefit of commercial interests like the railroads and telegraph companies. Almost everyone found the entire notion strange and puzzling, particularly those who lived on or near the prospective time zone borders. People in a place like North Platte, Nebraska, couldn't for the life of them understand why their neighbors down the road in Ogallala should get to rise an hour later than they each day.

Finally, in November 1883, after a meeting called the National Railway Time Convention, it was agreed to introduce time zones and synchronize clocks. November 18, dubbed "the day of two noons," was set for its inception. For two weeks, people everywhere fretted and fussed as if the country were about to be struck by an outsized meteor. Farmers worried that their hens would stop laying or that their cows would go dry. Workers in Chicago, suspecting they would be compelled to work an extra nine minutes on the big day, threatened to strike. By the dawn of the appointed day, the nation was in a fever of uncertainty. Just before noon, people everywhere began silently gathering by town halls and courthouses to watch the clocks change.

Although the time change had no legal authority—it was done solely at the behest of the railroads—it went ahead almost everywhere, and almost everywhere the event proved to be disappointingly anticlimactic. Millions watched as the hands on their courthouse clocks were summarily advanced or moved back a few minutes, and then quietly returned to business as it dawned on them that that was as exciting as it was going to get. Here and there, local difficulties cropped up. In Washington, a disagreement between the U.S. Attorney General and the head of the Naval Observatory meant that for several years government clocks in the city showed a different time from all others.[2] But for the most part,

America took to uniform timekeeping with barely a flutter and life grew easier because of it.

Money, too, was a feature of American life that did not become standardized until relatively late in the day. Only with the issuing of the first "greenbacks" during the Civil War did the federal government produce any paper money. Unlike coinage, paper money was left to banks. Through the first half of the nineteenth century, banks—and the word is used loosely to describe some of these institutions—were in the happy position of being able to print their own money. Types of bills proliferated wildly. In Zanesville, Ohio, to take one example, no fewer than thirty banks churned out money under such colorful appellations as the Virginia Saline Bank and the Owl Creek Bank. Such bills were often of such dubious value that they were referred to as *shinplasters*.[3] Some banks' money was more respected than others'. The Citizens' Bank of New Orleans issued a particularly sought-after $10 bill. Because the French word for ten, *dix*, was inscribed on the back, they became known as *Dixies*. As a descriptive term for the whole South, the word didn't really catch on until 1859, when Daniel Decatur Emmett, a Northerner, wrote the immensely successful song "Dixie's Land" (which almost everyone thinks, wrongly, is called "Dixie").[4]

Despite the confusing varieties of money floating about, the situation was in fact a great improvement on what had gone before. Throughout the colonial period, the British had allowed very little British specie to circulate in the colonies. Though businesses kept their accounts in pounds, shillings, and pence, they relied on whatever tender came to hand—Portuguese *johanneses* (familiarly known as *joes*), Spanish *doubloons* and *pistoles*, French *sous* and *picayunes*, Italian and Flemish *ducatoons*, American *fugios* (so called because the Latin *fugio*, "I fly," was inscribed on one side), and other types of coin almost without number. Businesspeople had to know that 1 shilling and 4 pence was equal in value to one-sixth of a milled *peso* (the original "piece of eight"), that a Spanish or Mexican *real* was worth 2½ cents, that a Portuguese *johannes* traded for $8.81, that 2 shillings and 3 pence was equivalent to half a Dutch *dollar*. Along the eastern seaboard, a *real* was generally called a shilling, but elsewhere it was more racily known as a *bit*. First found in English in 1688, *bit* may be a translation of the Spanish *pieza*, "piece" (which metamorphosed into *peso*), or it may be that the early coins were literally bits broken from larger silver coins. Because a bit was worth 12½ cents, a quarter dollar naturally became known as *two bits* and a half dollar as *four bits*, particularly west of the Mississippi. Ten cents was a *short bit*; a *long bit* was 15 cents. Even after the United States began minting its own coins, foreign coins remained such an integral part of American commerce that they weren't withdrawn from circulation until 1857.

To add to the confusion, values varied from place to place. In Pennsylvania and Virginia, a half *real* went by the alternative name *fipenny* (pronounced "fip-uh-nee") *bit* or *fip* because it was equivalent in worth to an English 5-penny piece. But in New York it was worth 6 pence and in New England 4 pence hapenny (pronounced "hape-nee"). It is something of a wonder that any business got done at all—and even more wondrous when you consider that until after the Revolution there wasn't a single bank in America. Philadelphia got the first, in 1781; Boston and New York followed three years later.[5]

Not surprisingly perhaps, many people dispensed with money and relied instead on barter, or *country pay* as it was often called. The goods used in barter were known as *truck* (from the Old French *troquer,* meaning to peddle or trade), a sense preserved in the expression *to have no truck with* and in *truck farm,* neither of which has anything to do with large wheeled vehicles. (In the vehicular sense, *truck* comes from the Latin *trochus,* "wheel.")

Our decimalized monetary system based on dollars and cents was devised by Gouverneur Morris as assistant to the superintendent of finances, in consultation with Thomas Jefferson, and adopted in 1784 against the protests of bankers and businessmen, most of whom wanted to preserve English units and terms such as *pound* and *shilling.* The names given the first official U.S. coins were something of an etymological ragbag. In ascending order they were *mill, cent, dime, dollars,* and *eagle.*

Dollar comes ultimately from *Joachimstaler,* a coin that was first made in the Bohemian town of Joachimstal in 1519 and then spread through Europe as *daler, thaler,* and *taler.* In an American context, *dollar* is first recorded in 1683.[6] *Dime,* or *disme* as it was spelled on the first coins, is a corruption of the French *dixième,* and was intended to be pronounced "deem," though it appears that hardly anyone did. The word is not strictly an Americanism. *Dime* had been used occasionally in Britain as early as 1377, though it had fallen out of use there long before, no doubt because in a nondecimal currency there was no use for a term meaning one-tenth. *Cent* comes from the Latin *centum,* "one hundred," and was rather an odd choice of term because initially there were 200 cents to a dollar.[7] Our custom of referring to a single cent as a *penny* is a holdover from the days of British control. No American coin has ever actually been called a penny. (The term appears to come from the Latin *pannus,* "a piece of cloth," and dates from a time when cloth was sometimes used as a medium of exchange.) A *mill,* from the Latin *millesimus,* "thousandth," was worth one-hundredth of a penny, and an *eagle* was worth $10.

A notable absentee from the list is *nickel.* There was early on a coin worth 5 cents, but it was called a *half dime* or *jitney,* from the French *jeton,* signifying a small coin or a token. When, in the opening years of this century, American cities began to fill with buses that charged a 5-cent fare, *jitney* fell out of use for the coin and attached itself instead to the vehicles. *Nickel* didn't become synonymous with the 5-cent piece until 1875; before that *nickel* signified either a 1-cent or 3-cent piece. The phrase "don't take any wooden nickels" dates only from 1915—and, no, there never was a time when wooden nickels circulated. Such a coin would have been immediately recognizable as counterfeit and in any case would have cost more to manufacture than it was worth.

One of the more durable controversies in the world of numismatics is where the dollar sign comes from. The first use of $ in an American context is in 1784 in a memorandum from Thomas Jefferson suggesting the dollar as the primary unit of currency, and some have deduced from this that he made it up there and then, either as a monogram based on his own initials (improbable; he was not that vain) or as a kind of doodle (equally improbable; he was not that unsystematic). A more widely held notion is that it originated as the letters *U* and *S* superimposed on each other and that the *U* eventually disintegrated into unconnected parallel lines. The problem with this theory is that $ as a symbol for *peso* far outdates its application to U.S. dollars. (It is still widely used as a peso sign throughout Latin America.) The most likely explanation is that it is a simplified depiction of the pillars of Hercules—twin pillars, wrapped around with a scroll—found on old Spanish pieces of eight.

Many of our slang terms and other like expressions associated with money date from the nineteenth century. Americans have been describing money as *beans* (as in "I haven't got a bean") since at least 1810 and as *dough* since at least 1851, when it was first recorded in the *Yale Tomahawk. Small change* has been with us since 1819, *not worth a cent* since the early 1820s, and *not worth a red cent* since 1839. *Upper crust* dates from 1832, *easy money* from 1836, *C-note* (short for *century note*) for a $100 bill from 1839, *flat broke* and *dead broke* from the 1840s. Americans have been referring to a dollar as a *buck* since 1856 (it comes from *buckskin,* an early unit of exchange). *Sound as a dollar, bet your bottom dollar, strike it rich, penny-ante,* and *spondulicks* or *spondulix* (a term of wholly mysterious origin) all date from the 1850s. A $10 bill has been a *sawbuck* since the early 1860s. It was so called because the original bills had a Roman numeral *X* on them, which brought to mind a sawhorse, or sawbuck. *Mazuma,* from a Yiddish slang term for money, dates from 1880, and *simoleon,* another word of uncertain provenance, dates from 1881.

But it wasn't just money terms that America developed in the nineteenth century. A flood, a positive torrent, of words and expressions of all types came out of the country in the period. The following is no more than a bare sampling: *to make the fur fly* (1804); *quick on the trigger* and *to whitewash* (1808); *to have an ax to grind* (1811); *to keep a stiff upper lip* (yes, it's an Americanism, 1815); *no two ways about it* (1818); *to fly off the handle* (1825); *to move like greased lightning* (1826); *to have a knockdown and dragout fight* (1827); *to sit on the fence* and *to go the whole hog* (1828); *firecracker, hornswoggle, noncommittal,* and *to be in cahoots with* (1829); *ornery* and *to talk turkey* (1830); *horse sense* and *nip and tuck* (often originally *rip and tuck;* no one knows why; 1832); *conniption fit, to bark up the wrong tree,* and *to keep one's eyes peeled* (1833); *close shave* and *rip-roaring* (1834); *hell-bent* (1835); *stool pigeon* (1836); *to have a chip on one's shoulders* and *to raise Cain* (1840); *to scoot* (1841); *to pull the wool over one's eyes* and *to get hitched,* in the sense of being married (1842); *to hold your horses* (1844); *beeline* (1845); *to stub one's toe* (1846); *to be a goner* (1847); *to back down, to dicker, by the great horn spoon,* and *highfalutin* (1848); *to face the music* (1850); *to paddle one's own canoe* and *to keep one's shirt on* (1854); *one-horse town* (1855); *to knock the spots off* and *stag party* (1856); *deadbeat* (1863); *to knuckle down* (1864); *to go haywire* (1865); *con man* and *to slather* (1866); *to go back on,* as with a promise (1868); *to get in on the ground floor* (1872); *to eat crow* (1877); *underdog* (1887); *cagey* in the sense of shrewd (1893); and *panhandler* and *to be out on a limb* (1897).

Scores more have since fallen out of use: *ground and lofty* (once a common synonym for *fine and dandy*), *happify, to missionate, to consociate* (that is, to come together in an assembly), *dunderment* (bewilderment), *puckerstoppled* (to be embarrassed), *from Dan to Beersheba.* This last, alluding to the northernmost and southernmost outposts of the Holy Land, was in daily use for at least two hundred years as a synonym for *wideranging, from A to Z,* but gradually, mysteriously, and rather regrettably dropped from view in the nineteenth century and hasn't been seen much since.

Sometimes the meaning of nineteenth-century neologisms is self-evident, as with *to move like greased lightning* and *to have a close shave. To go haywire* evidently alludes to the lacerating effect of that material once a tightly wound bale is loosed, and *to talk turkey* may owe something to a once-popular, if obviously apocryphal, story about an Indian and frontiersman who often went hunting together. According to this tale, each time they came to divide the kill, the frontiersman would say, "You may take the buzzard and I will take the turkey, or if you prefer I will take the turkey and you may take the buzzard." After several such episodes, the Indian interrupts the frontiersman and says, "But when do I get to talk turkey?" or words to that effect.

More often, however, we are left with words and phrases that seem to have sprung from the blue and do not appear to signify anything in particular—*even steven, fit as a fiddle, easy as a lead pipe cinch, to take a powder, to peter out, to paint the town red, to talk through one's hat, to josh, to root hog or die.* Explanations are frequently posited but all too often on unpersuasively flimsy evidence. The *Oxford English Dictionary* suggests that *josh* may be connected to the humorist Josh Billings, but in fact the term was current at least as early as 1845 and Josh Billings was unknown outside his neighborhood until 1860. *To face the music,* first recorded in a publication called the *Worcester Spy,* may allude to a soldier's being drummed out of service or possibly it may have some theatrical connection, perhaps to a nervous performer having to face the audience across the orchestra pit. But no one knows. The mild expletives *doggone* and *doggone it* both date from the early nineteenth century, though no one has any idea what they meant. The mystery deepens when you realize that the first recorded citation has it as *dog on't,* reminiscent of earlier formations like *a pox on't.*

Phony has been linked to everything from the Gaelic for *ring, fauney* or *fawney* (the explanation being that a street vendor known as a *fauney dropper* would show the gullible purchaser a ring of genuine quality, then slip him a cheap *fauney*), to an unscrupulous businessman named *Forney. Ballyhoo, blizzard, hunky dory, shanty, conniption fit* (at first also spelled *caniption* or *kniption*), *bogus, bamboozle,* and many other durable Americanisms are of unknown, or at least decidedly uncertain, derivation. *To root hog or die,* first found in *A Narrative Life of David Crockett* in 1834, is similarly bewildering. The expression, meaning to fend for oneself or perish, evidently refers to the rooting practices of hogs, but precisely what Mr. Crockett (or his ghostwriter) meant by it is uncertain. His contemporaries, it seems, were no wiser. They variously rendered the expression as "root, hog, or die" (as if it were an admonition to a pig) or as "root, hog or die" (as if presenting a list of three options). Clearly they hadn't the faintest idea what they wanted the poor hog to do, but the expression filled a gap in the American lexicon, and that is what mattered. As Gertrude Stein might have put it, an expression doesn't have to mean anything as long as it means something.

For a long time the most American of Americanisms, *O.K.,* fell resoundingly into this category. The explanations for its etymology have been as inspired as they have been various. Among the theories: that it is short for *only kissing,* that the semiliterate Andrew Jackson wrote it on papers as an abbreviation for *oll korrect* (in fact, he was not that ignorant), that it came from *Orrin Kendall* crackers, that it was an abbreviation for the Greek *olla kalla* ("all good"), that it was from a prized brand of Haitian rum called *Aux Cayes,* that it was an early telegraphic abbreviation for *open key,* that it was from the Choctaw affirmative *okeh,* that it came from the Indian chief *Old Keokuk,* and that it came from the nickname for Martin Van Buren, *Old Kinderhook* (he was from Kinderhook, New York).

Learned papers were written in defense of various contentions. The matter was discussed at conferences. By 1941, when Allen Walker Read, a professor at Columbia University, began looking into the matter, *O.K.* was already the most widely understood Americanism in the world and the search for its origins was the etymological equivalent of the search for DNA. It took Read some twenty years to nail the matter down, but thanks to his efforts we now know that *O.K.* first appeared in print in the *Boston Morning Post* on March 23, 1839, as a jocular abbreviation for "Oll Korrect." At the time there was a fashion for such, and often intentionally illiterate, concoctions—*K.Y.* for "Know Use," *R.T.B.S.* for "Remains to Be Seen," *K.G.* for "Know Go," *W.O.O.O.F.C.* for "With One of Our First Citizens." In 1840, when Martin Van Buren ran for President, the Democratic O.K. Club was formed to promote his election, evidently helping to consolidate *O.K.* in the national consciousness. Almost overnight the term raced into general usage, where it has remained ever since.[8]

As well as creating new words by the hundreds in the nineteenth century, Americans also gave new meanings to old ones. *Fix* and its offshoots accumulated so many uses that Craigie and Hulbert's *Dictionary of American English* needs nearly seven columns of text and some five thousand words to discuss their specifically American applications. They added prepositions to common verbs to give them new or heightened significance: *to pass out, to check in, to show off, to beat up, to flare up, to start off, to stave off, to cave in, to fork over, to hold on, to hold out, to stay put, to brush off, to get away with.* They cut long words down—turning *penitentiary* into *pen, fanatic* into *fan, reformation* into *reform*—and simplified constructions, preferring *to graduate* over *to be graduated.* They created nouns from verbs—*dump* and *beat,* for example. Above all, they turned nouns into verbs. The practice began as early as the late seventeenth century (*to scalp,* first noted in 1693, is one of the earliest) and reached a kind of fever pitch in the nineteenth. The list of American verb formations is all but endless: *to interview, to bankroll, to highlight, to package, to panic, to au-*

dition, to curb, to bellyache, to demean, to progress, to corner, to endorse, to engineer, to predicate, to resurrect, to notice, to advocate, to splurge, to boost, to coast, to oppose, to demoralize, to placate, to donate, to peeve (backformed from peevish), to locate, to evoke, to rattle, to deed, to boom, to park, to sidestep, to hustle, to bank, to lynch, to ready, to service, to enthuse—all of these, and many more, are Americanisms without which the language clearly would be very much the poorer.[9]

The nineteenth century was, in short, our Elizabethan age, and the British hated us for it. Among the many neologisms that stirred their bile were backwoodsman, balance for remainder, spell in the context of time or weather, round-up, once in a while, no great shakes, to make one's mind up, there's no two ways about it, influential, census, presidential, standpoint, outhouse, cross-purposes, rambunctious, scrumptious, loan for lend (not actually an Americanism at all), portage, immigration, fork as in a road, mileage, gubernatorial, reliable, and almost any new verb.

The first recorded attack on an American usage came in 1735 when an English visitor named Francis Moore referred to the young city of Savannah as standing upon a hill overlooking a river "which they in barbarous English call a bluff" and thereby, in the words of H. L. Mencken, "set the tone that English criticism has maintained ever since."[10] Samuel Johnson, who seldom passed up a chance to insult his colonial cousins (they were, in his much-quoted phrase, "a race of convicts, and ought to be grateful for anything we allow them short of hanging"), vilified an American book on geography for having the misguided audacity to use such terms as creek, gap, branch, and spur when they had not been given a British benediction. Another critic attacked Noah Webster for including the Americanism lengthy in his dictionary. "What are we coming to?" he despaired. "If the word is permitted to stand, the next edition will authorize the word 'strengthy.' "[11] A Captain Basil Hall, a professional traveler, writer, and, it would appear, halfwit, spoke for many when he remarked that America's penchant for neologisms was unnecessary because "there are enough words already."[12]

By the 1800s, the continent fairly crawled with British observers who reported with patronizing glee on America's eccentric and irregular speech habits. Captain Frederick Marryat, best known for the novels Mr. Midshipman Easy (1836) and Masterman Ready (1841), recounted how one American had boasted to him that he had not just trebled an investment but "fourbled and fivebled" it. It was Marryat who also reported the oft-recounted—and conveniently unverifiable—story of the family that clad its piano's legs in little skirts so as not to excite any untoward sexual hankerings among the more impressionable of its visitors.

The classlessness of U.S. English—the habit of calling every woman a *lady,* every man a *gentleman*—attracted particular vituperation. Charles Janson, a British writer, recorded how he made the mistake of referring to a young maid as a servant. "I'd have you to know, man, that I am no sarvant," she bristled. "None but negers are sarvants." She was, she informed him solemnly, her employer's *help.*[13] Though easy enough to mock, such semantic distinctions contributed mightily toward making America a less stratified society. Moreover they underscored the essential openness of the American character. As Henry Steele Commager put it: "The American was good natured, generous, hospitable and sociable, and he reversed the whole history of language to make the term 'stranger' one of welcome."[14]

Before long, it seemed, an American could scarcely open his mouth without running the risk of ending up mocked between hard covers. Abuse was heaped upon the contemptible American habit of shortening or simplifying words—using *pants* for *trousers, thanks* in favor of *thank you, gents* instead of *gentlemen.* "If I were naked and starving I would refuse to be clothed gratis in a 'Gent's Furnishing Store,' " sniffed one especially fastidious social commentator.[15] *Pants,* a shortening of *pantaloons,* is an Americanism first recorded in 1840 and attacked as a needless lexical affectation within the year. Incidentally, but not without interest, *panties* came into American English in 1845 and for a long time signified undershorts for males. They weren't regarded as a female article until 1908.

The British appeared unaware that their mockery had the capacity to make them look priggish and obtuse. Charles Dickens in his *American Notes* professed to have been utterly baffled when a waiter asked him if he wanted his food served "right away." As Dillard points out, even if Dickens had never heard the expression, he must have been a very dim traveler indeed to fail to grasp its meaning.[16]

Always there was a presumption that Americans should speak as Britons. In 1827, Frances Trollope, mother of the novelist Anthony Trollope, came to America at the rather advanced age of forty-seven to found a department store in Cincinnati. The enterprise failed and she lost everything, down to her household effects. But the experience gave her ample fodder for her enormously successful *Domestic Manners of the Americans*, published in 1832. Among her criticisms of American behavior, she was struck again and again by how rarely she had heard a sentence "correctly pronounced." It appears never to have occurred to her that Americans had a perfect right, and sometimes possibly even a sound reason, to pronounce words in their own way.

All this would have been fractionally more bearable had the commentators not so often been given to blithe generalizations and careless reporting. Emerson noted with more than a hint of exasperation that most

Americans didn't speak in anything like the manner that Dickens suggested. "He has picked up and noted with eagerness each odd local phrase that he met with, and when he had a story to relate, has joined them together, so that the result is the broadest caricature."[17] And all the while they were making capital out of America's foibles, the British observers were unwittingly picking up American habits. It was, ironically, Dickens's use of many Americanisms, notably *talented, lengthy, reliable,* and *influential,* which he had absorbed on his travels and unthinkingly employed in *American Notes,* that at last brought them a measure of respectability in his homeland.[18]

For their part, Americans showed a streak of masochism as wide as the Mississippi. When *American Notes* was published it was such a sensation that people lined up fifty deep to acquire a copy. In Philadelphia it sold out in thirty-five minutes. Mrs. Trollope's *Domestic Manners of the Americans* was even more successful, going through four editions in a year and so capturing America's attention that a British visitor was astonished to discover that her barbed observations on American social habits had almost entirely displaced a raging cholera epidemic as the principal topic of news in the papers and conversation in the taverns.

Attacks on the new national language came from within as well as from without. In 1781, the eminent president of Princeton, John Witherspoon, a Scot by birth but one of the signers of the Declaration of Independence—indeed, a fierce proponent of American independence from Britain in all things but language—wrote a series of articles for the *Pennsylvania Journal and Weekly Advertiser* in which he attacked the lax linguistic habits that predominated in his adopted country even among educated speakers: using *notify* for *inform, mad* for *angry, clever* for *good,* and other such "improprieties and vulgarisms which hardly any person in the same class in point of rank and literature would have fallen into in Great Britain."[19] In the course of these writings he became the first to use *Americanism* in a linguistic sense, but by no means the last to use it pejoratively.

There was, it must be said, more than a dollop of toadying to be found among many Americans. When the Scottish philosopher David Hume criticized Franklin for employing *colonize* and other New World novelties in his correspondence, Franklin contritely apologized and promised to abandon the practice at once. John Russell Bartlett compiled a *Dictionary of Americanisms,* but far from being a celebration of the inventive nature of American speech, the book dismissed Americanisms as "perversions." James Fenimore Cooper in *The American Democrat* opined: "The common faults of American language are an ambition of effect, a want of simplicity and a turgid abuse of terms."[20]

Many critics on both sides of the Atlantic feared that America would cut itself off from its linguistic and cultural database (as it were) by forming an effectively separate dialect. Linguistic isolation was not a sensible or desirable goal for a small, young nation if it wished to be heard in the wider world of commerce, law, and science. The *Knickerbocker Magazine* saw the "greatest danger" in America's tendency toward linguistic innovation and urged its readers to adhere to British precepts.

Several observers pointed out that the American continent required a more expansive vocabulary than the British Isles, like the anonymous essayist in the *North American Review* who plaintively noted: "How tame will his language sound, who would describe Niagara in language fitted for the falls at London bridge, or attempt the majesty of the Mississippi in that which was made for the Thames?"[21] Or as Jefferson put it with somewhat greater simplicity: "The new circumstances under which we are placed, call for new words, new phrases, and for the transfer of old words to new objects."

Others saw Britain's linguistic hegemony as presumptuous and imperious. We were not her children any longer. "Our honor requires us to have a system of our own, in language as well as government," argued Noah Webster in 1789. Echoing his sentiment, the writer Rupert Hughes asked: "Why should we permit the survival of the curious notion that our language is a mere loan from England, like a copper kettle that we must keep scoured and return without a dent?"[22]

Still others tried the defense—accurate if somewhat feeble—that many of the objectionable words were not Americanisms at all. Chaucer, it was pointed out, had used *gab;* Johnson had included *influential* in his dictionary; *afeared* had existed in English since Saxon times. *Son of a gun, to bite the dust, to beat it, I guess,* and scores of other detestable "Americanisms" all had existed in England, it was pointed out, long before there were any American colonies. As the poet James Russell Lowell dryly put it, Americans "unhappily could bring over no English better than Shakespeare's."[23] One dedicated scribbler named Alfred Elwyn compiled a *Glossary of Supposed Americanisms* in which he asserted passionately but wrongly: "The simple truth is, that almost without exception all those words or phrases that we have been ridiculed for using, are good old English; many of them are Anglo-Saxon in origin, and nearly all to be heard at this day in England."

This tack struck many as more than a little pathetic. Lowell acidly observed: "Surely we may sleep in peace now, and our English cousins will forgive us, since we have cleared ourselves from any suspicion of being original in the matter."[24]

Lowell had a particular reason for feeling protective about the

American dialect. His fame rested almost entirely on the creation of a fictional New England hayseed, Hosea Biglow, whose comically quaint speech formed the basis of the hugely popular *Biglow Papers.* Unfortunately, Lowell's effectiveness as a defender of American speech was somewhat diminished by his growing antipathy for his own creation. When the reading public continually ignored his more earnest poetical compositions (and rightly; they were unceasingly mediocre), he went so far as to preface a volume of Biglow poems with a veiled insult to the reader: *"Margaritas, munde porcine, calcâsti: en, siliquas accipe,"* which translates as "Oh, swinish world, you have trampled pearls; so take the husks."[25]

Nonetheless, he left behind an invaluable mass of material recording the habits of New England speech in the first half of the nineteenth century. As an extract shows, it was very different from that of today:

> *Ez fer war, I call it murder,—*
> *There you hev it plain an' flat:*
> *I don't want to go no furder*
> *Than my Testyment fer that;*
>
> *God hez sed so plump an' fairly*
> *It's ez long ez it is broad,*
> *An' you've gut to git up airly*
> *Ef you want to take in God.*

But this, it must be remembered, was the speech of an uneducated New Englander. Someone from a more refined background, like John Quincy Adams, say, would have sounded as different again. One of the paradoxes of the day was that as America was becoming more politically unified it was in danger of becoming linguistically fractured. Class differences and regional differences alike were acutely felt and remarked upon. The relative few who lived out along the frontier were cut off not only from changes in fashion but also from changes in language. So when, for instance, Britons and eastern Americans began to change the diphthong in words like *boil* and *join* from *bile* and *jine,* or to insert a voiced *r* in some words while removing it from others, the frontier people were less likely to adopt the new trends. They continued for much longer to say "bar" for *bear,* "consarn" for *concern,* "varmint" for *vermin,* "virtoo" for *virtue,* "fortin" for *fortune,* "enjīne" for *engine,* "cattel" or "kittle" for *kettle,* "cuss" for *curse,* "thrash" for *thresh,* "tetchy" for *touchy,* "wrastle" for *wrestle,* "chaw" for *chew,* "gal" for *girl,* "riled" for *roiled,* "critter" for *creature,* and so on.

As a new breed of frontier people like Andrew Jackson, Davy Crockett, and Abraham Lincoln brought their regional speechways to Washington with them, their distinctive turns of phrase and raw pronunciations increasingly grated on the sensibilities of their eastern colleagues and underlined the linguistic variability of the sprawling nation. Something of the flavor and pronunciation of frontier life is conveyed by a speech attributed to Davy Crockett (though in fact it was concocted on his behalf by a ghostwriter). "We are called upon to show our grit like a chain lightning agin a pine log, to extarminate, mollify and calumniate the foe like a niggar put into a holler log. . . . Cram his pesky carcass full of thunder and lightning like a stuffed sassidge and turtle him off with a red hot poker. . . . Split his countenance with a live airthquake, and tarrify him with a rale Injun yell. . . ." Though the words are not Crockett's, there is no reason to suppose that the spellings are unfaithful to his pronunciations.[26]

Much the same country air applied to Lincoln, if at slightly less than gale force. However sophisticated his prose style, Lincoln's spoken English always had a whiff of the backwoods about it. His invariable greeting was "Howdy," and his conversation was sprinkled with folksy colloquialisms like "out yonder" and "stay a spell," which must have caused at least some of Washington's more sophisticated politicos to cringe.[27] He very probably pronounced more than a few of his words in the antiquated frontier style. Certainly we know that he enjoyed an earthy story and took delight in showing his associates a letter he received from a disgruntled citizen in 1860. It read: "God damn your god damned old hellfired god damned soul to hell god damn you and goddam your god damned family's god damned hellfired god damned soul to hell and god damnation god damn them and god damn your god damn friends to hell."[28] The letter came, it hardly needs saying, from the frontier.

The friction between the direct, colorful, independent language of the West and the more reserved and bookish diction of the East was a constant leitmotif of American speech throughout the nineteenth century, and nowhere was it made more arrestingly manifest than at the commemoration of a cemetery for Civil War soldiers in the little Pennsylvania town of Gettysburg on November 19, 1863.

The main speaker of the day was not Lincoln, but the orator Edward Everett—an Easterner, naturally. As was the custom of the day, his speech was full of literary allusions, Ciceronian pomp, and obscure historical references that bore only the scantest significance to the occasion. The syntax was highflown and decked out with phalanxes of subordinate clauses, convoluted constructions, and parenthetical excursions. Almost every sentence had an acre of flowery verbiage between the subject and predicate. A single sentence gives some hint of its denseness:

> Lord Bacon, in "the true marshalling of the sovereign degrees of honor," assigns the first place to "the Condirotores Imperiorum, founders of States and Commonwealths"; and truly, to build up from the discordant elements of our nature, the passions, the interests and the opinions of the individual man, the rivalries of family, clan and tribe, the influences of climate and geographical position, the accidents of peace and war accumulated for ages—to build up from those often-times warring elements a well-compacted, prosperous and powerful State, if it were to be accomplished by one effort or in one generation would require a more than mortal skill.

And this was just one of some fifteen hundred equally windy sentences. At 2 P.M., two long, cold hours after starting, Everett concluded his speech to thunderous applause—motivated, one is bound to suspect, more by the joy of realizing it was over than by any message derived from the content—and turned the dais over to President Lincoln. The audience of perhaps fifteen thousand people had been standing for four hours, and was tired, cold, and hungry. Lincoln rose awkwardly, "like a telescope drawing out," as one contemporary put it, adjusted his glasses, held the paper directly in front of his face, and in a high, reedy voice delivered his address. "He barely took his eyes off the manuscript," according to one witness, as he intoned those famous words:

> Four score and seven years ago our fathers brought forth on this continent a new nation, conceived in liberty and dedicated to the proposition that all men are created equal.
> Now we are engaged in a great civil war, testing whether that nation or any nation so conceived and so dedicated can long endure. We are met on a great battlefield of that war. We have come to dedicate a portion of that field as a final resting place for those who here gave their lives that that nation might live. It is altogether fitting and proper that we should do this.
> But, in a larger sense, we cannot dedicate—we cannot consecrate—we cannot hallow—this ground. The brave men, living and dead, who struggled here have consecrated it far above our poor power to add or detract. The world will little note nor long remember what we say here, but it can never forget what they did here. It is for us, the living, rather, to be dedicated here to the unfinished work which they who fought here have thus far so nobly advanced.

It is rather for us to be here dedicated to the great task remaining before us—that from these honored dead we take increased devotion to that cause for which they gave the last full measure of devotion; that we here highly resolve that these dead shall not have died in vain; that this nation, under God, shall have a new birth of freedom; and that government of the people, by the people, for the people shall not perish from the earth.

Though Lincoln was never expected to provide anything other than some concluding remarks, this was breathtakingly brief. The Gettysburg Address contained just 268 words, two-thirds of them of only one syllable, in ten mostly short, direct, and memorably crystalline sentences. It took only a fraction over two minutes to deliver—so little, according to several contemporary accounts, that the official photographer was still making preliminary adjustments to his camera when the President sat down.

Far from taking the listener on a discursive trip through the majesties of imperial Rome or the glory that was Greece, the address contained no proper nouns at all. As Garry Wills notes, it doesn't mention Gettysburg or slavery or even the Union.[29] Lincoln thought it a failure. "I failed: I failed: and that is about all that can be said about it," he remarked forlornly to Everett. Many agreed with him. The *Chicago Times* wrote: "The cheek of every American must tingle with shame as he reads the silly, flat and dishwatery utterances of the man who has to be pointed out to intelligent foreigners as the President of the United States." Even newspapers sympathetic to Lincoln scarcely noted his address. Not until considerably later was it perceived as perhaps the greatest of American speeches.

The Gettysburg Address also marked a small but telling lexical transition. Before the Civil War, people generally spoke of *the Union,* with its implied emphasis on the voluntariness of the American confederation. In his first inaugural address, Lincoln invoked *the Union* twenty times, and *nation* not at all. Three years of bloody Civil War later, the Gettysburg Address contained five mentions of *nation* and not one of *union.*

We have come to take for granted the directness and accessibility of Lincoln's prose, but we should remember that this was an age of ludicrously inflated diction, not only among politicians, orators, and literary aesthetes, but even in newspapers. As Kenneth Cmiel notes in *Democratic Eloquence,* no nineteenth-century journalist with any self-respect would write that a house had burned down, but must instead say that "a great conflagration consumed the edifice." Nor would he be content with a sentiment as unexpressive as "a crowd came to see" but instead would write "a vast concourse was assembled to witness."[30]

In an era when no speaker would use two words if eight would do, or dream of using the same word twice in the same week, Lincoln reveled in simplicity and repetition. William Seward, his Secretary of State, drafted Lincoln's first inaugural address. It was a masterpiece of the times. Lincoln pruned it and made it timeless. Where Seward wrote "We are not, we must not be, aliens or enemies, but fellow-countrymen and brethren," Lincoln changed it to "We are not enemies, but friends. We must not be enemies."[31] Such succinctness and repetition were not just novel, but daring.

His speeches were constantly marked by a distinctive rhythm—what Wills calls "preliminary eddyings that yield to lapidary monosyllables," as in "The world will little note, nor long remember, what we do here," and "We shall nobly save, or meanly lose, the last best hope of earth."[32] Always there was a directness about his words that stood in marked contrast to the lofty circumlocutions of the East and marked him as a product of the frontier. "With malice towards none; with charity for all; with firmness in the right . . . let us strive . . . to do all which may achieve and cherish a just, and a lasting peace, among ourselves, and with all nations," from Lincoln's second inaugural address, may not seem on the face of it to have a great deal in common with Davy Crockett's "like chain lightning agin a pine log," but in fact it has precisely the same directness and simplicity of purpose, if phrased with somewhat more thoughtful elegance.

American English had at last found a voice to go with its flag and anthem and national symbol in the shape of Uncle Sam. But at the same time it had found something else even more gratifying and more certain to guarantee its prospects in the world. It had found wealth—wealth beyond the dreams of other nations. And for that story we must embark on another chapter.

Chapter 6

WE'RE IN THE MONEY: THE AGE OF INVENTION

On the morning of July 2, 1881, President James Garfield, accompanied by his Secretary of State, James G. Blaine, was passing through the central railroad station in Washington, D.C., to spend the Fourth of July holiday on the New Jersey shore with his family. His wife had only recently recovered from a nearly fatal bout of malaria, and he was naturally anxious to be with her. In those days there was no Secret Service protection for the President. On occasions such as this the President was quite literally a public figure. Anyone could approach him, and one man did—a quietly deranged lawyer named Charles Guiteau, who walked up to the President and calmly shot him twice with a .44 caliber revolver, then stepped aside and awaited arrest. Guiteau's complaint, it transpired, was that the President had ignored his repeated entreaties to be made chief consul in Paris.

The nation waited breathlessly for news of the President's recovery. Newspapers all over the country posted frequent, not to say strikingly candid, bulletins outside their main offices. "The President was somewhat restless and vomited several times during the early part of the night. Nutritious enemata were successfully employed to sustain him," read a typical one on the facade of the *New York Herald* office.[1]

As the President slipped in and out of consciousness, the greatest minds in the country were brought to his bedside in the hope that someone could offer something more positively beneficial than rectal sustenance. Alexander Graham Bell, at the peak of his fame, devised a makeshift metal detector, which he called an "induction balance" and which employed his recently invented telephone as a listening aid. The intention was to locate the bullets lodged in the President's frame, but to Bell's considerable consternation it appeared to show bullets practically everywhere in the President's body. Not until much later was it realized that the device had been reading the bedsprings.

The summer of 1881 was one of the sultriest in the nation's capital in years. To provide some relief for the stricken President, a corps of naval engineers who specialized in ventilating mine shafts was summoned to the White House and instructed to build a cooling device. They rigged up a large iron box filled with ice, salt, and water and a series of terry-cloth filters which were saturated by the melting ice. A fan drew in warm air from outside, which was cooled as it passed over the damp terry cloth, cleansed by charcoal filters, and propelled onward into the President's bedroom. The device was not terribly efficient—in fifty-eight days it consumed a quarter of a million pounds of ice—but it cooled the President's room to a more or less tolerable eighty-one degrees, and stands in history as the first air conditioner.[2]

Nothing, alas, could revive the sinking President, and on the evening of September 19, two and a half months after he had been shot, he quietly passed away.

The shooting of President Garfield was significant in two ways. First, it proved the folly of the *spoils system,* a term inspired by a famous utterance of New York politician William L. Marcy sixty years earlier: "To the victor belong the spoils."[3] Under the spoils system it fell to a newly elected President to appoint literally hundreds of officials, from rural postmasters and lighthouse keepers to ambassadors. It was a handy way to reward political loyalty, but a tediously time-consuming process for a President, and—as Charles Guiteau conclusively demonstrated—it bred dissatisfaction among disappointed aspirants. Two years later, Congress abolished the practice for all but the most senior posts. The shooting of the President—or more precisely the response to the shooting—was significant in another way as well. It underlined the distinctively American belief that almost any problem, whether it was finding a bullet buried in soft tissue or cooling the bedroom of a dying Chief Executive, could be solved with the judicious application of a little know-how.

Know-how, dating from 1857, is a quintessentially American term and something of a leitmotif for the nineteenth century. Thanks to it, and some other not insignificant factors like an abundance of natural resources and a steady supply of cheap immigrant labor, the United States was by 1881 well on its way to completing a remarkable transformation from an agrarian society on the periphery of world events to an economic colossus. In the thirty years that lay either side of Garfield's death the country enjoyed a period of growth unlike any seen anywhere in history.

In almost every area of economic activity, America rose like a giant, producing quantities of raw materials and finished products that dwarfed the output of other countries—sometimes dwarfed the output of all other countries combined. Between 1850 and 1900, American coal production rose from 14 million tons to over 100 million; steel output went from barely a million tons to over 25 million; paper production increased ninefold, pig iron production sevenfold, cottonseed oil by a factor of fourteen, copper wire by a factor of almost twenty. In 1850, America's 23 million people had a cumulative wealth of $7.1 billion. Fifty years later, the population had tripled to 76 million, but the wealth had increased thirteenfold to $94.3 billion. In 1894, the United States displaced Britain as the world's leading manufacturer. By 1914, it was the world's leading producer of coal, natural gas, oil, copper, iron ore, and silver, and its factories were producing more goods than those of Britain, Germany, and France together. Within thirty years of Garfield's death, one-fourth of all the world's wealth was in American hands.[4] For the average American, progress was not, in the words of Henry Steele Commager, "a philosophical idea but a commonplace of experience. . . . Nothing in all history had ever succeeded like America, and every American knew it."[5]

In no other country could the average citizen enjoy such an intoxicating possibility of accumulating wealth. An obsession with money had long been evident in the national speech. As early as the eighteenth century, Benjamin Franklin was reminding his readers that *time is money* and foreign visitors were remarking on the distinctly American expression *to net a cool thousand,*[6] and on the custom of defining a person as being *worth so-and-so many dollars.* Long before Henry Clay thought up the term in 1832, America was the land of the *self-made man.*[7] At about the same time, people began referring to the shapers of the American economy as *businessmen.* The word had existed in English since at least 1670, but previously it had suggested only someone engaged in public affairs.[8] In the sense of a person concerned with the serious matter of creating wealth, it is an Americanism. As the century progressed, people could be *well fixed* (1822), *well-to-do* (1825), *in the dimes* (1843), *in clover* (1847), *heeled* (1867; *well-heeled* didn't come until the twentieth century), a *high roller* (1881), or a *money bag* (1896 and made into the plural *money bags* in the first years of this century). As early as the 1850s they could hope *to strike it rich,* and by the 1880s they could dream of *living the life of Riley* (from a popular song of the period, "Is That Mr. Reilly?" in which the hero speculates on what he would do with a sudden fortune).[9]

Not everyone liked this new thrusting America. In 1844, Philip Hone, a mayor of New York and a noted social critic, wrote, "Oh, for *the good old days,*" the first recorded use of the phrase.[10] But most people, then as now, wanted nothing more than to get their hands on *the almighty dollar,* an expression coined by Washington Irving in 1836 in an article in *The Knickerbocker Magazine.*[11]

A great many of them did. As early as the mid-1820s, Americans were talking admiringly of *millionaires,* a term borrowed from the British, who had in turn taken it from the French, and by 1850 were supplementing the word with a more aggressive version of their own devising: *multimillionaires.*[12] An American lucky enough to *get in on the ground floor* (1872) with an arresting invention or a timely investment might reasonably hope to become a millionaire himself. Between 1840 and 1915, the number of millionaires in America went from just twenty to forty thousand.[13]

The new class of *tycoons* (from the Japanese *taikun,* military commander, and first applied to business leaders in the 1870s) enjoyed a concentration of money and power now almost unimaginable. In 1891, John D. Rockefeller and Standard Oil controlled 70 percent of the world market for oil. J. P. Morgan's House of Morgan and its associate companies in 1912 were worth more, according to the historian Howard Zinn, "than the assessed value of all the property in the twenty-two states and territories west of the Mississippi."[14]

With great wealth came the luxury of eccentricity. James Hill of the Great Northern Railroad reportedly fired an employee because the man's name was Spittles. The servants at J. P. Morgan's London residence nightly prepared dinner, turned down the bed, and laid out nightclothes for their master even when he was known beyond doubt to be three thousand miles away in New York. The industrialist John M. Longyear, disturbed by the opening of a railroad line beside his Michigan residence, had the entire estate packed up—sixty-room house, hedges, trees, shrubs, fountains, the works—and reerected in Brookline, Massachusetts.[15] James Gordon Bennett, a newspaper baron, liked to announce his arrival in a restaurant by yanking the tablecloths from all the tables he passed. He would then hand the manager a wad of cash with which to compensate his victims for their lost meals and spattered attire. Though long forgotten in his native land, Bennett and his exploits—invariably involving prodigious drinking before and lavish restitution after—were once world-famous, and indeed his name lives on in England in the cry "Gordon Bennett!"—usually uttered by someone who has just been drenched by a clumsy waiter or otherwise exposed to some exasperating indignity.

The indulgences of the rich become all the more insufferable when contrasted with the miserable condition of those whose labors sustained their wealth. Through the 1860s, workers in factories—or *manufactories* as they were still often called—routinely worked sixteen-hour days six days a week for less than 20 cents a day. Often they were paid in scrip, which they could spend only at the factory store. Workplaces were often ill lit, ill heated, and filled with dangerous machinery and perilous substances. A physician in the mill town of Lawrence, Massachusetts, noted just after the turn of the century that 36 percent of factory workers employed by one firm didn't live to see their twenty-fifth birthdays.[16]

As America prospered, less attractive words entered the language, like *slum* (of uncertain origin, but probably based on a British dialectal variant of *slime*) and *sweatshop*, commonly shortened to *sweater* and first recorded in 1867, and *tenderloin* for the less salubrious areas of cities. This last has been traced to a New York policeman who announced upon being assigned to the district around 42nd Street that the opportunities for graft would enable him to stop eating ground beef and switch to tenderloin. The obvious pun on a prostitute's salient anatomical feature no doubt helped to reinforce the term.[17] Older words, too, sometimes took on new, more sinister meanings. *Tenement* originally described any tenanted dwelling, but in America, where only the poor lived in shared housing, it had by the 1840s taken on the sense of a crowded, fetid building inhabited by the lowest orders.

Out in the sunshine of prosperity it was a dazzling age. A brief list of just some American inventions of the period may give an idea of the dynamism that seized the country: the passenger elevator, escalator, telephone, phonograph, air brake, cash register, electric light, fountain pen, linotype, box camera, pneumatic tire, adding machine, revolving door, safety pin, paper clip, and typewriter. All were invented in America, mostly in the frantic last quarter of the nineteenth century, and all were designed to relieve people of some everyday inconvenience. Where other countries tied their fortunes to the development of revolutionary industrial processes—Bessemer steel, Jacquard looms, steam presses—Americans primarily churned out appliances that made life easier. They took to heart Ralph Waldo Emerson's famous apothegm "Build a better mousetrap and the world will beat a path to your door." Or they would have had Emerson ever said any such thing. In fact, what Emerson said didn't mention mousetraps and was a good deal more prolix: "If a man has good corn, or wood, or boards, or pigs, to sell, or can make better chairs or knives, crucibles or church organs, than anybody else, you will find a broad hard-beaten road to his house, though it be in the woods."[18] But they took the sentiment to heart anyway.

America had a long tradition of productive tinkering. Jefferson invented a plow, which secured him a *prix d'honneur* from a French agricultural academy (though in fact it didn't work very well), and filled

Monticello with self-invented contrivances designed to thwart small everyday irritants. Franklin, as everyone knows, was a manic inventor. He gave the world bifocals, the lightning rod, extendable grippers for taking items off high shelves, possibly the rocking chair, and certainly the Franklin stove (though for its first forty years it was more generally known as the *Pennsylvania fireplace*)—and always, always with a practical bent. "What signifies philosophy that does not apply to some use?" he asked. Like Jefferson, he never profited from any of them.

It was at Jefferson's insistence that the U.S. Patent Office was set up in 1790. At first, the patent board consisted of the Attorney General, the Secretary of State, and the Secretary of War, who were given the job of vetting inventions as an extra little something to keep them occupied between more pressing assignments. They don't appear to have been run off their feet. In the first year just three patents were issued. (For the record, the first American patent went to a Samuel Hopkins for a new way of making potash.) But by 1802, patents were pouring in so fast that a proper patent board had to be organized. Suddenly the country teemed with tinkerer-inventors. In other nations, inventions emerged from laboratories. In America they came out of kitchens and toolsheds. Everyone, it seemed, got in on the act. Even Abraham Lincoln found time to take out a patent (No. 6469: A Device for Buoying Vessels over Shoals).[19]

Typical of the age was Charles Goodyear, the man who gave the world vulcanized rubber. Goodyear personified most of the qualities of the classic American inventor—total belief in the product, years of sacrifice, blind devotion to an idea—but with one engaging difference: he didn't have the faintest idea what he was doing. Described by one biographer as a "gentle lunatic," Goodyear in 1834 became fascinated with rubber. It was a wonderfully promising material—pliant, waterproof, rugged, and durable—but it had many intractable shortcomings. For one thing, it had a low melting point. Boots made of rubber were fine in winter, but at the first sign of warm weather they would gooily decompose and quickly begin to stink.

Goodyear decided to make it his life's work to solve these problems. To say that he became obsessed only begins to hint at the degree of his commitment. Over the next nine years, he sold or pawned everything he owned, raced through his friends' and family's money, occasionally resorted to begging, and generally inflicted loving but untold hardship on his long-suffering wife and numerous children. He turned the family kitchen into a laboratory and, with only the most basic understanding of the chemistry involved, frequently filled the house with noxious gases and at least once nearly asphyxiated himself. Nothing he tried worked.

To demonstrate the material's versatility, he took to wearing a suit made entirely of rubber, but this merely underlined its acute malodorousness and its owner's faltering grip on reality. Amazingly, everyone stood by him. His wife did whatever he asked of her, and relatives gladly handed him their fortunes. One brother-in-law parted with $46,000 and never whimpered when all it resulted in was tubs of noisome slop. With implacable resolve, Goodyear churned out one product after another—rubber mailbags, life preservers, boots, rainwear—that proved disastrously ineffective. Even with the lavish support of friends and relatives, Goodyear constantly lived on the edge of penury. In 1840, when his two-year-old son died, the family couldn't even afford a coffin.

Finally in 1843, entirely by accident, he had his breakthrough. He spilled some india rubber and sulfur on the top of his stove and in so doing discovered the secret of producing a rubber that was waterproof, pliant, and resistant to extremes of heat and cold, made an ideal insulator, didn't break when dropped or struck, and, above all, was practically odorless. Goodyear hastily secured a patent and formed the Naugatuck India-Rubber Company. At long last he and his family were poised for the fame and fortune that their years of sacrifice so clearly warranted.

It was not to be. Goodyear's process was so easily duplicated that other manufacturers simply stole it. Even the name by which the process became known, *vulcanization,* was coined by an English pirate. He had endless problems protecting his patents. The French gave him a patent but then withdrew it on a technicality, and when he traveled to France to protest the matter, he found himself tossed into a debtors' prison. He made more money from his autobiography—a book with the less than compelling title *Gum-Elastic*—than he ever did from his invention. When he died in 1860, he left his family saddled with debts.[20] The company that proudly bears his name, the Goodyear Tire and Rubber Company, had nothing to do with him or his descendants. It was named Goodyear by two brothers in Akron, Ohio, Frank and Charles Seiberling, who simply admired him.[21]

Many of the most prolific and important inventors of the age are now almost wholly forgotten. One such was Walter Hunt, who took out patents by the score on fountain pens, a process for manufacturing paper collars, a machine to make nails and rivets, and the prototype of the breech-loading Winchester rifle. Perhaps his most lasting invention was the safety pin, which he devised in 1849 after a couple of hours' fiddling with a piece of wire. Never much of a businessman, he immediately sold the rights to the device for $400. Slightly earlier, but in much the same mold, was Eli Whitney. While still a youth, he had devised novel processes for manufacturing nails, pins, and men's walking sticks, and later in life would be instrumental in developing the idea of interchangeable mass-produced parts, an approach that came to be known as the *uniformity system* or *Whitney system*. But what he is chiefly remembered for is the cotton gin, and rightly so. It was one of the great inventions of the age. If you have ever wondered how an intoxicating drink became associated with a device for combing cotton, the answer is it didn't. *Gin* is merely a shortening of *engine*.

Whitney hit upon the invention while visiting a cotton plantation in Georgia. As a New Englander unacquainted with the region, Whitney took a keen interest in how the plantation worked, and was immediately struck by how slow and labor-intensive was the process of deseeding cotton by hand. He knocked together a contraption that consisted essentially of two contrarotating drums with teeth that effectively parted the cotton from the seeds. It was ingeniously simple, but it transformed the plantation economy of the South. Indeed, perhaps no other simple invention in history except the wheel had a more sensational and immediate payback in terms of increased efficiency. A single gin could do the work of a thousand slaves. In ten years, exports of cotton from the South increased from 189,500 pounds to 41 *million* pounds. What is notable here is that Whitney wasn't thinking of a revolutionary device that would alter history or secure his fortune—at least not at first—but of a simple machine that would make a friend's life simpler and more efficient.

When it did occur to Whitney that the gin was revolutionary and that there ought to be money in it, he hastily secured a patent. But as so often with nineteenth-century inventors, he found himself cheated at every step and spent much of his life fighting costly court battles that gained him little but lawyers' bills. At least he had the satisfaction of being famed for his achievement, which is more than many got.

Consider the fate of poor Elias Howe, a young Boston native who in 1846 produced the first workable sewing machine. So revolutionary was Howe's machine that he couldn't find a clothing mill willing to try it. Depressed by his failure, Howe suffered a nervous breakdown and traveled to England, where he hoped his ingenious invention might be given a more congenial reception. It was not. After two years tramping the streets, he was so destitute that he had to work his passage home on a merchant ship. Arriving penniless in Boston, he discovered that in his absence one Isaac Singer had stolen his patent and set up a sewing machine factory and was making money hand over fist. Howe took Singer to court, where two things became clear: Singer was nothing more than a thief, but now an extremely rich one who could afford to hire the sharpest lawyers. After a protracted fight, Singer was eventually compelled to pay Howe a handsome royalty on every machine built. (Having thus secured his fortune, Howe promptly enlisted in the Union Army as a common foot soldier; it was an age of eccentrics as well as of inventors.) Nonetheless, it is Singer's name, not Howe's, that is indelibly associated in the popular mind with the sewing machine.[22]

Equally unlucky was J. Murray Spangler, who invented the vacuum cleaner—or *electric suction sweeper,* as he called it—at the turn of the century in New Berlin, Ohio. Unable to make a success of it, he turned for advice to W. H. Hoover, a local leather-goods maker who knew nothing about electrical appliances but did recognize a business opportunity when it fell in his lap. Before long there were Hoover factories all over the world, Hoover was credited with a great invention he had nothing to do with, the British were even turning his name into a verb (to this day they don't vacuum a carpet but hoover it), and J. Murray Spangler was forgotten.

But perhaps the greatest historical snub was that meted out to Professor Joseph Henry of Princeton, who in 1831 invented the telegraph. The word itself had been coined thirty-seven years earlier by a Frenchman named Claude Chappe, for a kind of semaphore system employed during the French Revolution, and by 1802 was being employed to describe long-distance messages of all types. Henry not only had the idea of transmitting messages as coded electrical impulses via wires, but worked out all the essentials that would be necessary to make such a system feasible. For some reason, though, he never bothered to perfect, or more crucially patent, the process.

That fell to a talented, well-connected, but generally unattractive fellow from Charlestown, Massachusetts, named Samuel Finley Breese Morse. Morse—Finley to family and friends—would have been a man of distinction even if he had never perfected the telegraph. The scion of a leading New England clan (his grandfather had been president of Princeton), he was an accomplished artist, a member of Britain's Royal Academy, a professor of fine arts at New York University, a dedicated dabbler in the creative sciences, and a would-be politician of distinctly reactionary bent. He ran twice for mayor of New York on a virulently anti-Catholic ticket and believed, among other things, that slavery was not just a good thing but divinely inspired. But his consuming passion was the idea of transmitting messages along wires, to the extent that he abandoned his career and spent five desperately impoverished years perfecting the telegraph and lobbying Congress for funding. Finally, in 1842, Congress—proving that it is seldom more than half smart—appropriated $30,000 for Morse's wireless experiments and $30,000 to be spent on the equally exciting new science of mesmerism.

With his share of the funds, Morse strung a wire between Washington and Baltimore and on May 11, 1844, sent the first telegraphic message (it would not be called a *telegram* for another twelve years). Every schoolchild knows that this first message was "What hath God wrought?" In fact, no. The first message was "Everything worked well." The more famous and ringing words, chosen not by Morse but by the daughter of the Commissioner of Patents, came at a later public demonstration. Morse's only real invention was the simple code that bears his name.* Much of the rest was utterly beyond him. To build a working telegraph, Morse not only stole lavishly from Henry's original papers, but when stuck would call on the eminent scientist for guidance. For years, Henry encouraged and assisted his efforts. Yet later, when Morse had grown immensely famous and rich, he refused to acknowledge even the slightest degree of debt to his mentor.

Throughout his career, Morse was the lucky beneficiary of men more generous and gifted than he. In Paris he persuaded Louis Daguerre to show him how his newly invented photographic process worked. He then took it back to America and handsomely supplemented his fortune by making pictures and selling them (becoming in the process the first person to photograph a living person). On the same trip, he actually stole a magnet crucial to long-distance telegraphy invented by Louis Breguet, and took it home with him to study at leisure.

It is almost impossible to conceive at this remove how the telegraph astonished and captivated the world. That news from remote places would be conveyed instantaneously to locations hundreds of miles away was as miraculous to Americans as it would be today if someone announced a way to teletransport humans between continents.

Within just four years of Morse's first public demonstration, America had five thousand miles of telegraph wire and Morse was widely regarded as the greatest man of his age.[23]

In 1876 came an invention even more useful and lasting, and far more ingenious, than the telegraph—the *telephone,* invented by Alexander Graham Bell and not strictly an American invention, since Bell, a native of Edinburgh, Scotland, didn't become a U.S. citizen until six years later. Bell did not coin the term *telephone.* The word had been around since the 1830s, and had been applied to a number of devices designed to produce noise, from a kind of musical instrument to a particularly insis-

---

*SOS, incidentally, does not stand for *save our ship* or *save our souls.* It stands for nothing. It was chosen as a distress signal at an international conference in 1906 only because its nine keystrokes (three dots, three dashes, three dots) were simple to transmit.[24]

tent foghorn. Bell described his appliance on the patent application as a new kind of "telegraphy" and soon afterward began referring to it as an "electrical speaking telephone." Others commonly referred to it in its early days as a "speaking telegraph."

Bell had become interested in the possibility of long-distance speech through his work with the deaf (a misfortune that extended to both his mother and wife). He was just twenty-eight and his assistant, Thomas A. Watson, just twenty-one when they made their breakthrough on March 10, 1876. Despite their long and close association, there was a formality in their relationship that is somehow touching. It is notable that Bell's first telephonic communication was not "Tom, come here, I want you," but "Mr. Watson, come here, I want you."

Flushed with excitement, Bell and Watson demonstrated their new device to Western Union, but the company's executives—why does this seem so inevitable?—failed to see its potential. "Mr. Bell," they wrote to him, "after careful consideration of your invention, while it is a very interesting novelty, we have come to the conclusion that it has no commercial possibilities," adding that they saw no future for "an electrical toy."[25] Fortunately for Bell, others were not so shortsighted. Within four years of its invention, America had sixty thousand telephones. In the next twenty years that figure would increase to over six million, and Bell's telephone company, renamed American Telephone and Telegraph, would become the largest corporation in America, with stock worth $1,000 a share. The Bell patent (No. 174,465) became the single most valuable patent in history.[26] The speed with which the telephone insinuated itself into American life is indicated by the fact that by the early 1880s when a person said "I'll call you" it was taken to mean by telephone—or *phone,* as it was already familiarly known. Bell sold his interests in the telephone in 1881 and devoted himself to other scientific pursuits. He invented ailerons for airplanes and made significant contributions to the phonograph, the iron lung, the photoelectric cell, and water desalination.[27]

The telephone not only brought instant communication to millions, but enriched American English in a way the telegraph never had. Scores of new words entered the language or were given new meaning. *Operator* was current by the late 1870s, as was "Hello, central," the phrase universally used before the introduction of dial phones. "Number, please?" dates from 1895, as does *telephone booth. Yellow pages* and *information* first appeared in 1906, *telephone directory* in 1907 (the first, listing fifty subscribers, appeared in New Haven, Connecticut), and *telephone book* in 1915.[28] That year also saw the introduction of *coast-to-coast service.*

It took almost half an hour to make all the connections and the minimum charge was $20.70.

At first people weren't sure what to say in response to a ringing phone. Thomas Edison is sometimes credited with inventing the word *hello* specifically for use on the telephone. In fact, *hello* (a variant of *hallo, halloo,* and other much older salutations) was current in English for at least twenty years before the telephone came along. What Edison actually favored was a jaunty "Ahoy!" and that was the word habitually used by the first telephone operator, one George Coy of New Haven. (Only male operators were employed at first. As so often happens with new technologies, women weren't allowed anywhere near it until the novelty had worn off.) Others said, "Yes!" or "What?" and many merely picked up the receiver and listened hopefully.

Such was the outpouring of inventions in the late nineteenth century that in 1899 Charles Duell resigned as head of the Patent Office, declaring that "everything that can be invented has been invented."[29] As patent applications proliferated and grew ever more arcane, the definition of what constituted a patentable invention had to be revised. In the early years a product or device had to be not only new but also demonstrably useful. From 1880 to 1952 the law was refined to require that an invention constitute a genuine breakthrough rather than a mere modification. By 1952 that definition was held to be too ambiguous and a new standard was adopted. Since then, an invention must merely be "nonobvious."[30]

From the linguistic point of view, it is interesting to note how seldom inventions were patented under the names by which we now know them. Bell, as we have seen, described his most famous invention as *telegraphy.* Hiram Maxim didn't use *machine gun* on his American patent application—and quite rightly, since all guns were machines—but the more precise *automatic gun.* Edison called his light bulb an *electric lamp.* Joseph Glidden showed a small stroke of genius in inventing barbed wire, a material that transformed the West, but rather less in naming it; he described it on the patent application as *wire-fences.* The cash register began life as the *Incorruptible Cashier*—so called because every dip into the till was announced with a noisy bell, thus making it harder for cashiers to engage in illicit delvings among the takings. (For much the same reason, early owners discovered that if they charged odd amounts like 49 cents or 99 cents the cashier would very probably have to open the drawer to extract a penny change, obviating the possibility of the dreaded unrecorded transaction. Only later did it dawn on merchants that $1.99 had the odd subliminal quality of seeming markedly cheaper than $2.) The escalator began life as the *Reno Inclined Elevator,* named for its inventor, Jesse Reno, who installed the first one at the Old Iron Pier on Coney Island in 1896. *Escalator* was the trade name used by the Otis Elevator Company when it joined the market with a version of its own in 1900, but for years most people called it a *movable stairway.* (The modern word *escalate,* incidentally, is a back-formation from *escalator*—an uncommon instance of a verb being back-formed from a trademark.)[31]

Among such company, the typewriter, patented in 1868 by Christopher Latham Sholes of Milwaukee as the *Type-Writer,* was unusual for remaining faithful to its original designation, though earlier models went by a variety of names, from *pterotype* to *mechanical chirographer,* and Sholes himself considered calling it a *writing machine* or *printing machine.* Sholes's earliest models had some notable drawbacks. They printed only capital letters and the keys tended to jam. At first, the letters were arrayed in alphabetical order, an arrangement hinted at on modern keyboards by the sequences *F-G-H, J-K-L,* and *O-P.* But the fact that no two other letters are alphabetical and that the most used letters are not only banished to the periphery but given mostly to the left hand while the right is assigned a sprinkling of secondary letters, punctuation marks, and little-used symbols are vivid reminders of the extent to which Sholes had to abandon common sense and order just to make the damn thing work. There is a certain piquant irony in the thought that every time you stab ineptly at the letter *a* with the little finger of your left hand, you are commemorating the engineering inadequacies of a nineteenth-century inventor.

To test the machines, a mechanic at Sholes's Milwaukee factory reportedly took to typing "Now is the time for all good men to come to the aid of the party"—no one knows why—which is apparently how this rousing sentiment became indelibly associated with testing a keyboard or limbering up the fingers.[32] Mark Twain, incidentally, was the first person to write a book on a typewriter, or *typemachine* as he insisted on calling it. He claimed in an autobiographical note that it was *The Adventures of Tom Sawyer,* but his memory was faulty. It was *Life on the Mississippi.*[33]

As the twentieth century dawned, still more terms designating wealth entered the language: *to be on easy street* (1901), *high flier* (1904), *sitting pretty* (1910). And inventors continued giving names to their processes that the world ignored. When a twenty-year-old recent graduate of Cornell named Willis Carrier developed the first modern air conditioner in 1902, he didn't call it that, but an "Apparatus for Treating Air."

The first electric stove was called a "fireless cooker." The first ballpoint pen was patented as a "non-leaking, high altitude writing stick." Radio and television, as we shall see elsewhere, went by any number of names before settling into their present, seemingly inevitable forms. Chester Carlson invented xerography in 1942, but called it *electrophotography,* while the transistor, invented by three researchers at AT&T Bell Laboratories in 1950, was described on its patent application as a "three-electrode circuit element utilizing semiconductive materials."[34]

Although America was unsurpassed at devising new conveniences, its constant bent on practicality—or *pragmatism,* a term coined by William James in 1863—meant that it wasn't always so good at dealing with more complicated systems. Many of the great technological breakthroughs of the nineteenth century didn't occur in America but in Europe. The car was invented in Germany and the radio in Italy, just as radar, the computer, and the jet engine would later be invented in Britain. But where Americans couldn't be touched was in their capacity to exploit new technologies, and no one was better at this than Thomas Alva Edison.

Edison was the archetypal American pragmatist. Latin, philosophy, and other such esoteric pursuits he dismissed as "ninny stuff."[35] What he wanted were useful inventions that would make life more agreeable for the user and bring untold wealth to him. With 1,093 patents to his name (though many of these were in fact attributable to his employees), Edison has almost twice as many patents as his nearest contender, Edwin Land (inventor of the Polaroid camera), and no one gave the world a greater range of products that have become central to modern life.

Edison's character was not, to put it charitably, altogether unflawed. He connived against competitors, took personal credit for inventions that were not his, drove his assistants to the breaking point (they were known as the *Insomnia Squad*),[36] and when all else failed did not hesitate to resort to bribery, slipping New Jersey legislators $1,000 each to produce laws favorable to his interests.[37] If not an outright liar, he was certainly often economical with the truth. The popular story, which he did nothing to dispel, was that a width of thirty-five millimeters was chosen for movie film because when one of his minions asked how wide the film should be he crooked a finger and thumb and said, "Oh, about this wide." In fact, as Douglas Collins points out, it is far more probable that, rather than devise his own film, he used Kodak film, which was not only seventy millimeters wide but fifty feet long. When cut down the middle it would conveniently yield a hundred feet of 35mm film—curiously, the precise dimensions of Edison's first reels.[38]

When George Westinghouse's novel and, in retrospect, superior alternating current electrical system began to challenge the direct current system in which Edison had invested much effort and money, Edison produced an eighty-three-page booklet entitled *A Warning! From the Edison Electric Light Co.* filled with alarming (and possibly fictitious) tales of innocent people who had been killed by coming in contact with Westinghouse's dangerously unreliable AC cables.★ To drive home his point, he paid neighborhood children 25 cents each to bring him stray dogs, then staged elaborate demonstrations for the press at which the animals were dampened to improve their conductivity, strapped to tin sheets, and slowly dispatched with increasing doses of alternating current.[39]

But his boldest—and certainly tackiest—public relations exercise was to engineer the world's first electrical execution using his rival's alternating current in the hope of proving once and for all its inherent dangers. The victim selected for the exercise was one William Kemmler, an inmate at Auburn State Prison in New York, who had gotten himself into this unfortunate fix by bludgeoning to death his girlfriend. The experiment was not a success. Strapped into an electric chair with his hands immersed in buckets of salt water, Kemmler was subjected to sixteen hundred volts of alternating current for fifty seconds. He gasped a great deal, lost consciousness, and even began to smolder a little, but conspicuously failed to die. Not until a second, more forceful charge was applied did Kemmler finally expire. It was a messy, ugly death and wholly undermined Edison's intentions. Alternating current was soon the norm.

Of linguistic interest is the small, forgotten argument over what to call the business of depriving a person of his life by means of a severe electrical discharge. Edison, always an enthusiast for novel nomenclature, variously suggested *electromort, dynamort,* and *ampermort* before seizing with telling enthusiasm on *to westinghouse,* but none of these caught on. Many newspapers at first wrote that Kemmler was to be *electrized,* but soon changed that to *electrocuted,* and before long *electrocution* was a word familiar to everyone, not least those on death row.

Edison was to be sure a brilliant inventor, with a rare gift for coaxing genius from his employees. But where he truly excelled was as an organizer of systems. The invention of the light bulb† was a wondrous thing,

<hr />

★Though Westinghouse is associated in the popular mind with electricity, his initial fame came from the invention of air brakes for trains. Before this useful development, trains could only stop in one of two ways: by having brakemen manually turn a handwheel on each car, a laborious process that took some time to implement, or by crashing into something solid, like another train.

†Curiously, although everyone refers to the object as a *light bulb,* few dictionaries do. The *American Heritage* (first edition) has *lighthouse, light-headed, light meter,* and

but of not much practical use when no one had a socket to plug it into. Edison and his tireless workers had to design and build the entire system from scratch, from power stations to cheap and reliable wiring to lamp-stands and switches. In this he left Westinghouse and all other competitors standing. The first experimental power plant was built in two semiderelict buildings on Pearl Street in lower Manhattan, and on September 4, 1882, Edison threw a switch that illuminated, if but faintly, eight hundred flickering bulbs all over southern Manhattan. With incredible speed, electric lighting became a wonder of the age.[40] Within months, Edison had set up no fewer than 334 small electrical plants all over the world. Cannily he put them in places where they would be sure to achieve maximum impact: in the New York Stock Exchange, the Palmer House Hotel in Chicago, La Scala opera house in Milan, the dining room of the House of Commons in London. All this made Edison, and America, immensely rich. By 1920 it was estimated that the industries spawned by his inventions and business pursuits—from electric lighting to motion pictures—were worth an aggregate $21.6 billion. No other person did more to make America an economic power.[41]

Edison's other great innovation was the setting up of a laboratory—the "invention factory" in Menlo Park, New Jersey—with the express purpose of making technological breakthroughs with commercial potential. Before long, many leading corporations, notably AT&T, General Electric, and Du Pont, were doing the same. Practical science, elsewhere the preserve of academics, had become in America the work of capitalists.

As small companies grew into mighty corporations, a new breed of magnates required increasingly grand and imposing headquarters. Fortunately, their need for office space coincided with the development of a radical type of building: the skyscraper. Before the 1880s, a building of more than eight or nine stories was impracticable. Such a structure, made of brick, would require so much support as to preclude openings for windows and doors on the lower floors. But a number of small innovations and one large one—curtain walling, a cladding of non-weight-bearing materials hung on a steel skeleton—suddenly made

---

many other words in similar vein, but no *light bulb*. If you wish to know what that object is, you must look under *incandescent light, electric light,* or *electric lamp. Funk & Wagnalls Revised Standard Dictionary* devotes 6,500 words to *light* and its derivatives, but again makes no mention of *light bulb. Webster's Second New International* similarly makes no mention of *light bulb*. The third edition does—although it has just this to say: "light bulb n: incandescent lamp." For full details you still have to turn to *incandescent lamp*. In my experience, most dictionaries are the same. I can't explain it.

skyscrapers a practical proposition. *Skyscraper* had existed in English since 1794, but had been applied to any number of other things: a top hat, a high popup in early baseball, the loftiest sail on a merchant ship. It was first used in the context of a building in 1888 (though *skyscraping building* had been used four years earlier), and not in New York, as one might expect, but in Chicago. Throughout the last quarter of the nineteenth century, Chicago led the world in the engineering of large structures, and for one very good reason: it had burned down in 1871. Its first skyscraper was the Home Insurance Building, built 1883–1885, soon followed by the Leiter Building (1889), the Reliance Building (1894), and the Carson, Pirie, Scott Building (1899). Soon skyscrapers were transforming *cityscapes* (an Americanism of 1850) across the nation and so altering people's way of looking at cities as to give new meaning to the word *skyline,* which originally was a synonym for *horizon* but took on its modern sense in 1896.

If Chicago was the birthplace of the skyscraper, New York soon became its spiritual home. The city's first skyscraper, the twenty-two-story New York World Building, opened in 1890, and soon Manhattan was gleaming with tall towers—the Pulitzer Building (1892, 309 feet), the Flatiron Building (1903, 285 feet), the Times Tower (1904, 362 feet), the Singer Building (1908, 600 feet), the Metropolitan Life Tower (1909, 700 feet), and finally the Woolworth Building, built in 1913 and soaring to 792 feet.[42]

With fifty-eight floors and space for fourteen thousand workers, the Woolworth Building seemed unsurpassable—and for seventeen years it remained the world's tallest building. Not until 1930 was it displaced by the Chrysler Building, which with seventy-seven stories and 1,048 feet of height was nearly half again as big. The Chrysler Building had been planned for a height of 925 feet, but when a rival developer began work on a building at 40 Wall Street, designed to be two feet higher, the architect William Van Alen hastily and secretly made plans for the 123-foot-high art deco spire that remains the building's glory. The spire was assembled inside the building and hoisted triumphantly into place just as 40 Wall Street was being completed.[43] The Chrysler Building's undisputed eminence was painfully short-lived. Before it was even completed, work had begun on an even more ambitious project on Fifth Avenue, on the site of the original Waldorf-Astoria Hotel. There, the Empire State Building began to rise. When completed the following year it soared 1,250 feet and 102 stories, a record that would stand for forty-three years until the erection in 1974 of the 110-story, 1,454-foot-high Sears Tower in Chicago, still the tallest building in the world.

Steel frame construction and curtain walling made tall buildings possible, but not necessarily usable. For that, countless secondary innovations were needed, among them the revolving door, without which drafts would be all but uncontrollable, heightening fire risks and making effective heating and cooling an impossibility, and, above all, swift, safe passenger elevators.

The elevator was not, as is commonly supposed and even sometimes stated, the invention of Elisha Graves Otis. Hoists and lifts of various types had been around for years when Otis sprang to fame in the late 1850s. Otis never pretended to have invented the elevator. His contribution was merely to come up with a simple, reliable safety device—a spring mechanism with gripper cogs—that made vertical passenger travel safe. A born showman, Otis traveled the world giving demonstrations of the safety of his elevators. Standing in a heavily weighted elevator, he would have himself hoisted thirty feet or so above the ground, and then call out to an assistant to cut the rope. The audience would gasp, but instead of crashing to the ground, the elevator would merely drop an inch or so and stay there. He sold the devices by the hundreds. (Even so, early passenger elevators were by no means foolproof. In 1911 the *New York Tribune* reported that in the previous two years at least 2,600 people had been injured or killed in elevator accidents.)[44]

Although skyscrapers transformed the appearance of the American city, they did surprisingly little for it linguistically. According to several sources, the Flatiron Building in New York was responsible for the expression *23 skiddoo,* the idea being that the curious angular geometry of the building created unusual drafts that lifted the skirts of women passing on 23rd Street, to such an extent that men began hanging out there in hopes of catching a glimpse of stockinged leg. The police, in response, took to moving them on with the growled entreaty "Hey, you—23 skiddoo!" Unfortunately, there is not a shred of evidence to support the story. *Skiddoo,* meaning "scram" or "scat," is known to have been the invention of the linguistically prolific cartoonist T. A. "Tad" Dorgan in the early years of this century, but how or why *23* became immutably associated with it is, like so much else, anybody's guess.

Chapter 7

NAMES

I

Soon after the Milwaukee Railroad began laying track across Washington state in the 1870s, a vice-president of the company was given the task of naming 32 new communities that were to be built along the line. Evidently not a man with poetry in his soul, he appears to have selected the names by wandering through his house and choosing whatever objects his eye happened to light on. He named the communities after everything from poets (*Whittier*) and plays (*Othello*) to common household foods (*Ralston* and *Purina*). One town he named *Laconia* "after what I thought was Laconia in Switzerland located high up among the Alps, but in looking over the Swiss map this morning I am unable to find a place of that name there."[1] Laconia was, in fact, a region of classical Greece, as well as a town in New Hampshire. Never mind. Wherever it was from, Laconia at least had a kind of ring to it, and was certainly better than being named for groceries.

This is by way of making the point that no people in modern history have been confronted with a larger patch of emptiness to fill with names than those who settled America, or have gone about it in more strikingly diverse ways. According to George R. Stewart, the great American toponymist (that is, one who studies place names), as of 1970 America had probably 3.5 million named places, plus another million or so that no longer existed (among them, Purina and Laconia, Washington). There is almost nothing, it would appear, that hasn't inspired an American place name at some time or other. In addition to breakfast foods and Shakespearean plays, we have had towns named for radio programs (*Truth or Consequences,* New Mexico), towns named for cowboy stars (*Gene Autry,* Oklahoma), towns named for forgotten heroes (*Hamtramck,* Michigan, named for a Major John Hamtramck), towns that you may give thanks you don't come from (*Toad Suck*, Arkansas, and *Idiotville*, Oregon, spring to mind), at least one town named for a person too modest to leave his name (*Modesto*, California), and thousands upon thousands of others with more prosaic or boring etymologies (not forgetting *Boring*, Maryland).

The first colonists were largely spared the immediate task of giving names to the land, since much of the eastern seaboard had been named already by earlier explorers. But as the colonists increased and formed new settlements, some system for labeling unfamiliar landmarks and new communities became necessary. The most convenient device was to adopt names from England. Thus the older states abound in names that have counterparts across the sea: *Boston, Dedham, Braintree, Greenwich, Ipswich, Sudbury, Cambridge,* and scores of others. An equally straightforward expedient was to honor members of the royal family, as with *Charlestown, Jamestown, Maryland,* and *Carolina.* Many of these names, it is worth noting, were pronounced quite differently in the seventeenth century. *Charlestown,* Massachusetts, was "charlton." *Jamestown* was "jimston" or even "jimson"—a pronunciation preserved in *jimson weed,* a poisonous plant found growing there in alarming quantities.[2] *Greenwich* was pronounced "grennitch," in the English fashion, but over time came to be pronounced as spelled: "green-witch." Only since about 1925, according to Krapp, has it reverted to the original.[3]

But the colonists employed a third, rather less expected method for place-naming. They borrowed from the Indians. As we know, the native languages of the eastern seaboard were often forbiddingly complex, and nowhere more so than in their naming practices, yet the colonists showed an extraordinary willingness not only to use Indian names but to record them with some fideltiy. Even now the eastern states are scattered with Indian names of arresting density: *Anasagunticook, Mattawamkeag, Nesowadnehunk, Nollidewanticook, Nukacongamoc,* and *Pongowayhaymock,* Maine; *Youghiogheny* and *Kishecoquillas,* Pennsylvania; *Quacumquasit* and *Cochichewick,* Massachusetts; *Wappaquasset,* Connecticut; *Nissequogue,* New York.

Once there were many more. Until 1916, New Hampshire had a stream called the *Quohquinapassakessamanagnog,* but then the cheerless bureaucrats at the Board on Geographic Names in Washington, D.C., arbitrarily changed it to *Beaver Creek.* In like fashion the much-loved *Conamabsqunooncant River* was transformed into the succinctly unmemorable *Duck.*[4] The people of Webster, Massachusetts (especially those who sell postcards), continue to take pride in the local body of water named on a signboard as *Lake Chargoggagoggmanchauggauggagoggchaubunagungamaugg,* which is said to be Nipmuck for "You fish on that side,

I'll fish on this side, and no one will fish in the middle." Such is the hypnotic formidableness of its many syllables that the sign painter added an extra one; the *gaugg* roughly midway along shouldn't be there. In any case, the name is no longer official.

Often, as you might expect, Indian names went through many mutations before settling into their modern forms. *Connecticut* was variously recorded as *Quonectacut, Quonaughticut, Qunnihticut, Conecticot,* and many other spellings before arriving at a permanent arrangement of letters. John Smith recorded *Susquehanna* as *Sasquesahanock* and *Potomac* as *Patowomek.*[5] *Kentucky,* from the Iroquoian *kentake,* appeared in a variety of guises—*Kaintuck, Caintuck, Kentuck,* and *Kentucke*—and was generally pronounced with just two syllables until the nineteenth century. More than 132 spellings have been recorded for *Winnipesaukee,* perhaps not surprisingly. *Minnesota* has been recorded as everything from *Menesotor* to *Menisothé* to *Minnay Sotor.*[6] *Oregon* has appeared as *Ouaricon, Ouragon, Ourgan,* and *Ourigan.* Even *Kansas* has had 140 spellings. *Milwaukee,* first recorded in 1679 as *Melleoki,* roamed freely through the alphabet as *Meleke, Millioki, Milwarik, Milwacky, Muilwahkie,* and many other forms before settling into its permanent spelling as recently as 1844. But probably the liveliest diversity of spellings belongs to Chicago, which in its early days was rendered as *Schuerkaigo, Psceschaggo, Shikkago, Tsckakko, Ztschaggo, Shecago, Shakakko, Stkachango,* and almost any other remotely similar combination you could think of.

Indian names often evolved into forms that disguised their native origins. *Kepaneddik* became *Cape Neddick. Norwauk* transmuted into *Norwalk.* The arresting *Waycake Creek,* New Jersey, grew out of *Waakaack,* while Long Island's *Rockaways* had their origins in *Rackawackes. Moskitu-auke* became, almost inevitably, *Mosquito Hawk. Oxopaugsgaug* became the jauntily accessible *Oxyboxy.* No Man's Land island in Massachusetts commemorates not some forgotten incident, but is taken from an Indian chief named Teque*noman.* The list goes on and on. *Ticklenaked, Smackover, Pohamoonshine, Poo Run, Zilly Boy,* and countless other resonant landmarks owe their names to the confusion or comic adaptability of early colonial settlers.

Non-Indian names likewise sometimes underwent a kind of folk evolution. *Burlington,* Delaware, was originally called *Bridlington,* after the town in Yorkshire.[7] *Newark* is a shortening of *New Ark of the Covenant. Teaneck* was a folk adaptation of the Dutch family name *Teneyck. Newport News* has nothing to do with news; it was originally *New Port Newce* and named for the Newce family that settled there.[8]

Although Indian names occasionally were lost in this process—as when *Cappawack* became *Martha's Vineyard* or *Mattapan* was turned into

Dorchester—for the most part Native American names have proved re-markably durable. You have only to flit an eye over a map of the United States to see how extraordinarily rich our heritage of Indian names is. In his classic study *Names on the Land*, George R. Stewart noted that "twenty-six states [now twenty-seven; Alaska has been added since he wrote], eighteen of the greatest cities, and most of the larger lakes and longer rivers" all owe their identities to the Indians.[9] The sentiment is true enough, but the specifics demand some qualifying. For one thing, many "Indian" names were never uttered by any Indian—*Indiana* being the most obvious example. *Oklahoma* was a word coined in Congress. It employed Choctaw elements but not in any way ever used by the Choc-taws themselves. *Wyoming* was taken from a sentimental poem of the early 1800s called "Gertrude of Wyoming," commemorating a massacre. The poem was so popular that communities all over the country were given the name before it was applied in 1868 to a western territory to which it had no linguistic relevance. *Idaho,* even more absurdly, had no meaning whatever. It simply sounded to nineteenth-century congress-men like a good Indian word.

Indian town names, too, often arose not out of any direct historical connection, but under the impulse of romanticism that swept the coun-try in the nineteenth century. All the many *Hiawatha*s owe their identi-ties not to the sixteenth-century Mohawk chief, but to the much later poem by Longfellow. The great Seminole chief Osceola never went anywhere near Iowa, but there is a town there named for him. Even when an Indian place-name has some historical veracity, it was often ap-plied relatively late. Agawam, Connecticut, for instance, took its place on the map two hundred years after the nearby town of Ipswich did.

As the nation spread west, the need for names grew apace. For a time, the fashion was to give classical names to new communities—hence the proliferation, particularly among those states that received the first west-ward migrations, of classical names: *Cincinnati, Troy, Utica, Athens, Cor-inth, Memphis, Sparta, Cicero, Carthage, Cairo, Hannibal.* The residents of one town in New York evidently grew so wearied by the various spellings that attached themselves to their town—*Sinneken, Sinnegar, Sennicky*—that they seized the opportunity to give the place both con-sistency and classical credibility by making it *Seneca.*

Another approach, and one that grew increasingly common, was to name places and landmarks after people, usually their founders but often someone deemed to have admirable qualities. In the Midwest especially, every state is dotted with communities bearing the name of some for-gotten pioneer or hero of the nineteenth century. In Iowa you can find *Webster City, Mason City, Ames, Charles City, Grinnell,* and perhaps two hundred others in a similar vein. A notable (if seldom noted) feature of American place-names is how many of our larger cities honor people hardly anyone has ever heard of. We have no great cities named *Franklin* or *Jefferson,* but we do have a *Dallas.* It was named for George Mifflin Dallas, who rose to the certain obscurity of the vice-presidency under James K. Polk and then sank from history like a stone dropped in deep water. *Cleveland* (originally spelled *Cleaveland*) is named for a forgotten Connecticut lawyer, Moses Cleaveland, who owned the land on which it stood but never bothered to visit the community that bears his name. *Denver* commemorates a governor of the Kansas Territory. It is not that these people were deemed especially worthy of having great cities named after them, but that the communities grew to greatness later.

Timing was all in these matters. Lewis Cass's nearest brush with immortality was to be defeated by Zachary Taylor in the 1848 presidential election, yet counties in nine states are named for him. Taylor had to be content with just seven county names—though that is perhaps seven more than a longer view of history would grant him. Henry Clay, the Kentucky senator and twice-failed presidential candidate, did better than both put together. He is honored with county names in no fewer than eighteen states. You can search the West for notable commemorations of Lewis and Clark and find almost nothing, but Zebulon Pike is grandly honored with a mountain peak he never climbed or even got very close to (he merely sighted it from afar). Even Warren G. Harding, a President whose greatest contribution to American history was to die in office, has a county named in his honor in New Mexico. Only George Washington got anything approaching his just reward, receiving the approbation of a state, the nation's capital, thirty-one counties, and at least 120 communities.[10] Once there were even more. Cincinnati, for example, began life as *Fort Washington.*

Often early colonists arrived in a place to find it already named by other Europeans. The process began with the names the Dutch left behind when they gave up their hold on Nieuw Amsterdam. The British hastily changed that to *New York*—in honor of the Duke of York, and not the historic English city—but others required a little linguistic surgery. *Haarlem* was shorn of a vowel, *Vlissingen* was transformed into *Flushing,* and *Breukelyn* became *Brooklyn* (and at one point looked like evolving further into *Brookland*).[11] *Deutel Bogt* begat *Turtle Bay, Vlachte Bosch* became *Flatbush, Thynevly* became *Tenafly, Bompties Hoek* became *Bombay Hook,* and *Antonies Neus* became *Anthony's Nose.* Like the English and French, the Dutch often took Indian names and rendered them into something more palatable to their tongues. Thus *Hopoakan,* a village across the river from Manhattan, became *Hoboken.*

Farther west, the French left hundreds of names. In a single summer in 1673, the explorers Marquette and Jolliet set down eleven important names that still live on in the names of rivers or cities (often both): *Chicago, Des Moines, Wisconsin, Peoria, Missouri, Osage, Omaha, Kansas, Iowa, Wabash,* and *Arkansas,* though those weren't quite the spellings they used. To Marquette and Jolliet, the river was the *Mesconsing.* For reasons unknown, this was gradually altered to *Ouisconsing* before eventually settling into English as *Wisconsin.* Similarly, *Wabash* evolved from *Ouabasche* and *Peoria* from *Peouarea. Iowa* began life as the decidedly more formidable *Ouaouiatonon.* The French shortened this to the still-challenging *Ouaouia* before English-speaking settlers finished the job for them.

In Marquette and Jolliet's wake came French trappers, traders, and explorers. For a century and a half, much of America west of the Appalachians was under French control, and the names on the landscape record the fact: *Michigan, Illinois, Louisiana, Detroit, Baton Rouge, St. Louis, Chicago,* and countless others. *Chicago* appears to be from an Indian word meaning "place that stinks of onions," and *Baton Rouge* was evidently so called because in 1700 a party of explorers came upon a red stake—a *baton rouge*—marking the boundary between two Indian hunting grounds and built a trading post there. Other names are uncertain. No one knows for sure what *Des Moines* might originally have signified, and *Coeur d'Alene* is wholly baffling. It translates as "heart of awl," and quite what the founders had in mind by that is anybody's guess.[12]

No less of a mark was made by the Spanish. Though we tend to associate the Spanish with the Southwest, Spain's American dominions at one time stretched across most of the continent, from the Florida Keys to California. Memphis was once known as San Fernando and Vicksburg as Nogales.[13] But, preoccupied with their holdings in Central and South America and convinced that North America was mostly worthless desert, the Spanish never made much of the lands to the north. By 1821, when Spain withdrew from North America, its estate north of the border consisted of only a few scattered garrisons and just three towns worthy of the name—Santa Fe, San Antonio, and St. Augustine, though even they couldn't muster ten thousand citizens between them. (Mexico City, by contrast, had a population comfortably above 150,000.) Even so, as I need hardly say, the Spanish left hundreds of names on the American landscape, including the oldest non-Amerindian place-name in the United States—*Florida,* or "place of flowers," so dubbed by Juan Ponce de León when he became the first known European to set foot on what would eventually become U.S. soil, on April 2, 1513. Missions and other small settlements soon followed, among them Tortugas (the second-oldest European place-name in North America), St. Augustine, and Apalchen. This last named was never anything more than an obscure hamlet, but the name somehow came to be applied to the vaguely defined mountainous interior. Eventually it attached itself to the mountains themselves—hence, *Appalachians.*

If the Spanish were modest in peopling their North American settlements, they were often lavish, not to say excessive, when bestowing names upon them. To them *Santa Fe* was, at least formally, *La Villa Real de la Santa Fe de San Francisco* ("The Royal City of the Holy Faith of Saint Francis"), while the community that we know as *Los Angeles* went by the dauntingly ambitious name *El Pueblo de Nuestra Señora la Reina de los Angeles del Río Porciúncula* ("The Town of Our Lady the Queen of the Angels by the Little-Portion River"), giving it nearly as many syllables as residents.

Often, as with *Los Angeles* and *Santa Fe,* these names were shortened, respelled, or otherwise modified to make them sit more comfortably on English-speaking tongues. Thus *L'Eau Froid* ("Cold Water"), a lake in Arkansas was turned into *Low Freight. Mont Beau,* North Carolina, evolved into *Monbo. Les Monts Verts* became *Lemon Fair.* Similarly the *Siskiyou Mountains* may be an adaptation of the French *six cailloux,* "six stones." *Waco,* Texas, began as the Spanish *Hueco,* while *Key West* was corrupted from *Cayo Hueso. Bob Ruly,* Michigan, started life as *Bois Brûlé.*[14] *Miguel Creek* in California became *McGill Creek* before reverting to the original. But more often the English-speaking settlers kept the spelling but adapted its pronunciation. *Des Moines, Detroit, St. Louis,* and *Illinois* are obvious examples of French words with non-French pronunciations, but there are countless lesser-known ones, like *Bois D'Arc,* Missouri, pronounced "bodark," and *De Blieux, Fortier,* and *Breazale,* Louisiana, pronounced respectively "double-you," "foshee," and "brazil."[15]

Odd pronunciations are by no means exclusive to communities with a foreign pedigree. Often founders of towns selected an exotic name and then either didn't know how to pronounce it or decided they had a better way. Thus we find *Pompeii,* Michigan, pronounced "pom-pay-eye"; *Russiaville* and *Peru,* Indiana, as "roosha-ville" and "pee-roo"; *Versailles,* Kentucky, as "vur-sales"; *Pierre,* South Dakota, as "peer"; *Bonne Terre,* Missouri, as "bonny tar"; *Beatrice,* Nebraska, as "be-*at*-riss"; *Dante* and *Fries,* Virginia, as "dant" and "freeze." (The joke in Fries is that it is "fries" in summer and "freeze" in winter.)

If America had a golden age of place-naming it would be the middle portion of the nineteenth century, when in quick order Oregon fever, the California gold rush, and the opening of a transcontinental railroad saw hundreds of new communities spring up practically overnight. The railroads not only often arbitrarily bestowed titles on new communities but sometimes took the opportunity to rename existing ones. Marthasville, Georgia, had its new name—*Atlanta*—forced on it entirely against its wishes by a railroad official in 1845. Occasionally, as H. L. Mencken notes, the first passengers on a new line were given the privilege of naming the stops they passed.[16] Post Office officials also enjoyed free rein. One official, Stewart relates, was said to have named post offices all over the West "for practically all the kids and babies in his immediate neighborhood."[17]

When the naming was left to unofficial sources, as with the towns that sprang up around the mining camps in California, the results were generally livelier. California briefly reveled in such arresting designations as *Murderer's Gulch, Guano Hill, Chucklehead Diggings, Delirium Tremens, Whiskey Diggings, You Bet, Chicken Thief Flat, Poker Flat, Git-Up-and-Git, Dead Mule, One Eye, Hell-out-for-Noon City, Puke,* and *Shitbritches Creek.*[18] But the practice was by no means confined to California. The whole of the West was soon dotted with colorful nomenclature—*Tombstone,* Arizona; *Cripple Creek,* Colorado; *Whiskey Dick Mountain,* Washington; *Dead Bastard Peak,* Wyoming; and others beyond counting. Often the more colorful of these names were later quietly changed for reasons that don't always require elucidation, as with *Two Tits,* California, and *Shit-House Mountain,* Arizona. Once, doubtless in consequence of the loneliness of Western life, the West had more *Nipple Mountains, Tit Buttes,* and the like than you could shake a stick at. Today we must make do with the *Teton Mountains,* whose mammary implications are evident only to French-speakers.

Colorful appellations are not a uniquely Western phenomenon, however. Lunenberg County, Virginia, once boasted a *Fucking Creek* and a *Tickle Cunt Branch,*[19] North Carolina had a *Coldass Creek,* and Kentucky still proudly boasts a *Sugar Tit.* Indeed, oddball names know no geographical bounds, as a brief sampling shows:

Who'd A Thought It, Alabama
Eek, Alaska
Greasy Corner and Turkey Scratch, Arkansas
ZZyzx Springs, California
Two Eggs, Florida
Zook Spur and What Cheer, Iowa
Rabbit Hash, Bug, and O.K., Kentucky
Lick Skillet, Bugtussle, Chocolate Bayou, Ding Dong,
    Looneyville, Jot 'Em Down, and Cut and Shoot, Texas
Knockemstiff, Pee Pee, Lickskillet, and Mudsock, Ohio

Bowlegs, Oklahoma
Teaticket, Massachusetts
Tightwad, Peculiar, and Jerk Tail, Missouri
Hot Coffee and Goodfood, Mississippi
Sleepy Eye and Dinkytown, Minnesota
Bald Friar and Number Nine, Maryland
Wynot, Nebraska
Brainy Boro and Cheesequake, New Jersey
Rabbit Shuffle, Stiffleknee Knob, and Shoofly, North Carolina
East Due West, South Carolina
Yell, Bugscuffle, Gizzards Cove, and Zu Zu, Tennessee
Lick Fork, Unthanks, and Tizzle Flats, Virginia
Humptulips and Shittim Gulch, Washington
Superior Bottom, West Virginia
Embarrass, Wisconsin

Often a prosaic explanation lies buried in an arresting name. *Goodnight*, Texas, has nothing to do with a memorable evening or bed-time salutation. It simply recalls a Mr. Goodnight. So, too, *Humble* and *Oatmeal* (named for a Mr. Othneil), Texas, and *Riddle*, Idaho. *Chagrin Falls*, Ohio, does not, as the name would seem to suggest, have any connection with some early exploratory setback, but is a misrendering of the surname of François Séguin, an early French trader who settled along the river from which the town takes its name.[20] In the eastern states, colorful names often have their roots in the name of a tavern or inn. Such is the case with *King of Prussia, Blue Ball, Bird-in-Hand, Rising Sun, Bishop's Head, Cross Keys*, and many other curiously named towns lying mostly in or between Pennsylvania and Virginia.

The twentieth century has seen an odd, and mercifully intermittent, fashion for giving towns names that it was hoped would somehow put them on the map. Breakthroughs in science often provided the spur, prompting towns to name (or more often rename) themselves *Xray, Radio, Gasoline, Electron*, and *Radium. Bee Pee*, Kansas, after putting up for years with jokes concerning the urinary habits of honey-making insects, decided to change its name to something less risible—and opted for *Chevrolet*.

Changing names is something that towns do more often than you might expect. Few communities haven't changed their name at least once. Scranton, Pennsylvania, has gone through no fewer than eight names, the most notable of which perhaps was its first: *Skunk's Misery*. Sometimes names are changed for reasons of delicacy—as when *Screamerville* became *Chancellor* or when *Swastika*, Arizona, transmuted into *Brilliant*—but just as often it was a desire by some real estate developer to make the place sound more attractive. Thus *Willmore City,* California, became *Long Beach, Roscoe* became *Sun Valley, Girard* became *Woodland Hills,* and parts of Van Nuys and North Hollywood declared independence as, respectively, *Chandler Estates* and *Valley Village.* Merely changing the name can give property values an instant boost of up to 15 percent.[21] Mellifluousness is generally given priority over etymological considerations, as with *Glendale,* California, a name that combines the Scottish-Gaelic *glen* with the northern England *dale* to form a name that means "valley-valley." Practically every city in America can boast subdivisions whose names owe nothing to any consideration beyond their developers' vision of what sounds prosperous, trim, and appealing: *Wellington Heights, Canterbury Hills, Vista View Estates,* and the like.

By the late nineteenth century, the United States had a confusing profusion of names for towns, lakes, mountains, and other topographical entities. Many states had as many as five towns with the same name, causing constant perplexity for the postal service. Hundreds of other features on the landscape went by two or more names, like the mountain near San Diego sometimes called *Cloud Peak* and sometimes called *Cuyamaca.* Then, too, there were hundreds of places with variant spellings, like *Alleghany,* Virginia, *Allegany,* New York, and *Allegheny,* Pennsylvania.

In 1890, to sort out the disorder, President Benjamin Harrison founded the ten-man Board on Geographic Names. The board was chronically underfunded—it didn't get its first paid secretary until 1929—and had no great authority. It could order government offices to use its spellings, but no one else had to, and at first many people didn't. Gradually, however, most communities gave in to its decisions whether they liked them or not, rather in the way that most people have quietly acceded to the Postal Service's insistence on two-letter abbreviations for state names.

Early on, the board established thirteen guiding principles. The first of these was the wholly sensible conclusion that in general it would be best to follow local custom. Unfortunately, the other twelve principles all contradicted the first by calling for some deviation from historic practice. One ruling was that places should be shorn of unnecessary punctuation, so that *Coeur d'Alêne* lost its stately circumflex (though not its apostrophe) and San José was deprived of a sliver of its Spanish heritage.[22] All towns terminating in *-burgh* were instructed to change to *-burg,* while those ending in *-borough* were henceforth to read *-boro.* Nonstandard spellings like *Centre* were ordered Americanized. *City* and

Town, the board decreed, should in general be removed from place-names, and names involving multiple words should be made into one word, so that every *New Castle* or *La Fayette* became at a stroke *Newcastle* or *Lafayette.* Above all, difficult names were arbitrarily changed or shortened, so that a name as phonetically formidable as *Popocatepetl Mount,* Oregon, or *Nunathloogagamiutbingoi Dunes,* Alaska (at twenty-three letters, the longest name on the American landscape officially recognized today), is now a rarity.

All of this would have been more tolerable had it been applied with some degree of consistency. But the board, alas, seemed wholly incapable. It couldn't even decide on a name for itself. After starting as the Board on Geographic Names, it became the Geographic Board, then the Board on Geographical Names, and now is once again the Board on Geographic Names.

Because of its decisions, American toponymic spelling lost much of its distinctiveness and charm, and a good deal of its clarity (an outsider could make a better stab at pronouncing *Wilkes-Barré* than *Wilkes-Barre*), without gaining anything much in the way of uniformity. Its decisions had a constant air of bewildering whimsicality. It took the apostrophe out of *Pikes Peak,* but left it in *Martha's Vineyard.* It ordered hundreds of communities to amalgamate their names—making all the *El Dorado*s into *Eldorado*s, for instance—but realized that no one would accept *Newyork, Losangeles,* or *Cedarrapids.* It threw out hundreds of Indian names, but allowed hundreds of others to stay. Almost its only act of incontestable virtue was to try to ameliorate racist names—changing *Chinaman's Springs* to *Chinese Springs, Nigger Creek* to *Negro Creek,* and so on—but even here it didn't generally begin to act until the 1960s, long after they had become an obvious embarrassment.[23]

On the matter of *-burg* and *-boro* terminations, however, the board was nothing short of relentless, and even now you can search a gazetteer long and hard before you find an exception to these two terminations. The main and most obvious one is *Pittsburgh,* which, curiously, often styled itself *Pittsburg* before the board came along and got the city's collective dander up. (Pittsburgh was named, incidentally, for the British statesman William Pitt by a Scottish immigrant who almost certainly intended it to be pronounced, on analogy with *Edinburgh,* "pittsburra.") In 1891, in one of its earliest decisions, the board ordered the city to call itself *Pittsburg.* The Post Office diligently followed its instructions, but almost everyone else became resentful, and most of the city's leading institutions—the University of Pittsburgh, the Pittsburgh Stock Exchange, the *Pittsburgh Gazette* newspaper—refused to buckle under. After twenty years of squabbling, the board finally reversed itself and on July 19, 1911, the city officially became Pittsburgh.[24]

Just as hundreds of towns have changed their names, so too have states. Maine was once *New Somerset*. New Jersey was briefly called *Albania* and later bore the alternative name *New Cesarea*. Vermont was called *New Connecticut* until the inhabitants came up with the contrived, and inescapably nonsensical, name *Vermont*. If their intention was to name it for the Green Mountains, they should have called it *Les Monts Verts*. As it is, according to George R. Stewart, insofar as it means anything at all, it means "worm-mountain."[25]

But then quite a number of our state names are, when you pause to consider them, at least faintly nonsensical. *Mississippi* is a curious name for a state that possesses neither the source nor the mouth of the river for which it is named and indeed owns only part of one bank. Missouri has more of the Mississippi River than Mississippi has—but then Missouri also has more of the Mississippi River than it has of the Missouri River, and yet we call it *Missouri*. You figure it. Rhode Island is not only not an island, but is not named for anyone or anything called *Rhode*. Nevada is named for a chain of mountains that lies almost entirely in California. Maine has no particular reason for being called that. Montana and Idaho are named for nothing at all.

The explanations behind all these are various. *Rhode Island* originally referred only to the island in Narragansett Bay on which Newport now stands. An early Dutch explorer called it *Roodt Eylandt* ("red island," from the color of its soil), and the name eventually evolved into a form more palatable to English sensibilities after Roger Williams founded Providence Plantation there in 1636. The state's full official name is *Rhode Island and Providence Plantations*. *Maine* comes from an archaic sense of *main* meaning great or principal. The Atlantic was sometimes referred to as the *Main Sea*—hence "to sail the Spanish Main." We retain the use in the term *mainland*—and, less explicitly, in the name of our twenty-third state. Missouri is named not directly for the river, but for the Missouri Territory of which it was the most important part, and *Mississippi* came about more or less because no one else had taken the name. It was nearly called *Washington*.

Many states almost went by other names. West Virginia was nearly called *Kanawha*. Washington State nearly became *Columbia*. Idaho might have been *Esmerelda, Oro Plata, Sierra Plata,* or *Humboldt.* Nevada might have been *Bullion* or *Washoe,* the name by which the region was generally known before Congress decided to name it *Nevada* after the mountains that feature only incidentally in its geography.

From the outset, the question of what names to bestow on new states was one that generated hot debate and exercised the minds of men whose talents might better have been applied to more consequential matters. In 1784, in one of his few truly misguided efforts, Thomas Jefferson drew up a list of fashionably neoclassical but pompously inane names that he suggested be bestowed on the territories of the West. Among his choices: *Polypotamia, Assenisipia, Pelisipia, Chersonesus, Macropotamia,* and *Metropotamia.*[26]

Jefferson never got his way with his fancy names, but he did have somewhat greater success with a second proposal, namely that western states be divided in a neat checkerboard pattern. Every state west of the Mississippi has at least two straight (or nearly straight) borders except for Oregon, Minnesota, and Texas, though only two, Colorado and Wyoming, are entirely rectangular. In terms of their interior organization, the western states had an almost brutal orderliness imposed upon them, and one that made little allowance for topographical features like rivers and mountains. Land was divided into one-mile squares, or 640-acre sections. Six sections formed a township. Sections were divided into sixteen forty-acre squares, which accounts for those familiar farm expressions like "north forty." One problem with such a setup is that a spherical planet doesn't lend itself to square corners. The nearer you move to the poles, the closer the lines of longitude grow—which is why, if you look at a map, Wyoming is perceptibly narrower at the top than at the bottom. To get around this problem, longitudinal lines were adjusted every twenty-four miles, which explains why north-south roads in places like Nebraska and Kansas so often take a mysterious jag where they intersect with east-west highways.

Debates over state names never failed to inflame passions. Among the names suggested for Colorado were *Colona* (a rather odd feminization of the Spanish for Columbus, *Colón*), *Jefferson, Franklin, Jackson, Lafayette, Yampa, San Juan, Lula, Arapahoe, Tahosa,* and *Idaho. Idaho* had a strange and almost mystical popularity among some congressmen. Despite having no meaning whatever, it was suggested over and over again for thirty-one years until it was finally adopted for the forty-third state in 1890. Once it was out of the way, other names took its place in the lineup of hopefuls. Among those considered for Arizona were *Gadsonia*—after James Gadsden of Gadsden Purchase fame—and *Pimeria.* For New Mexico the suggestions included *Hamilton, Lincoln, Montezuma,* and *Acoma* (a concocted name designed for no purpose other than that it would put the state first in the nation alphabetically).

Even more improbable in their way are state nicknames. Considering how widely known they are, the origins of state nicknames are often a mystery. No one can say for sure why Iowans are called *Hawkeyes,* why North Carolinians are *Tarheels,* why Kansans are *Jayhawkers* (there is no such bird), or why Indianans are *Hoosiers.* We know that Delaware has been called the Blue Hen State since at least 1840, but we don't know why. Various, sometimes ingenious explanations have been adduced— someone, for instance, traced *Hoosier* to a Cumberland dialect word, *hooser*—but the evidence in each case is at best inconclusive and often merely fanciful.[27]

Most states also have a discarded nickname somewhere in their past. Arkansas has been called the Hot Water State and the Toothpick State, Georgia the Buzzard State, Goober State, and Cracker State. (The cracker in *Georgia cracker* has nothing to do with crisp baked wafers. It comes from the practice of cracking corn to make cornmeal.) Missouri was once widely known as the Puke State, Illinois as the Sucker State, and Montana as the Stub-Toe State—though again in each case no one seems to know why. We do know, however, the derivation of Missouri's current slogan, the Show Me State. The expression was coined as an insult by outsiders and was meant to suggest that Missourians were so stupid that they had to be shown how to do everything. The state's inhabitants, however, contrarily took it as a compliment, persuading themselves that it implied a certain shrewd caution on their part.

As you might expect, state legislatures from time to time come up with more flattering nicknames for themselves, even at the risk of seeming a shade overambitious. New Jersey for a time called itself the Switzerland of America, while Arkansas opted for the Wonder State. New Mexico appears to have suffered from the most severe outbreak of narcissism, calling itself at various times the Land of Heart's Desire, the Land of Opportunity, the Land of the Delight Makers, and the Land of Enchantment.

For the honor of nickname *least* likely to make you pack up your bags and head on out, there has been no shortage of contenders. Among the perennial frontrunners in this category we find the Tree Planters State (Indiana), the Wheat State (Kansas), the Blizzard State (South Dakota), the Hog and Hominy State (Tennessee), the Iodine State (South Carolina), the Mosquito State (New Jersey), and the apt if resplendently self-evident Land of the Dakotas (North Dakota).

II

And so, more briefly, to personal names. One of the more striking features of life in the early colonial period is how casual people were with the spellings of their names. Sir Walter Raleigh, for instance, changed the spelling of his surname as one might change a shirt, some-times styling himself *Rawleyghe,* sometimes *Rawley,* sometimes *Ralegh.*★ His friends and associates were even less specific, addressing him as *Ralo, Ralle, Raulie, Rawlegh, Rawlighe, Rawlye,* and some sixty-five other seemingly whimsical variants. The one spelling he never apparently used is the one most commonly applied to him today: *Raleigh.*[28]

Abraham Lincoln's ancestors are recorded in early church and prop-erty rolls in such forms as *Lyncoln, Linccolne,* and *Linkhorn;* Jefferson's as *Giffersonne* and *Jeffreson;* and Andrew Jackson's as *Jaxon, Jackeson, Jakeson,* and *Jakson.* John Winthrop, first governor of Massachusetts (or *Masathusets,* as it appeared on the first colonial-minted coins, place-names being equally subject to orthographic variability), sometimes styled himself *Wyntropp,* which is in fact how he pronounced the name,[29] and early colonial town records are so full of multiple spellings for the same name—*Mayo/Mayhew, Smith/Smythe, Moore/Muir*—as to suggest that few in that busy age saw any special merit or purpose in consistency of spelling or even pronunciation.

As early colonists employed odd spellings, so too they often brought unexpected pronunciations with them. This was particularly the case in Virginia, where the leading families had a special fondness for pro-nouncing their family names in improbable ways, so that *Sclater* became "Slaughter," *Munford* became "Mumfud," *Randolph* was "Randall," *Wyatt* was "Wait," *Devereaux* was "Deverecks," *Callowhill* was "Carroll," *Higginson* was "Hickerson," *Norsworthy* was "Nazary," and *Taliaferro* be-came a somewhat less than self-evident "Tolliver." Still more unlikely were the Crenshaws, who were said to pronounce the name "Granger," and a branch of the Enroughty clan, which altered the pronunciation to "Darby," evidently as a way of distinguishing themselves from those members who said "Enruffty." Almost always these aberrant pronuncia-tions were brought from England, and presumably treasured as rather eccentric heirlooms. But in contrast to England, where bewildering pronunciations are affectionately preserved to this day, in most cases in America pronunciations gradually fell into line with spellings, as when the forebears of John Wilkes Booth stopped rhyming the name with *south* and instead made it rhyme with *truth.*

The practice was less common in the North but not unknown. Franklin Pierce of New Hampshire, the fourteenth President, pro-nounced the name "Purse" throughout his life, but even such modest

---

★Nearly all the spellings suggest, incidentally, that the modern American pronun-ciation of his name, "rawly," is more faithful to the original than the modern Brit-ish pronunciation, "rally."

phonetic unorthodoxy was rare. New Englanders saved their creative impulses for their first names, finding a certain comfort in endowing their children with names that denoted virtuous qualities. Among the *Mayflower* passengers we find Love and Wrastle Brewster, Resolved White, Humility Cooper, Desire Minter, and Remember Allerton. Such names, as far as we can tell, appear only among the *Mayflower* children, suggesting that in 1620 the practice was quite new. We can't be entirely sure, because the records are patchy. William Bradford compiled a "compleat" list of *Mayflower* passengers in which he recorded the names of all the men and most of the children and manservants, but only a few of the women, as if they were incidental to the enterprise. We therefore know, for instance, the name of Christopher Martin's two manservants, but have no idea what his wife was called. As wives gave up their surnames upon marriage, so it would appear that they relinquished their forenames except among their familiars, being known in the wider world—or at least to William Bradford—simply as "Mistress Martin" or "Mistress Jones."

At first descriptive names were confined to a single virtue: Faith, Hope, Love, Charity, Increase, Continent, and the like. But within a generation, Puritan parents were giving their children names that positively rang with righteousness: Flie-Fornication, Misericordia-Adulterina, Job-Raked-Out-of-the-Ashes, Small-Hope, Praise-God, Fear-Not, The-Lord-Is-Near. Names began to sound rather like cheerleaders' chants, so that among the early Pilgrims we find Fight-the-Good-Fight-of-Faith Wilson, Be-Courteous Cole, Kill-Sin Pemble, and the memorably euphonious Safely-on-High Snat. Occasionally the desire for biblical fidelity resulted in names of daunting sonorosity: Mahershalalhasbaz, Zaphenathpaneah, Zerubbabel, and Mene Mene Tekel Upharsin. And sometimes parents simply closed their eyes and stabbed blindly at the Bible, placing all their faith in the wisdom of Providence, which accounts for the occasional occurrence of such relative inanities as Maybe Barnes and Notwithstanding Griswold.[30]

Although these memorable appellations naturally attract our attention, they were not in fact all that numerous. Careful tabulation has shown that no more than 4 percent of Puritan children were given unconventional names. Most infants were in fact endowed with names that were unimaginative to the point of timidity. Just three names—Sarah, Elizabeth, and Mary—accounted for more than half of all the females christened in the Massachusetts Bay Colony in the 1600s.[31] Where parents applied more adventurous names, generally it was not to venerate the Bible, but to honor some progenitor—as with the celebrated clergyman and author Cotton Mather, who was named not for that useful fiber, but for his mother, Maria Cotton (who was, entirely incidentally, the stepsister of her husband, Increase Mather, and thus not only Cotton's mother but his aunt).[32]

By the turn of the eighteenth century, striking forenames had fallen out of use almost entirely. At the same time, there arose a tendency to encourage a measure of uniformity in surnames. In Britain, family names often came—indeed still come—with a variety of acceptable spellings: *Lea/Leigh/Lee, More/Mohr/Moore, Coke/Cook, Cooper/Cowper, Smith/Smythe* (and even in my acquaintance *Shmith*). But early on in America names tended to standardize around a single simplified spelling, so that *Browne* generally became *Brown, Hull* became *Hall, Newsholme* became *Newsom,* and so on.[33]

From the earliest days, immigrants from non-English-speaking countries likewise adapted their names to ease their way into American society. Paul Revere's father, a French Huguenot refugee, arrived in America as Apollos Rivoire.[34] James Bowdoin, the Massachusetts revolutionary leader and founder of Bowdoin College, was the son of Pierre Baudoin. George Armstrong Custer, of Last Stand fame, emerged from a long line of Kösters. The Rockefellers began as Roggenfelders, the Westinghouses as Wistinghausens. Buffalo Bill Cody's family name was adapted from Kothe. President Hoover's forebears were Hubers.[35]

Often the transition was relatively straightforward. *Langestraet* easily became *Longstreet,* as *Wannemacher* turned naturally into *Wanamaker, Schumacher* into *Shoemaker, Jung* into *Young, Schmidt* and *Müller* into *Smith* and *Miller, Braun* into *Brown, Grün* into *Green, Blum* into *Bloom, Fjeld* into *Field, Koch* into *Cook, Nieuwhuis* into *Newhouse, Pfoersching* into *Pershing, Jansson, Jonsson,* and *Johansson* into *Johnson, Olesen* and *Olsson* into *Olsen.* Occasionally slightly more ingenuity was required, as when *Bon Coeur* was turned into *Bunker* and *Wittenacht* became *Whiteneck.* When folk etymology wouldn't do, direct translation was often the most convenient solution, which is how the French *Feuillevert* evolved into the *Greenleaf* in John Greenleaf Whittier. The result is that American surnames often have an Anglo-Saxon homogeneity that belies their origins. Miller and Johnson, for instance, are far more common in America than in Britain, and almost entirely because of adoption by Germans and Scandinavians with similar, but other, names.

In the second half of the nineteenth century, European immigration increasingly moved away from the comfortably adaptable Germanic heartland of Europe to its southern and eastern fringes. People began arriving on American shores bearing names far less accommodating to English sensibilities and phonetics. Polish names like Krzyanowski, Szybczyński, Mikolajezyk, and Gwzcarczyszyn[36] clearly represented a greater linguistic challenge than Braun or Olesen. Even the shortest of East European names—notably such Czech manifestations as Krĉ, Chrt, Hnát, and Srch—often seemed to defy easy assimilation. In addition, some groups like the Hungarians put their last names first, and others, notably Armenians, didn't normally go in for last names at all. Sometimes a foreign name could be translated into an English equivalent, so that many Poles named Kowalczyk and Czechs named Kovář became Smiths. Long names were generally truncated, so that Greeks with names like Pappadimitracoupoulos became, almost inevitably, Pappas, and Poles named Mikolajezyk became Mikos (often further refined to some less visibly ethnic form like Michaels).

Sometimes the old name was abandoned altogether to be replaced with a shiny new name with a good American ring to it, as when the Italian boxer Andrea Chiariglione became the American boxer Jim Flynn. Not infrequently, some members of a family would adapt the new name while others would stay faithful to their cultural heritage. Thus the novelist Theodore Dreiser and the songwriter Paul Dresser ("On the Banks of the Wabash") were brothers.[37]

For Jewish immigrants the question of an American identity had an additional dimension. For those who wished to function in the wider world—for instance, in show business—an obviously Jewish name could be a handicap, so Israel Baline became Irving Berlin, Mendel Berlinger turned into Milton Berle, and Nathan Birnbaum took to the stage as George Burns. This was hardly a new problem for Jews. Mencken quotes a tale from Samuel Pepys's diary about a Dr. Levy who had petitioned a court to let him change his name to Sullivan and then a month later sought permission to change it again to Kilpatrick. "On request for ye reason, he telleth ye court that ye patients continually ask of him, 'What was your name *before?*' If granted ye change, he shall then tell them 'Sullivan.' "[38] Often, Jews had no particular attachment to their surnames. Those from Austria and parts of Germany had been compelled to adopt surnames only sixty or seventy years before. Often the names imposed on them had been unattractive to begin with, as with Geldwässer ("gold water"), a venerable euphemism for urine, Wanzenknicker ("louse picker"), and Eselkopf ("ass's head"), and they were only too glad to shed them.

Despite the manifold pressures to conform and the incontestable convenience that came with adopting a simple American name, millions stuck loyally to whatever name fate and geography had brought them. A glance through the index of a book on the history of American football, which I happen to have before me, throws up such uncompromisingly "un-American" names as Dick Modjelewski, Ed Abbatticchio,

Knute Rockne, Bronsilaw "Bronko" Nagurski, Fred Benirschke, Harry Stuhldreder, Zeke Bratkowski, W. W. Heffelfinger, Jim Kiick, Dan Pasquariello, and Alex Wojchiechowicz, and I daresay most other lists of Americans would show equal ethnic diversity.

There is, however, one group of Americans that did *not* enjoy the option of keeping their original surnames. I refer, of course, to enslaved American blacks, whose loss of liberty in the New World was so profound as to include even their personal identity. Few slaves enjoyed anything more than a single Christian name. Conventional wisdom has it that slaves conveniently took the names of their former owners upon being freed. However, the evidence—not to mention common sense— suggests that blacks showed no special affection for the names of their masters. Those names that feature most prominently among Southern slaveholders—Pinckney, Randolph, and Rutledge, for instance—appear only incidentally among any list of modern black names. It appears that most freed slaves either adopted an innocuous American name— Johnson, Jones, Smith, Robinson, and the like—or named themselves for a hero. Hence the relatively large number of African-Americans named Washington, Jefferson, Brown (from the abolitionist John Brown), and Howard (after General O. O. Howard, head of the Freedmen's Bureau in the years just after the Civil War)—but not, oddly and inexplicably, Lincoln.

Chapter 8

"MANIFEST DESTINY": TAMING THE WEST

In 1803, Thomas Jefferson made one of history's better buys. For about three cents an acre, he purchased from the French most of the North American continent between the Mississippi River and Rocky Mountains, at a stroke doubling the size of the United States. It was known as the Louisiana Purchase.

The natural thing was to commission someone to explore and chart the new territory. In fact, Jefferson already had. Months before the Louisiana Purchase had even been considered a possibility, he had authorized Meriwether Lewis to lead an illegal exploratory party across the western territories to find "the most direct and practicable water communication access across this continent for the purposes of commerce."[1] By the time word reached Lewis that most of the country to the west was now in American hands, he was already halfway to St. Louis.

Lewis had grown up near Monticello as Jefferson's protégé, "almost a son" to him, in the words of one biographer, and was something of an odd choice to lead the expedition.[2] Though he had military experience, he was not particularly acquainted with wilderness travel and for the past two years had led a decidedly soft life as Jefferson's private secretary in the White House. His schooling was minimal. He had no training as a botanist or cartographer and spoke no Indian languages. More ominously, he was given to disturbing mood swings euphemistically called "hypochondriac affections." For coleader he turned to his friend William Clark. Despite coming from a distinguished family (his brother was the Revolutionary War General George Rogers Clark), Clark had even less schooling than Lewis and had about him the perennial air of a frontiersman, but he was steady, resourceful, and brave. They made, almost miraculously, a perfect pair of leaders.

On May 14, 1804, they set off up the Missouri at the head of a ragtag party consisting of thirty-two soldiers, ten civilians, one slave (Lieutenant Clark's servant, York), a teenaged Shoshone Indian guide and interpreter named Sacagawea and her newborn baby, two other interpreters, and Lewis's dog, Scannon. They would be gone almost two and a half years and would travel some eight thousand miles through unknown and often hostile territory, yet just one member of the party would die, from a ruptured appendix.

They were by no means the first whites to venture into the vast North American interior. As early as 1680, some eight hundred French fur trappers were at work in the West, and by 1804 both French and English traders and trappers were a common sight all along the sprawling watershed of the Missouri River.[3] In 1792–1793, a Briton named Alexander Mackenzie had traveled over the Canadian Rockies to British Columbia, and in doing so had become the first person of European descent to reach the Pacific overland. Many more had reached the West Coast by sea, as Lewis and Clark discovered when Pacific Northwest Indians greeted their arrival with a hearty "son-of-a-pitch" in the evident belief that this was an English call of friendship.[4] They also encountered an Indian woman with the name of "Jonathan Bowman" crudely tattooed on her leg.[5] In 1801 the explorer Mackenzie published an influential book, *Voyages from Montreal . . . through the Continent of North America, to the Frozen and Pacific Oceans,* in which he suggested that the British preempt the United States in the western territories while the chance was there. It was this alarming prospect that had led Jefferson to initiate the Lewis and Clark expedition.

With unflagging diligence the two explorers labeled, mapped, and inspected everything that passed before them, recording their findings in their famous journals, which still make marvelous reading today. It is impossible to read Clark's notes in particular without developing a swift affection for his rough spelling and erratic grammar. From his first entry upon setting off—"We proceeded on under a jentle brease up the Missourie"[6]—his directness of description and eccentricity of composition make the whole hazardous undertaking come alive:

> Sunday 25th a fair morning river rose 14 Inch last night, the men find numbers of Bee Trees, & take great quantities of honey, at 11 oClock 24 Sauckees Came pass from St Louis, and asked for Provisions. . . . Guterge [his spelling of Goodrich] returned with Eggs & [illegible], Willard brought in 10 pr. Hinges George Shannon Caught 3 large Cat fish—The musquetors are verry bad this evening.[7]

Under his uncertain hand, *circumference* became *secumpherance, rheumatism* became *rhumertism,* and *Missouri* became almost anything—*Missouris, Missouries, Missourie*—often taking on two spellings in the same line. Sacagawea, the heroic Indian girl who guided the party across the wilderness, he wisely steered clear of, referring to her as "the squar." Lewis, though himself an erratic speller, brought a more assured style to the journals. Between them they coined almost a thousand terms for animals, plants, and features previously unrecorded on the landscape. They discovered 178 plants and 122 animals, among them the grizzly bear and great-tailed fox and several species of pike, catfish, and squirrels. No other explorers or scientists in American history have named more objects.

Among the terms not previously recorded in English were *great plains, prairie dog* (though Clark preferred *ground rat*), and *cache* for a secret hole in the ground (taken evidently from French trappers and spelled, almost inevitably, *carsh* by Clark). Some of their words didn't catch on. Their term *small wolves* was eventually displaced by the Mexican-Spanish *coyote* (from the Nahuatl *coyotl*). They also named every feature of the landscape that didn't have a known name already, though quite a number did. *Yellowstone,* for instance, is no more than Lewis's literal translation of the French trappers' *Roche Jaune.* Yet relatively few of their geographic names survived. They gave the noble name Philanthropy River to a tributary of the Missouri, but it didn't stick. Later passersby renamed it Stinking Water. The Lewis River later became the Shoshone. Philosophy River became Willow Creek.

Despite having three interpreters to call on, Lewis and Clark often encountered extraordinary language difficulties with the Native Americans. At one meeting, in a kind of pass-the-parcel round of translating, Lewis's English was translated into French by one listener, from French into Minitari by another, from Minitari into Shoshone by the next person in line, and finally from Shoshone into Nez Percé. The Indians themselves obviated such difficulties with a universal sign language of about a hundred gestures, which could communicate, at least baldly, most needs. The explorers also experienced remarkable good fortune, most notably during a potentially tense encounter with a party of natives when Sacagawea realized that one of the opposing braves was her brother.

After the expedition, Jefferson appointed Lewis governor of the Louisiana Territory. In October 1809, just three years after the expedition's completion and while aged just thirty-four, the great explorer died in exceedingly odd circumstances in a backcountry inn called Grinder's Tavern along the Natchez Trace in Tennessee. Clearly suffering a severe outbreak of his "hypochondriacal affections," he began behaving in an odd and paranoid manner—to the extent that the proprietor of the lodgings took refuge in an outbuilding. For hours Lewis could be heard talking and shouting to himself. Then late in the night shots rang out and all went quiet. In the morning, Lewis was found with terrible self-inflicted wounds to his head and body, but still conscious. He begged the proprietor to put him out of his misery, but the proprietor refused. Lewis died later that day. His friend and colleague William Clark fared better. He became governor of the Missouri Territory and commanded it with distinction, though he never did learn to spell.

For the better part of a century, Lewis and Clark's scientific and linguistic achievements went almost wholly unremarked. Not until 1893, when a researcher and naturalist named Elliott Coues rediscovered their all but forgotten manuscripts moldering in a cupboard at the American Philosophical Society in Philadelphia and produced an annotated edition of their journals, were they at last accorded recognition as naturalists, cartographers, and ethnologists.[8]

Jefferson thought it would take a thousand years for Americans to populate the vast emptiness of the West,[9] but he hadn't reckoned on the great waves of immigration of the nineteenth century and the odd "restlessness of character" that so fascinated Tocqueville.[10] From the start, Americans seldom stayed anywhere long. Jamestown was a ghost town less than a century after it was founded. Few states haven't seen their state capitals move at least once and often more. Just between the Revolution and the War of 1812, a period of roughly thirty-five years, eight of the original thirteen colonies moved their seats of government. Farther west, capitals changed location even more often. Indiana moved its capital from Vincennes to Corydon and finally to Indianapolis. Illinois went from Kaskaskia to Vandalia and on to Springfield.[11] *Frontier*, which meant (and still means) a national border in British English, took on in America the new sense of the ever-moving dividing line between wilderness and civilization.

Towns were established with high hopes and, if things didn't work out, abandoned without hesitation. In 1831, Abraham Lincoln moved to New Salem, Illinois. Six years later, trade on the nearby Sangamon River proving disappointing, he and everyone else abandoned the community and scattered to more promising parts. All over the West, towns came and went. For every Chicago and Milwaukee that thrived, thousands of others passed quietly away. Iowa alone had 2,205 communities fade into ghost towns in its first century.[12]

Before the 1800s, *city* was a term usually reserved for substantial communities. In nineteenth-century America, however, it could be applied to almost any cluster of houses, however modest. To this day the United States is dotted with "cities" for which the term is patently overambitious—places like Republican City, Nebraska (pop. 231), Barnes City, Iowa (pop. 266), and Rock City, Illinois (pop. 286). But in America, dusty hamlets *could* become cities, and sometimes almost overnight.

The boomtown par excellence was a little community on the shores of Lake Michigan called Fort Dearborn. In 1832, it had fewer than a hundred inhabitants. Sixty years later, renamed Chicago, it boasted a million inhabitants and was the largest grain market in the world.[13] No community in history had grown so big so swiftly. As Daniel Boorstin has noted: "Mankind had required at least a million years to produce its first urban community of a million people. Chicagoans accomplished this feat in less than a century."[14] What made it possible to house such a mass of people in so short a period was a Chicago invention that went by the odd name of *balloon frame construction*. This revolutionary method of building, in which light but sturdy timber frames are hammered together, then hoisted into place, was invented by Augustine Taylor in Chicago in 1833, and was so ingeniously unimprovable that it is still almost universally used in the building of American homes. *Balloon frame* was not Taylor's term. It was coined by skeptical carpenters to denigrate the method because of the extraordinary lightness and presumed frailty of the structures.[15] When Taylor used the method to construct Chicago's first Catholic church, nearly everyone thought that it would be carried off like a tent by the first strong winds. Needless to say, it was not, and soon the method was being copied everywhere.

To Americans, "the West" was an ever-changing concept. At the time of the first federal census in 1790, 95 percent of America's four million people lived hard by the eastern seaboard and "the West" was virtually everything else. By the 1820s, it extended not much beyond the Appalachians. Kentucky's leading paper of the day was called the *Argus of Western America*. Even as late as mid-century a chronicler like Charles Dickens could venture only as far as St. Louis, still the better part of a thousand miles short of the Rockies, and plausibly claim to have seen the West.

The move to the West as we now know it began in earnest in the mid-1840s when the expression *Oregon fever* erupted. Encouraged by the government to settle the northwestern territory claimed also by Britain, homesteaders set off in their thousands for a new life at the end of the Oregon Trail, following a route blazed by trappers twenty years before. The phrase that summed up America's new assertive attitude to western development was coined by the editor of the *Democratic Review*, John O'Sullivan, in 1845 when he wrote that it was "our manifest destiny to overspread the continent allotted by Providence for the free de-velopment of our yearly multiplying millions."[16] The peopling of the West became not just an opportunity to be seized, but a kind of mission.

Oregon Trail is a somewhat misleading term. For one thing, it wasn't a trail in the sense of a well-defined track. It was almost entirely a no-tional corridor, highly variable in width, across the grassy plains. More-over, after the first few years, relatively few of those who traveled the trail were heading for Oregon. Once past the Rockies, they instead broke off and made for the gold fields of California.

One of our more enduring images of westward migration, reinforced by a thousand movies, is of long, orderly lines of Conestoga wagons lumbering across the prairies. In fact, these sturdy vehicles were, in the words of one historian, "uselessly heavy for the long pull to Oregon or California."[17] They did haul some freight west, but almost never did they transport families. Instead, westward immigrants used lighter, smaller, and much nimbler wagons universally known as *prairie schooners.* These were hauled not by horses, but by mules or oxen, which could withstand the hardships of prairie crossings far better than any horse could. A final myth engendered by Hollywood was that wagons gath-ered in a circle whenever under attack by Indians. They didn't, for the simple reason that the process would have been so laborious and time-consuming to organize that the participants would very probably have been slaughtered long before the job was accomplished.

Wagons were covered with canvas, as in the movies, though that word was seldom used; the material was more generally known in the nine-teenth century as *twill.* Though *wagon train* was also used (it is first re-corded in 1849), the term wasn't particularly apt. For much of the journey the wagons fanned out into an advancing line up to ten miles wide to avoid each other's dust and the ruts of earlier travelers—providing yet another obstacle to forming into defensive circles.

Many early homesteaders had only the faintest idea of what they were letting themselves in for, often through no fault of their own. Until well into the third decade of the nineteenth century, ignorance of the West remained so profound that maps were routinely sprinkled with rumored and imaginary rivers—the Multnomah, the Los Mongos, the Buen-aventura—and with a great inland sea called the Timpanogos. Those who went west, incidentally, didn't think of themselves as still being in America. Until about the time of the Civil War, *America* was generally taken to signify the eastern states, so that accounts of the time com-monly contain statements like "Some people here [in Oregon] are talk-ing about going back to America" and "We'll go back to America.

Dressed up slick and fine" (from, respectively, the *New York Tribune* in 1857 and the *Rocky Mountain News* in 1860).

The landscape they found was so strikingly different that it required new words. Although *great plains* had been used as early as 1806, the grassy flatlands west of the Missouri were usually called *the barrens,* or sometimes *the great dismal,* until the French *prairie* began to supersede them. *Prairie,* from an old French word for meadow, was not a new word. It had been in use in America since colonial times, originally signifying a piece of wild open ground enclosed by forest. *Desert,* too, was modified to suit the particular landscape of the West. Originally it had signified any uninhabited place (a sense preserved in *deserted*). Thus, the *Great American Desert,* first noted in 1834, described not just the scrubby arid lands of the Southwest, but also the comparatively rich grasslands to the north. Much of the landscape that we now think of as desolate and forbidding was nothing like as barren then as it is today. When the western migrants arrived, much of the Southwest was covered in waving grass. They simply grazed it away.[18] Even so, there was no shortage of places that proved treacherous beyond endurance. One party that tried taking a short cut to California in 1849 discovered to its cost a killing expanse that they named *Death Valley.*

The traditional western stagecoach, notwithstanding its perennial role in movies and TV programs, saw active service for only a little over a decade. The first service was inaugurated in 1858 when the Overland Mail Company began twice-weekly trips from St. Louis to San Francisco. Its Concord coaches (named for Concord, New Hampshire, where they were developed) were intended principally to carry mail and freight but also carried up to nine passengers at $200 each for the westward trip and $150 for the eastward. (Eastward was cheaper because the traffic was largely one-way.) All being well, the trip took a little over three weeks. In 1866 the Overland Mail Company was sold to Wells, Fargo and Company, but it was put out of business by the opening of the first transcontinental railroad three years later.

Even shorter-lived was the Pony Express. Inaugurated on April 3, 1860, it was designed to carry mail as quickly as possible from St. Joseph, Missouri, to Sacramento, California. Riders rode in relays, each averaging fifty to eighty miles a day (though some occasionally went as far as three hundred miles without a rest), carrying a mail pouch or *mochila,* as it was more normally called. On an average run, seventy-five riders would cover the two thousand miles between Missouri and California in ten and a half days. It was a fabulous achievement, but economic folly. Setting up and maintaining riders, horses, and way stations was an exceedingly costly business. The express's investors sank $700,000 into the service and, despite charging a whopping $5 an ounce for letters, never made back more than a fraction of their costs. By late 1861, barely nineteen months after starting, the Pony Express was out of business, a victim of the newly installed telegraph and its own inescapable costs.

For those who wished not to face the perils and discomforts of traveling overland to California, the alternative was to go by sea. One option was to take a ship to Panama through the Gulf of Mexico, cross the fifty-mile-wide Isthmus of Panama (or Isthmus of Darien, as it was then commonly called) on horseback, and catch another ship up the Pacific coast. But connections were uncertain and it was not uncommon to be stranded in Central America for weeks at the mercy of steamy heat and yellow fever. The other option was to go by ship around Cape Horn, a fifteen-thousand-mile journey that seldom took less than six months and sometimes twice that in conditions that rarely rose above the squalid. Altogether, getting to California was a dangerous and uncomfortable affair.

But that didn't stop anyone—not at least after gold was found there in 1848. In the first four years of the gold rush, the population of California went from 20,000 to just under 225,000. In those same four years, $220 million in gold was pulled from the ground or sluiced from its glittering creeks. The gold rush not only enriched a fortunate few, but enlivened the language. Many of the terms that arose from it soon made their way into more general usage, among them *pay dirt, pan out, to stake a claim,* and *to strike it rich,*[19] all of which were soon being used in senses far removed from the idea of scrabbling in the earth for nuggets of gold.

One of the many side effects of the gold rush was the invention of hard-wearing canvas pants and bib overalls in San Francisco in the 1850s. The inventor was, of course, Levi Strauss, who had traveled west with a load of canvas (or twill) intending to make tents, but found a much greater demand for pants that would stand up to the wear and tear of life in the mining camps. He didn't call them *jeans.* In the 1850s the word signified not an item of apparel but a type of cloth. It is a corruption of *Genoa,* the Italian city where it was first woven. Not until' this century did denim (itself a corruption of *serge de Nîmes,* from the French city) pants become generally known as jeans and not until the 1940s were people calling them *Levi's.*

The traffic to California wasn't all from east to west. Many thousands came from China. At the beginning of the gold rush, just 325 Chinese lived in California; two years later the number had jumped to 25,000. In the next three decades it increased twelvefold, to over 300,000, or nearly one-tenth of the population. Because of political turmoil in

China, almost all the Chinese immigrants came from just six small districts in Guandong province. To them, America was *Gam Saan,* "Gold Mountain."[20]

The Chinese, who for entirely mysterious reasons were commonly known in the West as "Johnnies," were treated exceptionally badly. Because they were prepared to work hard for little, and because their appearance precluded easy assimilation, they were often pointlessly attacked and occasionally massacred. Even banding together didn't provide much protection. In 1885, in Rock Springs, Wyoming, a mob swooped on a community of five hundred Chinese for no reason other than that they didn't like them and left twenty-eight dead. Such was the prejudice against the Chinese that in some western courts they were not even permitted to plead self-defense. Thus there arose the telling western expression "He doesn't have a Chinaman's chance."

Many of the terms that we most closely associate with the West were not coined there at all. Abigail Adams used *desperadoes* to describe the participants in Shays's Rebellion long before the word attached itself to western bandits.[21] Though the *chuck wagon* (from a slang term for food, which survives in the expression *upchuck*) became widely used in the West—one of the most popular models was built by the Studebaker Company of Detroit—the term originated in Kentucky long before the Oregon Trail was even thought of. *Son of a gun* and *to bite the dust* were both anglicisms brought to America by early colonists. *Posse* has been in English since the Middle Ages. Much of the inflated speech that seems such a natural accompaniment to the high-spirited lifestyle of the West—formations like *absquatulate* and *rambunctious*—had originated long before in New England.[22] Likewise, the *Stetson* hat, also often called a *John B.,* was an eastern innovation. Its originator, John Batterson Stetson, was a Philadelphian who never intended the hat to be exclusively associated with guys on horses.

Even *cowboy* was an old term, first used during the Revolutionary War as a disparaging epithet for loyalists. In its modern sense it dates from 1867, when an entrepreneur named Joseph McCoy (another oft-named, but erroneous, candidate for the source of the expression *the real McCoy*) began employing cowboys to run longhorn cattle up the Chisholm Trail from Texas to his railhead at Abilene, Kansas. He became immensely successful and by the early 1870s was shipping out up to 500,000 head of cattle a year from the dusty town. (*Cow town* didn't enter the language until 1885.)

To distinguish one herd of cattle from another, ranchers began using brands, and these developed a complicated argot of their own. A letter tipped on its side was called *lazy.* A line underneath a letter was a *bar.* A letter written with curving lines rather than straight ones was called *running*. From these came the names of many ranches: the Lazy X Bar, the Running W, and so on.[23] There were literally thousands of brands—five thousand in Wyoming and nearly twelve thousand in Montana by the early 1890s—and a publisher could make a good income by producing annual brand books. Unmarked cattle were called *mavericks*. The name came from a Texas rancher named Samuel A. Maverick who refused to brand his cattle—though whether because he was eccentric or lazy or cagily hoped to claim *all* unmarked cattle as his own is a matter of long dispute among Western historians.[24]

Hollywood has left us with the impression that the West was peopled by little but cowboys. In fact, they were outnumbered by farmers by about a thousand to one. Even at their peak there were fewer than ten thousand working cowboys, at least a quarter of them black or Mexican (and the remainder not a great deal higher up the nineteenth-century social scale).[25]

The cowboy of popular imagination was largely the invention of two highly unlikely Easterners. The first was the artist Frederic Remington, whose action-filled, hyperrealist paintings were in fact largely studio creations based on a lively imagination. He never saw any real cowboys in action. For one thing, he was much too fat to get on a horse, much less ride it into the midst of Indian battles. Even more crucially, by the time he made his first trip to the West the age of the cowboy was all but over.

No less disconnected from life around the campfire was his close friend Owen Wister, who mythologized cowboys on paper in much the way that Remington mythologized them on canvas. Cowboys had begun to appear as heroes in dime novels as early as the 1880s (the genre appears to have been the invention of one Prentiss Ingraham), but it wasn't until Wister published *The Virginian* in 1902 that the cowboy (or *cow-boy,* as Wister insisted on spelling it) truly became a national figure. Wister was the quintessential *dude* (a word of unknown origin dating in a western context only from 1883, though it was used earlier in the East). Scion of a wealthy Philadelphia family and grandson of the celebrated actress Fanny Kemble, a Phi Beta Kappa at Harvard, and a close friend of Teddy Roosevelt, he was of a decidedly delicate disposition. Unlike Remington, he actually traveled in the West, though he hardly hit the dusty trail. He was sent west by his parents to recover from a nervous breakdown and was chaperoned throughout by two spinsters.

Although Wister introduced many of the conventions of cowboy fiction—the use of a hero without a name, the introduction of a climactic shootout between the hero and villain, the immortal line "When you call me that, *smile!*"—his main achievement was to make the cowboy a respectable figure for fictionalization. He began the process with a now forgotten novel called *Lin McLean*, but brought it to full fruition with *The Virginian*. The story of an Easterner (unnamed, of course) who goes west, it struck a chord with millions of Americans, but particularly the better-educated, at whom it was aimed. The book sold fifty thousand copies in its first four months and three million copies overall, went through fifteen printings in its first seven years, and was made into a Broadway play that ran for ten years, and subsequently into a seminal film.

The mythologizing of the West was consolidated in the immensely popular novels of writers like C. J. Mulford, creator of the absurdly uncowboylike Hopalong Cassidy, and Zane Grey, a New York dentist who knew almost nothing of the West but refused to let that get in the way of a good tale.[26] The first movie western, *The Great Train Robbery*, appeared in 1903. By the 1920s, westerns accounted for nearly a third of all Hollywood features. But their real peak came in the 1950s on television. During their zenith year, 1959, the American television viewer could choose among twenty-eight western series running on network television—an average of four a night.[27]

It is decidedly odd that these figures of the West, whose lives consisted mostly of herding cows across lonely plains and whose idea of ultimate excitement was a bath and a shave and a night on the town in a place like Abilene, should have exerted such a grip on the popular imagination. As the western historian William W. Savage, Jr., has put it: "The cattle business and cowboy life were hardly the stuff of which legends are made. . . . The cowboy is a symbol for many things—courage, honor, chivalry, individualism—few of which have much foundation in fact."[28]

They certainly didn't spend a lot of time shooting each other. In the ten years that Dodge City was the biggest, rowdiest cow town in the world, only thirty-four people were buried in the infamous Boot Hill Cemetery, and almost all of them died of natural causes. Incidents like the shootout at the O.K. Corral or the murder of Wild Bill Hickock became famous by dint of their being so unusual. Those who *were* shot seldom got up again. Scarcely a western movie has been made in which at least one character hasn't taken a bullet in the thigh or shoulder but shrugged it off with a manly wince and continued firing. As one critic put it: "One would think that the human shoulder was made of some self-healing material, rather like a puncture-proof tire."[29] In fact, nineteenth-century bullets were so slow, relatively speaking, and so soft that they almost never moved cleanly through the victim's body. Instead, they bounced around like a pinball and exited with a hole like a fist punched through paper. Even if they miraculously missed the victim's vital organs, he would almost invariably suffer deep and incapacitating shock and bleed to death within minutes.

For the most part, trust and goodwill were no more lacking in the lawless environment of the West than elsewhere. As Daniel Boorstin notes, it is no accident that the term *pardner*—originally implying a relationship much deeper and more trusting than a casual friendship—entered the language in the gold fields of California around 1850.[30] Justice was often peremptory and swift—thieves and cheats on riverboats were generally put down on the nearest sandbar and left to make their way back to civilization, if they could—but at least justice there was. Land-based miscreants were often dealt with by *kangaroo courts*—impromptu convocations that seldom bothered with the niceties of due process. This rather odd and interesting term has been traced to Texas, a place notably deficient in antipodean marsupials, and was first recorded in 1849. It appears to have no connection to Australia—the expression was unknown there until introduced from America—and may derive from the idea of a criminal being bounced like a kangaroo to the gallows, but that is no more than conjecture.

Among other terms that appear to have arisen in the West are *bogus, rip-roaring, joint* in the sense of a gathering spot, *piker* for an untrustworthy character (it is sometimes said to be a reference to the inhabitants of Pike County, Missouri, but more probably comes from *turnpike*), *to be caught between a rock and a hard place, six-shooter* for a Colt revolver, *gunplay, holdup,* and *crook,* plus scores of others that didn't survive into the twentieth century, including *dying with throat trouble* and *the big jump* for being hanged. *Bogus* is wholly mysterious and *crook* only slightly less so. *Crook* may have something to do with the fact that a shepherd's crook is not straight but bent (*bent* was in the nineteenth century a common adjective for a criminal, and still is in Britain), but written evidence is lacking.

Many of the terms we most closely associate with cowboys and life amid the purple sage didn't appear in the West until much later, if at all. *Dogy,* a motherless calf, memorialized in the song lyrics "git along, little dogy, git along," has not been found earlier than 1903.[31] *Hoosegow,* for a jail, didn't enter the language until 1920. Bandits were seldom called that; *banditti* was the more common term. *Bounty hunter, gunslinger,* and *to have an itchy trigger finger* were all the inventions of Hollywood scriptwriters.[32]

The lexical creations of cowboys, miners, and other western Americans became incidental when compared with the legacy of Spanish terms from the West. These at one time numbered well over a hundred. Among the more notable survivors we find *lasso* (1819), *sombrero* (1823), *patio* (1827), *corral* (1829), *lariat* (from *la reata,* "the rope," 1831), *canyon* (1834), *plaza* (1836), *burro, stampede* and *rodeo* (1844), *bonanza* (1844), *bronco* and *pronto* (1850), *alfalfa* (1855), *cinch* (from *cincha,* a saddle girth, 1859), *pinto* (1860), and *vigilante* (1865).[33]

Often these words had to be wrestled into shape. *Wrangler* comes from *caballerangero. Vamos* became *vamoose* and then *mosey. Vaquero,* literally "cow handler," went through any number of variations—*buckhara, bakkarer, backayro, buccahro*—before finally settling into English as *buckaroo.* The *ten-gallon hat* is named not for its capacity to hold liquids (it would have had to be the size of a washtub for that) but for the braid with which it was decorated; the Spanish for braid is *galón.*

Sometimes the English spellings of Spanish words took some time to become established. As late as the 1920s, *bronco* appeared in a famous ad for Jordan cars in this manner: "Somewhere west of Laramie, there's a broncho-busting, steer-roping girl who knows what I'm talking about." In the same way, G. M. Anderson, the first cowboy movie star, was sometimes represented to his fans as *Broncho Billy,* and the evidence suggests that it was pronounced by some as spelled. Meanwhile, *rancher,* from the Mexican-Spanish *rancho,* or "mess room," was often originally pronounced "ranker."

The early English-speaking immigrants to the Southwest also encountered Spanish-Mexican cuisine for the first time: tacos, enchiladas, tortillas, and the like. *Nachos* is said to honor a certain Ignacio who made them particularly well, but the story, if true, is unsubstantiated. Unquestionably apocryphal is the old tale that Mexicans began calling Americans *gringos* because a popular marching song during the Mexican War contained the words "Green grow the rushes." In fact, *gringo* is not a New World term at all. It was in common use in Spain in the eighteenth century. It is a corruption of *Griego,* "Greek," signifying unintelligible foreign babble, in much the same way as we say "It's Greek to me."[34]

Many other terms that are sometimes lumped in with Spanish expressions brought into English by cowboys and ranchers actually entered English much earlier, among them *adobe* and *mesa* as early as 1759, *calaboose* (from *calabozo,* "dungeon") by 1792, and *mustang* (from *mesteño* or *mestengo,* signifying stray animals) in 1808. One of the more breathtakingly complex of these early adaptations was *maroon.* In the sense of being stranded, it began life as the Spanish *cimarrón* (literally "one who lives on the mountaintops"), and originally signified a fugitive slave in the West Indies. Then it came to mean the offspring of such a slave. Finally it evolved into the sense of suffering abandonment. (The Spanish also applied *cimarrón* to a tribe of Muskhogean Indians, the ones we know as *Seminoles,* from which comes the name of the Cimarron River.) In the meantime, the French had picked up *cimarron* and changed it to *marron,* their word for chestnut, and it then passed into English as *maroon,* with two quite separate meanings—a chestnutlike color and the act of being abandoned. By such convoluted means do languages sometimes grow. Rather less challenging was *el lagarto,* "the lizard," which slipped into English as *alligator.*

Further north, French-speaking trappers provided many useful words to the settlers, notably *gopher, rendezvous, peak* for a mountaintop (from the French *pic*), *badlands* (translated literally from the French *mauvaises terres*), and *park* for a mountain valley, a sense that survives in a few place-names, such as *Estes Park,* Colorado. As with Spanish, many French words came into English well ahead of the western migrations, among them *chute* (1804), *butte* and *picayune* (1805), *coulee* (1807), *depot* (1832), and *to sashay* (1836). Often they, too, underwent complicated transformations. *Lagniappe,* usually attributed to the French of New Orleans, in fact originated among the Kechuan Indians of Peru as *yapa.* The Spanish adopted it as *ñapa.* The French then took it from the Spanish and we from the French.

If the English-speaking settlers of the West didn't much shoot each other, they did shoot a lot of buffalo. Between 1830 and 1895, the seventy million buffalo that roamed the Great Plains were reduced in number to just eight hundred, most of those in zoos or touring shows. During roughly the same period, the number of Indians fell from perhaps two million to no more than ninety thousand as war, disease, and poverty born of the loss of their lands and livelihood took their brutal toll.

To say that the Indians were often treated abysmally barely conveys the scale of the indignity heaped upon them. Again and again, tribes were uprooted and moved on until they were crowded onto *reservations* (in the sense of a place to confine natives, an Americanism of 1789) on the meanest, most unproductive land. Though the United States' wars with the Indians ended in 1886 with the surrender of the Apache chief Geronimo, their mistreatment did not end there. Between 1887 and 1934, they were deprived of a further 86 million acres. Altogether, as Howard Zinn notes, the United States made four hundred treaties with the Indians and broke every one of them. They weren't even made citizens until 1924.[35]

Today no one knows how many Indians there are. All we know is how many people think they are Indians, which of course is not the same thing. Some two million Americans claimed on the 1990 census to be Indian, a rise of almost 40 percent from the 1980 census—clearly not in line with population growth.[36]

Some three hundred tribes remain in America today, but much of the linguistic diversity that once existed is gone forever. According to Dr. Duane King of the National Museum of the American Indian, "fewer than two hundred [Native American] languages are spoken today, and eighty to one hundred of those will probably disappear within a generation."[37] Among those most perilously on the brink of extinction are Mandan (with only six known speakers left in 1991) and Osage (spoken by only five). Lakota, the language used in the movie *Dances with Wolves*, appears to be dead. No native speaker could be found to act as adviser to the film crew.

In only half a century or so, the new nation conquered the West and extended its hold over a vast continent, but at a terrible price to native cultures. For millions of Native Americans, *manifest destiny* came to suggest not so much the peopling of the West as the unpeopling of it.

Chapter 9

THE MELTING POT:
IMMIGRATION IN AMERICA

I

By the early 1830s, America's cotton trade with Britain had become so vast that up to a thousand ships at a time, a significant portion of the Atlantic fleet, were engaged in carrying cotton to Liverpool. The problem was that most made the return journey largely empty. Casting around for a convenient cargo for the return trip, the shipowners hit on an unusual one: people.

Never mind that their ships were never intended for passengers, that a crossing could take up to three months with the human freight crowded into fetid holds that were breeding grounds for diseases like trachoma and malignant typhus (which in the nineteenth century was so closely associated with Atlantic crossings that it was called *ship fever*). People were willing to endure almost any hardship to get to America if the price was right, and by packing the passengers in and giving them almost nothing in the way of civilizing comforts, the fares could be made not just low but effectively irresistible. By mid-century a one-way ticket in *steerage* (so called because it was near the ship's steering mechanism and thus noisy) could be had for as little $12 from Liverpool to New York, and for less than $10 from Dublin. All but the most miserably destitute could scrape together that.[1]

Millions did. From 150,000 in the 1820s, the number of immigrants to America climbed steadily with each successive decade: 600,000 in the 1830s, 1.7 million in the 1840s, 2.3 million in the 1850s. All this was happening in a much more thinly populated America, of course. The three million immigrants who came to the United States in the decade 1845–1855 arrived in a country that had a population of only twenty million. In just twenty years, 1830–1850, the proportion of foreign-born immigrants in America rose from one in a hundred to one in ten.

Never before had there been such a global exodus—and not just to the United States, but to Australia, Argentina, New Zealand, anywhere that showed promise, though the United States took by far the largest share. Between 1815 and 1915, it took in 35 million people, equivalent to the modern populations of Norway, Sweden, Austria, Ireland, Denmark, and Switzerland. Seven million came from Germany, roughly five million each from Italy and Ireland (1.5 million more than live in Ireland today), 3.3 million from Russia, 2.5 million from Scandinavia, and hundreds of thousands from Greece, Portugal, Turkey, the Netherlands, Mexico, the Caribbean, China, and Japan. Even Canada provided a quarter of a million immigrants between 1815 and 1860, and nearly a million more in the 1920s.[2] For smaller countries like Sweden, Norway, and Ireland, and for regions within countries, like Sicily and the Mezzogiorno in Italy, the numbers represented a significant drain on human resources. This was especially true of Ireland. In 1807 it was the most densely populated country in Europe; by the 1860s it was one of the least.[3]

Once across the ocean the immigrants tended to congregate in enclaves. Almost all the migrants from Norway between 1815 and 1860 settled in just four states, Wisconsin, Minnesota, Iowa, and Illinois. In much the same way, two-thirds of the Dutch were to be found in Michigan, New York, Wisconsin, and Iowa. Sometimes they were given active encouragement to congregate. In the first half of the nineteenth century, several German societies were formed with the express intention of so concentrating immigration in particular areas that they could, in effect, take over. One German spoke for many when he dreamed of Pennsylvania becoming "an entirely German state where . . . the beautiful German language would be used in the legislative halls and the courts of justice." Not just in Pennsylvania, but in Texas, Missouri, and Wisconsin there were earnest hopes of colonizing all or at least a significant part of those states.[4]

In factory towns, too, immigrant groups were often concentrated to an extraordinary degree. In 1910, Hungry Hollow, Illinois, a steel town, was home to 15,000 Bulgarians. At the same time, of the 14,300 people employed in Carnegie steel mills in western Pennsylvania, almost 12,000 were from eastern Europe.[5]

The bulk of immigrants settled in cities even when their backgrounds were agricultural, as was generally the case. So effortlessly did Irish, Poles, and Italians settle into urban life, we easily forget that most came from rural stock and had perhaps never seen a five-story building or a crowd of a thousand people before leaving home. Often they arrived in such numbers as to overturn the prevailing demographics. In a single year, 1851, a quarter of a million Irish came to America, and almost all of them settled in New York or Boston. By 1855, one-third of New York's population was Irish-born.[6] As immigration from northern Europe eased in the third quarter of the century, the slack was taken up by eastern European Jews. Between 1880 and 1900 an estimated one-third of the Jewish population of Europe came to America, and again settled almost exclusively in New York.[7]

By the turn of the century, New York had become easily the most cosmopolitan city the world had ever seen. Eighty percent of its five million inhabitants were either foreign-born or the children of immigrants.[8] It had more Italians than the combined populations of Florence, Genoa, and Venice, more Irish than anywhere but Dublin, more Russians than Kiev. As Herman Melville put it: "We are not so much a nation as a world." In 1908, a British Zionist named Israel Zangwill wrote a play about the immigration experience that gave Americans a term for the phenomenon. He called it *The Melting-Pot*.

The popular image, recreated in countless movies and books from *The Godfather* to *Kane and Able*, is of an immigrant arriving wide-eyed and bewildered at Ellis Island, being herded into a gloomy hall and subjected to an intimidating battery of medical tests and interviews, being issued a mysterious new name by a gruff and distracted immigration official, and finally stepping into the sunshine to realize that he has made it to the New World. Except possibly for the last part, it wasn't quite like that.

For one thing, until 1897 immigrants didn't pass through Ellis Island, but through Castle Garden, a former opera house on the Battery. Even after immigration facilities were transferred to Ellis Island, only steerage passengers were taken there. First- and second-class passengers were dealt with aboard their ships. Nor was Ellis Island (named for an eighteenth-century owner, Samuel Ellis) the drab, cheerless institution we might imagine. It was a beautiful, richly decorated complex with first-class health facilities, a roof garden with inspiring views of lower Manhattan and the Statue of Liberty, and good food for the relative few who were subjected to detention. Its Registration Hall with its brass chandeliers and vaulted ceiling containing 29,000 tiles handset by Italian craftsmen was possibly "the grandest single space in New York," according to *The New Yorker*.[9] Although immigration officials were unquestionably hard-worked—they processed up to five thousand arrivals a day and just over one million, four times Ellis Island's supposed capacity, in a single peak year, 1907—they performed their duties with efficiency, dispatch, and not a little compassion.[10] (Many were themselves immigrants.)

Though the list of those who could be denied admission was formidable—it included prostitutes, lunatics, polygamists, anarchists, those with "loathsome or contagious diseases," those deemed likely to become public charges, and some ninety other categories of undesirables—only about 2 percent of applicants were denied entrance, and so few were given names they didn't willingly accede to as to make the notion effectively mythical. Far from being a cold and insensitive introduction to the New World, it was a dazzling display of America's wealth, efficiency, and respect for the common person, one that made many truly believe that they had passed into an earthly paradise.

On landing in Manhattan the new immigrants would immediately find further manifestations of the wondrousness of America. Often they would be approached by fellow countrymen who spoke their language, but who were friendlier, easier in their manner, and far more nattily dressed than anyone they had seen at home. With astounding magnanimity, these instant friends, or *runners* as they were known, would offer to help the newly arrived immigrant find a job or lodgings and even insist on carrying their bags. Then at some point the immigrant would turn to discover that his new friend had vanished with his belongings, and that he had just learned his first important lesson about life in a new land. Few newly arrived travelers weren't fleeced in some way within their first days.

Most of the millions of lower-class immigrants settled in the four square miles that were the Lower East Side, often in conditions of appalling squalor, with as many as twenty-five people sharing a single windowless room. As early as the 1860s, three-fourths of New York City's population—more than 1.2 million people—were packed into just 37,000 tenements. By the end of the century the population density of the Lower East Side was greater than that in the slums of Bombay.[11] In an effort to improve conditions, a law was passed in 1869 requiring that every bedroom have a window. The result was the air shaft. Though a commendable notion in principle, air shafts turned out to be a natural receptacle for garbage and household slop, and thus became conduits of even greater filth and pestilence.

Crime, prostitution, begging, disease, and almost every other indicator of social deprivation existed at levels that are all but inconceivable now. (But not murder; the rate is ten times higher today.) A study of Irish immigrants to Boston around mid-century found that on average they survived for just fourteen years in America. In 1888, the infant death rate in the Italian quarter was 325 per 1,000. That is, one-third of all babies didn't survive their first year.[12]

Gangs with names like the Plug Uglies, Dead Rabbits, and Bowery

B'hoys roamed the streets, robbing and *mugging* (an Americanism dating from 1863; also sometimes called *yoking*) with something approaching impunity. Although New York had had a police force since 1845, by the second half of the century it was largely corrupt and ineffectual. Typical of the breed of nineteenth-century policeman was Chief Inspector Alexander "Clubber" Williams, who was brought up on charges no fewer than 358 times but was never dismissed or even apparently disciplined, and who was so magnificently talented at corruption that by the time of his retirement he had accumulated a yacht, a house in Connecticut, and savings of $300,000.[13]

Against such a background, it is hardly surprising that many immigrants fled back to Europe. At one point, for every one hundred Italians who arrived in New York each year, seventy-three left. Perhaps as many as a third of all immigrants eventually returned to their native soil.[14]

Nonetheless, the trend was relentlessly westward. The pattern for European immigrants was for one group to settle in an enclave and then disperse after a generation or so, with a new concentration of immigrants taking its place. Thus when the Irish abandoned their traditional stronghold of the Five Points area, their place was taken almost immediately by Italians. The old German neighborhoods were likewise taken over by Russian and Polish Jews. But there were finer gradations than this, particularly among the Italians. Natives of Genoa tended to accumulate along Baxter Street, while Elizabeth Street housed a large community of Sicilians. Calabrians congregated in the neighborhood known as Mulberry Bend. Alpine Italians—those from areas like Ticino in Switzerland and the Tyrol near Austria—were almost invariably to be found on 69th Street.

Immigrant groups had their own theaters, newspapers, libraries, schools, clubs, stores, taverns, and places of worship. Germans alone could choose from 133 German-language newspapers by 1850, some of them, like the *New York Staats-Zeitung* and *Cincinnati Volksblatt*, nearly as large and influential as their English-language counterparts.[15] Yiddish-speaking New Yorkers by the 1930s had a choice of a dozen daily newspapers, one of which, the *Jewish Daily Forward*, had a circulation of 125,000. Nationally, even Norwegians had forty papers in their own tongue. It was possible—indeed, in some cases not unusual—to live an entire life in the United States and never use English.

Dutch, for instance, remained widely spoken in rural New York well into the nineteenth century, some two hundred years after the Netherlands had retreated from the continent. The celebrated abolitionist, feminist, and public speaker Sojourner Truth, for instance, was raised as a slave in a Dutch household in Albany and spoke only Dutch until she reached adulthood.[16] According to Raven I. McDavid, Jr., "a few native speakers [of Dutch] survived in the remoter parts of the Hudson Valley as late as 1941."[17]

Though the Dutch were only a passing political presence in America, their linguistic legacy is immense. From their earliest days of contact, Americans freely appropriated Dutch terms—*blunderbuss* (literally "thunder gun") as early as 1654, *scow* in 1660, *sleigh* in 1703. By the mid-eighteenth century, Dutch words flooded into American English: *stoop, span, coleslaw, boss, pit* in the sense of the stone of a fruit, *bedpan, bedspread* (previously known as a *counterpane*), *cookie, waffle, nitwit* (the Dutch for I don't know is *Ik niet wiet*), the distinctive American interrogative *how come?* (a literal translation of the Dutch *hoekom*), *poppycock* (from *pappekak,* "soft dung"), *dunderhead,* and probably the *caboodle* in *kit and caboodle.* (*Boedel* in Dutch is a word for household effects, though J. L. Dillard, it is worth noting, mentions its resemblance to the Krio *kabudu* of West Africa.)[18]

Two particularly durable Americanisms that emanate from Dutch are *Santa Claus* (out of *Sinter Klaas,* a familiar form of *St. Nicholas*), first recorded in American English in 1773, and *Yankee* (probably from either *Janke,* a diminutive equivalent to the English *Johnny,* or *Jan Kees,* "John Cheese," intended originally as a mild insult).

Often Dutch words were given entirely new senses. *Snoepen,* meaning to slip candy into one's mouth when no one is watching, was transformed into the English *snoop,* meaning to spy or otherwise manifest nosiness.[19] *Docke,* "doll," became *doxy,* a woman of easy virtue. *Hokester,* an innocuous tradesman, became our *huckster,* someone not to be entirely trusted. *Doop* to the Dutch signified a type of sauce. In America, transliterated as *dope,* it began with that sense in 1807, but gradually took on many others, from a person of limited mental acuity (1851), to a kind of lubricant (1870s), to a form of opium (1889), to any kind of narcotic drug (1890s), to a preparation designed to affect a horse's performance (1900), to inside information (1910). Along the way it spawned several compounds, notably *dope fiend* (1896) and *dope addict* (1933).

Still other Dutch terms came to English by way of nautical contacts, reflecting the Netherlands' days of eminence on the seas, among them *hoist, bumpkin* (originally a short projecting spar; how it became transferred to a rustic character is unclear), *bulwark, caboose* (originally a ship's galley), *freebooter, hold, boom,* and *sloop.*

As Dutch demonstrates, a group's linguistic influence bears little relation to the numbers of people who spoke it. The Irish came in their millions, but gave us only a handful of words, notably *smithereens, lallapalooza, speakeasy, hooligan* (from Gaelic *uallachán,* a braggart),[20] and *slew*

(Gaelic *sluagh*), plus one or two semantic nuances, notably a more casual approach than in Britain to the distinctions between *shall* and *will* and the habit of attaching definite articles to conditions that previously lacked them, so that whereas a Briton might go into hospital with flu or measles, we go to *the* hospital and suffer from *the* flu and *the* measles.

The Scandinavians imparted even less. With the exception of a very few food words like *gravlaks* and *smorgasbord,* and a few regional terms like *lutfisk* (a fish dish) and *lefse* (a pancake) that are generally unknown outside the upper Midwest and the books of Garrison Keillor, their linguistic presence in America escaped emulation.

Italian was slightly more productive, though again only with food words—*spaghetti, pasta, macaroni, ravioli, pizza,* and the like. The few nonfood Italian terms that have found a home in English, like *ciao* and *paparazzo,* came much later and not through the medium of immigration.

German, by contrast, prospered on American soil. Germans had been present in America from early colonial times—by 1683 they had formed their own community, Germantown, near Philadelphia—but the bulk of their immigration came in two relatively short later bursts. The first, numbering some ninety thousand, happened mostly in the five years from 1749 to 1754 and was largely completed by the time of the American Revolution.[21] From 1830 to 1850 there was a second, larger influx focused mostly on urban areas like St. Louis, Cincinnati, Chicago, Milwaukee, Cleveland, Buffalo, and New York, in several of which the German cultural impact was not just enormous but dominant. An editorial writer for the *Houston Post* noted at the outbreak of World War I, "Germany seems to have lost all of her foreign possessions with the exception of Milwaukee, St. Louis, and Cincinnati."[22]

Only a few German words naturalized into English date from the earlier period of immigration, notably *sauerkraut* (1776), *pretzel* (1824), and *dumb* in the sense of stupid (1825). Most Americanized German terms arose during or soon after the second wave: *to loaf* and *loafer* (1835); *ouch, bub,* and *pumpernickel* (1839); *fresh* in the sense of being forward (1848); *kindergarten* (1852); *nix* (1855); *shyster,* probably from *Scheisse,* "shit" (1856); *check* in the sense of a restaurant bill (1868); and possibly *hoodlum* from the Bavarian dialect word *hodalump* (1872). Rather slower to assimilate were *delicatessen* (1889); *kaput* (1895); *fink,* from *Shmierfink,* a base character, literally "a greasy bird" (1892); *kaffeeklatsch* and *hockshop* (1903); and *scram* (1920). From German speakers, too, came our habit of saying *gesundheit* ("health!") after a sneeze and *so long* upon departing, of using *how* as an intensifier ("And how!"), and of putting *fest* on the ends of words (*songfest, foodfest, slugfest, talkfest*).

Many German terms underwent minor modifications of spelling to make them accord with English practice, so that *autsch* became *ouch,* *krank* (to be ill) became *cranky, zweiback* became *zwieback, Schmierkäse* became *smearcase,* and *Leberwurst* became *liverwurst.*

Equally productive, if somewhat less diffused through society, was Yiddish (from Middle High German *jüdisch diutsch,* "Jewish German"), brought to America by eastern European Jews beginning in about 1880. Though based on German, Yiddish uses Hebrew characters and is written from right to left like Hebrew. It originated in the early twelfth century in the Jewish ghettoes of central Europe. As Jews dispersed through Europe, they took Yiddish with them, enlivening it along the way with borrowings from Aramaic, Hebrew, various Slavic and Romance languages, and finally English. By the late nineteenth century it was the mother tongue of some eleven million people, a quarter of whom ended up in the United States.

As with the Germans, Jews came to America in well-defined but far more culturally distinct waves—first a small block of Sephardic Jews from Spain and Portugal (*Sephardic* means Spaniard in Hebrew) in the seventeenth and eighteenth centuries, then, from the 1820s through the 1880s, a much larger group of Ashkenazi Jews (named for the scriptural figure Ashchenaz) from elsewhere in western Europe, particularly Germany, and finally, from about 1880 to 1924, a tidal wave of eastern European Jews, most especially from Poland and Russia.

Members of the first two groups, generally educated and comfortably off, moved smoothly into American life. Many of the great names of American business and philanthropy—Guggenheim, Kuhn, Loeb, Seligman, Schiff, Lewisohn, Morgenthau, Speyer—trace their origins to the first and more particularly second waves. Those in the final diaspora were by contrast almost universally ragged and poor. At least one-quarter could not read or write. To the "uptown Jews," these new arrivals were something of an embarrassment. They referred to them as "barbarians" or "Asiatics," and regarded speaking Yiddish as a mark of poverty and ignorance.[23]

But it was these poor eastern Europeans who would more than any other group reshape America's concept of itself. They would help to create Hollywood and give us many of our most cherished creative talents, from the Marx Brothers to the composers George Gershwin and Irving Berlin. Both of the latter would get their start in the New York music district known as Tin Pan Alley (so called because of the cacophony to be heard there), Gershwin with "Swanee" and Berlin with the 1908 hit "Yidl with Your Fiddle, Play Some Ragtime," a song that, in the words of the writer Marvin Gelfind, "speaks volumes on the process called assimilation."[24]

Among the Yiddish words that found their way to a greater or lesser extent into mainstream English were *to kibbitz, schmaltz* (literally "chicken fat"), *schlemiel, schlock, keister* (rear end), *nosh, phooey, mashuggah* (crazy), *schmo* (a backward person), *schnozzle, to schlep, chutzpah, schikse* (a Christian female), *bagel, pastrami,* and *glitch* (from *glitschen,* "to slip"), plus a raft of expressions: *I should live so long, I should worry, get lost, I'm coming already, I need it like I need a hole in the head,* and others beyond counting.★

Many Yiddish terms convey degrees of nuance that make them practically untranslatable, except perhaps through humor, a quality never far off when Yiddish is under discussion. *Chutzpah,* for example, is usually defined in dictionaries as a kind of brazenness, but its subtleties cannot be better conveyed than by the old joke about the boy who kills his parents, then throws himself on the mercy of the court because he has only recently been orphaned.

Such was the scale of immigration that by 1930 more than 35 percent of white Americans were foreign-born or had at least one foreign-born parent.[25] Confined as they often were to ethnic enclaves by a combination of economics, prejudice, and convenience, it is a wonder that the country didn't splinter into scores of linguistic pockets. But it didn't, and for several reasons. First, as we have already seen, most people moved on as assimilation and economic circumstances permitted. An area like that around Hester Street in New York might remain Yiddish-speaking for several generations, but the speakers were a constantly changing mass. For the most part, foreign immigrants couldn't wait to learn English and circulate in the wider world. Indeed many, particularly among the children of immigrants, refused to speak their ancestral tongue or otherwise acknowledge their ethnic grounding. By 1927, *Time* magazine noted, older Jews were complaining that the younger generation didn't understand Yiddish.[26] At about the same time, H. L. Mencken was noting: "In cities such as Cleveland and Chicago it is a rare second-generation American of Polish, Hungarian, or Croatian stock who even pretends to know his parents' native language."[27]

Children not only refused to learn their parents' language but "would reprove their parents for speaking it in front of strangers."[28] As the his-

---

★It should be pointed out, however, that the closeness of German, Dutch, and Yiddish often makes it impossible to ascribe a term positively to one camp. *Spook* and *dumb* could be either Dutch or German in origin, and *nosh, schlemiel,* and *phooey,* among others, are as likely to have entered American English from German sources as Yiddish. More often than not, the influence probably came from two directions simultaneously.

torian Maldwyn Allen Jones has put it: "Culturally estranged from their parents by their American education, and wanting nothing so much as to become and to be accepted as Americans, many second-generation immigrants made deliberate efforts to rid themselves of their heritage. The adoption of American clothes, speech, and interests, often accompanied by the shedding of an exotic surname, were all part of a process whereby antecedents were repudiated as a means of improving status."[29]

"Every immigrant who comes here should be required within five years to learn English or leave the country," barked Theodore Roosevelt in 1918. In fact, almost all did. Of the 13.4 million foreign-born in the United States in 1930, all but 870,000 were deemed by census enumerators to have a workable grasp of English, and most of those who did not were recent arrivals or temporary residents (many Italians in particular came for a part of every year when there was no farm work to be had at home), or felt themselves too old to learn. Although many urban, nonnative speakers could get by without English, most chose not to. There were, to be sure, troubling disparities. Only 3 percent of German immigrants did not speak English in 1930, while almost 13 percent of Poles and 16 percent of Italians (rising to over 25 percent for Italian women) existed in linguistic isolation.[30] But even the worst of those numbers would become negligible within a generation.

The erosion of linguistic enclaves was inevitable in urban areas where the mingling of immigrant groups was necessary and unavoidable. But what of more isolated communities? At the turn of the century throughout the Midwest there existed hundreds of towns or clusters of towns inhabited almost exclusively by specific linguistic groups. Iowa, for instance, had Elk Horn (founded by Danes), Pella (by the Dutch), and the Amana Colonies (by Germans), among many others. In each of these places, the local populace was homogeneous and sufficiently isolated to escape the general pressure to become Americanized. Even if they learned English in order to listen to the radio and converse with outsiders, we might reasonably expect them to preserve their mother tongue for private use. Yet, almost without exception, they did not. By the 1930s in such towns, English was not just the main language spoken but the only one. Even those German immigrants who came to America with the intention of founding a *Kleinedeutschland,* or Little Germany, in Texas or Wisconsin eventually gave up the fight. Today, it is unusual to find almost anyone in any such town who knows more than a few words of his ancestors' tongue.

Only one group has managed to resist in significant numbers the temptations of English. I refer to the speakers of the curious dialect that is known generally, if mistakenly, as Pennsylvania Dutch. The name is an accident of history. From the early eighteenth century to almost the end of the nineteenth, *Dutch* in American English was applied not just to the language of Holland and its environs but to much else that was bewilderingly foreign, most especially Germans and their language—doubtless in confusion with the German word *deutsch*.

The Germans came to Pennsylvania at the invitation of William Penn, who believed that their ascetic religious principles fit comfortably with his own Quaker beliefs. The German influx, eventually comprising about 100,000 people, or a third of Pennsylvania's population, was made up of a variety of loosely related sects, notably Mennonites, Schwenkenfelders, Dunkards, Moravians, and Amish. It was the Amish in particular who spoke the Palatinate dialect of High German that eventually evolved into the tongue that most know as Pennsylvania Dutch. To the Pennsylvania Dutch the language is called *Mudderschprooch*. To scholars and the linguistically fastidious it is *Pennsylvania German*.

For a century and a half, Pennsylvania German was largely ignored by scholars. Not until 1924, when Marcus Bachman Lambert published his *Dictionary of the Non-English Words of the Pennsylvania-German Dialect*, with some seventeen thousand entries, did it at last attract serious attention. Even now it remains relatively neglected as a topic of academic interest, which is a pity, because few dialects provide a more instructive example of what happens to languages when they exist in isolation. As the linguist and historian C. Richard Beam has put it: "In an age when there are billions of dollars available for trips to the moon and destruction abroad, it is very difficult to procure even a few hundred dollars to help finance the production of a dictionary of the language of the oldest and largest German language island on the North American continent."[31]

Because it has always been primarily a colloquial, spoken dialect, very different in form and content from standard German, Pennsylvania German presents serious problems with orthography. Put simply, almost any statement can be rendered in a variety of spellings. Here, for instance, are three versions of the same text:

> *Die Hundstage kumme all Jahr un bleibe sechs . . .*
> *De hoons-dawga cooma alla yohr un bliva sex . . .*
> *Die Hundsdaage kumme alle Yaahr un blwewe sex . . .*[32]

During its long years of isolation, Pennsylvania German has become increasingly distinct from mainstream German. Many words bear the unmistakable mark of English influence, others preserve archaic or dialectal German forms, and still others have been coined *in situ*. The drift away from standard German can be seen in the following:

Pennsylvania German	Standard German	English
aageglesser	Brillen	eyeglasses
bauersleit	Bauern	farmers
bauerei	Bauernhöfe	farms
elfder	elf	eleven
feierblatz	Kamin; Feuerplatz	fireplace
eensich ebbes	etwas; irgend etwas	anything
Febber	Februar	February
dabbich	ungenschickt	clumsy
alde daage	Alter	old age
Schtaagefensich	zick zack	zigzag
Grischtdaag	Weihnachten	Christmas
Nei Yarick	New York	New York

A striking feature of Pennsylvania German is its wealth of curiously specific terms. Notions and situations that other languages require long clauses to convey can often be expressed with a single word. For example:

fedderschei—the condition of being reluctant to write letters
aagehaar—an eyelash hair that grows inwardly and irritates the sclera
dachdrops—water dripping from a roof
aarschgnoddle—the globules of dung found on hair in the vicinity of the anus (and, no, I cannot think why they might need such a word)

At its peak in the nineteenth century, Pennsylvania German was spoken in communities as far afield as Canada, the upper Midwest, and the deep South. Today, according to Beam, it constitutes "but the remnants of a unique German-American folk culture, so rapid has been the process of acculturation."[33] Estimates of the current number of speakers range as high as sixteen thousand—up to a quarter of the inhabitants of Lehigh, Lebanon, and Berks counties in Pennsylvania are said to still speak it[34]—but the trend is implacably downward.

II

If one attitude can be said to characterize America's regard for immigration over the past two hundred years it is the belief that while immigration was unquestionably a wise and prescient thing in the case of one's

parents or grandparents, it really ought to stop now. Succeeding generations of Americans have persuaded themselves that the country faced
imminent social dislocation, and eventual ruin, at the hands of grasping
foreign hordes pouring into its ports or across its borders.

At the turn of the nineteenth century, Thomas Jefferson responded to
calls for restrictions on immigration by asking, a trifle plaintively, "Shall
we refuse the unhappy fugitives from distress that hospitality which the
savages of the wilderness extended to our fathers arriving in this
land?"—though even he feared that immigrants with their "unbounded
licentiousness" would turn the United States into a "heterogeneous, in-
coherent, distracted mass."[35]

From the earliest days, immigrants aroused alarm and attracted epithets. For the most part, early nicknames for foreigners were only mildly
abusive—for example, calling the Germans *cabbageheads* or *krauts* (from
their liking for sauerkraut)—or even rather backhandedly affectionate.
This was particularly the case with the Irish, whose reputed fondness for
drinking and brawling and lack of acquaintance with the higher mental
processes inspired a number of mostly good-natured terms of deroga-
tion, so that a police station was an *Irish clubhouse,* a wheelbarrow was an
Irish buggy, bricks were *Irish confetti,* and an *Irish beauty* was a woman
with two black eyes.

But as time went on, such terms grew uglier and more barbed, and
tended to cluster around harsh mono- or dissyllables that weren't so
much spoken as spat: *chink, kike, dago, polack, spic, hebe.* Some of these
had been floating around in English long before they became common
in America. *Polack,* for a Pole, was current in Elizabethan England and
can be found in *Hamlet. Chink,* for a Chinese, appears to have been
coined in Australia. *Sheeny,* for a Jew, arose in the East End of London,
where it was first noted in 1824, but what inspired it is unknown. *Kike,*
an Americanism first recorded in 1917, is thought to come from the *-ki*
terminations on Jewish names like *Levinski. Bohunk,* probably a blend of
Bohemian and *Hungarian,* is also of American origin and dates from the
early 1900s. *Spic,* for Latin Americans, is said by Mencken to derive
from "no spik Inglis." *Wop,* from *guappo,* a Neapolitan expression for a
dandy or fop, was brought from Italy but took on its unseemly, more
generalized shadings in the New World. (The theory that *wop* is short
for "without passport" is simply wrong.)

Geographical precision has never been a hallmark of terms of abuse.
Guinea began, accurately, as a term to describe an African in the late
eighteenth century, then attached itself to Italians in the 1880s. *Dago*
originated as a shortening of *Diego* and was at first applied to Spaniards
before becoming associated with Italians, Greeks, Mexicans, and anyone

else suspiciously foreign and swarthy in the 1880s, as did *greaser* (dating from as far back as 1836) and the more recent *greaseball*. Many others are much less commonly heard now, notably *skibby* for a Japanese (possibly, if somewhat mysteriously, from *sukebei*, "lewdness"), and the even more obscure *gugu* for a Filipino, which some authorities believe is the source for *gook*.

Until the closing years of the nineteenth century, America reserved most of its official racist animus for blacks and Indians. But in 1882, it added a new category when Chinese were expressly denied entry to the United States through the Chinese Exclusion Act, and those already here were forbidden the rights and protections of citizenship. In 1908 the exclusion was extended to most Japanese immigrants through an arrangement known as the Gentlemen's Agreement. Throughout the early decades of this century, Orientals were compelled to attend segregated schools, and barred from owning property, providing landlords with considerable scope for abuse.[36] As late as the early 1950s, the immigration quotas for Asian countries were niggardly to say the least: 185 for Japan, 105 for China, 100 each for Korea and the Philippines.

But beginning in the 1890s, as the flood of immigrants from the poorer parts of Europe turned into a deluge, racism became more sweeping, more rabid, and less focused. Anti-immigrant fraternities like the American Protective Association and the Immigration Restriction League sprang up and found large followings, and books like Madison Grant's *The Passing of the Great Race* (which argued "scientifically" that unrestricted immigration was leading to the dilution and degeneration of the national character) became best-sellers. William J. H. Traynor of the American Protective Association spoke for the mood of the country when he argued against giving the vote to "every ignorant Dago and Pole, Hun and Slav" and all the other "criminal riffraff of Europe" that washed up on American shores.[37] Such sentiments appealed not only to the masses but to people of considerable eminence. The Immigration Restriction League numbered among its supporters the heads of Harvard, Stanford, Georgia Tech, the University of Chicago, and the Wharton School of Finance.[38]

Even Woodrow Wilson, who many would argue was as enlightened a President as we have had this century, could write in his *History of the American People* in 1902 that recent immigrations had been characterized by "multitudes of men of lowest class from the south of Italy, and men of the meaner sort out of Hungary and Poland" who collectively were endowed with neither skills nor energy "nor any initiative of quick intelligence." The Chinese, he added a trifle daringly for the time, "were more to be desired, as workmen if not as citizens."[39]

When several Italian immigrants were lynched in New Orleans for associating with blacks, President Theodore Roosevelt made appropriate lamentations in public, but remarked in a letter to his sister that he thought it was really "rather a good thing" and added derogatory comments about the tiresomeness of "various dago diplomats" who had protested to him about the lynchings.[40] Even Margaret Sanger, the esteemed birth control activist, was motivated not by a desire to give women more control over their destinies, but by a utopian urge to reduce the lower orders through carefully imposed eugenics. "More children from the fit, less from the unfit—that is the chief issue of birth control," she wrote.[41] Never before or since have intolerance and prejudice been more visible, fashionable, or universal among all levels of American society.

In 1907, to give vent to the growing concerns that America was being swept to oblivion by a tide of rabble, Congress established a panel called the Dillingham Commission. Its forty-two-volume report concluded essentially that immigration before 1880 had been no bad thing—the immigrants, primarily from northern Europe, were (by implication) industrious, decent, trustworthy, and largely Protestant, and as a result had assimilated well—while immigration after 1880 had been marked by the entrance into America of uneducated, unsophisticated, largely shiftless, and certainly non-Protestant masses from southern and eastern Europe. It maintained that the Germans and Scandinavians had bought farms and become productive members of American society, while succeeding waves of immigrants had merely soaked up charity and acted as a drug on industrial earnings.

As evidence the commission pointed out that 77 percent of arrested suspects in New York City were foreign-born, as were 86 percent of those on some form of relief, and the poor were not just overwhelmingly, but almost entirely, of immigrant stock.[42] When the commission investigators examined housing conditions in New York, they could not find a single case of a white native American living in a tenement. The commission concluded that immigrants from southern and eastern Europe had increased overall unemployment and depressed wages.

In fact, all evidence points in the opposite direction. It was *because* America had a base of low-wage, adaptable, unskilled labor that it was able to become an industrial powerhouse.[43] For over half a century, American business had freely exploited its foreign-born workers, paying them appalling wages, dismissing them wholesale if they agitated for better pay or conditions, and replacing them with new supplies of compliant immigrants when necessary. Now it was blaming them for being poor and alienated. It failed to note that those who turned to crime or sought relief were only a small part of the immigrant whole, most of whom were loyal, productive, law-abiding citizens.

Fired by the oxygen of irrationality, America entered a period of grave intolerance, not just toward immigrants but toward any kind of antiestablishment behavior. The Sedition Act of 1918 made it illegal, among much else, to make critical remarks about government expenditure or even the YMCA.[44] So low did standards of civil liberty fall that police routinely arrested not only almost anyone remotely suspected of sedition, but even those who came to visit them in jail.

In 1917, in an effort to weed out unfit immigrants, a literacy test of sorts was introduced. Most aspiring immigrants now had to show that they were capable of reading at least thirty words—though, oddly, the words didn't have to be English. Why a Croat who could read thirty words of Croatian was perceived to be better prepared for life in America than a fellow Croat who could not was never explained.

At the same time, the questions that were asked of immigrants at ports of entry became far more searching and insinuating. Arriving in America in 1921, G. K. Chesterton was astonished at the probing interview to which he had to submit. "I have stood on the other side of Jordan," he remarked later, "in the land ruled by a rude Arab chief, where the police looked so like brigands that one wondered what the brigands looked like. But they did not ask me whether I had come to subvert the power of the *Shereef;* and they did not exhibit the faintest curiosity about my personal views on the ethical basis of civil authority."[45] Finally, in 1924 a quota system was introduced and America's open-door policy became a part of history.

By this time, however, immigrants everywhere were proving the iniquity of the prejudice against them. Eastern European Jews in particular showed a model regard for education and self-improvement. By 1927, two-thirds of New York's twenty thousand lawyers were Jewish,[46] and thousands more had built distinguished careers as academics, musicians, playwrights, journalists, doctors, composers, entertainers—in almost every field of human endeavor not barred to them. Having faced four decades of complaints that they did not work hard enough, Jews now found themselves accused of working *too* hard.

A quiet drive began to ration Jewish admissions to many universities (echoing present-day concerns over Asian domination of institutions of higher learning), and there arose a new expression, *five-o'clock anti-Semitism,* by which was meant that people were prepared to work with Jews during the day, but would not dream of socializing with them at night. For at least another three decades, Jews would remain casually excluded from large parts of the American mainstream.

Not until the 1960s could they hope to be admitted to non-Jewish country clubs, college fraternities and sororities, and other bastions of gentile life.

But the prejudice the Jews experienced paled when compared to that meted out to the most visible, least voluntary of all minorities: black Americans. It may come as a surprise to learn that blacks were one of the *least* numerous of groups to enter the United States, exceeded in number of arrivals by Swedes, Sicilians, Poles, and most other national or ethnic blocks. Between 1505, when the first consignment of black slaves arrived in the Caribbean, and 1888, when slavery was finally outlawed in its last New World stronghold, Brazil, an estimated twelve million black Africans were transported across the Atlantic. The overwhelming majority, however, went to Brazil and the Caribbean. Just 5 percent—about half a million people—were imported into what was to become the United States.[47]

For obvious economic reasons, blacks were encouraged to propagate freely. As early as 1775, they accounted for 40 percent of the population of Virginia, 30 percent in North Carolina, Maryland, and Georgia, and well over 60 percent in South Carolina.[48]

Though the physical cruelties to which they were subjected have perhaps been somewhat inflated in the popular mind—most were at least passably fed and clothed by the standards of the day; it was, after all, in the slaveowner's interest to look after his property—the psychological humiliations to which they were subjected are immeasurable. It was not merely the imposition of involuntary servitude but the denial of even the most basic human dignities that made American slavery so singularly odious. David Hackett Fischer reports how a visitor to Virginia "was startled to see ladies buying naked male slaves after carefully examining their genitals."[49] Female slaves were routinely regarded as sexual playthings by owners and their overseers. Scarcely a plantation existed that didn't have a sprinkling of *mulattos* (originally a Spanish term denoting a small mule), and visitors from outside the South were often taken aback at encountering a light-skinned slave bearing a more than passing resemblance to their host. (Sally Hemings, the slave woman who may have been the long-standing mistress of Thomas Jefferson, was in fact his late wife's half sister.)

Slaves were commonly wrenched from their partners—about a quarter ended up so separated—and mothers divided from their children with a casualness that strains the heart even now. A typical advertisement of the time read: "NEGROES FOR SALE. —A negro woman 24 years of age, and two children, one eight and the other three years. Said negroes will be sold separately or together as desired."[50] In a thousand ways, black Americans were daily reminded of their subhuman status. As the words of a slave song had it:

> *We bake de bread,*
> *Dey gib us de crust,*
> *We sif de meal,*
> *Dey gib us de huss . . .*
> *We skim de pot,*
> *Dey gib us de liquor*
> *An say dat's good enough for nigger*[51]

Almost everywhere they were kept in a state of profound ignorance. Learning of any sort was assumed to be an invitation to insubordination. Joel Chandler Harris had his fictional creation Uncle Remus remark: "Put a spellin-book in a nigger's han's, en right den an dar' you loozes a plowhand. I kin take a bar'l stave an fling mo' sense inter a nigger in one minnit dan all de schoolhouses betwixt dis en de state er Midgigin."[52] In consequence, their awareness of the world beyond the plantation bounds was often stupefyingly limited. Frederick Douglass recounted in his autobiography that until he secured his freedom he had never even *heard* of New York and Massachusetts.[53]

Even if they managed to secure their freedom, they scarcely enjoyed the fruits of democracy. By 1820, America had 233,000 freed blacks, but they weren't in any meaningful sense free. White workmen refused to work alongside blacks or to allow them apprenticeships, so their prospects of worthwhile employment, much less advancement, were exceedingly meager. Iowa, Illinois, and Indiana would not allow even free blacks to settle within their boundaries. Even where they were allowed to settle, they were subjected to constant indignities, which they had to suffer in silence. Every child knew that he could pelt a black person with a snowball without fear of reprisal. Even in the case of the most serious grievances, blacks were often denied the rights of habeas corpus, trial by jury, or to testify in their own behalf. Almost nowhere were they allowed to testify against whites.

Though slavery was widely detested in the North, only a handful of idealistic eccentrics saw abolition as a prelude to equality of opportunity. Even Lincoln, in his debates with Stephen Douglas, made his position clear: "I am not, nor ever have been, in favor of bringing about in any way the social and political equality of the white and black races. . . . I am not, nor ever have been, in favor of making voters or jurors of negroes, nor of qualifying them to hold office, nor to intermarry with white people. . . ."[54]

Most preferred to think of blacks as happy-go-lucky, childlike creatures who wanted nothing more from life than something good to eat and a chance to sing and dance. The popular image was captured in the song "Jim Crow," popularized by Thomas D. Rice in the mid-1830s:

> Come, listen all you gals and boys,
> I'se just from Tucky hoe;
> I'm goin' to sing a little song,
> My name's Jim Crow.

What is remarkable is how long-lasting this imagery proved. Well into the 1940s, *Time* magazine was still commonly referring to blacks as "pickaninnies" and reveling in news snippets in which black people fell down wells or otherwise came amusingly a cropper. Hollywood roles for blacks were largely limited to the shuffling, eye-rolling, perennially timorous and befuddled types played by actors like Stepin Fetchit and Buckwheat Thomas. The 1950s saw the stereotype extended with television characters like Amos 'n' Andy and the faithful Rochester on the *Jack Benny Show*, while in the wider world of commerce almost the only black face one saw was the smiling countenance of Aunt Jemima, a fat and irrepressibly happy black woman who clearly saw no higher gratification in life than to fix pancakes for white folks. Elsewhere blacks simply didn't exist. Even a program like the *Andy Griffith Show*, set in the fictional arcadia of Mayberry, North Carolina, appeared to take place in a surreally all-white world.

On the few occasions when blacks were treated more seriously, it was almost always with a degree of patronizing ignorance that now simply takes one's breath away. As late as 1949, the author of a nationally syndicated newspaper science column could solemnly inform his young readers that the American Negro was constitutionally incapable of pronouncing *r*'s in words like *cart* and *horse* because "his lips are too thick." Almost no scholarly attention was devoted to black Americans. The few books that focused on them, like *The Negro in Africa and America* (1902) and *The Negro in American Life* (1926), took it as a given that blacks were incapable, except in certain exceptional cases, of higher cerebral activity. Often, it was asserted that their distinctive speech habits were an inevitable consequence both of their impaired mental powers and of their physiology, as in this passage from *The Negro in American Life* discussing the Gullah dialect:

> Slovenly and careless of speech, these Gullahs seized upon the peasant English used by some of the early settlers . . . wrapped their

clumsy tongues about it as well as they could, and, enriched with certain expressive African words, it issued through their flat noses and thick lips as . . . speech.[55]

And this, I urge you to bear in mind, was a scholarly work. Even the most eminent of linguistic scholars found it impossible to credit blacks with even the most modest capacity for linguistic innovation. In *The English Language in America*, George Philip Krapp contended: "American words brought into the language through the negroes have been insignificant in number. . . . A few words like *juba*, a kind of dance, *banjo*, *hoodoo*, *voodoo*, *pickaninny*, exhaust the list of words of non-English origin."[56] Of Gullah—now widely regarded as the richest, most expressive, and most ethnically pure of all the Afro-American dialects in America— Krapp contended that "very little of it, perhaps none, is derived from sources other than English."

Almost every term of black speech was claimed to have its roots in English. *Jazz*, Krapp insisted, was an old English dialectal word. Another scholar went so far as to pronounce that *moke*, once a common word for a black person, came from the Icelandic *möckvi*, "darkness."[57] That even an eight-year-old child could see a certain implausibility in the idea of black Americans picking up and employing a term that had originated on a chilly island two thousand miles away didn't matter. What was important was that the credit had to go to some source other than the blacks themselves.

Not until a black academic named Lorenzo Dow Turner and a Swede named Gunnar Myrdal began studying black speech in the 1940s was it accorded serious, scholarly investigation. Turner and Myrdal quickly established that certain syntactical features of Gullah, a dialect still spoken by some 250,000 people on the Sea Islands off South Carolina and among neighboring coastal communities, were clearly traceable to the languages of West Africa, and also appeared in other New World patois as far apart as Brazil and Haiti, which clearly precluded British dialectal origins. Turner's *Africanisms in the Gullah Dialect* (1949) suggested that as many as six thousand Gullah words showed signs of concordance with West African terms.[58]

Turner and Myrdal showed, among much else, that the Wolof *hipikat*, denoting a person who is attuned to his environment, literally "has his eyes open," is the most plausible source for *hepcat*, *hip*, and their many variants.[59] Other words almost certainly of ultimate African origin are *chigger*, *gumbo*, *banjo* (at first also spelled *banjou* or *bangy*), *jitter*, *cola*, *yam*, *zombie*, *juke*, *goober*, *tote*, *okra*, and *boogie-woogie*, though many of these, like *banjo*, *chigger*, and *gumbo*, reached America by way of the Caribbean, often after being filtered through an intermediate language.

Even Teddy Roosevelt's *speak softly and carry a big stick* appears to have its roots in a West African proverb. Likewise, "Yankee Doodle Dandy" shows a striking similarity to a slave song from Surinam, which goes

> *Mama Nanni go to town*
> *Buy a little pony.*
> *Stick a feather in a ring,*
> *Calling Masra Ranni.*[60]

Other terms that have been credited with African roots include *bogus, banana, gorilla, funky, phony,* and *jazz,* though in each instance the evidence is largely conjectural. *Jazz* is one of the most hotly disputed terms in American etymology. Among the suggested possibilities are that it comes from *Chaz,* the nickname of an early ragtime drummer named Charles Washington, or from *chasse,* a kind of dance step. Others have linked it to various African or creole sources. In any case, its first use, in the South among both blacks and whites, was to describe sexual intercourse. It wasn't until after World War I that it entered the wider world conveying the idea of a type of music. Quite a number of African-American terms contain some forgotten sexual association. *Boogie-woogie* appears originally to have signified syphilis. *Juke,* from the West African *dzugu,* "wicked," originally carried that sense in English. Eventually it came to signify a brothel and then, by about 1930, a cheap tavern where lively music was played—a *juke joint. Jukebox* dates from 1937. *Blues,* a term popularized if not invented by one of its greatest exponents, the cornet player W. C. Handy (his "Memphis Blues" was written in 1910; "St. Louis Blues" followed in 1914), also originally had "a strong sexual significance," according to Mencken, though he doesn't elaborate.[61] So, too, did *rock 'n' roll.*

Among the many neologisms that certainly or probably were created in America by blacks, and have subsequently filtered into the wider world, we find *to blow one's top, gimme five* for a handshake and *high five* for a congratulatory handslap, *ragtime* (also obscure, but possibly arising from its ragged syncopation; it was first recorded in 1896), *bad* in the sense of good, *cool* in the sense of being admirable, *def* for excellent, *to get down* in the sense of to attend to pleasures, *case* in the sense of personal business ("get off my case"), *square* for a boring person, *to lighten up* for relax, *right on, uptight, jive, to chill out, to bad-mouth,* and *geek.* In addition, there are scores, perhaps hundreds, of other terms that are used primarily by blacks: *hood* for neighborhood, *dippin'* for being nosy, *to beam on* for to stare impolitely ("you beaming on my girl?"), *honky* for a white person (of uncertain derivation, but possibly from *hunky,* a shortening of *Bohunk*), *blood* for a fellow black, *411* for reliable information (from a phone company number for directory assistance), and *fess* for an insincere promise.

Finally, a word about descriptive terms for black people. *Negro* is Spanish and Portuguese for "black," and was first noted in English in 1555. *Nigger* appeared in 1587 and was not at first a pejorative term but simply a variant pronunciation of *Negro*. *Sambo,* a Nigerian word meaning "second son," was not originally pejorative either. *Uncle Tom* comes, of course, from Harriet Beecher Stowe's popular novel *Uncle Tom's Cabin,* though its use in the general sense of a servile black hasn't been found earlier than 1922.

Blacks were generally called *blacks* or, more politely, *coloreds* until the 1880s, when *negro* increasingly became the preferred term. The National Association for the Advancement of Colored People was founded in 1909 and, despite its own choice of name, soon launched a campaign to have *negro* given the dignity of a capital letter and accepted as the standard designation for black people. By 1930, *Negro* had been adopted by almost every large disseminator of information in the United States with the single notable exception of the U.S. Government Printing Office.[62] *Black* made a resurgence during the early 1960s, almost entirely displacing *Negro* by about 1970, and has since been joined by many other suggested designations: *African-American, Afro-American, Afri-American, Afra-American,* and *Afrikan.*[63]

Chapter 10

WHEN THE GOING WAS GOOD: TRAVEL IN AMERICA

I

On January 8, 1815, General Andrew Jackson led American troops in a stormy rout of the British at the Battle of New Orleans. It was a decisive triumph—or would have been had there been anything to be decisive about. Unknown to the combatants on both sides, the War of 1812 had been amicably concluded over port and brandy two weeks earlier with the signing of the Treaty of Ghent. More than two thousand men died fighting a battle in a war that was over.[1]

I bring this up here to make the point that throughout the early American period, communications were a perennial problem. If winds were unfavorable it could take months to cross the Atlantic. In December 1606, when John Smith and his party set off to found Jamestown, the winds proved so "unprosperous," as he rather mildly put it, that it took them six weeks just to get out of sight of England. A good crossing, such as that of the *Mayflower,* would take eight or nine weeks. But crossings of six or seven months were by no means unknown.[2]

In such circumstances, food rotted and water grew brackish. If the captain or shipowner was unscrupulous, the food was often rotten to begin with. Journals of the time are full of baleful remarks. "What with the heat and dampness, even the biscuit was so full of worms that, God help me, I saw many wait until nightfall to eat the porridge made of it so as not to see the worms," wrote one dismayed mariner.[3] Personal hygiene became an impossibility. Lice grew "so thick that they could be scraped off the body."[4] Occasionally circumstances would be so dire that sailors would refuse to put to sea and would "strike," or lower, the sails to show their defiance—hence the modern term *to strike* in the sense of withholding labor.[5]

For mariners, conditions were challenging enough, but for passengers unaccustomed to the perils of the sea, the experience all too often proved unbearable. One ship sailing from Leyden to Virginia in the winter of 1618 set off with 180 people. By the time it reached the New World, all but fifty had perished.[6] The passengers of the *Sea-Flower,* sailing out of Belfast in 1741, were so consumed with hunger that they ate their dead. Throughout the early colonial period, the problem with populating the New World wasn't so much one of finding people willing to go but keeping them alive before and after they got there.

The Atlantic was an equally exasperating barrier to the spread of news. Rarely did a letter posted in Boston in November reach London before the following spring. In 1745, the Board of Trade in London wrote to the governor of North Carolina asking him, a trifle peevishly, why it hadn't heard from him for three years.[7] Even news of crucial import was frequently delayed. No one in America knew of the imposition of the Stamp Act, or its subsequent withdrawal, for two months after both events. The Bastille was stormed in July 1789, but President Washington, newly inaugurated, didn't learn of it until the autumn.

Within America, matters were, if anything, worse. Often letters never found their destination, and when they did, it was not uncommon for a year to elapse before a reply was received. Letters routinely began with a summation of the fate of previous correspondence, as in this note from Thomas Jefferson, writing from Philadelphia in 1776, to William Randolph in Virginia: "Dear Sir, Your's of August I received in this place, that of Nov. 24th. is just now come to hand; the one of October I imagine has miscarried."[8]

There was good reason for the difficulty: until well after the time of the Revolution, America had virtually no highways worthy of the name. Such roads as existed were often little more than Indian trails, seldom more than fifteen inches wide and fraught with the obvious peril that you might at any time run into a party of Indians, not necessarily a thing you would wish for in the middle of the wilderness even in times of peace. One such trail was the Natchez Trace—*trace* here being used in the sense of something that describes a line—which covered the five hundred miles of risky nowhere between Nashville and Natchez. It was principally used by boatmen who would float freight down the Mississippi on rough rafts, sell their goods, break up the rafts for lumber, and hike back. Even in the more built-up East, such roads as existed would routinely disappear at riverbanks or dissolve into a confusion of forks. Signposts, maps, and other aids to the bewildered traveler were all but unknown. (The first book of road maps would not be published until 1789.) When Jefferson traveled from Virginia to Philadelphia for the Second Continental Congress he twice had to employ guides to show him the way along particular stretches—and this on one of America's better-traveled routes.[9] Until well into the nineteenth century, it was as cheap to send a ton of goods across the Atlantic as it was to move it thirty miles overland.[10]

With no roads to speak of, people traveled by oceangoing coaster or, more often, didn't go at all. Samuel Adams did not set foot out of Massachusetts—indeed, didn't mount a horse—until he was in his fifties, and there was nothing especially unusual in that.[11] In 1750, the whole of Massachusetts could boast just six passenger coaches.[12] In Virginia, according to a contemporary account, most people had never seen any four-wheeled vehicle but a wagon and many had not seen even that.[13]

In the circumstances, it is perhaps not surprising that American English became particularly rich in terms for unsophisticated rustics. *Yokel,* a word of uncertain provenance (it may come from the German *Jokel,* a diminutive of *Jakob*), entered American English in 1812. *Hick,* an indirect shortening of *Richard,* is older still, dating from fourteenth-century England and common in America from its earliest days. Among other similar words were *hayseed, bumpkin, rube* (from *Reuben*), *country jake,* and *jay* (which eventually gave us the term *jaywalker*—that is, an innocent who doesn't know how to cross a city street). *Hillbilly,* perhaps surprisingly, doesn't appear to have entered the language until as late as 1904 and didn't become widespread until the 1930s. By 1905 such uninformed rustics were said to come from *the sticks.* The expression derives from a slang term used by lumbermen for a forest. (More recent still is *boondocks,* a Filipino word for "mountain" first recorded in English in 1944. *Boonies* didn't arrive until 1965.)

Until the closing years of the eighteenth century, the only real roads in America were the sixty-two-mile-long Philadelphia and Lancaster Turnpike (*turnpike* is a British term dating from 1678, and so called because the way was blocked by a studded pole, or *pike,* which was turned to allow passage once a toll was paid), the Boston Post Road between Boston and New York, the Wilderness Road blazed by Daniel Boone into the Kentucky territory, and the "Great Road" connecting Philadelphia with the mouth of the Conestoga River. The covered wagons built to negotiate the Great Road were at first called *freighters.* Later, they came to be known as Conestogas, after the Pennsylvania town where they were built. Coincidentally, the town also became famous for a distinctive torpedo-shaped cigar. It was called, naturally, the Conestoga cigar, but the name was soon shortened to *stogy* (or *stogie*), and, fittingly, became a favorite of the Conestoga drivers along the Great Road.[14] An unusual feature of Conestoga wagons was that they were built with their brakes and "lazy boards"—a kind of extendable running board—on the left-hand side. If there was a reason for putting them there, it has since been forgotten. With drivers effectively compelled to sit on the left, they tended to drive on the right so that they had an unimpeded view of the road, which is why, it appears, Americans abandoned the long-standing British custom of driving on the left.

Though it surprises most people to hear it, roads in America are effectively a twentieth-century phenomenon. Instead of having a lot of roads, America fell into the habit of having a few roads but giving them lots of names. The great National Road, the first real long-distance highway in America, was also variously known as the Cumberland Road, the Great Western Road, Uncle Sam's Road, the Ohio Road, and the Illinois Road. Begun in 1811 in Cumberland, Maryland, it ran for 130 miles to Wheeling, West Virginia, and eventually stretched on across Pennsylvania, Ohio, Indiana, and as far west as Vandalia, Illinois, which it reached in mid-century and then terminated, its function abruptly overtaken by steamboats and railroads. Much of this road would become Highway 40, but not for another seventy years. For the moment, the highway age in America was dead.

Such highways as existed were not only few and far between, but perilous, uncomfortable, and slow. Early coaches (the word comes from *Kocs,* a town in Hungary noted for its carriages; how it then came to describe a person who trains football players and the like is a mystery) were decidedly short on comfort, largely because a seemingly obvious invention—the elliptical spring—occurred to no one before 1804 and didn't become common on vehicles until much later. The best roads, called corduroy roads because they were made of felled trees laid side by side, giving a ribbed effect like corduroy, were torturous enough, but they were a rarity. Most were simply rough clearings through the wilderness. That perhaps doesn't sound too bad, but bear in mind that the technology of the time didn't allow the easy removal of tree stumps. Even on the great National Road, pride of the American highway system, builders were permitted to leave stumps up to fifteen inches high—slightly under knee height. Imagine, if you will, bouncing day after day over rocks, fallen branches, and tree stumps in an unsprung carriage and you may get some notion of the ardors of a long-distance trip in nineteenth-century America.

Something of the flavor of the undertaking is reflected in the candid name of the most successful of the stagecoach companies running along the National Road: the Shake Gut Line. (The Shake Gut's principal rival was the June Bug Line, so called because its rivals predicted that it would survive no longer than the average June bug. They were wrong.)

Coaches not only shook their occupants mercilessly but routinely over-turned. In 1829, according to Paul Johnson, "a man traveling from New York to Cincinnati and back reported the coach had been overturned nine times."[15]

It is perhaps little wonder then that when railroads (and to a lesser extent steamboats and canal barges) began to provide an alternative form of transportation, people flocked to them. Even so, early trains were also slow, uncomfortable, and dangerous. Cars were connected by nothing more sophisticated than chains, so that they were con-stantly shunting into one another, jarring the hapless occupants. Front-facing passengers had the choice of sitting with the windows closed—not an attractive option in hot weather—or suffering the as-sault of hot cinders, jocularly called *eyedrops,* that blew in a steady stream back from the *locomotive* (a word coined in 1657 to describe any kind of motion, but first applied to railroad engines in 1815). Fires, derailments, and breakdowns were constant possibilities, and until late in the nineteenth century even the food was a positive hazard. Until 1868, when a new term and phenomenon entered the language, the *dining car,* customers were required to detrain at way stations and given twenty minutes to throw a meal down their gullets. The proprietors of these often remote and godforsaken outposts offered what food they could get their hands on—or, more often, get away with. Diners at Sidney, Nebraska, were routinely fed what most presumed to be chicken stew; in fact, its basic component was prairie dog.[16] Some said they were lucky to get that.

Despite the discomforts, railroads became hugely popular, offering many thousands of people their first chance to leave home. By 1835, ac-cording to one estimate, fifty times as many people were traveling by railroad as had traveled by all other means put together just five years earlier. From virtually nothing in 1830, railroad mileage rose to 30,000 by 1860—that is, more than all the rest of the world put together[17]—and to a staggering 200,000 by 1890. Railroads so dominated American travel that for four generations *road* meant railroads.[18] What we would now call roads were more generally known as *trails,* as in the Santa Fe Trail. (In Britain, where *road* continued to signify a highway, *railroads* be-came *railways.*)

With the arrival of train travel, the stagecoach was instantly eclipsed, and little wonder. Trains were not only faster and increasingly more comfortable, but also cheaper. From coast to coast the trip took eight to ten days at an average speed of about twenty miles an hour (rising to a giddy thirty-five miles an hour on the faster stretches). The one-way fare from Omaha to Sacramento was $100 for first class (plus $4 a night for a berth in one of the new Pullman sleepers), $75 for second class, $40 for third.

Pullman cars, originally Pullman Hotel-Cars, were named for George M. Pullman, who developed them in 1865 and dining cars in 1868. To accommodate his twelve thousand workers, Pullman built a model community, Pullman, Illinois (now part of Chicago), where workers lived in company houses and shopped at company stores, thus ensuring that most of what they made returned to the company. That Pullman porters were nearly always black was not a result of enlightened employment practices, but a by-product of abysmal pay. The custom of calling porters "George," whatever their name, was apparently taken from Pullman's own first name.[19]

Among railroads terms that have passed into general familiarity were *caboose, iron horse, cow catcher, jerkwater town, to featherbed, to ball the jack, to ride the rails,* and *to ride the gravy train. A gravy train* was a good run, either because it paid well or it wasn't too taxing. Surprisingly, it isn't recorded before 1945. *To featherbed,* meaning to employ more workers than necessary, is also recent. It isn't found before 1943. *Caboose* is much older. From the Dutch *kabuis,* it was used to describe various parts of a ship, notably the galley, long before it was appropriated by the railroads. *A jerkwater town* was literally that—a place, usually desolate, where trains took on water from a trackside tank by jerking on a rope. The origin of *to ball the jack,* meaning to travel quickly, even recklessly, is uncertain, though it may have some connection with *high ball,* a signal to proceed.

Two other terms more loosely associated with railroad travel are *bum* and *hobo. Hobo* is first found in a newspaper in Ellensburgh, Washington, in 1891, but no one has ever come up with a certain explanation of its etymology. Among the theories: that it is a contraction of "homeward bound" or that it has something to do with the salutation "Ho! Beau!" which sounds a trifle refined for vagrants, but in fact was a common cry among railroad workers in the nineteenth century and would certainly have been familiar to those who rode the rails. *Bum* in the sense of a tramp appears to be a shortening of the German *Bummler,* a loafer and ne'er do well.

Though we tend to associate urban congestion with the automobile and the shortcomings of our own age, horse-driven traffic clogged cities long before cars came along. In 1864, New York City built two miles of underground tunnels through Central Park to try to keep things moving, and dubbed them *sub-ways.* The British still use *subway* in the sense of a subterranean passageway (or, a cynic might add, public housing for vagrants), but in the United States that sense lasted just twenty-nine years before being usurped, in 1893, by the new urban underground railroads.[20] The automobile may have its drawbacks, but at least it doesn't normally attract flies or drop things you need to step around. The filth of horses was a constant problem for cities well into this century, one that we can barely imagine now. In 1900, some dedicated official in Rochester, New York, calculated that the manure produced by the city's horses would in a year cover a one-acre square to a depth of 175 feet. Kept in often unsanitary conditions and worked hard through all weathers, horses not only drew flies but dropped like them. At the turn of the century, fifteen thousand horses a year died on the streets of New York, twelve thousand on the streets of Chicago.[21] Sometimes their carcasses were left for days. Between the flies, the manure, and the steaming corpses, there was no mistaking that you were in a city.

Thus the advent of the cable car and trolley car was not just a boon but a kind of miracle. The cable car was perfected by a Scottish immigrant named Andrew Smith Hallidie, who had something of a vested interest in its success: he ran a company that made cables. Cable cars moved by gripping underground cables that were in constant motion. When a driver wished to stop he pulled a lever that disengaged the grippers. If for some reason the grippers would not disengage—and this appears to have happened quite a lot—the result was a runaway car, which would trundle along inexorably, mowing down anything too slow or insensible to get out of the way, until the power station could be alerted to shut down the entire system.[22] It was not, as you can imagine, an altogether ideal form of transportation. Even so, cable cars were briefly very popular, though today San Francisco is the only American city where they are left, and even there the system is a shadow of its former self. In 1900 the city had 110 miles of line and six hundred cars; by 1980 it had just forty cars and a little over ten miles of line.

What rendered the cable car obsolescent was the trolley car, or *trawley car* as it was sometimes spelled in the early days. The trolley car was so called because the mechanism that connected the cars to the overhead wires was a *troller,* which in turn was ultimately derived from *troll,* a British dialect word meaning to move about. Trolley systems were easier to install and cheaper to run than any competing systems, and in consequence they thrived. Today, it is little known that the United States once had the finest system of public transportation in the world. At the turn of the century, Berlin had the most extensive streetcar network in Europe; but in America it would have come only twenty-second.[23] By 1922, the peak year, the United States had over fourteen thousand miles of streetcar track. The biggest system in the country was, you may be surprised to hear, that of Los Angeles.

Streetcars changed the way we lived. They opened up suburban life.

The population of the Bronx went from under 90,000 to 200,000 in the years immediately after the introduction of the streetcar.[24] By 1902, New York streetcars alone were carrying almost one billion passengers annually. Cities became bigger, busier, more confusing, and in consequence in the 1890s two new words entered the language: *rush hour* and *traffic jam*.

But streetcars also offered opportunities for pleasure. People were for the first time able to explore districts of their cities that they had only heard about. Wising up to the possibilities, streetcar companies began building amusement parks at the end of their lines as a way of boosting revenue—places like Willow Grove Park, twelve miles from downtown Philadelphia and now, almost inevitably, the site of a shopping mall.

Despite their popularity, streetcars were seldom profitable. In 1921, America's three hundred largest streetcar systems made a collective profit of $2.5 million—roughly $8,000 each—on an investment of $1.5 billion. With the rise of private car ownership and other forms of transport such as buses—or *trackless trolleys,* as they were sometimes called at first—their fate was sealed. Between 1922 and 1932 the number of streetcar miles in America almost halved. In that same decade, a company called National City Lines—a cartel made up of General Motors and a collection of oil and rubber interests—began buying up trolley lines and converting them to bus routes. By 1950 it had closed down the streetcar systems of more than a hundred cities, including those of Los Angeles, Philadelphia, Baltimore, and St. Louis. Its actions were unquestionably illegal, and the company was eventually taken to court and convicted of engaging in a criminal conspiracy. And the penalty for this serious crime? A fine of $5,000, less than the cost of a new bus.

II

Tempting as it is to blame a monolithic corporation for the downfall of public transportation in America, the real culprit was the automobile, or more specifically our abiding addiction to it. No innovation in history has more swiftly captured the affections of humanity or more radically transformed the way the world looks, behaves, and operates. Look at any urban scene and notice how totally our world is dominated by the needs of the automobile. Yet only about a century ago, this marvel of the age didn't even have a name.

Motorized vehicles have been around for longer than you might think—as early as 1770 a Frenchman named Nicholas Cugnot had a steam-powered behemoth called the *Fardier* lumbering through the streets of Paris at just over two miles an hour (considerably less than walking speed)—but most authorities agree that the first real, working car was one devised by the German engineer Gottlieb Daimler in 1884. He called it a *Mercedes,* after his daughter. Unaware of Daimler's creation, another German, Karl Benz, invented a second and very similar car at almost the same time. By this time, however, the concept of an automobile had already been patented in America. A sharp patent lawyer named George B. Selden had the prescience in 1879 to take out a patent on a largely notional vehicle he called a *road engine.* Selden was first not because he was a gifted inventor or even an inspired tinkerer—in fact, he never built a working vehicle—but because he was an opportunist who shrewdly anticipated the limitless possibilities inherent in controlling the patent on this budding technology. Because there was no money in "road engines" in 1879, he managed by various legal manipulations to delay the issuance of the patent for sixteen years until the market was at last poised to take off, and thus was positioned to enjoy royalties for seventeen years on a technology to which he had made absolutely no contribution. (He didn't do a great deal for the honor of patent lawyers either. The law was changed soon after his patent expired.)

Only by the merest chance do we call this central component of our lives an *automobile.* Scores of other names were tried and discarded before *automobile* hauled itself to the top of the linguistic heap. Among the other names for the early car were *self-motor, locomotive car, autobat, autopher, diamote, autovic, self-propelled carriage, locomotor, horseless carriage, motor buggy, stink chariot* (presumably coined by a nonenthusiast), and the simple, no-nonsense *machine,* which for a long time seemed poised to become the generic term for a self-propelled vehicle. *Automobile,* a French word concocted from Greek and Latin elements, was at first used only as an adjective, not only to describe cars ("an automobile carriage") but also other self-propelled devices ("automobile torpedo"). By 1899 the word had grown into a noun and was quickly becoming the established general term for cars—though not without opposition. The *New York Times* sniffed that *automobile,* "being half Greek and half Latin, is so near indecent that we print it with hesitation."[25] Before the year was out, the word was being shortened to *auto. Car,* from the Latin *carrus* ("two-wheeled wagon"), was first applied to the automobile in 1896, though it had existed in English as a term for various types of wagons since the sixteenth century. By 1910 it had more or less caught up *automobile* in popularity.

Although the early technological developments were almost exclusively German, it was the French who became the first big manufacturers of cars and thus gave us many of the words associated with motoring—*chassis, garage, chauffeur, carburetor, coupé, limousine,* and of course *automobile* itself. *Chauffeur* was a term for a ship's stoker and as such was applied to drivers of cars in at least a mildly sarcastic sense. *Limousine* meant originally a heavy shepherd's cloak from the Limousin region of France. The first chauffeurs, forced to sit in the open air, adopted this coat, and gradually the word transferred itself from the driver to the vehicle. By 1902 it was part of the English language.[26]

The first car most Americans saw was one designed by Karl Benz, which was put on display at the 1893 Chicago World's Fair. Before the year was out, two brothers in Springfield, Massachusetts, Charles and J. Frank Duryea, had built America's first gasoline-powered car, and the country never looked back.

No big technology in history has taken off more swiftly, more breathtakingly, than the car. And nowhere did it take off faster than in America. In 1898, there were not thirty working cars in the whole of the United States. Within a little over a decade there were not just seven hundred cars in America, but seven hundred car factories. In just the first four months of 1899, American investors provided no less than $388 million of start-up capital for new automobile companies.[27]

They came from every walk of life. John F. and Horace E. Dodge had run a Detroit machine shop. David D. Buick made plumbing supplies. Studebaker was the world's largest producer of horse-drawn carriages. Pope, Winton, and Rambler all started out as makers of bicycles. A striking number of the first manufacturers were from the Midwest and particularly from Michigan—Ransom Olds, creator of the Oldsmobile, from Lansing; David D. Buick and Henry Ford from Detroit; William C. Durant, founder of General Motors, from Flint—which helps to explain why Detroit became the Motor City. As well as the celebrated names of the early years like Packard, Duesenberg, and Cord, there were scores of companies now almost entirely forgotten—among them Pathfinder, Marmon, Haynes, Premier, McFarland, Maxwell, Briscoe, Lexington, and Ricker (which held the world speed record of twenty-six miles an hour in the late 1890s).★ Many of the early cars were named for explorers, reflecting the sense of adventure they imparted: De Soto, Hudson, La Salle, and Cadillac (named for a French nobleman, Antoine de la Mothe Cadillac, who would almost certainly have been long forgotten except that he had the good fortune to found Detroit). But buyers could choose among a positive galaxy of names now sadly forgotten: the Black Crow, the Bugmobile, the Averageman's Car, the Dan

---

★But this was nothing compared with the speeds achieved by steam-powered cars. The great Stanley Steamer reached 127 miles an hour in 1906. Unfortunately steam cars also tended to be unreliable and to blow up.[28]

Patch, the Royal Mail, the Lone Star, the Premier, the Baby Grand, the Hupmobile, the Locomobile.

It is not easy to conceive from this remove just how improbable was the success of the car. In 1900, cars were costly, unreliable, and fearsome. "You can't get people to sit over an explosion," remarked one observer sagely. Being in control of several hundred pounds of temperamental metal was a frightening challenge that proved too much for many. On her first attempt to drive, Mrs. Stuyvesant Fish, a wealthy socialite, switched on the engine and promptly ran over a servant who had been stationed nearby in case she required assistance. As the man struggled dazedly to his feet, Mrs. Fish threw the car into reverse and mowed him down again. Panicking, she changed gears and flattened him a third time. At this Mrs. Fish fled to the house and never went near a car again.[29] How the servant subsequently accommodated himself to the automotive age is not recorded.

All the infrastructure necessary to support an automobile society—gas stations, traffic signals, road maps, insurance policies, drivers' licenses, parking lots—was entirely lacking in the first years of this century. Cars were not just unnecessary but, since there was almost no place to go in them, effectively pointless. As late as 1905, America possessed not a single mile of paved rural highway. Such roads as existed were unmarked dirt tracks, which became swamps in the wet months and were hopelessly rutted for much of the rest. In many parts of the country even a dirt track would have been welcome. To drive through Nebraska or Kansas often meant to cross a trackless prairie.

Those who made long journeys were deemed heroic or insane, often both. In 1903, the year that the Ford Motor Company was incorporated, Dr. Horatio Nelson Jackson of Vermont, accompanied by a mechanic named Crocker and a dog named Bud (who, like his companions, wore goggles throughout the trip), made the first transcontinental crossing by car in a two-cylinder, open-top Winton. The trip took them sixty-five days, but made them heroes. For the most part, cars of the period simply weren't up to the challenge. Those who tried to drive through the Rockies generally discovered that the only way was to back up them; otherwise the fuel flowed away from the engine. Not only were there almost no decent roads but no prospect of them. The federal government long refused to provide highway funds, arguing that it was a matter for the states, and the states likewise showed the deepest reluctance to subsidize what might be a passing fad. In 1912, twenty of them spent not a penny on highway construction.

But the absence of highways didn't stop anybody. America's eight thousand motor vehicles of 1900 had jumped to almost half a million by

1910 and to two million by 1915. Infrastructure began to appear. License plates made their first appearance in 1901. Four years later, Sylvanus F. Bowser invented a workable gas pump and, with some prescience, called it a *filling station* (though the term would not become common for gas stations until the 1920s). In the same year, the Automobile Gasoline Company of St. Louis started the first chain of gas stations—already people were casually shortening *gasoline* to *gas*—and everywhere they were singing Gus Edwards's "In My Merry Oldsmobile":

> *Come away with me, Lucille*
> *In my merry Oldsmobile,*
> *Over the road of life we'll fly*
> *Autobubbling you and I.*

An exciting new vocabulary emerged. Not everyone could yet afford to go *autobubbling* (a racy if short-lived term for a pleasure spin, dated to 1900), but soon most people were bandying about expressions like *road-hog* (a term originally applied to bicyclists in 1893), *self-starter* (1894), *station wagon* (1904), *spark plugs* (1908), *joy ride* (1909), *motorcade* (1913), *car crashes* and *blowouts* (1915), *to step on the gas* (1916), *to jaywalk* (1917), *jalopy* (1924), *to hitchhike* (1925), and *rattletrap* (1929).[30] As early as 1910, people were *parking* in order to *neck* or *pet*. As time went on, slightly more sinister linguistic aspects of motoring emerged. *Speeding ticket* entered the language in 1930, *double-parking* in 1931, and *parking meters* in 1935. (The first meters were in Oklahoma City.)

Some words came into the language so quickly that no one seems to have noticed where they came from. *Jalopy*—in the early days often spelled *jolopy, jaloopy,* and in many other ways—is wholly unexplained. It just emerged. Much the same is true of *Tin Lizzie* (1915) and *flivver* (1920). *Flivver* was sometimes used in the general sense of being a failure before it became attached to Henry Ford's Model T. Mary Helen Dohan notes that "human flivver" appeared in Harry Leon Wilson's novel *Ruggles of Red Gap* in 1917,[31] but that would appear merely to muddy the question of how it originated and why it became attached to a car that was anything but a failure. *Tin Lizzie,* according to Stuart Berg Flexner, arose because *Lizzie* was a common name for maids, and both maids and Model Ts were black and made to look their best on Sundays.[32] An alternative theory is that it may be connected in some way to *lizzard,* a term once common for a kind of sledge.

The two million cars of 1915 rose to ten million by 1920, more than in all the rest of the world combined. By 1920, Michigan alone had more

cars than Britain and Ireland. Kansas had more cars than France. Before
the decade was half over, America would be producing 85 percent of all
the world's cars and the automobile industry, which hadn't even existed
a quarter of a century earlier, would be the country's biggest business.

Most of the credit for this can go to a single person, Henry Ford, and
a somewhat oddly named vehicle, the Model T. Ford always used initials
for his early cars, but in a decidedly hit-and-miss manner. For reasons
that appear to have gone unrecorded, he disdained whole sequences of
the alphabet. His first eight models were the A, B, C, F, K, N, R, and
S before he finally produced, on October 1, 1908, his first universal car,
the Model T. (When, nineteen years later, he ceased production of the
Model T, he succeeded it not with the Model U, but with another
Model A.)

By 1912, just four years after its introduction, three-quarters of the
cars on American roads were Model Ts.[33] Ford is often credited with introducing the world to the concept of the moving *assembly line* in 1913.
Though the term may be his, the idea wasn't. For decades scores of
other industries, from vegetable canning to meat wholesaling, had used
assembly-line methods, but had referred to them as "continuous process
manufacturing" or "flow production." Ford simply adapted the idea to
a much larger manufacturing process.[34] With his revolutionary methods
and by keeping the car basic—"You can have any color you want as long
as it's black" was his oft-repeated quip—Ford cut the time it took to
produce a Model T from fourteen man-hours in 1910 to just two man-
hours in 1913, and with that, of course, the price fell.[35] The first Model
T cost $850 and the price rose the next year to $950, but after that, with
Ford's novel and wondrously efficient production lines and increasing
economies of scale, the price fell continuously. By 1916, a new Model
T cost as little as $345. Even so, that was far more money than most
people could get their hands on. A new system of financing arose, and
with it came a raft of ominous new expressions: *installment plan, time
payment, one-third down, down payment,* and that perennial invitation to
ruin *Buy Now, Pay Later.*

A month before the first Model T was produced, another great name
of the industry was born: General Motors. The company, which had
begun life as the Flint Road Cart Company, was founded by William
Crapo "Billy" Durant, a mercurial figure described by one friend as "a
child in emotions, in temperament, and in mental balance." Durant
knew nothing of engineering and was not a gifted innovator. Indeed, he
wasn't even a particularly astute businessman. He was simply a great
accumulator. He bought companies indiscriminately, not just car
makers, but enterprises that were involved with the automobile busi-

ness only tangentially, if at all—companies like the Samson Sieve-Grip Tractor Company (which built tractors steered by reins on the dubious grounds that farmers would find them more horselike) and a one-man refrigerator company that would eventually become Frigidaire. Many of his automotive acquisitions became great names—Buick, Oldsmobile, Cadillac, Chevrolet—but many others, like Cartercar, Sheridan, Scripps-Booth, and Oakland, were never more than highly dubious. His strategy, as he put it, was to "get every kind of car in sight" in the hope that the successes would outweigh the failures. They didn't always. He lost control of General Motors in 1910, got it back in 1916, lost it again in 1920. By 1936, after more bad investments, he was bankrupt, with debts of nearly $1 million and assets of just $250.[36]

Many of his best people found his imperiousness intolerable and took their talents elsewhere. Walter Chrysler left to form the Chrysler Corporation. Henry and Wilfred Leland departed to create Lincoln. Charles Nash went on to build Nash-Rambler. Others were dismissed, often for trifling transgressions. In 1911, Durant hired a Swiss mechanic/racing driver named Louis Chevrolet. Unfortunately for them both, Durant couldn't abide smoking. When, shortly after joining the company, Chevrolet wandered into Durant's office with a cigarette dangling from his lips, Durant took the instant decision that the only thing he liked about the Swiss mechanic was his name. He dismissed Chevrolet, who thence dropped from sight as effectively as if he had fallen through a trapdoor, but kept his melodic monicker and built it into one of the great names of automotive history. (Durant was also responsible for the Chevrolet symbol, which he found as a pattern on wallpaper in a hotel room in Paris. He carefully removed a strip, took it home with him, and had his art department work it up into a logo.)

As the opening years of the twentieth century ticked by, two things became clear: America desperately needed better roads and they weren't going to be paid for with government money. Into this seeming impasse stepped Carl Graham Fisher, one of the most remarkable go-getters of his or any other age. A former bicycle and car racer (for a time he held the world automobile speed record over two miles), founder of the Indianapolis 500 Speedway, hugely successful businessman, and perennial daredevil—he once rode a bicycle along a highwire stretched between two of Indianapolis's tallest buildings to publicize a business venture—Fisher was, as you may surmise, something of a dashing figure. His fortune came from the Prest-O-Lites car headlight company—early cars didn't have sufficient oomph to run headlights, so these had to be powered, and purchased, separately—but his fame came from creating America's first coast-to-coast highway.

In 1912, Fisher proposed raising $10 million for a graveled two-lane road from New York to San Francisco through donations. Thousands of people sent money in. President Woodrow Wilson patriotically gave $5, though Henry Ford refused to cough up a penny. By 1915 the pot was sufficiently full to make a start. But there were two problems. The first was what to call the highway. A good name was important to galvanize support. Fisher's proposed name, the *Coast-to-Coast Rock Highway,* was apt but rather short on zip. Fisher toyed with the *Jefferson Highway,* the *Ocean-to-Ocean Highway,* and the *American Road* before finally settling on the *Lincoln Highway,* which had a solid patriotic ring to it, even if it alienated many Southerners. The second problem was that despite all the donations, there wasn't nearly enough money to build the necessary 3,389 miles of highway. Fisher hit on the idea of constructing what came to be called "seedling miles." He would find a section of dirt road roughly midway between two towns and pave it. The idea of building a mile of good road in the middle of nowhere may seem odd, but Fisher reasoned that once people got a taste of smooth highway they would want the whole concrete banquet. Soon towns all along the route were enthusiastically raising funds to connect themselves to that tantalizing seedling mile. A new slogan arose: "See America First."

In 1923, the Lincoln Highway—the first transcontinental highway in the world—officially opened. For the next forty years, it hummed with life as a daily cavalcade of cars and trucks brought commerce and the intoxicating whiff of a larger, livelier world to the hundreds of little towns (it mostly avoided cities) standing along its pleasantly meandering route. Almost overnight it became, as the postcards proudly boasted, America's Main Street.

Eventually the federal government decided to make money available for interstate highways, though the matter was given such a low priority that the task was handed to the Secretary of Agriculture as something to do in his free time. With the help of federal money, other great roads were built: the Jefferson Highway from Detroit to New Orleans, the Dixie Highway from Bay City, Michigan, to Florida, the William Penn Highway across Pennsylvania. The Dixie Highway was yet another Fisher inspiration, though here the motivation had more to do with self-interest than patriotism. In the late 1910s, Fisher became seized with the idea that Miami Beach—or Lincoln, as he wished for a time to call it— would make a splendid resort.

The notion was widely held to be deranged. Florida was, as far as anyone knew, a muggy, bug-infested swamp a long way from anywhere. But Fisher envisioned a great utopian city linked to the outside world by his Dixie Highway. The costs and logistics of building a resort in a distant swamp proved formidable, but Fisher persevered and by 1926 had nearly finished his model community, complete with hotels, a casino, golf courses, a yacht basin, and a lavish Roman swimming pavilion (which featured, a trifle incongruously, a Dutch windmill). Then a hurricane blew it all down. Barely had he absorbed the blow than the stock market crashed and the market for vacation homes dried up. Miami Beach did, of course, become a success, but not for Carl Graham Fisher. He ended his years living in a modest house on a side street in the city he had built from nothing.[37]

At about the same time that the tireless Fisher was tempting fate in southern Florida, the Secretary of Agriculture was deciding it was time to bring some order to American roads. He introduced uniform road signs—the octagonal red stop sign, the cross for a railroad junction, and so on—and instituted the system of numbering for interstate roads that is with us yet. North–south highways were given odd numbers, and east–west highways even numbers (with numbers of major transcontinental routes being multiples of ten). Names were ruthlessly abandoned. At a stroke, highways lost much of their romance. The Lincoln Highway, completed only two years before, became U.S. Route 30. The great Dixie Highway became the uninspiring Route 25. The William Penn became Route 22. Probably the most famous highway of them all, Route 66, never suffered the indignity of being stripped of its name for the simple reason that it never had one. It was not begun until 1926, in the post-name era. Its humiliation would have to wait until 1985, when the federal highway department removed all the Route 66 shield signs along its 2,200 storied miles from Michigan Avenue in Chicago to Ocean Avenue in Santa Monica. Overnight this once-great highway became a series of back highways and anonymous frontage roads.

III

As you would expect, it wasn't long before people outside the automobile business discovered that there was money to be made from America's growing tendency to take to the roads. In the mid-1920s a new expression entered the language: *drive-in*.

The drive-in experience was not in fact exclusive to the automobile age. Around the turn of the century a brief craze arose among drugstores to provide curbside soda-fountain service to buggies. But it took the long-range mobility of the internal combustion engine to really put the concept on its feet. The first modern drive-in is generally agreed to be the Pig Stand, a barbecue pit that was the brainchild of one Royce Hailey. It opened for business in September 1921 along the highway between Dallas and Fort Worth and was such a hit that soon there were Pig Stands all over the southern states and California. In 1924, a competitor called A&W, named for its founders, a Mr. Allen and a Mr. White, opened for business. Its main contribution to American culture was the invention of *tray girls,* who brought the food to patrons' cars, saving them the emotional upheaval of having to be parted even briefly from their surrogate wombs.[38]

Highways became lined with diners, roadhouses, *greasy spoons* (first recorded in 1925), and other meccas of cheap, breezy service. In the early 1930s, a survey of the highway between New York and New Haven revealed that there was on average a gas station every 895 feet and a restaurant or diner every 1,825 feet.[39] Every main highway had its famed establishments, like the Pig Hip Restaurant in Lincoln, Illinois, or the Cozy Dog Drive-In in nearby Springfield (whose proud boast it was to have invented that midwestern delicacy the *corn dog,* in 1949, though it called it a *crusty cur*), both on Route 66. Some of these establishments were so successful that they grew into national chains, like the Servistation Cafe in Corbin, Kentucky, on the Dixie Highway, which was founded in 1929 by Harland Sanders★ and evolved into Kentucky Fried Chicken, or Dairy Queen, founded in Moline, Illinois, in 1945.

Though highway eating places were plentiful, there was about them a certain worrying unpredictability. In 1929, a young drugstore owner in Massachusetts named Howard Johnson decided that what America's motorists craved was a safe, reliable uniformity of eating. He hit on the idea of franchising as a quicker, less risky way of building a chain. By 1940, 125 Howard Johnson's restaurants stood along the eastern seaboard, two-thirds of them owned by franchisees, or *agents* as Johnson called them. Most of his establishments were built in a homey, neocolonial style, with shutters on the windows, a rooftop cupola with a weather vane, and upstairs dormers that had no function beyond lending the structure an air of cozy domesticity. Only the busy parking lot and bright orange roof—designed to attract the attention of passing motorists—announced that this was not the home of a local dentist or other well-heeled citizen. Johnson's main breakthrough was to standardize the restaurant business. His operating manual—what he called "The Bible"—dictated everything from the number of French fries per por-

★Not until the 1940s did Sanders pretend to be anything other than the Indiana farmboy fate had made him. But upon being made an honorary colonel by the cherishably named Governor Ruby Laffoon of Kentucky, he took the role to heart. He grew a goatee and ever after affected the manner and attire of a southern gentleman.

tion to how high to pour the coffee in a cup (to within three-eighths of an inch of the top), an obsession with detail that was to be copied with even greater success by Ray Kroc of McDonald's.

As motorists required frequent infusions of food, so they also needed a place to sleep from time to time. Throughout the late 1910s and early 1920s, cabin camps or tourist courts—freestanding wooden huts, usually ranged in a semicircle and often given affectionately illiterate names like U Like Um Cabins, Kozy Kourt, and Para Dice[40]—began to appear on the landscape until by 1925 there were some two thousand of them, generally charging $2 to $3 night, a price downtown hotels couldn't compete with. Variations on *cabin camp* and *tourist court* began to appear—*tourist camps, motor courts,* even at least one *autel*—but the first place to style itself a *motel* was the Milestone Mo-tel, on Route 101 in San Luis Obispo, California, which opened its doors on December 12, 1925. (It is still in business, though operating now as the Motel Inn.) The term itself first appeared a few months earlier in *Hotel Monthly* magazine, in the same article in which *motor hotel* made its debut.[41] By the 1940s, *motel* had largely driven out the older *court* and *camp* almost everywhere.

Very early on, it became apparent that not every customer was coming for a good rest. The FBI's ever vigilant J. Edgar Hoover gravely announced that America's motels were "assignation camps" and "hotbeds of crime."[42] That may have been overstating matters, but if they weren't hotbeds, they certainly had them. A rather sneaky study by Southern Methodist University sociology students of the comings and goings at Dallas motels over one weekend in 1935 found that of the two thousand customers who used the city's thirty-eight establishments, most were registered under fictitious names and at least three-quarters of those so registered were there for illicit sex. (What then, we might reasonably wonder, were the remaining one-quarter up to—and how did the researchers determine who was doing what?) Terrific money was to be made in the "hot bed" or "Mr. and Mrs. Jones" trade, as it came to be known. One Dallas establishment was noted to have rented out a particular room no fewer than sixteen times in twenty-four hours, or once every ninety minutes.

By 1948, America had 26,000 motels. Unfortunately, a good many of them were a shade sleazy. Kemmons Wilson, a wealthy Tennessee businessman, had been disappointed by the standards of motels he had encountered during a family vacation and decided to offer an alternative. In 1952 he opened a bright, clean, fastidiously respectable establishment on Summer Avenue in Memphis, charging $4 for singles, $6 for doubles. Carefully avoiding the seedy connotations inherent in *motel,* he called it a Holiday Inn. Before long, Holiday Inns were going up at the rate of one every two and a half days. In 1954, Howard Johnson got in on the act, and soon big hotel chains like Hilton and Sheraton were pushing their way into the market.

But it was also a golden age for individually owned establishments—"ma-and-pa motels," as they were known in the trade. The fifties saw a wave of quality, privately owned motels, often L-shaped and generally built in the sleek style known as *moderne.* Increasingly they offered swimming pools, air conditioning, ice machines, king-sized beds with soothing coin-operated Vibro-Matic massagers, and other luxuries that made them considerably nicer than most of their patrons' own homes. Often they were given names that were at least as soothing as the massagers: Sleepy Hollow, Restwell Manor, Dreamland Inn, Memory Lane Motel.

In 1925, at about the same time that tourist courts were evolving into motels, another venerable institution made its first appearance on the American roadside: the Burma-Shave sign. Born in the early 1920s, Burma-Shave was a revolutionary product—the first brushless shaving cream that really worked—but before its distinctive signs began appearing along highways it was going nowhere. The name can't have helped. Few people equated a country in Indochina with a smooth, close shave. (It was called Burma-Shave because it was a sequel to a liniment, Burma-Vita, which *did* contain ingredients from Burma, or at least from the Malay Peninsula.)

Then in 1925 one of the company's traveling salesmen noticed that gas stations were increasingly announcing themselves to motorists with a series of strident signs: GAS AHEAD! CIGARETTES! EATS! STOP HERE! It seemed to work, and he put the idea to the head of the company. As an experiment, Burma-Shave erected signs along two Minnesota highways near its headquarters. The first signs didn't have a jingle. In fact, they could hardly have been less catchy. One set read: GOODBYE SHAVING BRUSH! / HALF A POUND FOR /HALF A DOLLAR / VERY FINE FOR THE SKIN / DRUGGISTS HAVE IT / CHEER UP FACE / THE WAR IS OVER/ *Burma-Shave.* By the early 1930s the company was beginning to find its metier and offering passing motorists such droll entertainments as:

SHAVING BRUSHES / YOU'LL SOON SEE 'EM / WAY DOWN EAST / IN SOME / MUSEUM / *Burma-Shave* (1930)

HE PLAYED / A SAX / HAD NO B.O. / BUT HIS WHISKERS SCRATCHED / SO SHE LET HIM GO / *Burma-Shave* (1933)

HE HAD THE RING / HE HAD THE FLAT / BUT SHE FELT HIS CHIN /
AND THAT / WAS THAT / *Burma-Shave* (1934)

WHEN CUTTING / WHISKERS / YOU DON'T NEED / TO LEAVE ONE
HALF / OF THEM FOR SEED / *Burma-Shave* (1934)

As Frank Rowsome, Jr., has put it in his engaging history of the
Burma-Shave signs, *The Verse by the Side of the Road,* humor in advertising in the Depression years "was so scarce as to be virtually a trace element."[43] Burma-Shave became the exception. Its signs were virtually
guaranteed to hold the attention of passing drivers for an average of
eighteen seconds—far longer than any other type of roadside ad could
count on. They not only effectively popularized the product, but by
promoting highway safety and other timely causes like War Bonds they
gave the company an air of kindly altruism, as in:

DON'T TAKE / A CURVE / AT 60 PER / WE HATE TO LOSE / A
CUSTOMER

PAST / SCHOOLHOUSES / TAKE IT SLOW / LET THE LITTLE / SHAVERS
GROW

Unable to come up with a steady stream of new verses, the company
began holding national contests, paying $100 for each winning entry. At
its peak, it was receiving over fifty thousand entries a year. A few were
decidedly daring for the times: SUBSTITUTES / CAN DO / MORE HARM /
THAN CITY FELLERS / ON A FARM. Others were distinctly morbid: HER
CHARIOT / RACED AT 80 PER / THEY HAULED AWAY / WHAT HAD BEN
HUR. Or HE LIT A MATCH / TO CHECK GAS TANK / THAT'S WHY / THEY
CALL HIM / SKINLESS FRANK.

Sites were selected with great care. They had to be level, straight, and
not cluttered with other signs. They were perfect for the Midwest,
though in fact they appeared in every state but four: Arizona, Nevada,
New Mexico, and Massachusetts. The number of signs and the fortunes
of the company both peaked in 1955. At sixty miles an hour or more
the signs became hard to read even when spaced farther apart, and
they seemed old-fashioned. Rent and maintenance for the signs cost
$200,000 a year by 1960, and besides, two-lane highways were increas-
ingly out of the mainstream. In 1963, the last Burma-Shave signs were
removed. America was no longer a nation of two-lane highways. A golden
age was over.

IV

In 1919, the U.S. Army sent a convoy of trucks cross-country from Camp Meade, Maryland, to San Francisco, just to see if it could be done. It could, but only just. The trip took two months at an average speed of less than seven miles an hour. The young officer in charge of the convoy was Dwight D. Eisenhower. Thirty-five years later as President of the United States, he appointed a committee to study America's transportation needs. As Kenneth T. Jackson has observed: "The committee considered no alternative to a massive highway system, and it suggested a major redirection of national policy to benefit the car and the truck."[44] This should have come as no great surprise; the chairman of the committee was on the board of directors of General Motors. In 1956, in response to the committee's urgings, Eisenhower signed into law the landmark Interstate Highway Act, inaugurating the construction of 42,500 miles of superhighway and kicking off an era when America would spend 75 percent of its transportation funds on highways and a slightly less than munificent 1 percent on mass transit for cities.

High-speed roads had already been around for some time by 1956. The first freeway (of sorts) was the fifteen-mile-long Bronx River Parkway, opened in the 1920s, with a speed limit of a then-breakneck thirty-five miles an hour. The word *parkway* was significant. These roads were designed for leisure driving for the middle classes. Commercial vehicles were prohibited, and bridge clearances were kept intentionally low to stop trucks and buses from sneaking onto them. They were lavishly landscaped and endowed with graceful curves and wooded medians to enhance their aesthetics. Billboards, gas stations, and other roadside detritus were ruthlessly excluded. They weren't so much highways as sylvan glades where you could exercise your car.

The great builder of parkways was Robert Moses, the New York City parks commissioner, who ironically never learned to drive a car. He presided over the construction of such roads as the Meadowbrook Parkway to Long Island, the Henry Hudson Parkway, and the Taconic Parkway through the Taconic River Valley. Constructed between 1940 and 1950, the Taconic was possibly the most beautiful American highway ever built, but already it was an anachronism. By 1950, Americans had stopped thinking of driving as something you did for fun. It was something you did to get to where you could have fun. For this new style of driving, something new was needed: the superhighway.

One of the enduring myths of American travel is that our *express highways,* as they were at first almost invariably called, were modeled on Germany's *Autobahnen.* In fact, it was the other way around. Dr. Fritz

Todt, Hitler's superintendent of roads, came to the United States in the 1930s, studied America's sparkling new parkways, and went back to Germany with a great deal of enthusiasm and a suitcase full of notes. Most people's first contact with superhighways were the models of Norman Bel Geddes's hugely popular Futurama exhibit at the 1939 New York World's Fair. Designed to show the world as it would be—or as General Motors wanted it to be—twenty-five years hence in 1964, the exhibit comprised a large layout of model towns, cities, and countryside, all linked by sleek multilane highways along which tiny cars glided with ceaseless speed and ease. It was remarkably prescient. (*Futurama* also had a linguistic impact, inspiring such compounds as *Shop-o-rama* and *Fisherama,* even *Kosherama* and *Striperama,* and eventually *Cinerama.*)

Within a year, Bel Geddes's vision became reality with the opening of the Pennsylvania Turnpike, running 160 miles from just west of Harrisburg to just east of Pittsburgh. Designed primarily to provide work for the unemployed during the Depression, it opened on October 1, 1940. For the first six months it had no speed limit. Motorists could drive the entire length in two and a half hours—half the time it had taken on the old Lincoln Highway—for a toll of $1.50. Features that would soon become familiar all over America—cloverleaf interchanges, long entrance and exit lanes, service areas—astounded and gratified the 2.4 million motorists who came to experience this marvel of the age in its first year.

Two months after the Pennsylvania Turnpike opened, and two thousand miles away, American motoring passed another milestone with the opening of the first true freeway in—it all but goes without saying—Los Angeles when the mayor cut a tape and a procession of dignitary-filled cars (three of which crashed in the excitement) rolled onto the eight-mile-long Arroyo Seco Parkway. Despite the semibucolic name, the Arroyo Seco Parkway wasn't a parkway at all but a sleek, brutally purposeful eight-lane artery designed to move high volumes of traffic at speed. Pleasure didn't come into it. The age of the *freeway*—a term first cited in *American City* magazine in 1930—had begun. As if in recognition of this, the Arroyo Seco was soon renamed the Pasadena Freeway. Ironically, it was intended to lure shoppers downtown, rather than help locals flee to the suburbs. By 1945, such roads were also being called *expressways.*

Conventional wisdom has it that Los Angeles' sprawl is a consequence of its extensive postwar freeway system. In fact, it was because the city was sprawling already that freeways were thought a practical way of connecting its far-flung parts. It sprawled because it had the finest public transportation network in America, if not the world, with over a thousand miles of rail and trolley lines.

Freeways, in fact, evolved slowly on the West Coast, at least at first. As late as 1947, the whole of California had just nineteen miles of them. Then along came State Senator Randolph Collier, from the remote town of Yreka, as far from Los Angeles as you can get in California. For forty years he dominated the California highway program, not just promoting the construction of freeways, but repeatedly blocking the funding of rail systems (which he called "rabbit transport"). By the mid-1950s most Californians had no choice but to take to the freeways. Today one-third of all the land in Los Angeles is given over to the automobile and the Los Angeles County Transportation Commission has a larger budget ($4.5 billion in 1991) than the city it serves.[45]

Soon every city had to have a freeway of its own, even if it meant scything through old neighborhoods, as with Boston's destructive Downtown Artery, or slicing into a beauty spot like Fairmont Park with the Schuylkill (popularly known as the "Sure-Kill") Expressway in Philadelphia. At one time there was even a plan to drive a freeway through the heart of New Orleans' historic French Quarter.

As the freeways remodeled cities, so the new interstates dealt a blow to the old two-lane highways that stretched between them. Had it not been for the distraction of the Second World War, America almost certainly would have had a network of superhighways much earlier. The idea was really the brainchild of Franklin Delano Roosevelt, who saw the construction of a national high-speed highway system as the ultimate public works project. By the 1950s, Eisenhower saw in it the additional virtue of enhancing America's defense capabilities. Bridge and tunnel clearances were designed for the movement of intercontinental ballistic missiles. During the quarter century beginning in 1956, America spent $118 billion on interstate highways. It was, as Phil Patton has put it, the "last program of the New Deal and the first space program."[46]

In less than two decades, America's modern interstate highways drained the life from thousands of towns. No longer was it necessary—and before long often not even possible—to partake of the traditional offerings of two-lane America: motels with cherishably inane names like the Nite-E-Nite Motor Court and the Dew Drop Inn, roadside diners with blinking neon signs and a mysterious fondness for meat loaf and mashed potatoes, two-pump gas stations built in the cozy style of a rustic cottage. Today in western Nebraska the old Lincoln Highway, or

Route 30, is so little used that grass grows in its cracks. At the state border with Wyoming, it disappears altogether, abruptly and unceremoniously buried beneath the white concrete of Interstate 80. Like Route 66, the Dixie Highway, and other once-great roads, it has become a fading memory.

Chapter 11

WHAT'S COOKING?: EATING IN AMERICA

I

To the first Pilgrims, the gustatory possibilities of the New World were slow in revealing themselves. Though the woods of New England abounded in hearty sustenance—wild duck and turkey, partridge, venison, wild plums and cherries, mushrooms, every manner of nuts and berries—and though the waters teemed with fish, they showed a grim reluctance to eat anything that did not come from their dwindling stockpile of salt pork (which they called *salt horse*), salt fish, and salt beef, hardtack (a kind of biscuit baked so hard that it became more or less impervious to mold, weevils, and human teeth), and dried peas and dried beans, "almost preferring," in the words of one historian, "to starve in the midst of plenty rather than experiment with the strange but kindly fruits of the earth."[1] Or as another put it: "The first settlers had come upon a land of plenty. They nearly starved in it."[2]

Lobster was so plentiful that "the least boy in the Plantation may both catch and eat what he will of them," but hardly any did. John Winthrop lamented in a letter home that he could not have his beloved mutton but only such impoverished fare as oysters, duck, salmon, and scallops. Clams and mussels they did not eat at all, but fed to their pigs. To their chagrin the colonists discovered that English wheat was unsuited to the soil and climate of New England. The crops were repeatedly devastated by a disease called smut. For the better part of two centuries, wheat would remain a luxury in the colonies. Even their first crop of peas failed, a consequence not so much of the challenges of the New England climate as of their own inexperience as farmers. With their foodstocks dwindling and their aptitude as hunter-gatherers sorely taxed, the outlook for this small group of blundering, inexperienced, hopelessly underprepared immigrants was bleak indeed.

Fortunately, there were Indians to save them. The Indians of the New World were already eating better than any European. Native Americans enjoyed some two thousand different foods, a number that even the wealthiest denizen of the Old World would have found unimaginably varied. Among the delicacies unique to the New World were the white and sweet potatoes, the peanut, the pumpkin and its cousin the squash, the persimmon (or *putchamin,* as the first colonists recorded it), the avocado, the pineapple, chocolate and vanilla, cassava (the source of tapioca), chili peppers, sunflowers, and the tomato—though of course not all of these were known everywhere. Even those plants that already existed in Europe were often of a superior variety in the New World. American green beans were far plumper and richer, and soon displaced the fibrous, chewy variety previously grown in Europe. Likewise, once Europeans got sight and taste of the fat, sumptuous strawberries that grew wild in Virginia, they gladly forsook the mushy little button strawberries that had theretofore been all they had known. The Indians' diet was healthier, too. At a time when even well-heeled Europeans routinely fell prey to scurvy and watched helplessly as their teeth fell from spongy gums, the Indians knew that a healthy body required a well-balanced diet.

But above all, their agriculture had a sophistication that European husbandry could not begin to compete with. They had learned empirically to plant beans among the corn, which not only permitted a greater yield from the same amount of land but also replenished the nitrogen the corn took away. As a result, while Europeans struggled even in good years to scrape a living from the soil, the Indians of the New World enjoyed a constant bounty. That a single tribe in New England had sufficient surpluses to support a hundred helpless, unexpected visitors for the better part of a year is eloquent testimony of that.

The Indians' single most important gift to the colonists—apart from not wiping them out—was corn. Corn began as a wild grass, probably in the Tehuacán Valley of central Mexico. Converting a straggly wild grass into the plump and nutritious foodstuff we know today was possibly the greatest of all precolonial achievements. Corn will grow almost anywhere, and by 1620 was a well established crop throughout the New World. To the original colonists, *corn* signified any common grain, as it still does in Britain. So they adopted the Spanish name *maize* (after a West Indian Taino word, *mahiz*). But since maize was in effect the only type of grain there was, *corn* gradually came to signify it alone. Corn has been domesticated for so long—some seven thousand years—that it is now totally dependent on humankind for its continued existence. Left on its own, the kernels of each cob—its seeds—would be strangled by the husk. Even in colonial times it was a far more demanding plant than the colonists were used to. With their usual vexing ineptitude the first colonists tried sowing it by broadcast method, as they did with other grains, and were baffled when it didn't grow. It took the natives to show them that corn flourished only when each seed was planted in a mound and helped along with a little fishmeal fertilizer.

By the early seventeenth century, many New World foods were already known in Europe, though not necessarily to the early English colonists. The first Pilgrims may have heard of, but almost certainly had never tasted, two New World foods: the tomato and the white potato. Nor did they get the opportunity in their newfound land, since these plants were unknown on the eastern seaboard. The Indians of the East Coast did, however, have the sweet potato, and for almost two centuries when Americans talked of potatoes that was what they meant.

The white potato had reached England, via Spain, in the sixteenth century but suffered a crippling setback when the queen's cook, with that knack for culinary misapprehension with which the English have long distinguished themselves, discarded the tubers and cooked the leaves. The white potato was grown strictly as an ornamental plant for well over a century before Europeans at last began to appreciate its manifold possibilities as a foodstuff. The Irish developed a particular attachment to it, not so much because of its agreeable versatility as because it was one of the few edible plants that would prosper on Irish soil. Elsewhere in the British Isles it remained largely unknown. Not until 1719 did it make its first recorded appearance in the American colonies, in Boston, though it was not until a gentleman farmer in Virginia named Thomas Jefferson tried cultivating the white potato—which he called the Irish potato—that it began to attract any attention in North America as a potential food. Jefferson also appears to have been the first American to serve French fried potatoes*—rather a daring thing to do, since it was generally accepted that the tubers were toxic and that the only way to avoid a long and agonizing death was to boil them mercilessly. Until well into the 1800s almost no one dared to eat them any other way. It appears that the whole of Europe's potato output at this time came from just two plants brought back by the Spanish; this lack of genetic diversity is very probably what led to Ireland's devastating potato blight in the nineteenth century, with obvious consequences for Amer-

---

*The *French* in *French fries* does not necessarily mean that they were a French invention (though they may have been). *To French* originally meant merely to cut into strips or slices. Strips of tenderloin beef, for example, were said to be *Frenched*.[3]

ican immigration. The word *spud,* incidentally, comes from the kind of spade with which potatoes were dug out. Though the word itself dates from the Middle Ages, it became associated with potatoes only in the 1840s.

The history of the tomato (from *tomatl,* like so many other food words a Nahuatl term) in the New World is strikingly similar to that of the potato. It was carried to Europe from South America by the Spanish, widely regarded as poisonous, treated for two centuries as a decorative curiosity, and finally rescued from obscurity by the ever-industrious Thomas Jefferson, who made the first recorded mention of it in North America in 1781. He referred to it as the *tomata.* Until well into the nineteenth century it was regarded as dangerously exotic on its native soil, though a degree of caution is understandable, since the tomato is, after all, a member of the nightshade family.

The colonists were, however, well acquainted with a New World food that abounded along the eastern seaboard: the turkey. A not unreasonable question is how a native American bird came to be named for a country four thousand miles away. The answer is that when turkeys first appeared in England, some eighty years before the *Mayflower* set sail, they were mistakenly supposed to have come from Turkey. They had in fact come from Spain, brought back from Mexico by Hernán Cortés's expedition of 1519. Many other European nations made a similar geographical error in naming the bird. The French thought they came from India and thus called them *poulets d'Inde,* from which comes the modern French *dindon.* The Germans, Dutch, and Swedes were even more specifically inaccurate in their presumptions, tracing the bird to the Indian city of Calicut, and respectively named it *Kalekuttisch Hün, kalkoen,* and *kalkon.* By the 1620s, the turkey was so well known in Europe, and its provenance had so long been assumed to be the Near East, that the Pilgrims were astounded to find it in abundance in their new land. A similar linguistic misunderstanding occurred with another native American food, the Jerusalem artichoke, which is not an artichoke at all—indeed, it doesn't even look like an artichoke—but rather is the root of the sunflower *Helianthus tuberosus. Jerusalem* is merely a corruption of the Italian word for sunflower, *girasole.*

Under the patient tutelage of the Indians, the colonists gradually became acquainted with, and even developed a fondness for, native products like pumpkins, at first generally called *pompions,* from an old French word for *melon,* and squashes, which the colonists confusingly also called *pompions.* Pumpkin pie became a big hit after the Pilgrims were introduced to it at their second Thanksgiving feast in 1623, but the conventional spelling didn't become established until much later. As late as

1796, the first American cookbook—a slender volume with the dauntingly all-embracing title *American Cookery, or the Art of Dressing Viands, Fish, Poultry and Vegetables, and the Best Modes of Making Pates, Puffs, Pies, Tarts, Puddings, Custards and Preserves and All Kinds of Cakes, from the Imperial Plumb to Plain Cake, Adapted to This Country and All Grades of Life, by Amelia Simmons: An American Orphan*—called the dish *pompkin pie,* and elsewhere it was sometimes referred to as *punkin pie.* Until the mid-1600s the dish was also commonly called *pumpkin pudding,* the word *pudding* then suggesting a pie without a top crust.

The Indians introduced the colonists not only to new foods, but to more interesting ways of preparing them. Succotash, clam chowder, hominy, corn pone, cranberry sauce, johnnycakes, even Boston baked beans and Brunswick stew were all Indian dishes. In Virginia, it was the Indians, not the white settlers, who invented Smithfield ham.[4] Even with the constant advice and intervention of the Indians, the Puritans stuck to a diet that was for the most part resolutely bland. Meat and vegetables were boiled without pity, deprived of seasonings, and served lukewarm. Peas, once they got the hang of growing them, were eaten at almost every meal, and often served cold. The principal repast was taken at midday and called dinner. *Supper,* a word related to *soup* (and indeed at the time still often spelled *souper*), was often just that—a little soup with perhaps a piece of bread—and was consumed in the evening shortly before retiring. Lunch was a concept yet unknown, as was the idea of a snack. To the early colonists, *snack* meant the bite of a dog.

Johnnycake is sometimes said to be a contraction of *journey cake,* the idea being that it was a food packed for journeys. But since it is a kind of cornbread, and cornbread patently is *not* a traveling food, the explanation is unconvincing. Another suggestion is that it is a corruption of *Shawnee cake.* In New England it was called *jonakin* or *jonikin* long before it was called *johnnycake,* suggesting that *johnnycake* is a folk etymology based on some earlier, forgotten Indian term.[5] Two native American foods that *were* designed for traveling were pemmican and jerked beef. Despite the name, nothing is jerked to make jerked beef. The word comes from *charqui,* a Spanish adaptation of a Peruvian Indian word. Though the variant name *jerky* is etymologically closer to the Spanish original, it actually entered the language much later. *Jerked beef* was well established in the colonies by the early eighteenth century. *Jerky* isn't attested before 1850. *Pemmican,* more straightforwardly, is from the Cree *pimikân.*

The Pilgrims naturally brought many Old World dishes with them, among them *flummery* (a sweet dish made of flour or cornstarch, sufficiently insipid to still be eaten in England, where it is called *blancmange*), *loblolly* (a kind of gruel fractionally enlivened with molasses), *frumenty* (a milky mush), *hoecake* (another kind of mush), *burgoo* (yet another), and that mysterious compound of the Little Miss Muffett nursery rhyme *curds and whey.* (For the record, curds are the coagulated residue of milk and whey the watery remains created while making cheese.) Curds were also used to make *syllabub,* another sweet dish.

Pudding signified not just a dessert (a word that had recently entered the language from France and was pronounced "duh-*zart*") but a wider range of dishes, from *black* or *blood pudding* (a sausage made from congealed blood) to *hasty pudding* (a cornmeal mush so named because it could be prepared quickly). Cranberries were at first also called *craneberries, cramberries,* or *bounceberries* because you bounced them to see if they were fresh. *Fool,* as in gooseberry fool, meant clotted cream. *Duff,* as in plum duff, merely reflected a variant pronunciation of *dough. Doughnuts,* which the Puritans had discovered from the Dutch during their years in Holland, did not have the hole with which we associate them now, but were small balls—"nuts" in the parlance of the time—of fried dough. They also ate *doughboys,* often spelled *dowboys,* a dumpling made of flour or cornmeal.

Until 1624, when the first shipment of cows reached Plymouth, the colony's supply of livestock consisted of only half a dozen goats, fifty pigs, and about as many chickens. But by the mid-1630s things were improving rapidly—with the population of Massachusetts standing at more than four thousand, the colony could boast fifteen hundred cows, four thousand goats, and "swine innumerable." Cows primarily had a dairy role. For a very long while, meat came almost exclusively in the form of pork. Indeed, in the South *meat* and *pork* were used interchangeably.

As time moved on, the diet of the average American became heartier if not a great deal more appealing. In an environment where women devoted their lives to an endless, exhausting round of activity, from weaving and making soap and candles to salting and pickling anything that could be preserved, it is hardly surprising that quality cooking was at a premium and that most people were, in the words of Thomas Jefferson, "illy fed." Nonetheless, by the late eighteenth century, portions for almost everyone were abundant, and visitors from the Old World commonly remarked on the size of meals in even the humblest households. For the wealthier families, dishes were varied and, by earlier standards, exotic. The cookbook kept at Mount Vernon, written by George Washington's mother, tells us much about both the variety of foods eaten and their sometimes curious spelling and pronunciation, notably *mushrumps, hartichocke pie, fryckecy of chicken,* and *lettice tart.*

By the time of the Revolution, the main meal was taken between 2 and 4 P.M. A typical meal might consist of salted beef with potatoes and peas, followed by baked or fried eggs, fish, and salad, with a variety of sweets, puddings, cheeses, and pastries to finish, all washed down with quantities of alcohol that would leave most of us today unable to rise from the table—or at least to rise and stay risen.[6] Meat was consumed in quantities that left European observers slack-jawed with astonishment. By the early 1800s the average American was eating almost 180 pounds of meat a year, 48 pounds more than people would consume a century later, but fresh meat remained largely unknown because of the difficulty of keeping it fresh. Even city people often had chickens in the yard and a hog or two left to scavenge in the street. Until well into the nineteenth century, visitors to New York remarked on the hazard to traffic presented by wandering hogs along Broadway. Even in the more temperate North, beef and pork would go bad in a day in summer, chicken even quicker, and milk would curdle in as little as an hour. And even among the better classes, spoiled food was a daily hazard. One guest at a dinner party given by the Washingtons noted with a certain vicious relish that the General discreetly pushed his plate of sherry trifle to one side when he discovered that the cream was distinctly iffy but that the less discerning Martha continued shoveling it in with gusto. Ice cream was a safer option. It was first mentioned in America in the 1740s when a guest at a banquet given by the governor of Maryland wrote about this novelty, which, he noted, "eat most deliciously."

Thomas Jefferson, thanks to his scrupulous—one might say obsessive—record-keeping (for eight years, while helping to run a new nation, he found time to track the first and last appearances on Washington market stalls of thirty-seven types of vegetable), has left us the most complete chronicle of the life of a farmer in colonial times, but also the least typical. As we have already seen with the tomato and potato, Jefferson was a tireless experimenter with foods and grew any number of plants that most Americans had never heard of, among them such exotica as eggplants, damson plums, Savoy cabbages, sugar beets, cauliflower, endive, chicory (which he called *succory*), broccoli, celery, and a kind of squash called cymling. Only grapes of a sufficient caliber to make a palatable wine eluded him, to his unending despair.[7]

Other planters were less adventurous, but compensated with quantity. Diners at the finer homes were commonly offered eight or ten kinds of meat or fish, a galaxy of vegetables, and half a dozen desserts, all washed down with copious quantities of wine, porter, rum, beer, or Madeira. Jefferson, in his first year in the White House, spent $2,800—more money than many people saw in a lifetime—on wine alone.

For farmers, food was almost entirely homegrown. As late as 1787, even a prosperous yeoman farmer in New England might spend no more than $10 a year on all outside purchases. This might include a little tea or coffee, a good deal of salt, and perhaps some molasses. In all other respects he and his household were entirely self-contained.

By the mid-1800s, many Americans were eating well enough to give foreign critics something new to be appalled at. A correspondent for *The Times* of London recorded with amazement a "typical" American breakfast—"black tea and toast, scrambled eggs, fresh spring shad, wild pigeons, pigs' feet, two robins on toast, oysters"—and that, he implied, was one of the lighter repasts.[8] If such breakfasts were eaten, and a touch of skepticism might not be misplaced here, they weren't eaten by everyone. The bulk of urban dwellers ate poorly, partly because their meager wages didn't permit better, but also because such medical advice as filtered down to them suggested that most fresh foods were hazardous. Until the mid-nineteenth century, received wisdom had it that anyone reckless enough to consume an apple or pear or indeed almost any other vegetative product was all but asking for a speedy death at the hand of typhoid, dysentery, or cholera.[9] During cholera epidemics city councils routinely banned the sale of fruits and salads, but even during comparatively safe periods most people thought it imprudent to feed almost any plant food (with the exception of a well-boiled potato) to the more susceptible members of the community, especially children, who of course most needed the vitamins. As a result, diseases associated with malnutrition stalked even the better-off families.

Milk, too, was widely regarded as perilous, though with some justification, since it spoiled quickly and was processed and delivered in a manner that owed little—actually, that owed almost nothing—to modern standards of hygiene. Almost everyone knew somebody who had died of "milksick" or "the trembles" after drinking tainted milk.

As the nineteenth century progressed, diet evolved into two camps— the few who ate well and the many who did not—and class antagonisms were not long in emerging. The patrician New Yorker Martin Van Buren was ousted from the presidency in 1840 in part because one of his Whig opponents made a celebrated speech attacking him for serving such delicate and unmanly fare in the White House as strawberries, cauliflower, and celery. (Van Buren gained a sort of vicarious revenge when, at the subsequent inauguration, the crusty William Henry Harrison refused to don an overcoat, contracted pneumonia, and with alarming haste expired; his tenure as President was just thirty days, much of that spent unconscious.) Gradually even poorer Americans became acquainted with a wider variety of fruits and vegetables, though the linguistic evidence shows that they weren't always quite sure what to make of them. For the potato alone, the *Dictionary of American English on Historical Principles* records such arresting nineteenth-century concoctions as potato custard, potato chowder, potato pone, potato pudding, and even potato coffee. We can assume that most of these were consumed in a spirit of either experimentation or desperation and didn't survive long in the native diet.

Only a relative handful of new foods entered the American vocabulary in the nineteenth century, among them *pretzel* (1824), *pumpernickel* (1839), *liverwurst* (1869), *tutti-frutti* (1876), and *spaghetti* (1880). What changed was the way Americans ate. In particular they began to eat out. Before the 1820s, dining out was an activity reserved almost exclusively for travelers. Though it was possible to eat in hotels and taverns, there were no places dedicated to the public consumption of food for the mere pleasure of it, nor any word to describe them. Then, in 1827, a new word and concept entered American English from France: *restaurant*.

It was in that year that two Swiss-born brothers, Giovanni and Pietro Del-Monico, opened a coffee and pastry shop in the Battery district of New York City. The enterprise was sufficiently successful that in 1831 they invited their nephew Lorenzo to join them. Though just nineteen and with no experience in catering, Lorenzo was born to culinary greatness. He did none of the cooking, but he did buy the food, and made a point of arriving before dawn at the city's main markets to acquire the best and freshest provisions, a practice now routine but at the time unheard of. He transformed Del-Monico's pastry shop into America's premier restaurant (actually a series of restaurants: the enterprise moved frequently and sometimes operated under as many as four roofs at once), bringing a dimension of elegance to American dining that it had theretofore lacked. Under the new, unhyphenated name Delmonico's, the restaurant introduced Americans to many unfamiliar dishes, ranging from artichokes and mayonnaise (named originally for the Minorcan port Mahón)[10] to fricasseed calf's head, and invented several as well, notably *lobster Newburg,* which began life as *lobster à la Wenburg.* It was so called in honor of an esteemed client, Ben Wenburg, until he disgraced himself through some unseemly (but intriguingly unspecified) altercation on the premises, and the dish was abruptly anagramized. A similar transformation happened with another Delmonico's creation, *chicken à la Keene,* named for one Foxhall Keene, which became over time (for reasons that appear to have gone unnoted) *chicken à la king.*

Inspired by Delmonico's example, restaurants sprouted everywhere. By the 1870s, New York City alone had over five thousand restaurants, many of them, like La Maison Dorée, Louis Sherry's, and Lüchows, of a standard comparable to the finest restaurants of Europe. With the new restaurants came new dishes, like *Waldorf salad* and *eggs Benedict,* both created at the Waldorf-Astoria in the 1890s. The latter was designed as a hangover cure for one Samuel Benedict, though how anyone with a hangover could face poached eggs swimming in hollandaise sauce and think it recuperative will forever be a mystery to me.[11]

For many immigrants, and for Italians in particular, the restaurant business became an attractive way to establish a foothold in the New World. *Trattorie*—family-run restaurants—became a feature on street corners in every large city, some of them growing into large and celebrated establishments like Mama Leone's and Sardi's in New York and Colisimo's in Chicago. But most stayed small, like G. Lombardi's on Spring Street in New York, which would now be forgotten to history except that one of its early proprietors had the uncommon prescience in 1905 to introduce Americans to a dish for which they would develop an abiding addiction: the pizza.[12]

Many "classic" Italian dishes are in fact New World creations. *Chicken tetrazzini*—chicken in a cream sauce on spaghetti—was named for the Italian soprano Luisa Tetrazzini but invented in New York. The *Caesar salad* comes from Tijuana. It was devised by a restaurateur named Caesar Cardini who, so the story goes, whipped up the salad from leftover ingredients when a party of hungry guests descended on him late one night. *Fettucine primavera* was born in the kitchen of New York's Le Cirque restaurant. *Veal parmigiana, clams Posillipo, fettucine Alfredo* even *spaghetti and meatballs* were all products designed to satisfy the American palate. "By the 1950s," one writer notes, "Italian-American food was all but unrecognizable to visitors from Italy. A businessman from Turin might peruse a menu in an Italian restaurant in Chicago and not be able to decipher a single item."[13]

A similar situation obtained with many other well-loved "foreign" foods. *Russian dressing* is unknown to the Russians, as is the American variety of *French dressing* to the French. *Vichyssoise* was invented not in France but in New York in 1910, and *Liederkranz cheese* sprang not from Germany, or even from Austria or Switzerland, but from Monroe, New York, in 1892. (The name, meaning "wreath of song," commemorates a local choral society.) *Chili con carne* was unknown in Spain until introduced there from the New World. *Salisbury steak* has nothing to do with the English cathedral city (it was named for an American, Dr. J. H. Salisbury), nor does *Swiss steak* have even the tiniest alpine pedigree. *Chop suey* (based on the Cantonese for "miscellany") first saw light not in China but in San Francisco in the late 1800s, though the term itself does not appear in print until 1903. The fortune cookie was invented in Los Angeles in the second decade of this century. More recent still is *chow mein,* which first appeared in 1927, though the pidgin word *chow* dates in print from 1856 and the slightly more emphatic *chowchow* is first recorded in 1857.[14]

As America became increasingly urbanized, people more and more took to eating their main meal in the evening. To fill the void between breakfast and dinner, a new and essentially American phenomenon arose: lunch. The words *lunch* and *luncheon* (often spelled *lunchon, lunchen, lunchion,* or *lunching*) have been around in English since the late 1500s. Originally they signified lumps of food—"a luncheon of cheese"—and may have come from the Spanish *lonja,* a slice of ham. The word was long considered a deplorable vulgarism, suitable only to the servants' hall. In America, however, "lunch" became respectable, and as it dawned on opportunistic restaurateurs that each day millions of office workers required something quick, simple, and cheap, a wealth of new facilities sprang up to answer the demand. In short order Americans got *diners* (1872), *lunch counters* (1873), *self-service restaurants* (1885), *cafeterias* (1890s), *automats* (1902), and *short-order restaurants* (1905).

The process began in 1872 in Providence, Rhode Island, when one Walter Scott loaded a wagon with sandwiches, boiled eggs, and other simple fare and parked outside the offices of the *Providence Journal.* Since all the restaurants in town closed at 8 p.m., he had no competition and his business thrived. Soon wagons began appearing all over. By the time Scott retired forty-five years later he had fifty competitors in Providence alone. They were called *lunch wagons,* which was a little odd, since lunch was one thing they didn't serve. A few, seeking greater accuracy, called themselves *night lunch wagons* or *night cafés.* When residents complained about having food sold outside their houses, cities everywhere enacted ordinances banning the wagons. So lunch wagon proprietors hit on the idea of moving their wagons to vacant lots, taking off the wheels, and calling them restaurants, since restaurants were immune from the restrictions. By the 1920s, several companies were mass-producing shiny, purpose-built restaurants known everywhere as *diners.* From a business point of view, diners were an appealing proposition. They were cheap to buy and maintain. You could set them up in hours on any level piece of ground, and if trade didn't materialize you loaded them onto a flatbed truck and moved them elsewhere. A single diner in a good location could turn a profit of $12,000 a year—a lot of money in the 1920s. One of the more enduring myths of American eating is that diners were built out of old railway dining cars. Hardly any were. They were just made to look that way.

The first place known to be called a *cafeteria*—though the proprietor spelled it *cafetiria*—was opened in Chicago in the early 1890s. The word came from Cuban Spanish and as late as 1925 was still often pronounced in the Spanish style, with the accent on the penultimate syllable. Cafeterias proved so popular that they spawned a huge, if mercifully short-lived, vogue for words of similar form: *washeteria, groceteria, caketeria, drugeteria, bobateria* (a place where hair was bobbed), *beauteria, chocolateria, shaveteria, smoketeria, hardware-ateria, garmenteria, furnitureteria*—even *casketeria* for a funeral home and the somewhat redundant *restauranteria*.

The *automat*—a cafeteria where food was collected from behind little windows after depositing the requisite change in a slot in each—was not an American invention but a Swedish one. In fact, they had been common in Sweden for half a century before two entrepreneurs named Horn and Hardardt opened one in Philadelphia in 1902 and started a small, lucrative empire.

Luncheonette (sometimes modified to *lunchette*) entered American English in about 1920 and in its turn helped to popularize a fashion for words with *-ette* endings: *kitchenette, dinette, usherette, roomette, bachelorette, drum majorette,* even *parkette* for a meter maid and *realtyette* for a female real estate agent.[15]

The waitresses and *hash slingers* (an Americanism dating from 1868) who worked in these establishments evolved a vast, arcane, and cloyingly jocular lingo for the food they served and the clients who ate it. By the 1920s if you wanted to work behind a lunch counter you needed to know that *Noah's boy* was a slice of ham (since Ham was one of Noah's sons) and that *burn one* or *grease spot* designated a hamburger. *He'll take a chance* or *clean the kitchen* meant an order of hash, *Adam and Eve on a raft* was two poached eggs on toast, *cats' eyes* was tapioca pudding, *bird seed* was cereal, *whistleberries* were baked beans, and *dough well done with cow to cover* was the somewhat labored way of calling for an order of toast and butter. Food that had been waiting too long was said to be *growing a beard*. Many of these shorthand terms have since entered the mainstream, notably *BLT* for a bacon, lettuce, and tomato sandwich, *over easy* and *sunny side up* in respect of eggs, and *hold* as in "hold the mayo."

Eating out—usually quickly, cheaply, and greasily—became a habit for urban workers and a big business for the providers. Between 1910 and 1925 the number of restaurants in America rose by 40 percent. A hungry New Yorker in 1925 could choose among seventeen thousand restaurants, double the number that had existed a decade before.[16] Even drugstores got in on the act. By the early 1920s, the average drugstore, it was estimated, did 60 percent of its business at the soda fountain.[17] They had become, in effect, restaurants that also sold pharmaceutical supplies.

As the American diet grew livelier, it inevitably sparked alarm among those who believed that sensual pleasures were necessarily degenerate. There arose, in the second half of the nineteenth century, mighty bands of men and women who believed with a kind of religious fervor that the consumption of the wrong foods would lead to the breakdown of the nation's moral fiber. One man went so far as to form a Society for the Suppression of Eating, which would appear to be taking matters about as far as they will go. Others were only slightly more accommodating to the need for sustenance. Typical of the breed was the Reverend Sylvester Graham, who connected insanity with eating ketchup and mustard, and believed that the consumption of meat would result in the sort of hormonal boisterousness that leads men to take advantage of pliant women. Many believed him—so many indeed that by mid-century the nation was not only following his cheerless recipes, but many thousands of people were living in Graham boardinghouses, where his dietary precepts were imposed with rigor. His one lasting contribution to the American stomach was the graham cracker. Then there was Horace Fletcher, who gave the world the notion that each bite of food should be chewed thirty-two times. Though he had no standing as a nutritionist—he was an importer by trade—that didn't stop him from disseminating his theories in a phenomenally successful book, *The ABC of Nutrition*, published in 1903.

But the zenith of America's long obsessive coupling of food with moral rectitude came with a Seventh-Day Adventist doctor named John Harvey Kellogg who in 1876 took over the failing Western Health Reform Institute in Battle Creek, Michigan, renamed it the Medical and Surgical Sanitarium (though everyone soon knew it as the Battle Creek Sanitarium or simply the Kellogg), and introduced a regime of treatments that was as bizarre as it was popular. Possibly the two were not unconnected.

Patients who were underweight were confined to their beds with sandbags on their abdomens and forced to eat up to twenty-six meals a day. They were not permitted any physical exertion. Even their teeth were brushed by an attendant lest they needlessly expend a calorie.[18] The hypertensive were required to eat grapes and nothing else—up to fourteen pounds of them daily. Others with less easily discernible maladies were confined to wheelchairs for months on end and fed experimental foods such as gluten wafers and "a Bulgarian milk preparation known as yogurt." Kellogg himself was singular in his habits. It was his practice to dictate long tracts on the evils of meat-eating and masturbation (the one evidently led to the other) while seated on the toilet or while riding his bicycle in circles around the lawn. Despite—or very possibly because of—these peculiarities, Kellogg's "Temple of Health" thrived and grew into a substantial complex with such classy amenities as elevators, room service, and a palm house with its own orchestra. Among its devoted and well-heeled patrons were Teddy Roosevelt and John D. Rockefeller.

Throughout much of his life, Kellogg nurtured a quiet obsession with inventing a flaked breakfast cereal. One night the process came to him in a dream. He hastened to the kitchen in his nightshirt, boiled some wheat, rolled it out into strips, and baked it in the oven. It was not only tasty but sufficiently unusual to be unquestionably good for you. Dr. Kellogg's patients simply couldn't get enough of it. One of these patients was a young man named C. W. Post, who spent nine months at the sanitarium sitting listlessly and needlessly in a wheelchair before abruptly embracing Christian Science and fleeing. One thing Post took away with him was a profound respect for the commercial possibilities of Dr. Kellogg's cereal. Unable to get a license from Kellogg, he decided to make his own, and in a breathtakingly short time became one of America's wealthiest men. Among Post's inventions were *Grape-Nuts* (a curious name, since it contained neither grapes nor nuts) and *Post Toasties,* or *Elijah's Manna* as it was known until 1908.

As it dawned on people that breakfast cereals were awfully easy to make, innumerable imitators sprang up. By the turn of the century at least forty-four companies in Battle Creek were churning out breakfast cereals with names like *Grip Nuts, Hello-Billo, Malt-Ho, Flake-Ho, Korn Kure, Tryabita, Tryachewa, Oatsina, Food of Eden,* and *Orange Meat* (which, like Grape-Nuts, contained neither of the specified ingredients).[19] Without exception these products were sold as health foods.★ Each packet of Grape-Nuts contained an illustrated leaflet, *The Road to Wellville,* explaining how a daily dose of the enclosed toasted wheat-and-barley granules would restore depleted brain and nerve cells and build strong red blood. For a short but deliriously exciting time, fortunes were there for the taking. A Methodist preacher named D. D. Martin cooked up some healthful goop on the kitchen stove, dubbed it *Per-Fo,* and immediately sold the formula for $100,000. Curiously almost the only person in Battle Creek unable to capitalize on Kellogg's

---

★Compared with later cereals they certainly were. Kellogg's Sugar Smacks, introduced in 1953, were 56 percent sugar.

invention was Kellogg himself. Not until 1907, when he at last brought to market his cornflakes, did he begin to get the credit and wealth his invention merited.

Preoccupation with health-enhancing qualities became a theme for all manner of foods. Moxie, known for its soft drinks, was founded in 1885 as the Moxie Nerve Food Company of Boston, and Dr Pepper, founded in the same year, was so called not because the name was catchy but because it sounded sternly healthful. For a time, it seemed that no food product could hope to sell unless it dealt vigorously with a range of human frailties. Quaker Oats claimed to curb nervousness and constipation. Fleischmann's Yeast not only soothed frayed nerves and loosed the bowels, but also dealt vigorously with indigestion, skin disorders, tooth decay, obesity, and a vague but ominous-sounding disorder called "fallen stomach." Fleischmann's kept up these sweeping claims— occasionally added to them—until ordered to desist by the Federal Trade Commission in 1938 on the grounds that there wasn't a shred of evidence to support any of them.[20]

Against such a background it is little wonder that Americans turned with a certain enthusiasm to junk food. The term *junk food* didn't enter the American vocabulary until 1973, but the concept was there long before, and it began with one of the great breakthroughs in food history: the development of a form of edible solid chocolate.

Though a New World food (the Mayas and Aztecs so prized it that they used cocoa beans as money), chocolate took a long time to become a central part of the American diet. Not until just before the Revolution did it become known in colonial America, and then only as a drink. At first chocolate was so exotic that it was spelled and pronounced in a variety of ways—*chockolatta, chuchaletto, chocholate, chockolatto*—before finally settling in the late eighteenth century into something close to the original Nahuatl Indian word, *xocólatl*. Chocolate came from the cacao tree, which somehow became transliterated into English as *cocoa* (pronounced at first with three syllables: "co-co-a").[21] The chocolate bar was invented in England in the 1840s and milk chocolate in Switzerland some thirty years later, but neither became popular in America until Milton Stavely Hershey gave the world the nickel Hershey bar in 1903. (The price would stay a nickel for the next sixty-seven years, but only at a certain palpable cost to the bar's dimensions. Just in the quarter century following World War II, the bar shrank a dozen times, until by 1970, when it was beginning to look perilously like a chocolate credit card, the bar was reinvigorated in size and the price raised accordingly.)

As is so often the case with American entrepreneurs, Milton Hershey was an unlikely success. His formal education ended with the fourth grade and he spent decades as a struggling small-time candy maker before suddenly and unexpectedly striking it rich in middle age with caramels, a new sensation that swept the country in the late nineteenth century.

In 1900, he sold his caramel business for $1 million—this at a time when $10 was a good weekly wage—and turned his attentions to the still fairly novel process of making milk chocolate. This new venture was such a huge and instantaneous success that within three years he was able to embark on building his own model community, complete with streets named Chocolate Avenue and Cocoa Avenue, near his birthplace of Derry Church in central Pennsylvania. Among the names Hershey considered for the new town were *Ulikit, Chococoa City,* and *Qualitytells,* but eventually he decided on *Hersheykoko.* For reasons lost to history, the postal authorities refused to countenance the name and he was forced to settle on the more mundane, but unquestionably apt, name *Hershey.* As well as the world's largest chocolate factory, the town of Hershey boasted several parks, a boating lake, a museum, a zoo, a professional ice hockey team, and the usual complement of banks, stores, and offices, all owned by Mr. Hershey.

Hershey ran the town as a private fiefdom. He prowled the streets looking for malingering municipal workers, whom he would instantly dismiss, and personally supervised (with presumed keenness) the censoring of movies at the local bijou. But he also engaged in many charitable works, notably the building of one of the world's largest orphanages for boys (and boys alone; orphan girls would have to look elsewhere) and endowing it with most of his fortune, some $66 million (today worth $1.7 billion).

The first true candy bar—that is, one containing ingredients additional to chocolate—was the Squirrel Brand peanut bar. Introduced in 1905, it sold well, but was quickly overtaken by an innovation of 1912, the *Goo Goo Cluster.* But the golden age of candy bars was the 1920s. Several classics made their debut in that busy decade—the *Oh Henry!* and *Baby Ruth* bars in 1920, the *Milky Way* and *Butterfingers* in 1923, *Mr. Goodbar* in 1925, *Snickers* in 1930. The Baby Ruth was originally called the *Kandy Kake,* but in 1920 the Curtiss Candy Company changed the name. The company steadfastly maintained that the change had nothing to do with the baseball hero Babe Ruth—who just happened to be the hottest thing in baseball in 1920—but rather was in honor of a daughter of President Grover Cleveland. This bonny infant had indeed captured America's heart and gained the affectionate sobriquet Baby Ruth, but that had been more than twenty years earlier. By 1920 she had been dead for sixteen years, and thus would not appear to have been an obvious candidate for gustatory immortalization.[22] Still, if the Curtiss story is to be believed, Baby Ruth was no odder a designation for a candy bar than *Oh Henry!*—said to be named for a fresh-faced youth whose droll quips to the girls at the George Williamson candy factory in Chicago provoked the constant cry, "Oh, Henry!"

Among the many hundreds of other candy bars loosed on a willing nation during the decade were *Big Dearos, Fat Emmas,* the *Milk Nut Loaf,* and the intriguing *Vegetable Sandwich.* Made of chocolate-covered vegetables, it was sold with the solemn assurance that "it will not constipate." As might have been predicted, constipation was not a compelling preoccupation among America's children and the Vegetable Sandwich soon disappeared from the scene. Equally improbable was the *Chicken Dinner* candy bar, so called because it was supposed to engender the feeling of well-being provided by a steaming roast chicken dinner. Though few people were able to make the leap of imagination necessary to equate a 5-cent chocolate peanut roll with a well-balanced meal, the Chicken Dinner sold well and survived into the 1960s. Curiously, none of these products were known as *candy bars.* The term is not recorded in print until 1943.

The 1920s saw the birth of many other well-loved snack foods, including such perennial mainstays of the American diet as the *Good Humor* bar in 1920, the *Eskimo Pie* a year later, *Popsicles* in 1924, *Milk Duds* in 1926, *Hostess Cakes* in 1926 (with *Twinkies* to follow in 1930), and *Dubble Bubble Gum* in 1928. This last was invented by Frank H. Fleer, whose earlier bubble gum, *Blibber-Blubber,* was something of a failure—it tended to dissolve in the mouth but to stick tenaciously to everything else, including Junior's face, when popped—but who had made a fortune with an earlier invention, *Chiclets.* But the runaway success of the decade was the *Eskimo Pie* (originally called the *I-Scream-Bar* by its inventor, a high school teacher and part-time ice cream salesman in Onawa, Iowa). So immensely popular was the Eskimo Pie that within three months of its introduction more than a million bars a day were being sold and the price of cocoa beans on the open market had leaped 50 percent in response.

But all of these paled in comparison with a dietary behemoth that emerged from the shadows in the 1920s and took its place at the top of the table. I refer of course to the hamburger. No one knows where the first hamburger was made. The presumption has always been that it came to America from Hamburg, Germany, in the same way that the frankfurter came from Frankfurt and baloney from Bologna. But this overlooks the niggling consideration that Hamburg has never had any tradition of serving such a dish. Considering its central role in the American diet, the evidence as to when the hamburger first appeared and why it was so called is vexingly uncertain, though there is no shortage of claimants for the title. Among the more insistent, if not necessarily most likely, contenders have been the towns of Seymour, Wisconsin, and Hamburg, New York, both of which claim to have been the birthplace of the hamburger in 1885. Seymour attributes the invention to one Charles Nagreen and unequivocally advertises itself as the "Home of the Hamburger," though its supporters tend to grow quiet when asked to explain on what basis Nagreen chose to commemorate a distant German city. More plausible, on the face of it, would appear to be the claim of Hamburg, New York, whose proponents believe that it was the inspired creation of the brothers Frank and Charles Menches, who developed it at the Erie County Fair in 1885.

Unfortunately for both claims, the etymological evidence suggests an earlier birth for the name, if not the dish. There is some evidence to suggest that it may have appeared as *Hamburg steak* on a Delmonico's menu as early as 1836 or 1837. The first undisputed sighting has been traced to the *Boston Journal* of February 16, 1884, which wrote in passing, "We take a chicken and boil it. When it is cold we cut it up as they do meat to make a Hamburg steak." As so often happens with first citations, the context makes it clear that by this time the dish was already well known. Unfortunately, it also indicates that it was a different dish from the one we know today, involving as it did beef cut up rather than ground, and eaten cold. What is certain is that *Hamburg steak* was widely called *hamburger steak* by 1889 (the first reference was in a newspaper in Walla Walla, Washington, suggesting that by this time it was eaten nationwide). That term in turn was generally being shortened to *hamburger* by 1901, by which time it had come to signify a patty of ground beef fried on a grill.

But it was still not a sandwich. It was, rather, a lump of ground beef served bare and eaten with a knife and fork. Who first had the idea of serving it in a bun is unknown and essentially unprovable, though once again there is no shortage of claimants. One such is Louis' Lunch of New Haven, Connecticut, which claims to have invented the true article in 1900, though some purists dismiss Louis' on the grounds that it served its burgers (indeed still does) on toasted bread rather than buns. Kaelin's Restaurant in Louisville, meanwhile, claims to have concocted and named the first cheeseburger in 1934, and I've no doubt that there are many other places around the country making similar heartfelt assertions. In any case, we can safely say that by about 1910 the object that we now know and venerate as the hamburger was widely consumed and universally known by that name. Even so, it had yet to fully establish itself in the hearts, and stomachs, of Americans.

In its early years the hamburger was often regarded by short-order cooks as a convenient way of passing off old or doubtful meat, and by its consumers, in consequence, as an item to be approached with caution. Not until 1921, with the rise of two entrepreneurs in Wichita, Kansas, did the hamburger begin to take its first vigorous strides toward respectability. The men in question were a former insurance executive named E. W. "Billy" Ingram and a short-order cook named Walter A. Anderson, and their brilliant stroke was to offer the world decent hamburgers using fresh meat. Not much fresh meat, mind you. Their steamfried hamburgers cost a nickel and weren't much larger. Ingram and Anderson managed to squeeze eighteen hamburgers from a pound of ground beef, significantly less than one ounce each. Nonetheless, people were soon flocking to their tiny cubicle, built of rock-faced concrete shaped vaguely, and a little preposterously, in the image of a castle. They called it White Castle because, they explained, *white* symbolized purity and cleanliness, and *castle* suggested permanence and stability.

Anderson and Ingram hit on three novelties that sealed their success and have been the hallmarks of fast-food service ever since. They offered a limited menu, which promoted quick service and allowed them to concentrate on what they were good at; they kept their premises spotless, which encouraged confidence in their hygienic integrity; and they employed a distinctive, eye-catching design for the building, which made it instantly recognizable from blocks away. Soon there were White Castles all over the country and a following throng of eager imitators— White Tower, White Diamond, Royal Castle, and White Crest—some of which are said to survive yet. The age of fast food was upon us, though no one would know it as such for another thirty years. *Fast food* first appeared in 1954 (as an adjective it had appeared three years earlier). *Takeout food* was even slower to arrive; its first recorded appearance was not until 1962.[23]

Before we part temporarily from the delights of handheld comestibles, two other linguistic novelties of the early 1900s need mentioning. The first is the *hot dog*. Memorably defined by H. L. Mencken as "a cartridge filled with the sweepings of abattoirs," the hot dog had been part of the American scene since the early 1800s, but had gone under the name *frankfurter* or *wienerwurst* (literally "Vienna sausage," and corrupted to *wienie* as early as 1867). The modern name didn't arise until a popular cartoonist named T. A. "Tad" Dorgan drew a picture of a dachshund in an elongated bun in the early 1900s and the term caught on in a big way.

It was also helped by the fact that *Hot dog!* as a cry of delight or approbation was also sweeping the nation as a catchphrase.

Dorgan was responsible for a slew of catchphrases, among them *cat's pajamas, yes man, skiddoo, you said it, drugstore cowboy,* and *yes, we have no bananas,* which he had picked up from an Italian fruit-seller and used in one of his cartoons. It became a national catchphrase (one wonders how anyone found a context in which to employ it) and was soon set to music loosely plagiarized from "I Dreamt That I Dwelt in Marble Halls" and became a national sensation.[24] (It is striking how many words have come into American English through comic strips. *Heebie-jeebies, hot mama, hotsy-totsy, bodacious,* and *horsefeathers* were all either coined or popularized by W. B. "Billy" DeBeck in his comic strips involving the characters Barney Google and Snuffy Smith. *Hooligan* became familiar to most Americans through the comic strip *Happy Hooligan. Keeping up with the Joneses* was an expression inspired by a strip by I. Bacheller begun in 1911. *Popeye* popularized *goon* and *jeep.*)

At about the time that *hot dog* was taking its place in the language, another much-loved snack came to prominence: the ice cream cone. Its invention is commonly traced to the 1904 St. Louis World's Fair. According to one story (and there are many to choose from), a waffle vendor and ice cream seller were stationed side by side on the grand concourse and discovered that if they combined their products they could not only produce an appealing and portable treat but one that also eliminated the trouble, expense, and hygienic uncertainty of having to supply dishes and spoons. Unfortunately for this story, the ice cream cone already existed in 1904. A patent had been taken out a decade earlier by an Italian-American named Italo Marchiony. The ice cream cone may have become popular at the fair—though that in itself is by no means certain—but it wasn't invented there. In any case, *ice cream cone* isn't recorded in general usage before 1909.

II

And on to drinking. One of the more enduring misconceptions concerning our Puritan forebears is that they abjured alcohol. In fact, they liked a good drink—or even a not-so-good one. One of the more popular tipples of early America, especially at weddings and other big social occasions, was *sack posset,* a concoction made by combining any handy intoxicant, usually ale or wine, with thick clots of curdled milk, which may explain why no one any longer drinks it. The *sack* in the name has nothing to do with a cloth container, incidentally. It is a corruption of the Latin *siccus,* meaning dry.

If colonial Americans were not adventurous eaters, they evidently had no hesitation about taking their drinks from almost anywhere. The international pedigree of drinking terminology is evidenced by, among many others, *julep,* from the Arabic *julab;* *sangría* (often called *san garee* in eighteenth-century America), from the Spanish word for blood; *toddy* from the Hindi *tārē* or *tārī,* a kind of palm tree sap; and *beer,* from the Germanic *bēor* (and ultimately from the Latin *bibere,* "to drink").

The early colonists showed a particular fondness for blending odd ingredients—eggs with milk and beer, for instance—and employed a variety of names to describe the result: *mum, perry, switchel, metheglin, egg pop, balderdash* (from which comes our word for nonsense), *cherry bounce,* any number of *flips,* and *cock ale.* This last named—a somewhat less than beguiling mixture of chicken soup and beer—is sometimes cited as the source for *cocktail.* Though *cocktail* is indubitably an Americanism—its first known appearance was in a newspaper in Hudson, New York, in 1806—its similarity to *cock ale* is probably coincidental. Cock ale was never a popular drink—even in that adventurous age few thought of chicken soup as a distinguished addition to the punch bowl—and there is no known link between the two words. So where then does *cocktail* come from? According to Stuart Berg Flexner, the term "almost certainly" evolved from the French *coquetier,* or egg cup, after a New Orleans apothecary who dispensed concoctions in egg cups. Other, more literal-minded observers suggest that it has some connection with the tail of a rooster, though quite why the tail of a rooster would suggest a potent beverage is anyone's guess. A more ambitious—and almost certainly fanciful—theory is that the cocktail was invented for the daughter of King Oxolotl VIII of Mexico. Her name was Xochitl, which the Spanish translated as Coctel.[25] The word also bears a striking, but apparently coincidental, resemblance to a word from the Krio language of Sierra Leone, *kaktel,* meaning a scorpion, a creature with a notorious sting in its tail. One possibility that seems not to have been considered by any authority, so far as I can tell, is that it might refer to a stiff drink's capacity to make one's tail cock up. Applied to horses, the word took on that sense in England at almost exactly the time that it first appeared in a drinking context in America. In any case, for most of its early life, *cocktail* didn't have the whiff of sophisticated refinement now associated with it. In the 1820s, a Kentucky breakfast was defined as "three cocktails and a chew of terbacker."[26]

Through most of the eighteenth century the principal strong drink in America was rum, a shortening of *rumbullion,* a word whose origins are entirely obscure. But toward the end of the century a new drink came along that rapidly displaced it—bourbon. Bourbon was a by-product of the Whiskey Rebellion of 1794, when the federal government imposed a bitterly opposed tax on domestic rye whiskey. In an effort to evade taxation, some two thousand distillers fled to Kentucky—which was not yet a state and thus, they hoped, not subject to the tax—and set up their stills there. When the rye crop failed, they turned as an expedient to corn and found to their gratification that it produced a drink of uncommon smoothness. They called it after the county in which they had settled, though in fact it was not bourbon as we now know it. It was only later, after the 1820s, that distillers took to aging it in oak casks, a process that gives modern bourbon its agreeable color and flavor. Although there is still a Bourbon County in Kentucky, none of the state's bourbon is produced there (at least not legally). To say that it was popular barely hints at its effect. By the 1830s, the average adult American was drinking six gallons of bourbon a year—twenty-four times more than today.

Saloon, in the sense of a place to drink, is not recorded until 1848, though, oddly, *saloon-keeper* goes back to the eighteenth century.[27] From the French *salon,* it originally signified any large hall or other public gathering place. *Bootleg,* first used in 1855, comes from the American West. According to J. L. Dillard, enterprising traders sold liquor illegally to the Indians by putting it in a flat bottle that they could slip into their boot.[28] I have no grounds to dispute this, but it does seem to me evident that the amount of liquor one could transport in this way would be hardly worth the bother. Certainly there must have been more commodious places to hide illicit alcohol on any wagon. I suspect the term was metaphorical.

Rotgut, often shortened to *rot,* dates from 1819. Those who drank too much would get the *jitters,* or *shakes.* For a time, strong drink was known as *jitter sauce,* and one who took to it too heartily was a *jitterbug,* a sense resurrected by Cab Calloway in 1934 for a type of dance music. Chronic drinkers faced the prospect of ending up on *skid road,* a term that came from western logging camps, where logs were slid down a track called a skid road. Eventually the word was transferred to the shanty towns that grew up nearby and, misheard by Easterners, was altered to *skid row.*[29]

In response to the increasing sottedness of Americans, there arose a vigorous temperance movement in the early nineteenth century and with it a new word: *teetotal.* No one knows where the word comes from, but, as ever, there is no shortage of theories. The most plausible is that it was simply a jocular way of emphasizing the *total* in *total abstinence.* It appears to have first been used at a New York temperance meeting in 1827 and was common in both Britain and America by the 1830s.

Booze is not recorded in America before 1890, in a *Webster's Diction-*

ary, which is surprising, since the word has existed in the shadows of re-spectability since Chaucer's time. We can assume that it was used in America long before 1890, but just didn't find its way into print. *Manhattan, highball, hangover, daiquiri,* and *gin rickey* are all also first attested in the 1890s. *Daiquiri* comes from Daiquirí, Cuba, where a potent form of rum was made. *Gin rickey* evidently commemorates a certain Colonel Rickey, but beyond that the story grows vague. Equally murky is the derivation of *Tom Collins.* According to Mencken the drink was named for a "distinguished bartender," though tantalizingly he gives no further clues as to the gentleman's identity.

Drinking terms then grow quiet for a time, but on January 16, 1920, three ominous terms became suddenly fixed in the American con-sciousness: *the Eighteenth Amendment, the Volstead Act,* and *Prohibition.* The first was the Constitutional amendment that made the whole thing possible, the second the law that laid down the terms of punishment, and the third the generic term for the whole business. Considering its impact on American habits, Prohibition slipped into law with remark-able ease. As Frederick Lewis Allen put it: "The country accepted it not only willingly, but almost absentmindedly."[30] Many, including quite a few in the temperance movement, were under the impression that Pro-hibition would affect only hard liquor and that milder tipples like beer would be safe. How wrong they were.

The new law had a devastating effect on restaurants, particularly at the classier end of the market. Deprived of bar earnings, many had no choice but to close down or to tempt fate by quietly offering bootleg liquor. In 1921, Delmonico's suffered the mortal humiliation of being noisily raided after an undercover agent attending an afternoon *thé dansant* was served something with more kick than tea. The restaurant eventually gave up the fight on May 21, 1923, just short of its hundredth birthday. The same fate befell scores of other famous establishments across the land.

Winegrowers, to their dismay, were reduced to producing harmless grape concentrate, which of course almost no one wanted. But they re-covered their composure, and their fortunes, when they discovered that there was nothing illegal about pasting a prominent label on each bottle announcing boldly, "WARNING: WILL FERMENT AND TURN INTO WINE," and providing step-by-step instructions on how a careless consumer might inadvertently convert this healthful beverage into something with the power to make his legs wobble. Sacramental wine, excluded from the strictures of the Eighteenth Amendment, also showed a curious leap in sales, with some cynics suggesting that not all of it—or even much of it—was ending up in devout stomachs. In the years 1925 to 1939,

American wine consumption actually trebled, and California's vineyards expanded from less than 100,000 acres before Prohibition to almost 700,000 acres afterward.[31]

Seldom has any law anywhere led to greater hypocrisy or been more widely flouted. People not only continued to drink, but in greater numbers than ever. Before Prohibition, New York had fifteen thousand legal saloons; by the end of Prohibition, it had over thirty thousand illegal ones. Detroit had no fewer than twenty thousand *speakeasies,* as illegal drinking establishments became rather curiously known. Boston was rather primmer with just four thousand illicit watering holes, but that was four times the number of legal saloons in the whole of Massachusetts before Prohibition. Hardly anyone took the law seriously. In 1930, a journalist testified to the House Judiciary Committee that he had attended a lively party at a Detroit roadhouse at which he had seen the governor of Michigan, the chief of police of Detroit, and four circuit court judges drinking lavishly and enjoying the entertainment of a troupe of young ladies dancing the *hootchy-kootchy* (another new word of the age, based on the earlier *coochee-coochee*) without benefit of clothing. They couldn't even have been wearing *G-strings,* since this device of minimal attire would not become known to strippers until 1936. Although the term is often said to have arisen as a jocular allusion to the thinness of the G-string on a violin, it actually has a more noble pedigree. In the nineteenth century it described the leather string Indians employed to hold up their loincloths and was spelled *geestring* (probably a folk translation of a more complicated, and now forgotten, Indian term).

All this is by way of reaching the point that Prohibition—or more correctly the Volstead Act—was a law without teeth. Congress appropriated just $5 million to enforce the act and employed just 1,520 agents to protect America's frontiers from smugglers—or one man for every twelve miles of border.[32] A small but curiously durable myth is that President Herbert Hoover stoutly defended Prohibition as "a noble experiment." In fact, he called it "a great social and economic experiment, noble in motive and far-reaching in purpose," which isn't quite the same thing and actually falls considerably short of a ringing endorsement. He wasn't praising Prohibition itself, but merely the motives of those who had foisted it on the nation. In point of fact, by the election campaign of 1928, when Hoover made his utterance, Prohibition was an obvious disaster.

Prohibition may have been an inconvenience to drinkers, but it enriched the vocabulary. *Bootlegger, speakeasy, hip flask,* and many other terms associated with illicit behavior became part of the common par-

lance. So, too, did the expression *the real McCoy*. Although often supposed to date from a much earlier period, it is a Prohibition catchphrase.
No one knows who or what this McCoy was—explanations range from
the name of a now-forgotten but presumably talented bootlegger to
some connection with opiates from Macao—but there is no documentary evidence to favor any particular claim.

The more sinister side of Prohibition also gave new meaning to such
words as *gangster* (originally in the nineteenth century it denoted mem-
bership in political gangs, not criminal ones), *moll* (an Old English term
for a girl, which was given an unexpected boost as the word for a gangster's distaff sidekick), and *racket* (an English word for shady dealings dating back to 1812, but long dead there, which was resurrected in
America in 1927). The growing importance of the car to criminals, as
well as to everyone else, is reflected in *getaway car* and *to be taken for a ride*.

Brewers didn't have nearly as easy a time of it as winegrowers. In desperation they turned to producing a product they hopefully called *near
beer*—which was rather like calling bathwater *near ice*—and soft drinks
with names like *Howdy, Chero-Cola,* and *Lithiated Lemon* (which would
eventually evolve into *7UP,* so called because it came in seven-ounce
bottles).

Soft drinks were already an old tradition in America, having first appeared as flavored soda water in Philadelphia in either 1825 or 1838, depending on which source you credit. Throughout the nineteenth
century, root beer, sarsaparilla, ginger beer, spruce beer, and other non-
intoxicating beverages became increasingly popular. But it was not until
the seminal year 1886—the year that the Statue of Liberty and Sherlock
Holmes also entered the world—that America got its quintessential soft
drink when John Styth Pemberton, an Atlanta pharmacist and patent
medicine man whose earlier, less inspired inventions had included *Globe
of Flower Cough Syrup* and *French Wine Coca,* brewed up a concoction of
cola nuts, coca leaves, caffeine, and other similarly dubious condiments
in an iron tub in his backyard, stirred it with a wooden oar from an old
boat, and called it *Coca-Cola.*

His bookkeeper, Frank Robinson, who was adept at calligraphy, drew
up the florid italic logo that Coke uses to this day. Pemberton viewed his
invention not as the refreshing thirst-quencher that the world has come
to love, but as an efficacious tonic for hangovers and other ills of the upper body.[33] (It was also discreetly hinted that it was a potent aphrodisiac.)
Pemberton, alas, failed to see Coca-Cola's true potential. In 1887, he
sold a two-thirds interest in the company for the curiously precise but
decidedly shortsighted sum of $283.29. It took another Atlanta pharma-
cist, Asa G. Candler, to capitalize on Coca-Cola's true possibilities as a

money-making refreshment. Just before the turn of the century he bought the formula from its new owners for $2,000 and with canny marketing converted his investment into a fortune. By 1919, when the company was sold again, this time to a consortium of Atlanta business-men, Candler's $2,000 outlay had grown in value to $25 million.

Such success naturally encouraged imitation, and soon American purchasers could try competing brands like *Co Kola, Coke-Ola, Coke, Koke, Klu-Ko Kola, Afri-Cola, Okla-Cola, Carbo-Cola, Sola Cola, Pepsi-Cola,* and even *Celery-Cola.* Many copied not only its famous name and italic logo, but also its distinctive bottle. Coke took them all to court. By 1926 it had resorted to law no fewer than seven thousand times to pro-tect its trademark, including one fight that went to the Supreme Court. Not only did it destroy almost all its challengers, but in 1930 it won the exclusive right to its alternative name, *Coke,* making it the world's only successful product with two names.[34]

The one competitor it notably failed to quash was *Pepsi-Cola,* in-vented in 1898 by Caleb D. Bradham and so called because it was in-tended to combat dyspepsia. Despite going bankrupt twice in its formative years, PepsiCo is now actually a larger company than Coca-Cola, thanks to its diversifications—it owns, among much else, Pizza Hut and Taco Bell, which is why you needn't bother asking for Coke there—and by having the good sense not to tamper with its formula as Coke did, with disastrous results, in 1985, when it introduced *New Coke.* (Marketing disasters are something of a tradition at Coke. It once launched Coca-Cola–flavored cigars, with results not unlike those that greeted New Coke.)

Despite its occasional setbacks, Coke has long been a symbol of American culture in a way that Pepsi has never managed. As long ago as 1950, it inspired a word for the American cultural takeover of the planet: *Coca-Colonization.* Today, Coke is sold in 195 countries (giving it a bigger following than the United Nations, with 184) and is claimed to be the second most universally understood term in English, exceeded only by *O.K.*—an expression that conveniently carries us back to the nineteenth century and the start of the next chapter.

Chapter 12

DEMOCRATIZING LUXURY: SHOPPING IN AMERICA

In 1846, an Irish immigrant in New York named Alexander Stewart opened a business on Broadway called the Marble Dry-Goods Palace and in so doing gave the world a new phenomenon: the department store. Never before had a single enterprise tried to bring together such a range of merchandise under one roof. The business thrived. Soon it covered a whole block on Broadway and had a staff of two thousand. But even that was not enough. In 1862, Stewart relocated to an eight-story building nearby, and renamed it A. T. Stewart's Cast-Iron Palace. It was, and for many years would remain, the largest retail operation in the world.

In its wake came scores of other similar emporia—Field, Leiter & Co. (later Marshall Field) in Chicago, Jordan Marsh in Boston, John Wanamaker's in Philadelphia, Hudson's in Detroit, and R. H. Macy's, E. V. Haughwout's, and Lord & Taylor in New York.

We don't know when people started calling them *department stores*. The term isn't found in print until 1893 (in *Harper's Magazine*), but, as so often, the context makes it clear that it was already widely used and understood: "They [Brooklyn stores] compare favorably with the best and largest department stores of New York."[1]

What is certain is that department stores transformed the shopping experience for millions of urban Americans. *Palace* was scarcely an exaggeration for these new establishments. They offered not only an unprecedented range of goods, but also levels of comfort, luxury, and excitement previously unknown to consumers. Three things made this possible: the development of cast-iron architecture, allowing the construction of more open interiors; the arrival of the safety elevator, giving stores the option of expanding upward; and, above all, the increasing prosperity of Americans.

Compared with previous retail establishments, these new bazaars were airy and spacious and marvelously self-contained. Almost from the start they boasted restaurants, tearooms, rest rooms, and other conveniences, eliminating the need to go elsewhere for anything. As early as the 1850s, Stewart's emporium was entertaining shoppers with fashion shows and organ recitals. You could, as millions remarked in wonder, spend a whole day there. But what truly distinguished department stores was that they were the first grand commercial enterprises open to anyone. In the words of Emile Zola, they "democratized luxury."[2] A secretary or clerk might live a lifetime in a city and not once go into a swank hotel or restaurant, see the inside of a concert hall or opera house, or venture into a fashionable milliner's. But such a person could experience something of the same intoxicating whiff of elegance and possibility in a department store, and mingle on equal terms with what was known in the business as the *carriage trade,* those wealthy enough to arrive in their own conveyances.

Department stores offered millions their first look at wonders of the age like the passenger elevator (the world's first permanent safety elevator was installed in the Haughwout Department Store in New York in 1857), electric lighting, public telephones, and escalators (the last so novel and giddying that some stores stationed nurses at the top to minister to those made light-headed by the experience). By the turn of the century the department stores' services were almost limitless. They had post offices, branch libraries, lost-and-found departments, hair salons, roof gardens, first-aid stations, information bureaus, "silence rooms for nerve-tired shoppers," even their own in-store radio stations. They would sew on missing buttons, bandage a cut, amuse a lost child, answer any question—and all without charge. Some put on lectures, concerts, and plays. Most provided demonstrations of new products. Shopping had become a social experience.

By 1900, Marshall Field was serving as many as a quarter of a million customers a day and had become one of Chicago's biggest employers with a staff of eight thousand. Wanamaker's in Philadelphia took orders twenty-four hours a day. Its Crystal Tea Room could handle ten thousand customers at a time. America had embraced with both arms the idea of *conspicuous consumption,* a term coined in 1899 by the sociologist Thorstein Veblen in his *Theory of the Leisure Class*, and much needed ever since.

One man more than any other was responsible for the modern look of department stores. He was Harry G. Selfridge, a Wisconsin native who took a job as a stock boy with Marshall Field in 1879 and quickly rose through the ranks. One of his first acts was to take goods down from the high shelves and put them on counters and tables where customers could peer at them, touch them, and, as critics noted, shoplift them (though this was by no means a new activity; *shoplifting* has been part of the English vocabulary since 1680). Among Selfridge's many other innovations were the bargain basement, annual sales, gift certificates, the practice of reminding customers how many shopping days were left till Christmas, the custom of keeping the ground-floor windows lighted at night, thus encouraging evening strollers to browse and plan their next day's shopping, and the now universal practice of putting the perfumes and cosmetics departments on the ground floor by the main entrance where they would sweeten the atmosphere and act as a magnet for passersby.

Retiring from Marshall Field, Selfridge moved to Britain and at the age of fifty founded the London department store that bears his name. Though most British observers felt certain that such a crassly commercial undertaking would never succeed in London, it not only thrived but made Oxford Street into London's premier shopping thoroughfare. Selfridge was obsessively devoted to his store. He concerned himself with everything from the sharpness of sales clerks' pencils to the quality of their teeth. With the death of his wife in 1918, however, Selfridge abruptly changed character. He began to go nightclubbing, fell in with a pair of Hungarian-American vaudeville stars known as the Dolly Sisters, and neglected his business. He bought racehorses, gambled and lost spectacularly at Monte Carlo, chartered airplanes to bring cartons of ice cream to the Dollys and breasts of chicken for their lapdog, bought a castle on England's south coast, and laid plans to build a 250-room, $15 million estate nearby.

In ten years, he ran through $8 million. Unfortunately, not all of it was his. Unable to pay back the debts he owed to his own store—for a decade he and the Dollys had been helping themselves to whatever they fancied without troubling to pay for it—he was ignominiously retired from the Selfridge's board of directors and given a pension of $25,000 a year (later cut to $12,000 and then to $8,000), from which he was expected to pay back debts of $2 million. On May 8, 1947, he died nearly destitute and virtually forgotten.[3]

More successful at keeping his hands on his money was Frank W. Woolworth. Where Selfridge had created the bargain basement as a sideline—a useful way of generating money from otherwise unsellable goods—Woolworth had the idea of building a store that was in effect nothing but a bargain basement. He opened the first Woolworth's store in Utica, New York, in 1879. Everything cost 5 or 10 cents—a proposition scarcely less incredible then than it would be now. The store was immediately successful, and by 1900 Woolworth had fifty-nine stores with annual sales of over $5 million. By 1913, he was so rich that he was able to pay with cash for the construction of the $13.5 million Woolworth Building in New York.[4] By then people everywhere were shopping at *bargain counters* (an expression first used in 1888) and *five and tens* or *five and dimes* (1905).

Actually, not everywhere. Well into the 1900s, America remained largely a rural country. Farm families and small-town folk longed to consume and possess like everyone else, but for years there was no way to reach them. In 1872, a former traveling salesman named Montgomery Ward hit on the idea of selling goods by mail. He suggested the idea to a farming organization formally called the Patrons of Husbandry but better known as the *Grange* (an old English word, etymologically related to *grain* and signifying a farmstead), and the two struck up a long and lucrative relationship. The Grange supplied the potential customers; Ward provided the goods. The combination was a hit. Within a little over a decade, Ward's catalogue, which had begun as a single sheet of paper, had grown to nearly ten thousand items, bringing a new world of choice and possibility to thousands of rural customers.[5] For over a decade it had the market almost entirely to itself, but in 1886 two men in Chicago formed a business partnership that would eventually grow into a retail monolith that would dwarf even the mighty Montgomery Ward.

Their names were Richard Sears and Alvah Roebuck, though the latter was never much of an active partner and sold out altogether in 1893. Sears, Roebuck & Co. offered essentially the same service as Montgomery Ward, but with greater flair. Its catalogues were livelier, its claims more sweeping, its products consistently cheaper and more alluring. By 1900 it had surpassed Ward in size and by 1906 it was so mammothly successful that it needed two thousand workers to process the 900 sackloads of orders it received each day. Such was the volume of business that the post office, railroads, and telegraph companies all opened branch offices at the company's Chicago headquarters.[6] By the early 1900s it was possible to buy almost anything from Sears, from a packet of thumbtacks to a car (called, naturally, the *Sears*). Customers could even buy a house and all its furnishings from the company. The semiannual receipt of its catalogues was among the high points of the year. The people of one North Dakota town were so taken with the company that they renamed their community Seroco, for *Sears, Roebuck*

& *Co.,* and would have been more explicit had the U.S. Postal Service let them.

The quarter century or so from 1885 saw the refinement of another venerable component of American retailing: the brand name. Although a few durable brand names date from even earlier—*Smith Brothers Cough Drops* from 1866, *Arm & Hammer Baking Soda* from 1867, *Ivory Soap* from 1878—the closing years of the nineteenth century and opening years of the twentieth saw the birth of a positive blizzard of famous products, particularly in the food industry: *Morton Salt* (1885); *Coca-Cola* (1886); *Log Cabin Syrup* (1887); *Aunt Jemima* pancake mix (1889); *Shredded Wheat* (1892); *Cream of Wheat* (1893); *Tootsie Rolls* and *Cracker Jack* (1896); *Jell-O* gelatin (1897); *Pepsi-Cola* and *Campbell's Soup* (1898); *Fig Newtons* (1900); *Animal Crackers,* originally intended as a Christmas novelty—the string handle was to allow them to be hung on trees (1902); *Post Toasties* (1904); *Planters Peanuts* (1906); *Sunkist* fruit (1907); *Life Savers* and *Crisco,* originally intended to be called *Krispo* until it was discovered that another manufacturer owned that name (1911); and *Oreo* cookies (1912).

What made all this possible, in large part, was the development of secure packaging such as the National Biscuit Company's patented (and much misspelled) *In-er-Seal* wrap, which not only ensured freshness but also enabled manufacturers to turn from selling in bulk out of boxes and barrels to providing small, individualized packages. Often the packaging was all that stood between success and failure. Clarence Crane, father of the poet Hart Crane, invented *Life Savers* in 1911, punching them out on a pharmacist friend's pill-making machine, but they were a flop because the mints went stale inside their paper wrappers and tended to absorb the flavor of the glue with which the wrappers were sealed. Only after a New York businessman bought the company and began wrapping the mints in tinfoil did Life Savers take off—and take off they did. In just over a decade his initial investment of $1,500 in the company was worth $3.3 million.

Etymologically, one of the mysteries of the period is where the name *Oreo* came from. The dedicated archivists at Nabisco can tell you almost everything there is to know about the Oreo—that it is the largest selling cookie in the world, that more than six billion of them are produced each year, that 10 cents of every dollar spent on cookies in America goes for Oreos. They can even tell you where and when the first *Oreo Biscuit* (as it was then called; today it is officially the *Oreo Chocolate Sandwich Cookie*) was sold: at S. C. Thuesen's grocery store in Hoboken, New Jersey, on March 6, 1912. But what they cannot tell you is where the name comes from. It may have something to do with the French word for gold (*or*) or the Greek word for hill (*oreo*), but more probably it is a meaningless concoction that some forgotten employee in the marketing department found pleasing to the ear. In any case, no one thought to make a record at the time, and the reasoning behind it is lost to us forever.[7]

As foods and other household products came to be individually wrapped and more conveniently transportable, it was only a matter of time before someone thought of a new way of selling them. In 1916, Clarence Saunders of Memphis, Tennessee, hit on a novel proposition that he patented under the name the *Self-Serving Store*.

Grocery stores and other such businesses had been around in America for a long time—long enough for the terminology of shopping to take on a slightly different hue than in Britain. Whereas the British tended then (and still tend now) to refer to retail establishments in the possessive singular—*grocer's, baker's, stationer's*—Americans, possibly under the influence of the Dutch and Germans, were inclined from colonial times to give a -*y* ending to retail establishments: *grocery, bakery, bindery, wiggery. Grocery store* first appeared in print in America in 1774, though the term is probably even older.

The first well-known grocery store group in America was the Great Atlantic and Pacific Tea Company, founded in 1859. As the name suggests, it began as a tea importer but was stocking groceries as early as 1865. By the outbreak of World War I, A&P, as it was by then known, had two thousand stores all over the United States, but they were stores of the old-fashioned type in which clerks fetched requested items from high shelves.[8] Clarence Saunders changed all that with his Memphis store. He called it a *Piggly-Wiggly*. When asked why he had given it such an odd name, he replied: "*That's* why—because it makes people curious!" Customers entered through a turnstile, picked up a basket, made their selections, and eventually arrived at the "settlement and checking" desk, where the selections were "checked up" and wrapped. A reporter for *The New York Times*, clearly agog at this revolutionary concept, described how a customer "rambles down aisle after aisle, on both sides of which are shelves. The customer collects his purchases and pays as he goes out." The motivation behind the stores was not so much to provide a convenience for the customers as to deal with a shortage of clerks occasioned by the First World War. But it soon became evident that shoppers liked being able to squeeze the bread and handle the soup cans, and the idea took off in a big way. By 1929, America had three thousand Piggly-Wigglys, though even at its peak in the late 1930s, Piggly-Wiggly was considerably smaller than the still old-style A&Ps, with sixteen thousand outlets. Others followed Piggly-Wiggly's lead, often with names that seemed equally remote from the business of buying food, among them *Humpty Dumpty, Hinky Dinky, Alpha Beta, Jitney Jungle, Bull Market* and *Giant Tiger.*[9]

A&P opened its first real supermarket in Ypsilanti, Michigan, in 1936. Saunders was not a player by this time. He had lost control of Piggly-Wiggly while playing the stock market in 1923 and devoted his remaining years to an even more ambitious, but ultimately harebrained, scheme called *Keydoozle* (for which read: "Key Does All") *Markets,* a kind of automated grocery store in which the customers would make their selections by inserting keys into slots beside a specimen product. Behind the scenes an assortment of clattering machinery and flapping conveyor belts would sort the products and carry them, bagged and ready to take home, to the checkout counter. The system never really worked, and no more was heard of Clarence Saunders.[10]

In one important respect, Saunders's store represented no advance on the old-style grocery stores. They were small, often no more than fifteen hundred square feet, with no more than three or four aisles. The credit for creating the first true supermarket is usually given to Michael Cullen, who opened a "grocery warehouse" or "food market"—he used either name freely—in Jamaica, New York, in 1930. It wasn't the first big food store in America. As early as 1923, San Francisco had a grocery store called the Crystal Palace with parking for 4,350 cars★ and 68,000 square feet of retail space. But Cullen's outlet did offer several features that would become standard in the business—evening hours, self-service, strident advertising, and a practically irresistible impulse to put a misspelled word in the title. He called it *King Kullen.* The first company to use the word *supermarket* in its title appears to have been Albers Super Markets., Inc., of Cincinnati, which registered the name in 1933.[11] The same decade saw the development of an appliance to help shoppers deal with the increasing volume of goods on offer: the *shopping cart.* Although a grocery store in Houston had for years been offering its customers the use of children's wagons with a basket attached to help them manage their purchases, it wasn't until 1936 when a store owner in Oklahoma City named Sylvan Goldman invented the modern shopping cart—which he called a *basket carrier*—that bulk buying became a possibility. (At first, customers showed great reluctance to use the new contraptions. It wasn't until Goldman employed half a dozen people to do nothing but push the carts around all day, pretending to shop, that others began to imitate them.)

★Or so most books on retailing history say, though it seems an awfully large number. Many modern shopping centers can't take that many cars.

In terms of numbers, supermarkets were relatively slow to penetrate the marketplace. As late as 1955, 95 percent of America's 360,000 grocery stores were mom-and-pop corner businesses or medium-sized stores known as *superettes*. But although supermarkets accounted for just 5 percent of grocery outlets, they already had half of America's food sales. Supermarkets today are defined as stores with at least $2 million in annual sales.[12] The average supermarket customer, you may be interested to know, takes twenty seconds to negotiate each aisle and spends just four seconds deciding on any particular purchase.[13]

Supermarkets changed not only the way America shopped but the way America ate. As women increasingly went out to work, convenience foods took on an ever more important role. Frozen foods were developed by a small company called Birds Eye, which took its oddly unappetizing name from Clarence Birdseye, a naturalist from Gloucester, Massachusetts, who accidentally discovered the potential of flash-freezing food while out ice fishing. The first Birds Eye frozen foods came onto the market in 1930, though they weren't called that. They were sold as *frosted foods* because it was thought that *frozen* would suggest flesh burns and other spoilage. It quickly became apparent that people were even more baffled by *frosted*—they weren't sure if it meant partially frozen or even that it was covered in some kind of icing—and *frozen food* it became. Birdseye's first range of frosted/frozen offerings consisted of a range of eighteen meats, three seafoods, two vegetables, and three fruits. Suddenly in the middle of January America's housewives could, as the ads gushed, buy "June peas as gloriously green as any you will buy next Summer."

Frozen prepared foods followed just before the outbreak of World War II. Baked beans was the first, rather improbable, offering, though soon you could get more exotic dishes like chicken à la king and lobster Newburg. The first frozen dinners were produced in 1945, for use by the army, and a year later the concept was offered to the public under the buckle-your-seatbelt name *Strato Meals*. Another early competitor made *Frigidinners* before C. A. Swanson & Sons of Omaha swept all before it with its *TV Brand Dinners,* launched in 1954.[14]

The phenomenon that made supermarkets bloom—namely, the rise of suburbia—was responsible for another development without which modern life for millions would be unendurable: the shopping mall. Malls of a sort have been around for a long time. The prototypes were European *arcades* (from the Italian *arcata,* "arch"), starting with the Burlington Arcade in London in 1819 and followed soon after by the Galeries Saint Hubert in Brussels and the cathedral-like Galleria Vittorio Emanuele II in Milan, which Mark Twain found so enchanting that he declared he would happily live in it for the rest of his life. It is still probably the most beautiful shopping center in the world. The fashion soon spread across the Atlantic. By the 1830s, beginning with the Weybosset Arcade in Providence, Rhode Island, most large American cities could boast an arcade or two.

Arcades never became anything but an incidental feature in American retailing. For most Americans, shopping implied department stores and smaller businesses inhabiting the ground floors of downtown office buildings. Often these went through certain linguistic vogues. The fashion for -eria terminations started by cafeteria in the 1920s gave way in the following decade to a rash of -orium endings: suitatorium, shavatorium, corsetorium, hairitorium, shoetorium, pantatorium, even hot-dogatorium. These in turn were followed by brief fashions for -rama (shop-a-rama, hair-o-rama) and -ette (washerette, superette, drugette) before the infatuation with odd terminations ran its course in the 1950s.

As America spread into the suburbs, businesses naturally followed. Soon every residential area had a row of little businesses—a barbershop, a corner grocery, a drugstore perhaps—standing beside popular streetcar stops as a kind of prototype shopping center. These early assemblages of suburban stores were known variously as shopping strips, string streets, or taxpayer blocks (so called because they were often intended only as temporary improvements, the hope being that they would generate enough revenue to pay the taxes on the land until something grander could be erected).

Such was the proliferation of strips, triangles, squares, and other collections of retailers that the argument over who built the first true shopping center in America is all but unanswerable. As far back as 1907 a Baltimore businessman named Edward H. Bouton erected a development of six stores, slightly set back from the street and with space for parking out front, which he called the Roland Park Shopping Center. The National Register of Historical Places recognizes Market Square, built in 1916 in Lake Forest, Illinois, as the first planned shopping mall.[15] Others give the honor to Country Club Plaza in Kansas City, built by J. C. Nichols in 1922 as part of a huge housing development. It was the first to contain a few areas exclusively for the use of pedestrians, though its layout was otherwise strictly conventional, with the stores facing onto the street. Highland Park Shopping Village in Dallas, built in 1931, was the first to completely segregate shoppers and motorists by turning its back on the street. With the exception of the Roland Park Shopping Center, most of the early complexes were called neither shopping centers nor malls, but something rather cozier, usually incorporating in their titles the word square or village, as with the Highland Park Shopping Village, Suburban Square (built in 1928 in Ardmore, Pennsylvania), and Hampton Village (erected in St. Louis in 1941).

The shopping center was, however, essentially a 1950s phenomenon. By the close of World War II there were just eight shopping centers in the United States and as late 1949 no more than a dozen. Then, in 1950, came the Northgate Center in Seattle, followed the next year by Shoppers' World in Framingham, Massachusetts, and the floodgates opened. Shopping centers began to go up all over. Such was the rate of development that by 1956, *Business Week* was headlining a story "Too Many Shopping Centers" and noting with alarm that in just two months of 1956 more shopping center space opened in America than in the eight preceding years.[16]

In the generic sense for shopping center, *mall* isn't recorded until as late as 1967. The word has a curious history. It comes from a game popular in Europe in the sixteenth and seventeenth centuries. Called *palla a maglio* ("ball to mallet") in Italy and *pallemaille* in France, it became in England *pall-mall* (but pronounced "pell mell"). The game involved knocking a wooden ball along a leafy alley and chipping it through a hoop—a sort of early hybrid of golf and croquet. By the mid-eighteenth century it had fallen out of fashion, but the name lives on in two London streets: Pall Mall and the parallel avenue called the Mall (which by analogy ought to be pronounced "mell" but isn't). The Mall in particular became associated with aristocratic strolling. By 1784, *mall* had found a place in the American lexicon as a fashionable name for any green place suitable for perambulations, notably for the sweep of grass that features in the center of Washington, D.C.

The man responsible for the layout and ambience of the modern shopping center was not an American but a Viennese named Victor Gruen, who fled the Austrian Anschluss in 1938 and arrived in America with just $8 in his pocket. Within twelve years he had become one of the country's leading urban planners. Ironically, Gruen's intention was not to create a new and more efficient way of shopping but to recreate in America something of the unrushed café-society atmosphere of European city centers. Shopping centers—or *shopping towns,* as he preferred to call them—were to be gathering places for the neighborhood, focal points of the community where people could stroll and meet their friends, dally over a coffee or an ice cream, and only incidentally shop. Gruen was convinced that he was designing a system that would slow suburban sprawl and tame the automobile. How wrong he was.

"We must sensitively observe the colorful, stimulating, and commercially busy urban scenes in the market squares in Central European cities in order to understand the contribution to community life the open spaces in our new shopping towns can make," he wrote in his 1960 book *Shopping Towns USA*.[17] He "systematized" the shopping center and developed the idea of an anchor store at each extremity to encourage people to stroll from one to another. The idea was to get shoppers out of their cars and onto their feet. He insisted on having public gathering places at strategic spots—open areas with benches, fountains, and perhaps a piece of sculpture or two to encourage social interaction and a sense of community.

In 1956, the year that the British novelist Aldous Huxley coined the much-needed term *spending spree*,[18] Gruen's utopian vision was given tangible shape with the construction of the Southdale Center in the Minneapolis suburb of Edina. Built at a cost of $20 million, it was the biggest shopping center in the world, and the commercial wonder of its age. Reporters from almost every large newspaper and magazine in America came to marvel at its ten acres of enclosed shopping area, seventy-two stores, and forty-five acres of parking with space for 5,200 cars. It became the model from which almost all other malls in America were cloned. Gruen followed Southdale with other malls in a similar vein—the Northland and Eastland shopping centers near Detroit, the Southland Shopping Center near Minneapolis, Valley Fair in San Jose, the Bay Fair Center in San Leandro, California, and the South Bay Shopping Center in Redondo Beach, California.

Shopping mall design became a science. At their conferences, mall planners bandied about new concepts like *Reilly's Law of Retail Gravitation* (essentially, the mix of stores necessary to keep people moving) and *optimal positional isochrones* (another way of saying that the best location for a shopping center is near a highway interchange). No one any longer thought about the idea of encouraging people to linger or socialize. Benches were built without backs so that people *wouldn't* linger on them, and food court tables given just enough crampedness to induce a sense of discomfort after about ten minutes. Victor Gruen's vision of people sitting with cappuccinos, reading newspapers on gripper rods provided by a thoughtful management, or playing chess beside whispering fountains never materialized.

Shopping centers didn't just transform towns, they often effectively created them. In the late 1940s, Paramus, New Jersey, was a dying little community with no high school, no downtown to speak of, and almost no industry or offices. Then two shopping centers were built along Route 4—Macy's Garden State Plaza and Allied Stores' Bergen Mall. Within a decade, Paramus's population had more than quadrupled to 25,000 and its retail sales had shot up from $5 million to $125 million.

Much the same thing happened to Schaumburg, Illinois. In 1956, it had 130 people. Then two things happened: O'Hare became Chicago's main airport and the Woodfield Shopping Center, with over two million square feet of retail space, was opened. By 1978, Schaumburg's population had increased almost four-hundred-fold to fifty thousand and it was on course to become the second-biggest city in Illinois after Chicago by the turn of the century.[19]

As shopping centers blossomed, downtowns began to die. Between 1948 and 1954, at the height of America's postwar economic boom, downtown retailers in America's thirteen largest cities lost on average a quarter of their business.[20] One by one, downtowns grew more lifeless as stores and offices fled to the suburbs. Hudson's Department Store in Detroit closed after watching its annual sales fall from $153 million in 1953 to $45 million in 1981, its last year—the victim, ironically, of the automobile, the product that had brought Detroit its wealth.[21] Sears closed its flagship store on State Street in Chicago in 1983. All over America, where downtown department stores survived it was as a matter of pride or of tax breaks, and seldom one of commercial logic.

By the early 1980s, the United States had twenty thousand large shopping centers, which between them accounted for over 60 percent of all retail trade. They employed 8 percent of the workforce—nine million people—and were generating sales of $586 billion—13 percent of the nation's gross national product.[22] By 1992, the number of shopping centers had almost doubled again, and new malls were opening at the rate of one every seven hours. Four billion square feet of America's landscape was shopping centers, two-thirds of it built in the previous twenty years.[23] Shopping centers weren't just growing in numbers, but elaborating new forms. One was the *large regional center*—that is, a shopping center with at least 400,000 square feet of shopping space, or more than most downtowns. There were almost two thousand of these by 1990. Another type came to be known, somewhat ominously, as *power centers,* unenclosed developments, usually built in a U-shape around a central parking lot and containing at least one *category killer* store—a place like Toys 'Я' Us or Circuit City selling a particular type of product in such volume and at such low prices as to deter any nearby competition.

Mall shopping had become America's biggest leisure activity. Mall of America of Minneapolis, the country's biggest mall with 4.2 million square feet of consumer-intensive space (still considerably less than the world's biggest, the West Edmonton Mall in Canada, with 5.2 million square feet), was forecast to attract more people than the Grand Canyon in its first year of business.[24] By the early 1990s, Americans were spending on average twelve hours a month in shopping malls, more than they devoted to almost any activity other than sleeping, eating, working, and watching television.[25]

And what of Victor Gruen, the man who had started it all? Appalled at what he had unleashed, he fled back to Vienna, where he died in 1980, a disappointed man.

Chapter 13

MANNERS AND
OTHER MATTERS

If the English disliked Americans for their use of English, they liked them no more for their habits. In book after book through the nineteenth century—William Cobbett's *A Years* [*sic*] *Residence in the United States of America*, Harriet Martineau's *Society in America*, Dickens's *American Notes*, Frances Trollope's *Domestic Manners of the Americans*, Frances Wright's *Views of Society and Manners in America*, Thomas Hamilton's *Men and Manners in America*—the British showed a strange and unfriendly preoccupation with American life and habits.

"In regard to the passengers," wrote Thomas Hamilton in typical vein, "truth compels me to say, that any thing so disgusting in human shade I had never seen. Their morals and their manners were alike detestable."[1] William Cobbett offered the opinion that "the natives are by nature idle, and seek to live by cheating." Frances Trollope detested almost everything: "The total want of all the usual courtesies of the table, the voracious rapidity with which the viands were seized and devoured, the strange uncouth phrases and pronunciation; the loathsome spitting, from the contamination of which it was absolutely impossible to protect our dresses; the frightful manner of feeding with their knives, till the whole blade seemed to enter into the mouth; and the still more frightful manner of cleaning the teeth afterwards with a pocket knife, soon forced us to feel that we were not surrounded by the generals, colonels, and majors of the old world; and that the dinner hour was to be anything rather than an hour of enjoyment."[2] Americans, she felt, suffered from a "universal deficiency in good manners and graceful demeanour."

The haste and indelicacy of American dining habits was a constant theme. Observed Isabella Lucy Bird in 1856: "I cannot forbear mentioning the rapidity with which Americans despatch their meals. My next neighbour has frequently risen from his seat after a substantial and varied dinner while I was sending away my soup-plate."

Robert Louis Stevenson, generally a sympathetic observer, was startled in North Platte, Nebraska, when a fellow diner asked another to pass a jug of milk and was turned on in a fury and told there was a waiter for passing things. "I only asked you to pass the milk," replied the first man meekly. To which the second cried: "Pass? Hell! I'm not paid for that business; the waiter's paid for it. You should use civility at table, and, by God, I'll show you how!" To Stevenson's considerable relief, and presumably that of the milkless fellow, the threat was not carried out, and the meal was concluded in silence.[3]

The widespread American habit of chewing tobacco and disposing of the juice by expectorating in the approximate direction of a brass spittoon also excited much comment. Both houses of Congress, Dickens recorded in *American Notes*, "are handsomely carpeted; but the state to which these carpets are reduced by the universal disregard of the spittoon with which every honorable member is accommodated, and the extraordinary improvements on the pattern which are squirted and dabbled upon it in every direction, do not admit of being described." (In fact, of course, he had just described them.)

To be sure, there was something in this. Americans did often lack certain refinements. Louis Philippe, the future king of France, reported with dismay during a trip through the States in 1797 that when he asked for a chamber pot his host told him there were none available but invited him to make free use of the window.[4] Even when they tried to haul themselves to a higher level of gentility, Americans often betrayed a certain misapprehension in regard to the conventions of society. A junior army officer named Nathaniel Tracy, charged with entertaining a visiting delegation of French officers, and being hazily aware of the peculiarities of French dietary habits, sent his men to a nearby swamp to gather a sackful of frogs, which were then boiled whole and served floating in a soup.

Only recently had Americans become generally acquainted with an appliance that had been around in Europe for some time: the fork. (Something of its bewildering unfamiliarity in its early days is indicated by the fact that it was also known as a *split spoon*.) Before the rise of the fork, diners in the New World got by with knives, which often had two small prongs on the end for spearing meat, spoons, and fingers. Because they were accustomed to using the right hand for both cutting food and hoisting it to the mouth, they developed the habit—curious to the rest of the world—of transferring the fork from left hand to right between actions.[5] But even as late as the mid-1840s, many Americans were still struggling with the concept, as *The Art of Good Behavior*, a best-selling etiquette guide of the day, tacitly acknowledged when it cautioned: "If possible, the knife should never be put in the mouth at all."

This said, the Europeans' own manuals of decorum—such as the French tome that instructed its readers, "When the fingers are very greasy, wipe them first on a piece of bread"[6]—invite speculation as to the standards in their own dining salons.

What is certain is that until about the 1840s, levels of hygiene and social sophistication did generally lag in America. Well into the nineteenth century, the bulk of Americans lived lives that were, in the words of one historian, "practically medieval."[7] Most Americans were by modern standards abysmally poor. A survey of Delaware farmers in 1800 found that only 16 percent had a barn and only half had even one horse. A farmer who could not afford a horse was unlikely to invest much in hygienic niceties. Although several words associated with cleanliness first appeared in America at about the same time as they did in England—*bathing-house* in 1760, *bathing-room* in 1791—the contexts almost always make clear that these were wonders enjoyed only by the very rich.

Even among the middle classes, bathing was a novel experience until well into the 1800s. At the turn of the century an Elizabeth Drinker noted in her diary that she had just had her first bath in twenty-eight years, and the tone with which she recorded the fact indicates that there was nothing particularly remarkable in allowing a quarter century or so to pass between immersions.[8] Not until the 1820s did bathtubs begin to be produced commercially, though for their first half century they would be called *bathing-tubs*. *Bathtub* is not recorded until 1870, when it appears in a story by Mark Twain.

At about the time that bathtubs first became commercially available, the toilet began its long, slow move indoors. At first it was generally installed in a small room separate from the bathroom, and was normally called the *water closet* in the British fashion, though there was a vogue—unfortunately short-lived if you ask me—for calling it a *quincy* after John Quincy Adams installed the first one in the White House. *Bathroom* is first noted in 1836, though *toilet paper,* intriguingly, isn't found before 1880. *Washroom* also first appeared in 1880 and had been further euphemized into *rest room* by 1900.

If America got off to a slow start in terms of civilizing comforts, by the 1840s it was racing ahead of Europe and the rest of the world—ironically at just about the time that British criticisms of American life were reaching full shriek. Department stores and restaurants brought a measure of democratic luxury and convenience to the middle classes that their European counterparts would not enjoy for at least another half century. American trains were plusher and faster and equipped with lavatories at a time when Europeans had to hope for either a strong bladder or a short trip, and America's city streets were better lit at night. Above all, where America began to stand out was in the quality of its hotels.

In the sense of a place to stay for the night, *hotel* is, rather surprisingly, an Americanism. In French, *hôtel* signified a grand structure (as in *hôtel de ville,* "town hall"), but as early as the eighteenth century, Americans were using it to describe hostelries.[9] America's first grand hotel was the City Hotel in Baltimore, built in 1826. Three years later, Boston's Tremont House opened. Soon palatial hotels were opening all over the country—the Astor House in New York, the Burnet House in Cincinnati, the St. Charles in New Orleans, the Maxwell House in Nashville.

These establishments led the way in the development of all manner of comforts—central heating, spring beds, elevators (New York's Fifth Avenue Hotel was the first hotel to get one, in 1859), and, toward the end of the century, electric lighting and telephones. Just as elevators made department stores possible, so too did they transform hotels. Previously rooms on the upper floors had to be let at a discount, since few guests wished to drag suitcases up and down several flights of stairs. Suddenly, thanks to elevators, rooms on the upper floors could be let at a premium. As the Otis Elevator Company's sales literature persuasively cooed, guests could now "enjoy a purity and coolness of atmosphere, an extended prospect, and an exemption from noise, dust and exhalations of every kind."[10] Even the most critical foreign observer was hard pressed to find complaint with American hotels. Anthony Trollope, the novelist son of Frances, was so impressed that he devoted a whole chapter of one of his travel books to this most marvelous of New World innovations.[11]

Homes, too, became notably better equipped with conveniences like furnaces and artificial lighting than those of Europe, though the severity of the American climate could make comfort an elusive goal even among the wealthier classes. In January 1866, the businessman George Templeton Strong lamented that even with both his furnaces and all the fireplaces going he couldn't get the temperature in his house above thirty-eight degrees.[12] Even so, foreign observers continually remarked about the intolerable warmth and stuffiness of American households. The British consul general in Massachusetts noted with quiet wonder that in the finer American houses "an enormous furnace in the cellar sends up, day and night, streams of hot air, through apertures and pipes, to every room in the house" to the extent that "casual visitors are nearly suffocated."[13]

Summers could be equally unbearable. Not only was there no practical way of getting rid of the heat, but the lack of proper sanitary services in towns and the proliferation of horses and other animals meant that flies, mosquitoes, and other insects thrived to an extent unthinkable now. At least food could now be kept, however. By the 1840s, many middle-class homes enjoyed the benefits of an *icebox* (an Americanism first recorded in 1839), and the ice industry was huge. Ice would be cut in blocks from New England ponds in winter and stored in icehouses. The development of new means of insulation meant that losses from melting could be held to under 10 percent even in the hottest summer. By mid-century, Boston alone was shipping out 150,000 tons of ice a year, some of it going as far as India and China.

Improved lighting remained a constant preoccupation. Until the late 1700s, illumination was limited to tallow candles and whale oil, but both were inefficient—it would take a hundred candles to create as much light as a single modern light bulb—and beyond the means of most households. Until the early 1800s the average American home existed in nearly total darkness once night fell. For the middle classes, illumination improved dramatically with the invention in 1783 of the Argand lamp (named for its Swiss creator), which had greater intensity and less flicker. The next step forward was the invention of kerosene by a Canadian, Abraham Gesner, in 1858.[14]

But the big transformation came with gas. Initially gas was used to light streets—Baltimore had gas lamps as early as 1816, before Paris or Berlin—but the dirt, odors, and volatility of gas meant it could not be safely relied on for domestic purposes until after the Civil War. Once these problems were dealt with, gas swept the nation. Each gas outlet, or *gasolier,* provided as much light as a dozen candles. By 1895, it was estimated, the average middle-class home was twenty times better lit than it had been at mid-century.[15] But even cleaned up and made more stable, gas remained dirty and dangerous. It emitted unpleasant, potentially lethal fumes that required special vents to clear the air. Even in the best-ventilated homes the carbonic acid and smoke that seeped from gas lamps took a heavy toll on books, drapes, wallpaper, and soft furniture, as well as the eyes, lungs, and clothes of the inhabitants.

What was really needed was electricity, not just for lighting but for scores of other appliances that Americans had the prosperity to buy if only the means existed to make them practical. Before electricity, labor-saving devices often had about them a certain air of the ridiculous. One manufacturer devised a rudimentary vacuum cleaner consisting of two bellows that the user wore like shoes. As the user plodded about the room, her exertions on the bellows created a suction action of sorts, which could be used to sweep up dust and crumbs. It was, as you might imagine, not terribly efficient. Other offerings of the pre-electrical age were a gas-heated iron and an elaborate contraption called the "Water Witch," which operated with pressurized water and which, the makers boasted, not only would vacuum the carpets, but could be employed to dry one's hair and massage aching muscles.[16]

In 1882, domestic electricity at last became a possibility when Thomas Edison began providing electricity on a commercial basis. By mid-decade, two hundred of New York City's wealthiest households were enjoying the illumination of five thousand light bulbs—or *electric lamps,* as the Edison company called them. Only the very wealthiest could afford such an indulgence. A single bulb cost a dollar—half a day's earnings for the average working person—and cost up to twenty cents an hour to run.[17] Nor was household electricity a hit with everyone. After spending thousands of dollars and suffering much disruption to walls, floorboards, and ceilings having electricity installed, Mrs. Cornelius Vanderbilt ordered every inch of her new wiring torn out when it was implicated (possibly wrongly) in a small fire.[18]

Outdoors, however, it was another matter. Almost overnight, America became the most illuminated country in the world. By the 1890s, Broadway was already being described as "the Great White Way" because of its dazzling lights (almost all of them advertising products). People came from all over just to see the lights, which included the world's first flashing sign, for Manhattan Beach and its hotels. Standing fifty feet high and eighty feet wide, the sign would light up line by line and then flash rhythmically before starting the cycle over again. It seemed a wonder of modern technology. In fact it was manually operated by a man in a rooftop shack.

In 1910, Broadway got a sign that *was* a wonder of electrical engineering. Rising the equivalent of seven stories above the rooftop of the Hotel Normandie and incorporating twenty thousand colored light bulbs, it offered in intricate detail the illusion of a thirty-second chariot race, complete with cracking whips and flying dust. People were so agog over it that squads of police had to be assigned to the area to keep pedestrians and traffic moving lest the whole of Manhattan grind to a halt.[19] Almost as arresting were the lights of Luna Park on Coney Island. Two hundred thousand bulbs picked out ornamental patterns and the outlines of the towers and minarets at the amusement park, turning it into a nighttime wonderland.[20] Even now it looks quite wonderful in pictures.

By 1896, electricity had become such an accepted part of life that people were familiarly referring to it as *juice*. But the expense held people back. In 1910, just one home in ten had electricity. By 1930, however, 70 percent of American households, some twenty million homes, were electrified—more than in the rest of the world combined. The proportion would have been higher still except that rural electrification took so long to complete. As late as 1946, barely half of American farm homes had electricity. (But then only a tenth had an indoor flush toilet.)

As electricity became more widely available, electrical products began to come onto the market. Singer introduced the first electric sewing machine in 1889. The electric fan appeared in 1891, the electric iron in 1893, the electric vacuum cleaner in 1901, the electric stove—sometimes called a *fireless cooker*—in 1902, the electric washing machine in 1909, the electric toaster in 1910, and the electric dishwasher in 1918. By 1917, the American householder could choose between fifty types of electrical appliances—and eagerly did so. In that year, Americans spent $175 million on them.[21] Within a little over a decade, that figure would rise to no less than $2.4 billion a year.[22]

The new and fast-changing market for electrical appliances often gave small companies a chance to thrive. After General Electric turned down the idea of an automatic washing machine, a small outfit named Bendix, which had no experience of manufacturing household appliances, took up the idea and within a decade had become one of America's biggest manufacturers of appliances. Much the same happened with a small subsidiary of General Motors called Frigidaire, which saw an opening for domestic refrigerators and so successfully seized it that the name almost became generic.[23] The idea of the refrigerator might have been new, but the word wasn't. It had existed in English since 1611, applied to various types of vessels and chambers used for cooling, and had been used to describe a box for keeping food cool since 1824.[24]

Refrigerators, rather surprisingly, were among the last common electrical appliances to catch on. Frigidaire began production in 1918, but the first models were ungainly and expensive. The cheapest cost $900—as much as a good car. As late as 1921, just five thousand were made in America. But then things took off. By 1931 a million refrigerators were being produced every year, and by 1937, at the height of the Great Depression, the number was nudging three million.[25]

But no product was more successful than the radio. *Radio,* in the form of *radio-receiver,* entered the language in 1903. Earlier still there had been such specialized forms as *radiophone* (1881) and *radioconductor* (1898). As late as 1921 the *New York Times* was referring to the exciting new medium as "wireless telephony." Others called it a "loud-speaking telephone" or simply a "wireless" (as it is still often called in Great Britain). When a leading golf club, the Dixmoor, installed radio speakers around the course so that its members could listen to church services (honestly) while playing their Sunday-morning round, it referred to the system simply as a "telephone." *Radio* in the sense of a means of communication and entertainment for the general public didn't enter the language until 1922, and it took a decade or so before people could decided whether to pronounce it *rādio* or *rădio*.

Until as late as 1920, all private radio receivers in America were homemade. A crystal set involved little more than some wire, an oatmeal box, an earphone, and a piece of crystal. The earliest commercial sets were bulky, expensive, and maddeningly difficult to tune. The big breakthrough for radio was the Dempsey-Carpentier fight of July 2, 1921—which is a little odd, since it didn't actually involve a radio transmission, though it was supposed to.

It is difficult to conceive now how big an event like a heavyweight boxing fight could be in the 1920s, but the Dempsey-Carpentier fight was *huge*—so huge that *The New York Times* devoted virtually the whole of its first thirteen pages to reporting it (though it did find a small space on the front page to note the formal ending of the World War). The day before the fight, under the lead page 1 headline "Radio Phones to Tell Times Square of Fight," it noted that an operator at ringside in New Jersey would speak into a "wireless telephone transmitter" and that his words would be transmitted instantly to halls in several cities and to crowds outside the New York Times Building on Times Square. Although the headline used the word *radio,* the article never did.

On the day of the fight, ten thousand people jammed Times Square, but because of technical difficulties the radio transmitter wasn't used. A ticker tape was pressed into service instead. Even so, most of the people in the crowd *thought* they were receiving their eyewitness account live by the miracle of radio from New Jersey.[26] The very notion of instant, long-distance verbal communication was so electrifying that soon people everywhere were clamoring to have a radio. (Dempsey knocked Carpentier out in the fourth round, incidentally.)

In just three years, beginning in 1922, over four million radio sets were sold, at an average price of $55. In 1922 only one home in five hundred had a radio. By 1926, the proportion was one in twenty, and by the end of the decade, saturation was nearly total. Radio sales went from $60 million in 1922 to almost $850 million by 1929.[27] Radio buffs pored over specialized magazines and formed clubs where they could swap tips and bandy about terms like *regenerative circuits, sodion tubes, Grimes reflex circuits, loop aerials, rotary sparks,* and *neutrodynes.* Companies that made radios became monolithic corporations seemingly overnight. In one heady year the stock of Radio Corporation of America went from 85¼ to 549. By 1928, people could even listen to broadcasts in their cars after a little company called Motorola invented the car radio.[28]

If you have ever wondered why radio and television stations always have call signs beginning with *W* or *K,* the answer is that those letters were assigned to American airwaves by an international convention held in London in 1912. The United States was given the call letters *A, N, W,* and *K. A* and *N* were reserved respectively for the army and navy. The other two were given to public broadcasters. Generally—though there are many exceptions—*W* was assigned to stations east of the Mississippi and *K* to stations to the west. Call signs with three letters usually, but again not invariably, indicate older stations. Old slogans, now generally forgotten, are sometimes encrypted in station call letters. WGN, owned by the *Chicago Tribune,* stands for "World's Greatest Newspaper." WIOD in Miami is short for "Wonderful Isle of Dreams."

The first broadcasters were ham operators using Morse code. But by the 1910s, experimental stations were springing up all over. KDKA of East Pittsburgh, Pennsylvania, opened by Westinghouse in 1920, has the distinction of being the first true radio station in America, though the credit is sometimes given to a station without call letters operated by the San Jose College of Engineering and Wireless, which began regular transmissions of news reports and music to receivers set up in local hotel lobbies in 1909. The station eventually moved to San Francisco and became KCBS. Most of the early stations were distinctly amateurish. KDKA featured musical renditions by the chief engineer's young (and not notably gifted) sons. Another early Westinghouse station, WJZ of Newark, broadcast from a curtained-off area of the ladies' rest room at a Westinghouse factory, apparently because it was the quietest place in the building. To say that most of these early stations were low-powered would be to engage in riotous understatement. Many transmitters used less wattage than a single light bulb.[29]

By the middle of the decade, however, radio was taking on a more professional air and even producing its first celebrities, like Harold W. Arlin of KDKA. For reasons that seem deeply unfathomable now, Arlin and most other broadcasters developed the custom of donning a tuxedo for evening broadcasts, even though—patently—no one could see them.[30]

In 1926, RCA, General Electric, and Westinghouse got together to form the National Broadcasting Company. (It actually comprised two networks, one known as the Red network, the other as the Blue.) A year later, the Columbia Phonograph Broadcasting System was born. (The "Phonograph" was later dropped.) At first, some effort was made to bring higher values to radio. In the 1920s and early 1930s, the government issued 202 licenses for educational stations, but by 1936, 164 of those—some 80 percent—had closed down or become commercial. "Accordingly," in the somewhat ponderous words of a radio historian, "in the critically formative first two decades of its utilization, the radio spectrum had only the most limited opportunity to demonstrate its capabilities for human resource enhancement."[31]

If radio's resource enhancement capabilities were underutilized, they were as nothing compared with television once it got going. Most of us think of television as a comparatively recent development. In fact, in terms of its practical applications, it is nearly as old as radio. It just took longer to get established. As early as the 1880s, what was required to make a working television was known in theory, though the necessary valves and tubes had yet to be invented.[32] The word *television* dates from 1907, but in the early days it went by a variety of alternative names— *electric eye, iconoscope, image dissector, electric telescope, televisor, picture radio, visual wireless, electric vision,* and *radio vision.*

Unlike other technologies, television was the result of work by numerous inventors in different places—Herbert Ives, Charles Jenkins, and Philo T. Farnsworth in America, John Logie Baird in Britain, Boris Rosing in Russia. The first working television—that is, one that broadcast something more profound than silhouettes and shadows—was demonstrated by Charles Jenkins in Washington in 1925. Baird, a Scotsman, demonstrated a similar model, but with sound, four months later.

Television didn't attract much public notice until Bell Telephone demonstrated its new system in New York in April 1927. Shown on a screen two inches high by three inches wide—roughly the dimensions of a modern credit card—the broadcast consisted of a brief speech of encouragement from Washington by Secretary of Commerce Herbert Hoover, followed by some entertainment from the AT&T studio in Whippany, New Jersey—a vaudeville comic who first told some Irish jokes and then changed into blackface and told some "darky" jokes. (It is curious that from its inception, people instinctively grasped that this was a medium built for trivializing; when Baird demonstrated the first color transmission in London in 1928—yes, 1928—his viewers were treated to the sight of a man repeatedly sticking out his tongue.)

The New York Times gave much of page 1 and almost the whole of page 20 to this big event under an excited stack of headlines:

FAR-OFF SPEAKERS SEEN
AS WELL AS HEARD HERE
IN A TEST OF TELEVISION

Like a Photo Come to Life

Hoover's Face Plainly
Imaged as He Speaks
in Washington

The reporter marveled that "as each syllable was heard, the motion of the speaker's lips and his changes of expression were flashed on the screen . . . with perfect fidelity." Nonetheless the *Times* man considered television's prospects doubtful. Its future, "if it has one, is thought to be largely in public entertainment—super-news reels flashed before audiences at the moment of occurrence, together with dramatic and musical acts shot on the ether waves in sound and picture at the instant they are taking place at the studio."[33]

In 1928, Baird made the first transatlantic broadcast from a studio near London to one in Hartsdale, New York, and the following year the cumbersomely named W2XCW in Schenectady, New York, became the country's first "regularly operating television station," though its telecasts consisted of just three thirty-minute programs a week—usually just shots of an unidentified head talking, laughing, or smoking—and, of course, there was almost no one to watch them. By the end of 1929 there were twenty-six stations in America, though only those that were supported by big corporations, such as W2XBS in New York (which evolved into WNBC), were destined to survive through the 1930s. There was no great impetus to promote the industry in America because of the lack of a market during the Great Depression and the government's refusal to allow commercials until 1941.

Many people got their first glimpse of television at the New York World's Fair in 1939. *The New York Times*, with what was threatening to become a customary lack of prescience, forecast that it would never be a serious competitor for radio because "people must sit and keep their eyes glued on a screen; the average American family hasn't time for it."[34]

The year 1939 also saw the first television sets go on sale to the public, but still there wasn't much to watch (as there was in Britain, where the BBC was celebrating its tenth anniversary). During the war years, America had just nine television stations in five cities—New York, Chicago, Philadelphia, Los Angeles, and Schenectady—and just seven thousand sets on which to watch the meager programming available. In the autumn of 1944, for instance, on Wednesday and Saturday nights there was no television at all in America. On Thursdays, only CBS was on the air, with fifteen minutes of news followed by an hour of local programming where available and a half-hour show called *Missus Goes a Shopping*. On Sundays the American viewer could watch DuMont Labs' *Thrills and Chills* followed by *Irwin Shane's Television Workshop,* or nothing.[35]

With the end of the war, American TV at last was unleashed. By 1947, the number of television sets in American homes had soared to 170,000. In that same year a program called *Puppet Television Theater* made its debut. A year later it was renamed *Howdy Doody,* and television had its first hit.

As late as 1949, radio was still turning over profits of over $50 million, while TV was losing $25 million.[36] But as the 1950s opened, television became a kind of national mania. As early as 1951, advertisers were rushing to cash in on the craze. McGregor Sportswear took a full-page ad in *Life* to unveil its new sportswear range for go-ahead guys, called "Videos," which featured such televisually appropriate fare as the reversible "Visa-Versa Jacket," "the Host Tri-Threat Jacket," and the "Durosheen Host Casual Jacket" and matching "Durosheen Host Lounge Slacks," all expressly designed for wear in front of the TV. Soon people everywhere were buying folding tray-tables so they could eat their TV Dinners while glued to the box. America was well on its way to becoming a nation of *couch potatoes,* though that expression would not, of course, be used for many years. (Its first appearance has been traced to the rather unlikely forum *American Banker* magazine of December 30, 1980, but the context suggests that it was already current, at least in California.)[37]

By 1952, the number of sets had soared to eighteen million, 105 times as many as there had been just five years earlier. The seminal date for television was Monday, January 19, 1953, the date on which Lucille Ball gave birth to "Little Ricky" on national television (by happy coincidence she gave birth to the real Desi Arnaz, Jr., on the same day).[38] The first television networks were run by NBC, CBS, ABC (which had evolved from the NBC Blue radio network), and the now largely forgotten DuMont Labs, a leading electronics company of the 1930s and 1940s. As a television network it struggled for years—by 1955 it had just two shows on the air—and finally expired altogether in 1957, though the company itself, renamed Metromedia, lives on as a chain of television and radio stations.

Many early television programs were simply lifted from radio. *The*

Lone Ranger, Sergeant Preston of the Yukon, Sky King, Meet the Press, Queen for a Day, Stop the Music, and *Gunsmoke* had all begun life as radio shows, though the transition to a visual medium often required alterations of cast. The squat and portly William Conrad, who played Marshal Matt Dillon on the radio, was replaced on TV by the more slender figure of James Arness. A more telling alteration was the adaptation of the popular *The $64 Question* from radio, but with the payoffs raised a thousand-fold, reflecting television's sudden, staggering wealth. The show became not so much a a hit as a phenomenon. When a Marine Corps captain named Richard S. McCutchen won the $64,000 payoff, the story made the front page of *The New York Times.* By the middle of the decade there were at least half a dozen quiz shows on the air—*Dotto, Twenty-One, Tic Tac Dough, Name That Tune* (one of whose early contestants, Marine Major John Glenn, won $15,000 by correctly naming twenty-five tunes), and *The $64,000 Challenge.* Almost all relied on a formula in which each show ended with the winning contestant having to defer until the following week the agonizing decision of whether to take his or her winnings or press on at the risk of losing all. This not only guaranteed a week of hot debate in barbershops and barrooms, but ensured that viewers would be glued to the set for the next installment.

The difficulty was that contestants had an exasperating tendency to blow an answer late in the program, precluding the possibility of an even more exciting return performance. To get around this problem, the producers of several shows hit simultaneously on a simple expedient. They cheated. Each week they supplied selected contestants—among them a respected minister from New Jersey and a college professor—with the correct answers, which made the results rather easier to forecast. Unfortunately they failed to consider that some contestants, having gotten a taste of success, would grow disgruntled when the producers decided that their reign should end. A contestant named Herbert Stempel blew the whistle on *Twenty-One* when its producers told him to "take a dive," and soon contestants from several other quiz shows were sheepishly admitting that they too had been supplied with answers. And that was pretty much the end of such shows. Nonetheless, the expression *the $64,000 question* has shown a curious durability and remains current even in countries like England where those who utter it have not the faintest idea what it alludes to.

Perhaps not coincidentally, the boom years of the 1950s saw the development of another great electrical breakthrough: the home air conditioner. Air conditioning had been around for a long time. It was developed in 1902 by a twenty-year-old fresh out of Cornell named

Willis Carrier. As we have seen, Carrier didn't call it an air conditioner but an *apparatus for cooling air.* The term *air conditioner* was coined four years later by a North Carolina textile engineer named Stuart Cramer, who invented a device designed not to cool textile mills but to humidify them.[39]

By the 1920s, air conditioning was being widely used for specific applications—in hospitals and movie theaters, for instance—but the considerable cost and the need for outsized ducts acted as a disincentive for its use in most homes and office buildings. As late as the late 1940s, a home air-conditioning unit—which Carrier called an *Atmospheric Cabinet*—was as big as an upright piano and as noisy and as expensive to run as you would expect a piano-sized appliance to be. The development of small window models in 1951 made the industry take off. In 1952, sales of home units went from virtually nothing to $250 million, and the industry has never looked back. Today Americans spend $25 billion a year, more than the gross national products of some fair-sized countries, just on the electricity to run their air conditioners.

Three years after the window air conditioner made its debut, another durable household appliance entered the world: the microwave oven. First called the *Radarange,* it weighed over seven hundred pounds, required a lot of complicated cooling apparatus, and didn't cook food very well. Renamed the *microwave oven,* the first consumer unit was produced in 1955 by Tappan, but the product and word didn't become familiar to most Americans until the late 1960s, when further improvements and advanced miniaturization of components—not to mention the increasing busyness of American women—made it at last a realistic proposition for home use.[40]

Such was the proliferation of gadgets and appliances that by the 1960s it was possible to perform almost any daily household task while scarcely rippling a muscle—from opening cans to brushing one's teeth to juicing an orange to carving a turkey. Instead of becoming more versatile and innovative, household appliances mostly just became more complex. Blenders accumulated a dazzling array of buttons. One had no fewer than sixteen that the user could activate in an almost infinite series of permutations, though, in the candid words of one executive, it still "couldn't do much more than whip cream." Labeling the buttons presented a linguistic as well as marketing challenge. A manufacturer, quoted in Susan Strasser's history of domesticity, *Never Done,* recalled that "eight of us sat up two nights straight, trying to get words with five letters, each one sounding a bit higher than the other."[41]

Perversely, this plethora of labor-saving devices didn't translate into greater leisure. The average "nonworking mother," as they are so inaccurately called, spends as much time doing housework now as fifty years ago—about fifty-two hours a week.[42] Although she has the benefits of countless appliances, the increased productivity they have brought her has been effectively offset by the larger size of modern houses, more wide-ranging lifestyles (her great-grandmother didn't run children everywhere in the family mini-van and her groceries were probably delivered), and more scrupulous standards of household cleanliness.

Leisure in any meaningful sense is actually quite a modern concept. *Sight-seeing* didn't enter the language until 1847 and *vacation* not until 1878. Even then, both were diversions for the well-off few. For millions of people a vacation was a once-in-a-lifetime indulgence experienced only on a honeymoon, or *bridal tour,* as it was often called until about 1900. *Honeymoon* has existed in English since 1546, but originally signified only the first month of marriage. It didn't become associated with a trip away from home until about the middle of the nineteenth century.

Weekend is an even more recent concept. The word was coined in 1879 in England, but didn't become part of the average American's vocabulary until as recently as the 1930s. Well into the 1900s, most people worked a sixty-hour, six-day week, and thus terms like *Monday-to-Friday* and *weekend* had no particular significance to them. The five-day, forty-hour week is often attributed to Henry Ford, but in fact it was introduced by the steel industry in 1923. Ford followed in 1926. Most of the rest of the nation didn't catch up until the Great Depression, when a shorter working week became a convenient way of dealing with falling demand.[43] Though 9 A.M. to 5 P.M. had become the standard working day for most Americans by the early 1940s, the term *nine-to-fiver* isn't recorded before 1959.

Today, according to some studies, Americans work harder—or at least longer—than at any time since the forty-hour week became standard. According to Juliet B. Schor in *The Overworked American,* the amount of leisure time has fallen by almost 40 percent since 1973[44] as people have been driven to seek overtime, take second jobs, or simply show a zealous commitment to the workplace lest they find themselves the sudden victims of *restructuring, downsizing, premature retirement, coerced transition, constructive dismissal, skill mix redeployment,* or any of the other forty or so euphemisms for being laid off that *Executive Recruiter News* found in current use in 1991.[45] (Of which Digital Equipment Corporation's *involuntary methodologies* was perhaps the most chillingly recondite.)

Across the economy as a whole, it has been estimated, the average American works 163 hours more per year today than two decades ago. Men are working 98 hours more, and women no less than 305 extra hours.[46] The burden is particularly heavy on working mothers, who put in, on average, an eighty-hour week when cleaning, cooking, and child care are included. Not surprisingly, nearly all the recent neologisms relating to work and the workplace are negative: *workaholic* (1968); *3-o'clock syndrome,* i.e., the tendency to grow drowsy in midafternoon (1980); *information overload* (1985); *sick building syndrome,* a feeling of general malaise generated by a poorly designed environment, first noted in *Industry Week* (1983); *time squeeze* (1990); and so on.

According to Schor, the average American adult enjoys just sixteen and a half hours of leisure a week after disposing of work and household commitments—though it must be said that such a claim appears dubious when you consider that other studies show that the average American also devotes over twenty-eight hours a week to watching television, spends three hours in shopping malls, and presumably manages to find at least a few hours for sex, eating, and socializing.

What is certain is that Americans work longer hours and more days than their counterparts in almost any other nation in the developed world. Principally as a result of shorter vacations and fewer national holidays, the average manufacturing employee in the United States puts in the equivalent of eight extra weeks a year at the workplace compared with a manufacturing employee in France or Germany.[47]

Thanks to all that hard work, the United States produces twice the goods and services per person that it produced in 1948. Everyone in the country could, in principle at least, work a four-hour day or a six-month year and still maintain a standard of living equivalent to that enjoyed by our parents. Almost uniquely among the developed nations, America took none of its productivity gains in additional leisure. It bought consumer items instead.[48] And that, if it is any comfort to you, explains why you have a houseful of labor-saving appliances and are more tired than ever.

Chapter 14

THE HARD SELL:
ADVERTISING IN AMERICA

I

In 1885, a young man named George Eastman formed the Eastman Dry Plate and Film Company in Rochester, New York.[1] It was rather a bold thing to do. Aged just thirty-one, Eastman was a junior clerk in a bank on a comfortable but modest salary of $15 a week. He had no background in business. But he was passionately devoted to photography and had become increasingly gripped with the conviction that anyone who could develop a simple, untechnical camera, as opposed to the cumbersome, outsized, fussily complex contrivances then on the market, stood to make a fortune.

Eastman worked tirelessly for three years to perfect his invention, supporting himself in the meantime by making dry plates for commercial photographers, and in June 1888 produced a camera that was positively dazzling in its simplicity: a plain black box just six and a half inches long by three and a quarter inches wide, with a button on the side and a key for advancing the film. Eastman called his device the *Detective Camera*. Detectives were all the thing—Sherlock Holmes was just taking off with American readers—and the name implied that it was so small and simple that it could be used unnoticed, as a detective might.[2]

The camera had no viewfinder and no way of focusing. The *photographer* or *photographist* (it took a while for the first word to become the established one) simply held the camera in front of him, pressed a button on the side, and hoped for the best. Each roll took a hundred pictures. When the roll was fully exposed, the anxious owner sent the entire camera to Rochester for developing. Eventually he received the camera back, freshly loaded with film, and—assuming all had gone well—one hundred small circular pictures, two and a half inches in diameter.

Often all didn't go well. The film Eastman used at first was made of paper, which tore easily and had to be carefully stripped of its emulsion before the exposures could be developed. It wasn't until the invention of celluloid roll film by a sixty-five-year-old Episcopal minister named Hannibal Goodwin in Newark, New Jersey—this truly was the age of the amateur inventor—that amateur photography became a reliable undertaking. Goodwin didn't call his invention *film* but *photographic pellicule,* and, as was usual, spent years fighting costly legal battles with Eastman without ever securing the recognition or financial payoff he deserved—though eventually, years after Goodwin's death, Eastman was ordered to pay $5 million to the company that inherited the patent.

In September 1888, Eastman changed the name of the camera to *Kodak*—an odd choice, since it was meaningless, and in 1888 no one gave meaningless names to products, especially successful products. Since British patent applications at the time demanded a full explanation of trade and brand names, we know how Eastman arrived at his inspired name. He crisply summarized his reasoning in his patent application: "First. It is short. Second. It is not capable of mispronunciation. Third. It does not resemble anything in the art and cannot be associated with anything in the art except the Kodak."[3] Four years later the whole enterprise was renamed the Eastman Kodak Company.

Despite the considerable expense involved—a Kodak camera sold for $25, and each roll of film cost $10, including developing—by 1895, over 100,000 Kodaks had been sold and Eastman was a seriously wealthy man. (A lifelong bachelor, he lived with his mother in a thirty-seven-room mansion with twelve bathrooms.) Soon people everywhere were talking about *snapshots,* originally a British shooting term for a hastily executed shot. Its photographic sense was coined by the English astronomer Sir John Herschel, who also gave the world the terms *positive* and *negative* in their photographic senses.[4]

From the outset, Eastman developed three crucial strategies that have been the hallmarks of virtually every successful consumer goods company since. First, he went for the mass market, reasoning that it was better to make a little money each from a lot of people rather than a lot of money from a few. He also showed a tireless, obsessive dedication to making his products better and cheaper. In the 1890s, such an approach was widely perceived as insane. If you had a successful product you milked it for all it was worth. If competitors came along with something better, you bought them out or tried to squash them with lengthy patent fights or other bullying tactics. What you certainly did not do was create new products that made your existing lines obsolescent. Eastman did. Throughout the late 1890s, Kodak introduced a series of increasingly cheaper, niftier cameras—the Bull's Eye model of 1896, which cost just $12, and the famous slimline Folding Pocket Kodak of 1898, before finally in 1900 producing his eureka model: the little box Brownie, priced at just $1 and with film at 15 cents a reel (though with only six exposures per reel.)

Above all, what set Eastman apart was the breathtaking lavishness of his advertising. In 1899 alone, he spent $750,000, an unheard-of sum, on advertising. Moreover, it was *good* advertising: crisp, catchy, reassuringly trustworthy. "You press the button—we do the rest" ran the company's first slogan, thus making a virtue of its shortcomings. Never mind that you couldn't load or unload the film yourself. Kodak would do it for you. In 1905, it followed with another classic slogan: "If It Isn't an Eastman, It Isn't a Kodak."[5]

Kodak's success did not escape other businessmen, who also began to see virtue in the idea of steady product refinement and improvement. AT&T and Westinghouse, among others, set up research laboratories with the idea of creating a stream of new products, even at the risk of displacing old ones. Above all, everyone everywhere began to advertise.

Advertising was already a well-established phenomenon by the turn of the twentieth century. Newspapers had begun carrying ads as far back as the early 1700s, and magazines soon followed. (Benjamin Franklin has the distinction of having run the first magazine ad, seeking the whereabouts of a runaway slave, in 1741.)[6] By 1850, the country had its first *advertising agency,* the American Newspaper Advertising Agency, though its function was to buy advertising space rather than come up with creative campaigns. The first advertising agency in the modern sense was N. W. Ayer & Sons of Philadelphia, established in 1869. *To advertise* originally carried the sense of to broadcast or disseminate news. Thus a nineteenth-century newspaper that called itself the *Advertiser* meant that it had lots of news, not lots of ads. By the early 1800s the term had been stretched to accommodate the idea of spreading the news of the availability of certain goods or services. A newspaper notice that read "Jos. Parker, Hatter" was essentially announcing that if anyone was in the market for hats, Jos. Parker had them. In the sense of persuading members of the public to acquire items they might not otherwise think of buying—items they didn't know they needed—advertising is a phenomenon of the modern age.

By the 1890s, advertising was appearing everywhere—in newspapers and magazines, on *billboards* (an Americanism dating from 1850), on the sides of buildings, on passing streetcars, on paper bags, even on matchbooks, which were invented in 1892 and were being extensively used as an advertising medium within three years.

Very early on, advertisers discovered the importance of a good slogan. Many of our more venerable slogans are older than you might think. Ivory Soap's "99 $^{44}/_{100}$ percent pure" dates from 1879. Schlitz has been calling itself "the beer that made Milwaukee famous" since 1895, and Heinz's "57 varieties" followed a year later. Morton Salt's "When it rains, it pours" dates from 1911, the American Florist Association's "Say it with flowers" was first used in 1912, and the "good to the last drop" of Maxwell House coffee, named for the Maxwell House Hotel in Nashville, where it was first served, has been with us since 1907. (The slogan is said to have originated with Teddy Roosevelt, who pronounced the coffee "good to the last drop," prompting one wit to ask, "So what's wrong with the last drop?")

Sometimes slogans took a little working on. Coca-Cola described itself as "the drink that makes a pause refreshing" before realizing, in 1929, that "the pause that refreshes" was rather more succinct and memorable. A slogan could make all the difference to a product's success. After advertising its soap as an efficacious way of dealing with "conspicuous nose pores," Woodbury's Facial Soap came up with the slogan "The skin you love to touch" and won the hearts of millions.[7] The great thing about a slogan was that it didn't have to be accurate to be effective. Heinz never actually had exactly "57 varieties" of anything. The catchphrase arose simply because H. J. Heinz, the company's founder, decided he liked the sound of the number. Undeterred by considerations of verity, he had the slogan slapped on every one of the products he produced, already in 1896 far more than fifty-seven. For a time the company tried to arrange its products into fifty-seven arbitrary clusters, but in 1969 it gave up the ruse altogether and abandoned the slogan.

Early in the 1900s, advertisers discovered another perennial feature of marketing—the *giveaway,* as it was called almost from the start. Consumers soon became acquainted with the irresistibly tempting notion that if they bought a particular product they could expect a reward—the chance to receive a prize, a free book (almost always ostensibly dedicated to the general improvement of one's well-being but invariably a thinly disguised plug for the manufacturer's range of products), a free sample, or a rebate in the form of a shiny dime, or be otherwise endowed with some gratifying bagatelle. Typical of the genre was a turn-of-the-century tome called *The Vital Question Cook Book,* which was promoted as an aid to livelier meals, but which proved upon receipt to contain 112 pages of recipes all involving the use of shredded wheat. Many of these had a certain air of desperation about them, notably the "Shredded Wheat Biscuit Jellied Apple Sandwich" and the "Creamed Spinach on Shredded Wheat Biscuit Toast." Almost all involved nothing more than spooning some everyday food on a piece of shredded wheat and giving it an inflated name. Nonetheless the company distributed no fewer than four million copies of *The Vital Question Cook Book* to eager consumers.

The great breakthrough in twentieth-century advertising, however, came with the identification and exploitation of the American consumer's Achilles' heel: anxiety. One of the first to master the form was King Gillette, inventor of the first safety razor and one of the most relentless advertisers of the early 1900s. Most of the early ads featured Gillette himself, who with his fussy toothbrush mustache and well-oiled hair looked more like a caricature of a Parisian waiter than a captain of industry. After starting with a few jaunty words about the ease and convenience of the safety razor—"Compact? Rather!"—he plunged the reader into the heart of the matter: "When you use my razor you are exempt from the dangers that men often encounter who allow their faces to come in contact with brush, soap, and barbershop accessories used on other people."

Here was an entirely new approach to selling goods. Gillette's ads were in effect telling you that not only did there exist a product that you never previously suspected you needed, but if you *didn't* use it you would very possibly attract a crop of facial diseases you never knew existed. The combination proved irresistible. Though the Gillette razor retailed for a hefty $5—half the average workingman's weekly pay—it sold by the millions, and King Gillette became a very wealthy man. (Though only for a time, alas. Like many others of his era, he grew obsessed with the idea of the perfectibility of mankind and expended so much of his energies writing books of convoluted philosophy with titles like *The Human Drift* that he eventually lost control of his company and most of his fortune.)[8]

By the 1920s, advertisers had so refined the art that a consumer could scarcely pick up a magazine without being bombarded with unsettling questions: "Do You Make These Mistakes in English?"; "Will Your Hair Stand Close Inspection?"; "When Your Guests Are Gone—Are You Sorry You Ever Invited Them?" (because, that is, you lack social polish); "Did Nature fail to put roses in your cheeks?"; "Will There be a Victrola in Your Home This Christmas?"★ The 1920s truly were the Age of Anxiety. One ad pictured a former golf champion, "now only a wistful onlooker," whose career had gone sour because he had neglected his teeth. Scott Tissues mounted a campaign showing a forlorn-looking businessman sitting on a park bench beneath the bold caption "A Serious Business Handicap—These Troubles That Come from Harsh Toilet Tissue." Below the picture the text explained: "65% of all men and women over 40 are suffering from some form of rectal trouble, estimates a prominent

---

★The most famous 1920s ad of them all didn't pose a question, but it did play on the reader's anxiety: "They Laughed When I Sat Down, but When I Started to Play . . ." It was originated by the U.S. School of Music in 1925.

specialist connected with one of New York's largest hospitals. 'And one of the contributing causes,' he states, 'is inferior toilet tissue.' " There was almost nothing that one couldn't become uneasy about. One ad even asked: "Can You Buy a Radio Safely?" Distressed bowels were the most frequent target. The makers of Sal Hepatica warned: "We rush to meetings, we dash to parties. We are on the go all day long. We exercise too little, and we eat too much. And, in consequence, we impair our bodily functions—often we retain food within us too long. And when that occurs, poisons are set up—*Auto-Intoxication begins.*"[9]

In addition to the dread of auto-intoxication, the American consumer faced a gauntlet of other newly minted maladies—*pyorrhea, halitosis* (coined as a medical term in 1874, but popularized by Listerine beginning in 1922 with the slogan "Even your best friend won't tell you"), *athlete's foot* (a term invented by the makers of Absorbine Jr. in 1928), *dead cuticles, scabby toes, iron-poor blood, vitamin deficiency* (*vitamins* had been coined in 1912, but the word didn't enter the general vocabulary until the 1920s, when advertisers realized it sounded worryingly scientific), *fallen stomach, tobacco breath,* and *psoriasis,* though Americans would have to wait until the next decade for the scientific identification of the gravest of personal disorders—*body odor,* a term invented in 1933 by the makers of Lifebuoy soap and so terrifying in its social consequences that it was soon abbreviated to a whispered *B.O.*

The white-coated technicians of American laboratories had not only identified these new conditions, but—miraculously, it seemed—simultaneously come up with cures for them. Among the products that were invented or rose to greatness in this busy, neurotic decade were *Cutex* (for those deceased cuticles), *Vick's Vapo Rub, Geritol, Serutan* ("Natures spelled backwards," as the voiceover always said with somewhat bewildering reassurance, as if spelling a product's name backward conferred some medicinal benefit), *Noxzema* (for which read: "knocks eczema"), *Preparation H, Murine* eyedrops, and *Dr. Scholl's Foot Aids.*★ It truly was an age of miracles—one in which you could even cure a smoker's cough by smoking, so long as it was Old Golds you smoked, because, as the slogan proudly if somewhat untruthfully boasted, they contained "Not a cough in a carload." (As late as 1953, L&M cigarettes were advertised as "just what the doctor ordered!")

By 1927, advertising was a $1.5-billion-a-year industry in the United States, and advertising people were held in such awe that they were

---

★And yes there really was a Dr. Scholl. His name was William Scholl, he was a real doctor, genuinely dedicated to the well-being of feet, and they are still very proud of him in his hometown of La Porte, Indiana.

asked not only to mastermind campaigns but even to name the products. An ad man named Henry N. McKinney, for instance, named *Keds* shoes, *Karo* syrup, *Meadow Gold* butter, and *Uneeda Biscuits*.[10]

Product names tended to cluster around certain sounds. Breakfast cereals often ended in *-ies* (*Wheaties, Rice Krispies, Frosties*); washing powders and detergents tended to be gravely monosyllabic (*Lux, Fab, Tide, Duz*). It is often possible to tell the era of a product's development by its termination. Thus products dating from the 1920s and early 1930s often ended in *-ex* (*Pyrex, Cutex, Kleenex, Windex*), while those ending in *-master* (*Mixmaster, Toastmaster*) generally betray a late-1930s or early-1940s genesis.[11] The development of *Glo-Coat* floor wax in 1932 also heralded the beginning of American business's strange and long-standing infatuation with illiterate spellings, a trend that continued with *ReaLemon* juice in 1935, *Reddi-Wip* whipped cream in 1947, and many hundreds of others since, from *Tastee-Freez* drive-ins to *Toys 'Я' Us*, . along with countless others with a *Kwik, E-Z,* or *U* (as in *While-U-Wait*) embedded in their titles. The late 1940s saw the birth of a brief vogue for endings in *-matic,* so that car manufacturers offered vehicles with *Seat-O-Matic* levers and *Cruise-O-Matic* transmissions, and even fitted sheets came with *Ezy-Matic* corners. Some companies became associated with certain types of names. Du Pont, for instance, had a special fondness for words ending in *-on*. The practice began with *nylon*—a name that was concocted out of thin air and owes nothing to its chemical properties—and was followed with *Rayon, Dacron, Orlon,* and *Teflon,* among many others. In recent years the company has moved on to what might be called its *Star Trek* phase with such compounds as *Tyvek, Kevlar, Sontara, Condura, Nomex,* and *Zemorain*.

Such names have more than passing importance to their owners. If American business has given us a large dose of anxiety in its ceaseless quest for a healthier *bottom line* (a term dating from the 1930s, though not part of mainstream English until the 1970s), we may draw some comfort from the thought that business has suffered a great deal of collective anxiety over protecting the names of its products.

A certain cruel paradox prevails in the matter of preserving brand names. Every business naturally wants to create a product that will dominate its market. But if that product so dominates the market that the brand name becomes indistinguishable in the public mind from the product itself—when people begin to ask for a *thermos* rather than a "Thermos brand vacuum flask"—then the term has become generic and the owner faces the loss of its trademark protection. That is why advertisements and labels so often carry faintly paranoid-sounding lines like "Tabasco is the registered trademark for the brand of pepper sauce made by McIlhenny Co." and why companies like Coca-Cola suffer palpitations when they see a passage like this (from John Steinbeck's *The Wayward Bus*):

> "Got any coke?" another character asked.
> "No," said the proprietor. "Few bottles of Pepsi-Cola. Haven't had any coke for a month. . . . It's the same stuff. You can't tell them apart."[12]

An understandable measure of confusion exists concerning the distinction between patents and trademarks and between trademarks and trade names. A *patent* protects the name of the product and its method of manufacture for seventeen years. Thus from 1895 to 1912, no one but the Shredded Wheat Company could make shredded wheat. But because patents require manufacturers to divulge the secrets of their products—and thus make them available to rivals to copy when the patent runs out—companies sometimes choose not to seek their protection. *Coca-Cola,* for one, has never been patented.[13] A *trademark* is effectively the name of a product, its *brand name.* A *trade name* is the name of the manufacturer. So *Ford* is a trade name, *Taurus* a trademark. Trademarks apply not just to names, but also to logos, drawings, and other symbols and depictions. The MGM lion, for instance, is a trademark. Unlike patents, trademark protection goes on forever, or at least as long as the manufacturer can protect it.

For a long time, it was felt that this permanence gave the holder an unfair advantage. In consequence, America did not enact its first trademark law until 1870, almost a century after Britain, and then it was declared unconstitutional by the Supreme Court. Lasting trademark protection did not begin for American companies until 1881. Today, more than a million trademarks have been issued in the United States and the number is rising by about thirty thousand a year.

A good trademark is almost incalculably valuable. Invincible-seeming brand names do occasionally falter and fade. *Pepsodent, Rinso, Chase & Sanborn, Sal Hepatica, Vitalis, Brylcreem,* and *Burma-Shave* all once stood on the commanding heights of consumer recognition but are now defunct or have sunk to the status of what the trade calls "ghost brands"—products that are still produced but little promoted and largely forgotten. For the most part, however, once a product establishes a dominant position in a market, it is exceedingly difficult to depose it. In nineteen of twenty-two product categories, the company that owned the leading American brand in 1925 still has it today—*Nabisco* in cookies, *Kellogg's* in breakfast cereals, *Kodak* in film, *Sherwin Williams* in paint, *Del Monte* in canned fruit, *Wrigley's* in chewing gum, *Singer* in sewing machines, *Ivory* in soap, *Campbell's* in soup, *Gillette* in razors. Few really successful brand names of today were not just as familiar to your grandparents or even great-grandparents, and a well-established brand name has a sort of self-perpetuating power. As *The Economist* has noted: "In the category of food blenders, consumers were still ranking General Electric second twenty years after the company had stopped making them."[14]

An established brand name is so valuable that only about 5 percent of the sixteen thousand or so new products introduced in America each year bear all-new brand names. The others are variants on an existing product—*Tide with Bleach, Tropicana Twister Light Fruit Juices,* and so on. Among some types of product a certain glut is evident. At last count there were 220 types of branded breakfast cereal in America. In 1993, according to an international business survey, the world's most valuable brand was *Marlboro,* with a value estimated at $40 billion, slightly ahead of *Coca-Cola.* Among the other top ten brands were *Intel, Kellogg's, Budweiser, Pepsi, Gillette,* and *Pampers. Nescafé* and *Bacardi* were the only foreign brands to make the top ten, underlining American dominance.[15]

Huge amounts of effort go into choosing brand names. General Foods reviewed 2,800 names before deciding on *Dreamwhip.*[16] (To put this in proportion, try to think of just ten names for an artificial whipped cream.) Ford considered more than twenty thousand possible car names before finally settling on *Edsel* (which proves that such care doesn't always pay), and Standard Oil a similar number of names before it opted for *Exxon.* Sometimes, however, the most successful names are the result of a moment's whimsy. *Betty Crocker* came in a flash to an executive of the Washburn Crosby Company (later absorbed by General Mills), who chose *Betty* because he thought it sounded wholesome and sincere and *Crocker* in memory of a beloved fellow executive who had recently died. At first the name was used only to sign letters responding to customers' requests for advice or information, but by the 1950s, Betty Crocker's smiling, confident face was appearing on more than fifty types of food product, and her loyal followers could buy her recipe books and even visit her "kitchen" at the General Foods headquarters.

Great efforts also go into finding out why people buy the brands they do. Advertisers and market researchers bandy about terms like *conjoint analysis technique, personal drive patterns, Gaussian distributions, fractals,* and other such arcana in their quest to winnow out every subliminal quirk in our buying habits. They know, for instance, that 40 percent of all people who move to a new address will also change their brand of toothpaste, that the average supermarket shopper makes fourteen impulse decisions in each visit, that 62 percent of shoppers will pay a premium for mayonnaise even when they think a cheaper brand is just as good, but that only 24 percent will show the same largely irrational loyalty to frozen vegetables.

To preserve a brand name involves a certain fussy attention to linguistic and orthographic details. To begin with, the name is normally expected to be treated not as a noun but as a proper adjective—that is, the name should be followed by an explanation of what it does: *Kleenex facial tissues, Q-Tip cotton swabs, Jello-O brand gelatin desert, Sanka brand decaffeinated coffee.* Some types of products—notably cars—are granted an exemption, which explains why General Motors does not have to advertise *Cadillac self-propelled automobiles* or the like. In all cases, the name may not explicitly describe the product's function, though it may hint at what it does. Thus *Coppertone* is acceptable; *Coppertan* would not be.

The situation is more than a little bizarre. Having done all they can to make their products household words, manufacturers must then in their advertisements do all in their power to imply that they aren't. Before trademark law was clarified, advertisers positively encouraged the public to treat their products as generics. Kodak invited consumers to "Kodak as you go," turning the brand name into a dangerously ambiguous verb. It would never do that now. The American Thermos Product Company went so far as to boast, "Thermos is a household word," to its considerable cost. Donald F. Duncan, Inc., the original manufacturer of the *Yo-Yo,* lost its trademark protection partly because it was amazingly casual about capitalization in its own promotional literature. "In case you don't know what a yo-yo is . . ." one of its advertisements went, suggesting that in commercial terms Duncan didn't. Duncan also made the elemental error of declaring, "If it isn't a Duncan, it isn't a Yo-Yo," which on the face of it would seem a reasonable claim, but was in fact held by the courts to be inviting the reader to consider the product generic.[17] Kodak had long since stopped saying "If it isn't an Eastman, it isn't a Kodak."

Because of the confusion, and occasional lack of fastidiousness on the part of their owners, many dozens of products have lost their trademark protection, among them *aspirin, linoleum, yo-yo, thermos, cellophane, milk of magnesia, mimeograph, lanolin, celluloid, dry ice, escalator, shredded wheat, kerosene,* and *zipper.* All were once proudly capitalized and worth a fortune.

II

On July 1, 1941, the New York television station WNBT-TV interrupted its normal viewing to show, without comment, a Bulova watch ticking. For sixty seconds the watch ticked away mysteriously, then the picture faded and normal programming resumed. It wasn't much, but it was the first television *commercial*.

Both the word and the idea were already well established. The first commercial—the term was used from the very beginning—had been broadcast by radio station WEAF in New York on August 28, 1922. It lasted for either ten or fifteen minutes, depending on which source you credit. Commercial radio was not an immediate hit. In its first two months, WEAF sold only $550 worth of airtime. But by the mid-1920s, sponsors were not only flocking to buy airtime but naming their programs after their products—*The Lucky Strike Hour, The A&P Gypsies, The Lux Radio Theater*, and so on.[18] Such was the obsequiousness of the radio networks that by the early 1930s, many were allowing the sponsors to take complete artistic and production control of the programs. Many of the most popular shows were actually written by the advertising agencies, and the agencies naturally seldom missed an opportunity to work a favorable mention of the sponsor's products into the scripts.

With the rise of television in the 1950s, the practices of the radio era were effortlessly transferred to the new medium. Advertisers inserted their names into the program title—*Texaco Star Theater, Gillette Cavalcade of Sports, Chesterfield Sound-Off Time, The U.S. Steel Hour, Kraft Television Theater, The Chevy Show, The Alcoa Hour, The Ford Star Revue, Dick Clark's Beechnut Show,* and the arresting hybrid *The Lux-Schlitz Playhouse,* which seemed to suggest a cozy symbiosis between soapflakes and beer. The commercial dominance of program titles reached a kind of hysterical peak with a program officially called *Your Kaiser Dealer Presents Kaiser-Frazer "Adventures in Mystery" Starring Betty Furness in "Byline."*[19] Sponsors didn't write the programs any longer, but they did impose a firm control on the contents, most notoriously during a 1959 *Playhouse 90* broadcast of *Judgment at Nuremberg,* when the sponsor, the American Gas Association, managed to have all references to gas ovens and the gasing of Jews removed from the script.

Where commercial products of the late 1940s had scientific-sounding names, those of the 1950s relied increasingly on secret ingredients. Gleem toothpaste contained a mysterious piece of alchemy called GL-70.* There was never the slightest hint of what GL-70 was, but it would, according to the advertising, not only rout odor-causing bacteria but "wipe out their enzymes!"

---

*For purposes of research, I wrote to Procter & Gamble, Gleem's manufacturer, asking what GL-70 was, but the public relations department evidently thought it eccentric of me to wonder what I had been putting in my mouth all through childhood and declined to reply.

A kind of creeping illiteracy invaded advertising, too, to the dismay of many. When Winston began advertising its cigarettes with the slogan "Winston tastes good like a cigarette should," nationally syndicated columnists like Sydney J. Harris wrote anguished essays on what the world was coming to—every educated person knew it should be "as a cigarette should"—but the die was cast. By 1958, Ford was advertising that you could "travel smooth" in a Thunderbird Sunliner and the maker of Ace Combs was urging buyers to "comb it handsome"—a trend that continues today with "pantyhose that fits you real comfortable" and other grammatical manglings too numerous and dispiriting to dwell on.

We may smile at the advertising ruses of the 1920s—frightening people with the threat of "fallen stomach" and "scabby toes"—but in fact such creative manipulation still goes on, albeit at a slightly more sophisticated level. *The New York Times Magazine* reported in 1990 how an advertising copywriter had been told to come up with some impressive labels for a putative hand cream. She invented the arresting and healthful-sounding term *oxygenating moisturizers* and wrote accompanying copy with references to "tiny bubbles of oxygen that release moisture into your skin." This done, the advertising was turned over to the company's research and development department, which was instructed to come up with a product that matched the copy.[20]

If we fall for such commercial manipulation, we have no one to blame but ourselves. When Kentucky Fried Chicken introduced "Extra Crispy" chicken to sell alongside its "Original" chicken, and sold it at the same price, sales were disappointing. But when its advertising agency persuaded it to promote "Extra Crispy" as a premium brand and to put the price up, sales soared. Much the same sort of verbal hypnosis was put to work for the benefit of the fur industry. Dyed muskrat makes a perfectly good fur, for those who enjoy cladding themselves in dead animals, but the name clearly lacks stylishness. The solution was to change the name to *Hudson seal*. Never mind that the material contained not a strand of seal fur. It sounded good, and sales skyrocketed.

Truth has seldom been a particularly visible feature of American advertising. In the early 1970s, Chevrolet ran a series of ads for the Chevelle boasting that the car had "109 advantages to keep it from becoming old before its time." When looked into, it turned out that these 109 vaunted features included such items as rearview mirrors, backup lights, balanced wheels, and many other components that were considered pretty well basic to any car. Never mind; sales soared. At about the same time, Ford, not to be outdone, introduced a "limited edition" Mercury Monarch at $250 below the normal list price. It achieved this, it turned out, by taking $250 worth of equipment off the standard Monarch.[21]

And has all this deviousness led to a tightening of the rules concerning what is allowable in advertising? Hardly. In 1986, as William Lutz relates in *Doublespeak*, the insurance company John Hancock launched an ad campaign in which "real people in real situations" discussed their financial predicaments with remarkable candor. When a journalist asked to speak to these real people, a company spokesman conceded that they were actors and "in that sense they are not real people."[22]

During the 1982 presidential campaign, the Republican National Committee ran a television advertisement praising President Reagan for providing cost-of-living pay increases to federal workers "in spite of those sticks-in-the-mud who tried to keep him from doing what we elected him to do." When it was pointed out that the increases had in fact been mandated by law since 1975 and that Reagan had in any case three times tried to block them, a Republican official responded: "Since when is a commercial supposed to be accurate?"[23] Quite.

In linguistic terms, perhaps the most interesting challenge facing advertisers today is that of selling products in an increasingly multicultural society. Spanish is a particular problem, not just because it is spoken over such a widely scattered area but also because it is spoken in so many different forms. Brown sugar is *azucar negra* in New York, *azucar prieta* in Miami, *azucar morena* in much of Texas, and *azucar pardo* pretty much everywhere else[24]—and that's just one word. Much the same bewildering multiplicity applies to many others. In consequence, embarrassments are all but inevitable.

In mainstream Spanish, *bichos* means *insects,* but in Puerto Rico it means *testicles,* so when a pesticide maker promised to bring death to the *bichos,* Puerto Rican consumers were at least bemused, if not alarmed. Much the same happened when a maker of bread referred to its product as *un bollo de pan* and discovered that to Spanish-speaking Miamians of Cuban extraction that means a woman's private parts. And when Perdue Chickens translated its slogan "It takes a tough man to make a tender chicken" into Spanish, it came out as the slightly less macho "It takes a sexually excited man to make a chick sensual."[25]

Never mind. Sales soared.

Chapter 15

THE MOVIES

In 1877, in one of those instances of one thing leading to another, the railroad tycoon Leland Stanford and a business crony were lounging with drinks on the veranda of Stanford's California stud farm when the conversation turned to the question of whether a galloping horse ever has all four hooves off the ground at once. Stanford was so sure that it did—or possibly didn't; history is unclear on this point—that he laid his friend a bet of $25,000. The difficulty was that no matter how carefully you watch the legs of a galloping horse, you cannot tell (particularly, we might suppose, when you have had a number of drinks on the veranda) whether the horse is at any point momentarily suspended in air. Determined to find an answer, Stanford called in his chief engineer, John D. Isaacs, who in turn summoned the services of the photographer Eadweard Muybridge.

Muybridge was a self-created exotic (his real name was the rather more plebeian Edward Muggeridge) and an accomplished landscape photographer, though in 1877 his fame rested chiefly on having managed to get himself acquitted of murdering his wife's lover in one of the more sensational cases of the age. Isaacs and Muybridge deployed twenty-four cameras along a racetrack and with the aid of tripwires executed a series of photographs of a horse galloping past. This had two effects. It proved beyond question that a galloping horse *does* get all four hooves off the ground, and for quite a lot of the time, and it marked the beginning of motion picture photography.[1]

Motion pictures of a type had been around since the late eighteenth century. Usually they involved cutout silhouettes, pictures painted on disks or cylinders, or some other simple device, which could be backlit and spun to throw a moving image onto a wall or screen. Despite their primitiveness, these early devices went by a variety of scientifically impressive names: the *phenakistoscope,* the *animatoscope,* the *thaumatrope,* the *phantascope,* the *stroboscope.* Inspired by their linguistic inventiveness, Muybridge constructed a projector of his own and called it a *zoopraxiscope.* Soon other similar devices were crowding onto the market: the *mutascope,* the *kinematoscope,* the *kinematograph,* and *theatrograph,* the *projectoscope.*

All of these had certain deficiencies, primarily that they relied on stringing together sequences of still photographs, a process that required either a lot of cameras or careful orchestration of movements on the part of the subjects. What was really needed was moving film. Thomas Edison saw himself as the man to provide it—or at least as the man to provide the man to provide it. He gave the task to a young Scotsman in his employ named W.K.L. Dickson. Dickson (who would later go on to found Biograph, one of the first Hollywood studios) studied the competitors' machines, considered the problem, and in short order devised an entire motion picture system, the first in the world (which perhaps makes him the true father of the movies). The camera was called a *kinetograph,* the projection device a *kinetoscope,* and the films thus made were *kinetophones.* (I mention them specifically because books of film history sometimes confuse them.) Nothing that Dickson came up with was particularly new. He essentially put together, albeit in an ingenious way, existing technologies.

Edison didn't envision kinetophone viewing as a shared, public experience, but rather as a home entertainment system—one whose primary purpose would be to provide an extra, incidental use for his recently invented phonograph. Some of the early motion pictures even had sound. (What slowed the progress of sound movies wasn't the problem of synchronization but that of amplification.) He suspected the whole thing would prove a passing fad and had so little confidence in it that he decided against spending $150 on an international patent, to his huge eventual cost.[2]

The first public demonstration of Dickson's new system was on April 14, 1894, on Broadway in New York. Despite an admission charge of 25 cents, people lined up around the block for the chance to take a look at this marvelous new peepshow.[3] (The invention may have been new, but the word wasn't; *peepshow* had first been used in 1861 in reference to kinematoscope viewers.) Projected through fifty-foot loops of film, each kinetophone show lasted no more than a minute and sometimes as little as sixteen seconds, with obvious consequent limitations on narrative possibilities. That the camera that recorded the moving images weighed five hundred pounds and was the size of a modern refrigerator acted as a further deterrent to adventurous scenarios. As a result, the first kinetophone films consisted of simple amusements: quick vaudeville turns, pratfalls, dancing bears, and—something of a surprise hit—a brief but lively feature called *Fred Ott's Sneeze* (Fred Ott being an Edison employee), which has the distinction of being the first copyrighted motion picture.

The shortcoming of the kinetoscope was that it could be viewed by only one person at a time. Unwilling or unable to see its potential, Edison failed to exploit his head start and was soon left behind in the hunt for a projection system that would allow motion pictures to become a shared experience. Rival systems began to sprout up everywhere, particularly in Europe, where there were no copyright problems, thanks to Edison's miserly failure to secure a patent. In one of the more intriguing developments, an inventor named Louis Aimé Augustin le Prince briefly excited Paris in 1890 by demonstrating a fully developed system in which moving film was projected onto a screen, to the delight and astonishment of an invited audience. Shortly after this acclaimed performance, Le Prince left his house on some errand and was never seen again. Another inventor in Paris, one Jean Leroy, thereupon demonstrated a rival system, again to great acclaim, and likewise mysteriously vanished.[4]

Not until 1895 did anyone else crack the problems of projecting film. Then in quick succession came three workable systems, all developed independently. One was the *cinématographe,* invented by the brothers Auguste and Louis Lumière (an apposite name, since *lumière* is French for "light"). From this evolved both the French and British words for the movies (respectively *cinéma* and *cinema*) as well as such terms as *cinematography, cinematographer,* and, much later, *Cinerama.* The word occasionally appeared in the United States in the early days, though usually spelled *kinema.* In Germany, meanwhile, the brothers Max and Émile Skladanowsky developed their *Bioskop,* anglicized in America to *Bioscope.* In England, Robert Paul invented the *Theatrograph* or *Animatographe,* which was as technically sophisticated as the other two, but failed to prosper and soon dropped from contention.

At last it dawned on Edison that there was money to be made in the film game. Unable to invent his own projection system, he did the next-best thing. He bought one and claimed to have invented it. The system was in fact the invention of C. Francis Jenkins and Thomas Armat. The only thing Edison invented was the name: *Vitascope.* Jenkins and Armat based their system on Edison's kinetophone, but improved it substantially. One improvement was the addition of a small reel that gave the film an extra loop. Called the *Latham loop* after its American inventors, the brothers Otway and Greg Latham, it didn't look like much, but it transformed the history of the movies. Before the Latham loop, movies of more than a minute or so were impossible because the film would so often break. The Latham loop eased the tension on the film and in doing so made it possible to create films of more than a hundred feet. For the first time real movies, with plots, were possible.

The first public display of this new wonder was on April 23, 1896, as an added attraction between live shows at Koster & Bial's Music Hall on 34th and Broadway (a site now occupied by Macy's).[5] Not having enough films of his own to show, Edison illegally copied some of the Lumière brothers' early works.[6] *Motion picture* was coined in 1891, but wasn't used much at first. The earliest movies were called *life portrayals* or *mechanically reproduced theater entertainment,* though by the end of 1896 people were calling them *moving pictures* and by the early 1900s had shortened this almost everywhere to *movies* (though until as late as the 1920s, people sometimes referred to them as *movie plays*). People who took the pictures were called *camerists. Cameraman* didn't occur to anyone until 1905.

The first real movie—that is, one with a story line—was *The Great Train Robbery* by Edwin S. Porter, who had begun in the Edison studios in Paterson, New Jersey, as a general handyman and *camerist* before rising to become head of production. Running eleven minutes and containing fourteen scenes, *The Great Train Robbery* was revolutionary not only in its sophisticated editing and pacing, but also in its content. It was both the first true movie and the first *western*—though that word wouldn't become general until about 1928; before that they were *cowboy movies* or *gun operas*—and the first to explore the exciting possibilities of violent crime.[7] It was a sensation. The excitement it generated and its sense of wondrous novelty are difficult to conceive now. When one of the characters fired a gun at the camera, many members of the audience gasped and recoiled. (This may not seem quite so ridiculous if you pause to consider your own response the first time you saw a 3-D movie.) A few even fainted. It became one of those things that simply everybody had to see.

Almost overnight, movies went from being a craze to a compulsion. By 1905, people everywhere were flocking to *store theaters* (so called because they were usually set up in vacant stores) or *nickelodeons,* where viewers were treated to a half hour of escapism for a nickel. *Nickelodeon* had been used as a word for peepshow arcades since 1888, though the first purpose-built movie theater, in Pittsburgh, styled itself not a nickelodeon but a *Nicolet.* Within two weeks of the Nicolet's opening, people were flocking to the theater from eight in the morning until midnight to see Edwin S. Porter's sensational *Great Train Robbery*, and the proprietors were clearing profits of $1,000 a week. By 1906, America had a thousand nickelodeons; by 1907, five thousand. Film was designed to run at a speed of sixteen frames per second, but nickelodeon operators quickly discovered that if they speeded things up slightly they could pack in more shows.

For millions, attending the nickelodeon became a kind of addiction. By 1908, New York City's *movie theaters*—the word had been coined the year before; in 1914 it would be joined by *movie houses*—were clocking up 200,000 admissions every day, including Sundays when they were required by law to be closed. Many non-moviegoers considered the phenonemen alarming if not distasteful. Partly this was because of the mildly risqué nature of some of the shows—within two weeks of Edison's launching the first kinetophone parlor in 1894, some enterprising opportunist was offering a peepshow called *Doloria in the Passion Dance*, which was not terribly titillating by modern standards but was certainly a step up on *Fred Ott's Sneeze*—and partly because the movies attracted a disproportionate number of lower-class immigrants (for whom language problems often made other, more verbal forms of entertainment impractical), and anything that gave pleasure to lower-class immigrants was almost by definition suspect. There was, however, something less specific as well—a sense that going to the pictures was somehow immoral and conducive to idleness—and authorities sometimes organized sudden, unprompted purges on the early movie houses, as in 1908 when New York Mayor George B. McLellan ordered all 550 of that city's establishments shut for no particular reason other than that he didn't like them.[8]

The word *movies* even began to take on a slightly unsavory tone. In 1912 a studio called Essanay invited fans to come up with a better name. The winning entry was *photoplay*. It never caught on as a word for the pictures, but it did become the name of a hugely successful magazine.[9] (Hollywood's curious disdain of the word *movies* is reflected in the decidedly inflated title of its most vaunted institution: *The Academy of Motion Picture Arts and Sciences*.)

Among the scores of words and expressions generated by the new industry, we find *mob scene* (1908), *screen* (1910), *flashback* (1912), *close-up* (1913), *to pan* (1915), *double bill* (1917), *fade-in* and *fade-out* (1918), *movie star* (1919), *dissolve* (1920), *silver screen* (1924), *documentary* (1926), and *trailers* (early 1920s), so called because in the early days they followed, or *trailed,* the main film. The frames of written dialogue or explication that were inserted into the film at intervals were at first called *captions,* but by 1913 were generally referred to as *subtitles* or *titles.* Some of these captions were used so often that they passed into the language as stock phrases, notably "Comes the dawn" and "Meanwhile, back at the ranch."[10]

Many other movie words were taken from the stage. *Slapstick* was originally a vaudeville term. It described two sticks that were literally slapped together offstage to accentuate an onstage pratfall (*prat* being an old slang term for the buttocks). *Ham actor,* first recorded in 1875, originally alluded to lesser performers' having to use ham fat rather than cold cream to remove their makeup. Soon a second-rate actor was known as a *hamfatter,* by 1902 he was just a *ham. Grips,* the term for scenery shifters, was also originally a theatrical term. They were so called because they gripped the sets and props when they moved them.

By 1925, the movies had become not only America's most popular form of entertainment, but its fifth-biggest industry, and people everywhere dreamed of making it big in Hollywood. How a dusty, misnamed southern California hamlet that never had much to do with the making of movies became indelibly fixed in the popular consciousness as the home of the entertainment industry is a story that takes a little telling.

Let's start with the name. Hollywood never had any holly or even much wood to speak of. Originally called Cahuenga Valley, it was principally the site of a ranch owned by a Mr. and Mrs. Harvey Henderson Wilcox. The more romantic name came after Mrs. Wilcox, on a trip back East, fell into a conversation with a stranger on a train and was so taken with the name of her new acquaintance's summer home, *Hollywood,* that she decided to rename the ranch. That was in 1887, and in the general course of things that would very probably have been that. Hollywood would have been an anonymous piece of semiarid real estate waiting to be swallowed up by Los Angeles.

But between 1908 and 1913, something else happened. Many small independent film companies like Nestor, Biograph, and Mack Sennett's Keystone Studios began moving to southern California. Partly they were drawn by the weather, which permitted year-round filming without a lot of expensive lighting, but more crucially they were also trying to escape the threats, legal and physical, of the Motion Pictures Patents Company, a consortium of eight studios led (inevitably) by Thomas A. Edison. The MPPC had been trying for years to gain monopoly control of the movie business and had developed increasingly aggressive tactics to encourage competitors to join the consortium and pay its hefty licensing fees. Its idea of exploratory negotiations was to send in a party of thugs with baseball bats. Hence the appeal of a locale three thousand miles away on another coast.

Only one of the studios actually set up in Hollywood—the Nestor Film Company in 1911. Locals were so upset at the sudden appearance of ramshackle film sets and the louche aspect of actors that they enacted an ordinance forbidding the erection of further studios. So, Hollywood has never really had a film industry. The studios that began to dot the landscape in the following years were all elsewhere—in Culver City, Edendale, Boyle Heights, Burbank, Santa Monica, and indeed almost anywhere but Hollywood. As late as 1913, when Cecil B. DeMille filmed *The Squaw Man* in a studio at the corner of Sunset Boulevard and Vine, Hollywood was a country hamlet and Hollywood Boulevard, not yet so named, was just a dirt road.[11] Nonetheless, by 1915 the term *Hollywood* had become so identified with the movie business that neighboring communities scrambled to associate themselves with its magic. Ivanhoe and Prospect Park reincorporated as East Hollywood, and Lankershim became North Hollywood.[12] Laurelwood, not to be outdone, transformed itself into Studio City.

Beverly Hills, the other southern California name that most of us automatically associate with the movies, and more particularly with *movie stars* (a term coined in 1919), was likewise named on a whim. It was christened in 1907 by a property developer, who named his 3,200-acre housing development (although it had just one house at the time) Beverly Hills after his hometown of Beverly, Massachusetts. It became especially fashionable with the stars after Mary Pickford and Douglas Fairbanks married in 1920 and moved into a Beverly Hills mansion they called Pickfair.

In 1917, the Motion Picture Patents Company was declared an illegal cartel and ordered to disband. It hardly mattered. By that time, Hollywood (and from here on out I use the term generically) all but owned the movie business. It is a curious fact that this most American of phenomena was created almost entirely by non-Americans. Apart from Mack Sennett and Mary Pickford (who were, in any case, both Canadian), the early studios were run by a small band of men who had begun life from strikingly similar backgrounds: they were all eastern European Jews, poor and uneducated, who had left Europe in the same decade (the 1880s) and had established themselves in the New World in mostly lowly trades before they all abruptly—almost instinctively, it would seem—abandoned their careers in the first decade of this century and moved into the nickelodeon business.

Consider: Louis B. Mayer of Metro-Goldwyn-Mayer was a scrap merchant from Lithuania. The Hungarian-born Adolf Zukor of Famous Players Studios was a janitor and later a furrier. Samuel Goldwyn of the Goldwyn Picture Company was a glove salesman from Warsaw. Carl

Laemmle, founder of Universal, was a German who had run a clothing store in Oshkosh, Wisconsin. William Fox (real name Wilhelm Fried) was a Hungarian who worked in the garment industry before founding Fox Pictures. Joseph M. Schenk, creator of Twentieth Century Productions, was a Russian-born fairground showman and pharmacist. The Warner brothers—Albert, Harry, Jack, and Sam—were from Poland and had worked at various mostly menial jobs. None had any link to the entertainment industry. Yet in the first years of the century, as if answering an implanted signal, they all migrated to New York City and became involved in the nickelodeon business—some as owners of nickelodeon parlors, some as makers of films. In the second decade of the century, another signal appears to have gone off in their heads and they decamped en masse for Hollywood.

Some understandable confusion exists concerning Samuel Goldwyn and Metro-Goldwyn-Mayer. Though his name accounts for the middle initial in MGM, Goldwyn was never part of the company. In 1924, he sold out to the Metro studios and Louis B. Mayer, and was astonished to discover that they took his name with them. But then that was no more than Goldwyn himself had done. The Goldwyn Picture Company was not in fact named for Goldwyn, but rather he for it. His real name was Schmuel Gelbfisz, though for his first thirty years in America he had called himself—perhaps a little unwisely—Samuel Goldfish. *Goldwyn* was a portmanteau of the names of the studio's two founders: Samuel Goldfish and Edgar Selwyn. It wasn't until 1918, tired of being the butt of endless fishbowl jokes, that he named himself after his corporation. After the MGM takeover, he had to go to court to win permission to continue making movies under the Goldwyn name.

It would be putting it mildly to say that Goldwyn never entirely mastered the nuances of English. Though many of the expressions attributed to him are apocryphal—he never said "If you want to send a message call Western Union" to a pretentious director who wanted to make a movie with a message—he did actually say "I was on the brink of an abscess," "Gentlemen, include me out," and "You've bitten the hand of the goose that laid the golden egg." Warned that a Broadway production to which he had acquired rights was "a very caustic play," he shot back: "I don't give a damn how much it costs." And a close friend swore that once when they were walking on a beach and the friend said, "Look at the gulls," Goldwyn stopped in his tracks and replied in all seriousness, "How do you know they're not boys?" He had a particular gift for mangling names. He always referred to Mervyn LeRoy as "Moiphy" LeRoy, to Preston Sturges as "Preston Sturgeon," and to Ernst Fegte as "Faggoty."[13]

Not just the studio chiefs but directors, composers, art directors, musicians, and actors were as often as not foreigners working in this quintessentially American medium. The 1938 movie *The Adventures of Robin Hood*, for instance, starred an Australian, Errol Flynn, and an Englishman, Basil Rathbone, was directed by a Hungarian, Michael Curtiz, scored by a Czech, Erich Wolfgang Korngold, and had sets designed by a Pole, Anton Grot. Consider the backgrounds of just a few of those who made Hollywood pulse in its early years: John Ford (born Sean O'Fearna) was Irish, Greta Garbo Swedish, Charlie Chaplin, Alfred Hitchcock, Cary Grant, and Stan Laurel English, William Wyler Alsatian, Billy Wilder Hungarian, Frank Capra Italian (at least by birth), Fred Zinnemann and Erich Von Stroheim Austrian, Ernst Lubitsch German. Never has an industry been more international in its composition or more American in its output.

As the years passed, studios endlessly formed and reformed. Mutual, Reliance, and Keystone formed the Triangle Film Corporation, which, despite having America's three leading directors—D. W. Griffifth, Mack Sennett, and Thomas H. Ince—soon went under. RCA and the Keith Orpheum theater chain teamed up to form RKO. Joseph Schenk's Twentieth Century Pictures and William Fox's Fox Film Corporation merged into Twentieth Century–Fox. Many more fell by the wayside: Star, Biograph, General Film, and even the Edison Company. But Hollywood itself went from strength to strength, filling the world with a distinctively American mix of glamour, adventure, and moral certitude.

If the stars hadn't changed their names already, the studios often did it for them to make them fit more neatly into the pleasantly homogenized heaven that was Hollywood. Names were changed for almost any reason: because they were too dull, too exotic, not exotic enough, too long, too short, too ethnic, too Jewish. Generally, it must be said, the studio bosses knew what they were doing. Who, after all, could imagine John Wayne as Marion Morrison, Judy Garland as Frances Gumm, or Mary Pickford as dowdy Gladys Smith? Spangler Arlington Brugh is a name for a junior high school shop teacher; change it to Robert Taylor and you are already halfway to stardom. Archie Leach might pass muster as the kid who delivers groceries, but if you want a man of the world it's got to be Cary Grant. Doris Kappelhoff is the two-hundred-pound chocoholic who baby-sits your little brother; Doris Day dates the quarterback. Even little Mortimer Mouse had his name changed to Mickey just four years after his creation in 1923.

In the very early days of the movies, stars hadn't had to change their names because they weren't allowed any, at least not as far as their fans were concerned. Until the second decade of the century, actors and actresses weren't billed at all. For years, Mary Pickford was known only as "Little Mary" and Florence Lawrence as "the Biograph girl." Then as producers realized that audiences were drawn to certain faces and even to certain styles of filmmaking, they began billing not just the featured players, but also directors and even sometimes cameramen. The first actress to have her name changed for purposes of enhanced aura (*sex appeal* wouldn't come into general use until the 1940s) is thought to have been one Theodosia Goodman from Cincinnati. Seeking a persona better suited to her dark, exotic looks, someone at the William Fox Company in 1914 played around with the words *Arab* and *death,* and came up with *Theda Bara.* Soon all the studios were at it. Among the stars who found immortality with someone else's name, we can count the following. (Their original names are on the right.)

Rudolph Valentino	Rodolpho d'Antonguolla
Joan Crawford	Lucille Le Sueur
Al Jolson	Asa Yoleson
Bert Lahr	Isidore Lahrheim
Paul Muni	Muni Weisenfreund
Gilbert Roland	Luis Antonio Damoso De Alonzo
Lauren Bacall	Betty Jean Perske
Tony Curtis	Bernard Schwarz
Jack Benny	John Kebelsky
Barbara Stanwyck	Ruby Stevens
Veronica Lake	Constance Ockleman
Susan Hayward	Edyth Marrener
Fredric March	Frederick Bickel
Don Ameche	Dominic Amici
Red Buttons	Aaron Chwatt
Ed Wynn	Isaiah Edwin Leopold
Melvyn Douglas	Melvyn Hesselberg
Kirk Douglas	Issur Danielovitch Demsky
Lee J. Cobb	Leo Jacoby
June Haver	June Stovenour
Rita Hayworth	Margarita Carmen Cansino
Ginger Rogers	Virginia McMath
Mickey Rooney	Joe Yule, Jr.
Jane Wyman	Sarah Jane Faulks
John Garfield	Julius Garfinkle
June Allyson	Ella Geisman
Danny Kaye	David Daniel Kaminsky
Sterling Hayden	Sterling W. Relyea

Rock Hudson	Roy Scherer
Cyd Charisse	Tula Ellice Finklea
Troy Donahue	Merle Johnson
Anne Bancroft	Anna Maria Italiano
Jerry Lewis	Joseph Levitch
Dean Martin	Dino Crocetti
Tab Hunter	Andrew Arthur Kelm
Virgina Mayo	Virginia Jones
W. C. Fields	W. C. Dukinfield
Clifton Webb	Webb Parmelee Hollenbeck
Dorothy Lamour	Dorothy Kaumeyer
Hedy Lamarr	Hedwig Kiesler
Walter Matthau	Walter Mattaschanskayasky
Boris Karloff	William Pratt

No, I don't know why Boris Karloff was thought to be an improvement on Bill Pratt.

In 1926, two new terms entered the language, *Movietone* from the Fox studios and *Vitaphone* from Warner Brothers, and sound movies were on their way. Both employed music and sound effects, but not speech. The *talkies* (often also called the *speakies* in the early days) would have to wait till the following year and the release of *The Jazz Singer*, though even it was only partly speaking. The first all-talking film, a gangster feature called *The Lights of New York*, came in 1928, but such was the quality of sound reproduction that it came equipped with subtitles as well. With sound, movies became not only more popular but immensely more complicated to make.

As the industry evolved through the 1920s and 1930s, still more words were created to describe the types of films Hollywood was making—*cliffhangers, weepies, sobbies* and *tearjerkers, spine-chillers, westerns, serials*—and to denote the types of roles on offer. A character who wept freely was a *tear bucket*. An actress in a melodrama was a *finger-wringer*. A villain was, of course, a *baddie*. Sexy actresses were, by 1933, known as *bombshells*.

Many movie terms, particularly portmanteau words like *cinemaestro* and *cinemactress* and fractured spellings like *laff* and *pix,* originated or were widely popularized by the bible of the movie business, the newspaper *Variety*. Many were short-lived. *Oats opera* for a western, *clicko* for a success, *eight ball* for a failure, *bookritic,* and many others died in infancy, but scores more prospered in the wider world, notably *whodunit,* tie-in, *socko, rave* (in the sense of a review), *flopperoo, palooka* (a word of uncertain derivation), *belly laugh, newscaster, to scram,* and *pushover.*

Behind the scenes, the development of increasingly arcane apparatus brought a rash of new terms: *scrims, flags, gobos, skypans, inky dinks, century stands, flying rigs, match boxes, lupes,* and so on. A *gobo* is a type of black screen (no one seems to know why it is so called), a *skypan* is a big light, an *inky dink* a small one, and a *match box* one smaller still. A *scrim* is a type of light diffuser. The handlers of this equipment enjoyed job titles that were no less strange and intriguing: *focus puller, juicer, Foley artist, gaffer, best boy, supervising drape, inbetweener, wrangler, post-punch surpervisor, swing-gang,* and so on. A *gaffer* (a corruption of *godfather,* originally a sarcastic term for an old person) is the head electrician. *Best boy* is the chief electrician's chief assistant. *Juicers* are those who move electrical equipment around. The *Foley artist* is in charge of sound effects; he's the one who adds the "toosh!" to punches and the "gerdoings!" to ricocheting bullets. The name commemorates Jack Foley, one of the great sound recordists. *Supervising drape* is the person in charge of drapes, rugs, and other such inanimate objects. An *inbetweener* is an animator's assistant—one who draws the frames between the main action frames. *Swing-gangs* are those who build or rebuild sets overnight. *Wranglers* handle the animals, or indeed any living creatures. "Cockroach wrangler" has been recorded in the credits of at least one film. As you will have gathered, often the title is more impressive than the job, and nowhere perhaps more so than with the *post punch supervisor,* whose responsibility essentially is to look after the photocopying.

With so many exotic professions involved, it is little wonder that the credits nowadays often seem to roll on forever. The longest credits yet—for *Who Framed Roger Rabbit?*—lasted for six and a half minutes and saluted 763 creative artists, technicians, and other contributors—without mentioning Kathleen Turner, the voice of Jessica Rabbit, who opted not to be credited.

Huge amounts of effort and emotion go into deciding the order of billing for movie stars—whether the name goes above the title, whether it is larger than the title and by what percentage, and so on. When Paul Newman and Steve McQueen starred in *The Towering Inferno*, the problem of which of these superstars was to enjoy top billing led to protracted negotiations between agents and producers. Eventually it was decided that Newman's name would take the left-hand, pole position, but would be positioned fractionally lower than McQueen's, a practice that has been followed and elaborated on to the point of tedium in movie posters and advertising materials ever since. In 1956, Otto

Preminger appalled the Hollywood community by announcing *The Man with the Golden Arm* as "A Film by Otto Preminger." No one had ever displayed such audacity before, and few have failed to engage in it since. Occasionally a director is so miffed with the handling of a film in postproduction that he demands to have his name removed. The Directors Guild hit on the convention of crediting such disowned movies to the fabled and wholly fictional Allen Smithee, who is thus responsible for such classics as *Ghost Fever, Student Bodies, Morgan Stewart's Coming Home, City in Fear,* a Whitney Houston video, and some two dozen other efforts.[14] The ultimate in screen credits, though, was almost certainly the 1929 production of *The Taming of the Shrew,* starring Douglas Fairbanks and Mary Pickford, which contained the memorable line "By William Shakespeare, with additional dialogue by Sam Taylor."[15] Possibly the most choleric credit line appeared on the 1974 movie *The Taking of Pelham 123*, which concerned the hijacking of a New York subway train and finished with the closing line: "Made without any help whatsoever from the New York Transit Authority."

No discussion of the lexicon of Hollywood would be complete without at least a passing mention of the Oscars and how these golden statuettes got their name. Few terms in any creative field have engendered more varied etymological explanations. The most plausible story perhaps is that the figure was named by Margaret Herrick, a librarian at the Academy of Motion Pictures Arts and Sciences, who said upon seeing the prototype, "Oh, that reminds me of my Uncle Oscar" (whose surname, for the record, was Pierce).[16] What is certain is that the figure of a naked man with a long sword standing on a film can originated as a doodle by Cedric Gibbons, the MGM art director, and that the first one was awarded in 1929.

In 1949, after nearly half a century of seemingly unstoppable growth, Hollywood's executives got a shock when movie attendance slumped from ninety million to seventy million in a single year. Matters would grow increasingly more worrisome for them as the 1950s unfolded and Americans abandoned the movie theaters for the glowing comforts of their own televisions. In desperation, the studios tried to make the most of whatever advantages they could muster. One was color. Color movies had been possible since as far back as 1917, when a Dr. Herbert Kalmus invented a process he called *Technicolor.* The first Technicolor movie was *Toll of the Sea*, made by MGM in 1922. But the process was expensive and therefore little used. In 1947, only about a tenth of movies were in color. By 1954, well over half were. Hollywood studios also responded by forbidding their stars to appear on the new medium, and by denying television networks access to their libraries of films, until it gradually dawned on them that old movies generated money when shown on television and didn't when locked in vaults.

What the studios needed was some new technique, some blockbuster development, that television couldn't compete with. In September 1952 the world—or at least an audience at New York's Broadway Theater—got it with the introduction of a startling new process called *Cinerama*. Employing a curved screen, stereophonic sound, and three projectors, it provided watchers with the dizzying sensation of being on a Coney Island roller coaster or whizzing perilously through the Grand Canyon. People loved it. But Cinerama had certain intractable shortcomings, notably distractingly wobbly lines where the three projected images joined, and an absence of theaters in which it could be shown. It cost $75,000 to convert a theater to Cinerama, more than most could afford. There was also the problem that the process didn't lend itself to narrative performances, and the few Cinerama movies that were made, such as *This Is Cinerama, Cinerama Holiday,* and *Cinerama South Seas Adventure,* consisted mainly of a succession of thrills. In 1962, as a kind of last-gasp effort to save the process (theater owners who had invested heavily in the massive screens and projector systems naturally wanted to put them to use), two narrative films were made, *How the West Was Won* and *The Wonderful World of the Brothers Grimm,* but having to swivel your head to follow a conversation between characters separated by sixty feet of screen was something that audiences failed to warm to. Today, there is just one functioning Cinerama screen in the world, in (of all places) Bradford, England.

In the same year that Cinerama was born, the world was also given 3-D movies. The first was a film called *Bwana Devil,* apparently one of the worst movies ever made. The process involved slightly overlapping images that melded into a three-dimensional whole once the viewer donned special Polaroid glasses with one red and one green lens. Originally called *Natural Vision,* it enjoyed a huge if short-lived vogue—sixty-nine Natural Vision movies were made in 1953 alone—and people flocked in the millions to features like *The Creature from the Black Lagoon* and *The Charge at Feather River* for the dubious thrill of having barge poles thrust at them and, in one particularly memorable scene, having a character appear to spit in their faces. So promising did the process seem at first that some quite respectable movies, notably Hitchcock's *Dial M for Murder,* were filmed in 3-D, though the fad was so short-lived that most, including *Dial M,* were released in the normal flat form.

Before long it was all but impossible to go to a movie that didn't involve some impressive-sounding new technical process. One after another came *Vistarama, Vista Vision, Superscope, Naturama,* even *Aroma-Rama* and *Smell-O-Vision,* in which, as you might surmise, the theater was pumped full of appropriate odors at regular intervals. The problem was that the odors tended to linger and mingle in a perplexing manner, and the members of the audience situated nearest the smell dispensers weren't particularly gratified to find themselves periodically refreshed with a moist outpouring of assorted scents.

A year after Cinerama made its debut, Twentieth Century–Fox came up with a slightly more sophisticated, and certainly less gimicky, process called *CinemaScope,* which required just a single camera with a special anamorphic lens. The first CinemaScope picture was *The Robe.* CinemaScope screens were roughly double the width of a normal movie screen and were slightly curved to give some illusion of depth.[17] CinemaScope's one serious challenger was *Todd-AO* (named for the producer Michael Todd and its developer, the American Optical Company), but it was CinemaScope that won out. By 1955, just two years after its introduction, more than twenty thousand movie theaters throughout the world had installed the CinemaScope system.[18] Hollywood would live to fight another day.

Chapter 16

THE PURSUIT OF PLEASURE: SPORT AND PLAY

The abiding impression of life in Puritan New England that most of us carry with us is that it wasn't a great deal of fun. "Sad-visaged people moving always with sober decorum through a dull routine of work unrelieved by play" is the traditional view expressed by the historian John Allen Krout in 1929.[1]

In fact, it wasn't quite like that. Though they could scarcely be described as a bunch of cutups, the Puritans were not averse to pleasure. They smoked and drank, and enjoyed games and contests as much as anybody, particularly those involving physical challenges like footraces and wrestling, or that honed useful skills like archery. Increase Mather called recreation "a great duty," and at Harvard College the students were not merely permitted but actively encouraged to take part in "lawful" games.[2]

And *lawful* is the operative word. What the Puritans didn't like were activities deemed to be an encouragement to idleness or ungodliness—and of these, it must be said, they found many. Among the amusements they forbade at one time or another were quoits, ninepins, bowls, stoolball, and even shuffleboard. Games involving dice and cards were entirely out of the question. Plays, entertainments, "dancing and frisking," and "other crafty science" were equally abhorrent to them. Maypoles were cut down and even Christmas was abjured. Smoking was acceptable only within certain well-prescribed bounds. Connecticut had a statute forbidding inhabitants from taking "tobacco publiquely in the street, nor shall any take yt in the fyelds or woods."[3] On Sundays, no recreation of any sort was permitted. Even going for a stroll was forbidden. Indeed, even sitting quietly could land you in trouble. One hapless couple found themselves hauled before magistrates for no graver offense than being found "sitting together on the Lord's Day, under an apple tree."[4]

Oddly, none of this was inherent in Calvinist doctrine. Calvin himself was known to enjoy a lively game of bowls on a Sunday afternoon. Nothing in their pre-American experience had suggested that the Pilgrims would institute such an aggressive crackdown on fun.

To understand why this happened in New England, it is necessary to reexamine two commonly held conceptions about the Puritans. The first is the belief that they had come to America to establish freedom of religion. In truth, freedom of worship was the last thing they wanted. Having suffered years of persecution on their native soil, they desired nothing from America so much as the opportunity to establish a system of equal intolerance of their own. The second misconception is the belief that the colonization of New England was primarily pious in its impulse. In fact, throughout the early period, Puritans were decidedly—indeed, uncomfortably—in the minority. The great bulk of early Pilgrims were attracted to America not by religious zeal but by the hope of a better life. Between 1630 and 1640, of the sixteen thousand immigrants to Massachusetts, only one in four was a Puritan.[5] Even on the *Mayflower,* the Saints had been outnumbered sixty-one to forty-one by Strangers. Both of these considerations worked powerfully on the Puritan psyche. From the outset they became jealously possessive of their moral authority in the New World, and in consequence they showed a decidedly neurotic preoccupation with activities that might be construed as a challenge to their preeminence.

But beyond this there was a practical side to their detestation of idleness. Building a community in a wilderness was a terribly earnest undertaking, and one that did not admit of much leisure. Yet many of the non-Puritan settlers showed a vexing willingness to down tools and engage in play on any convenient pretext. Thus when on Christmas Day 1621 (almost precisely a year after their landing), Governor William Bradford found a group of impious Strangers "in the streete at play, openly; some pitching the barr and some at stoole-ball," and huffily took their implements from them, he was offended not merely by their celebration of a holiday not recognized by his sect, but at the wanton and dangerous frittering away of time and energy that might have been directed to securing their survival.

Such concerns were far from unique to New England. In Virginia, too, outsiders were often appalled at how little the inhabitants attended to their well-being and security. Thomas Dale, arriving with supplies in 1611, found the residents on the brink of extinction but playing at bowls. Soon after, the Virginia Assembly enacted restrictive laws very similar to those of New England, making it illegal to gamble, to be found incapacitated by drink, to fail to observe the Sabbath, even to dress "in excess." None of this was motivated by a desire to help them tread the narrow path to heaven, but rather by the need to bring order and discipline to a vulnerable community.

When a celebration was deemed in order, the Puritans were delighted to let their hair down. The first Thanksgiving feast went on for three full days and involved, in addition to copious eating and drinking, such diversions as stoneball, a game similar to croquet, and competitions of running, jumping, arm wrestling, shooting, and throwing. No one knows quite when this first Thanksgiving took place, other than that it was sometime between the beginning of October and the first week of November 1621. Nor was it regarded as the start of an annual tradition. No Thanksgiving appears to have been held the following year, and the Plymouth colony would not begin regular celebrations until almost the end of the century. For the rest of New England, Thanksgiving didn't become an annual tradition until about the 1780s. For the nation as a whole, Thanksgiving wasn't fixed as a holiday until President Lincoln so decreed it in 1863. The date he chose was August 6. The following year it was moved, arbitrarily, to the last Thursday in November, where it has remained ever since, apart from a brief period during the Depression when it was brought forward seven days to give stores an extra week of potential Christmas shopping.[6]

Christmas likewise got off to an erratic start in America, not least because the Puritans disdained it, regarding it (not altogether inaccurately) as a pagan festival. In 1659, they went so far as to ban it, and it remained widely suppressed in New England into the 1800s.[7] Partly because of this interruption of tradition, Christmas as we celebrate it now is a mongrel accumulation of practices from many lands.

Gift-giving, which has no intrinsic connection with Christmas, we borrowed from Holland. From the Middle Ages, the Dutch had made a custom of giving presents to children on December 6, St. Nicholas Day. St. Nicholas was a shadowy figure from Asia Minor whose many kindly deeds included bestowing bags of gold on three young women who otherwise faced a life of prostitution. Over time these three bags evolved into three golden balls and became, by some complicated leap of logic, the three balls associated with pawnbroking. In the late eighteenth century, St. Nicholas and the presents that went with him were borrowed from the Dutch but transferred to the nearest Anglican holiday, December 25. At the same time, the now wholly secular figure of Santa Claus became bizarrely bound up with *Christkindlein,* the Christ child, and thus took on the alternative designation *Kris Kringle.*

The Christmas tree and the practice of sending greeting cards arrived from Germany—they are often attributed to Queen Victoria's German consort, Prince Albert—and gradually became part of the Christmas tradition in the nineteenth century. The first mention of a Christmas tree in America is 1846. Carols (etymologically related to *choral*), mistletoe, holly, and the yule log all come from Britain, mostly as survivors of a pre-Christian past. (*Yule* itself is pre-Saxon Germanic and evidently commemorates a forgotten pagan festival.)

The American attitude toward Christmas and how to celebrate it was long ambivalent. On the one hand, Macy's was staying open till midnight on Christmas Eve as far back as 1867 in order to deal with the clamor to buy presents; on the other, the practice of decorating trees was so late in developing that even in 1880 a manufacturer of ornaments could persuade F. W. Woolworth to take no more than $25 of his stock. (Before the decade was out, however, Woolworth had upped the order to $800,000.)[8]

Many of our other holidays didn't come into existence until comparatively recent times. Memorial Day, at first called Decoration Day, dates from 1868. Labor Day didn't exist until 1894. Veterans Day (until 1954 called Armistice Day) began in 1918, and Columbus Day is as recent as 1934. It may come as a surprise to learn that officially there are no national holidays in America. One of the rights reserved to the states was the prerogative to decree holidays. The President can, with the assent of Congress, declare "legal public holidays," but these apply only to the District of Columbia and federal employees and have no formal sanction elsewhere. One of the odder features of national holidays in America is that only one, New Year's, is associated with drinking and general carousing, and none goes on for more than a day. Elsewhere drunken revels lasting up to a week are common. Even the pleasure-cautious British make Christmas into a two-day event with the addition of Boxing Day, December 26 (so called because menials were traditionally given boxes of food and other gifts on that day), and generally drink themselves silly throughout this agreeably extended period.

In America, if revelries were seldom given official sanction, they generally found private outlets. Though those who governed the early American colonies tried almost everywhere to subdue the national impulse to engage in dissolute pursuits, they didn't often succeed. Cockfighting, dogfighting, bearbaiting, drinking to excess, and gambling were available to anyone who wished to find them, and not just on scattered feast days. Horse racing, too, was widely popular, especially in Virginia, though suitable venues that offered a level surface and a measure of privacy were not always easy to find. Outside Jamestown there existed a particularly favorable stretch of road a quarter of a mile long. It became so popular as a location for illicit races that it led to the breeding of a new strain of horse, the quarter horse, which lacked stamina but could sprint at enormous speed for short distances.[9] Horse racing would later endow the American vocabulary with a wealth of terms, among them *frontrunner, inside track, to win by a nose, sure thing, also-ran,* and *bookie,* though some of these would have to wait a while before finding general acceptance. *Bookie,* for instance, isn't found in print before 1885.[10]

In the Appalachian region, wrestling—or *wrassling*—of a particularly brutal nature became popular early on and evidently stayed both brutal and popular up to this century. Many of those who settled the region hailed from northern England, home of Cumberland and Westmorland wrestling, a contest that is thought to date from Viking times and remains popular to this day at country fêtes and other such gatherings throughout the English Lake District and slightly beyond. In it, two men embrace in a standing position, and with occasional bursts of grunting exertion, mixed with longer periods of strategic stillness (during which a spectator could be excused for thinking that they had temporarily nodded off), try to throw each other to the ground. It was, and in England remains, a gentlemanly pursuit. In the more rough-and-tumble environment of Kentucky and Virginia, however, Cumberland and Westmorland wrestling evolved into something considerably more aggressive. Anything was permissible—biting, maiming, gouging, kicking—so long as it was done without weapons. Competitors grew long curved thumbnails, the better to gouge out eyes, and sometimes filed their teeth to sharp points for more destructive biting.

Fischer recounts the story of a fight between two men—and if you are squeamish you might just want to flit your eyes to the next paragraph—in which the winner secured an early advantage by gouging his opponent's eyes from his head with his thumbs. "The sufferer roared aloud, but uttered no complaint," recorded an eyewitness, and astonishingly refused to give up the fight. Not until his opponent had additionally bitten off his nose and torn his ears from his head did he at last conclude that discretion and the loss of a usable face were the better part of valor.[11]

Naturally, large sums of money changed hands at these spectacles. The Puritan ethic notwithstanding, Americans evinced an irrepressible urge to wager from the earliest days. Early gambling pursuits gave us many terms that have since passed into general usage. *Tinhorn,* meaning cheap or disreputable, comes from a metal cylinder of that name used to shake dice in games like *chuck-a-luck* (or *chutter-luck*) and *hazard. Pass the buck* came from the custom of passing a buckhorn knife as a way of keeping track of whose turn it was to deal or ante, and thus it is etymologically unrelated to *buck* as a slang term for dollar. The American passion for gambling made *bet* a commonplace in the wider language in expressions like *you bet I do, you bet your life,* and so on, which foreign observers commonly noted as a distinguishing characteristic of American speech by the early nineteenth century. Mark Twain told the story of a Westerner who had to break the news of Joe Toole's death to his widow. "Does Joe Toole live here?" the Westerner asks, and when the wife answers in the affirmative, he says, "Bet you he don't!"[12]

Among the favorite card games until about the time of the American Revolution were *whist* (a word of unknown derivation, but possibly related to *whisk*), *brag* (so called because of the bravado required of bettors), and *muggins* (source of a once-common expression for a gullible person or victim of fate). By the closing years of the century, these were giving way to *faro,* a game first mentioned in Britain in 1713. Corrupted from *pharaoh* (a pharaoh was pictured on one of the cards of a faro deck; it later evolved into the king of hearts), faro was a dauntingly complicated game in terms of equipment, scoring, betting, and vocabulary. Each card dealt had a name of obscure significance. The first was the *soda card,* the second the *loser,* and so on to the final card, the *hock;* hence the expression *from soda to hock,* and also *to be in hock.*[13] Scoring was kept track of on an abacuslike device called a *case,* from which is said to come the expression *an open and shut case. To break even* and *to play both ends against the middle* also originated in faro, as did the practice of referring to counters as *chips* (previously they had been called *checks*). Thus most of the many expressions involving *chips*—*to cash in one's chips, to be in the chips, a blue-chip investment*—owe their origins to this now forgotten game.[14]

Gradually faro was displaced by *poker.* Dispute surrounds the origins of the name. The most plausible guess is that it comes from a similar German game called *pochspiel,* in which players who passed would call "Poche," pronounced "polka."[15] Others have suggested that it may have some hazy connection to *poke* or *puck* (an English dialectal word meaning to strike, whence the name of the hard black disk used in ice hockey) or to the Norse-Danish *pokker,* "devil," from which comes the *Puck* of English folklore. At all events, *poker* is an Americanism first recorded in 1848. In its very early days it was also commonly referred to as *poko* or *poka.*

Among the many terms that have passed into the main body of English from poker are *deal* in the sense of a transaction (e.g., *business deal*), *jackpot, penny-ante, to stand pat, just for openers,* and *four-flusher* (that is, one who tries to make a flush with four cards rather than the requisite five).

Jackpot is of uncertain provenance. The *jack* may refer to the card of that name or to the slang term for money, or possibly it may be simply another instance of the largely inexplicable popularity of *jack* as a component with which to build words: *jackhammer, jackknife, jackboot, jackass, jack-in-the-box, jack-o'-lantern, jack-of-all-trades, jackrabbit, jackstraw, jackdaw, jackanapes, lumberjack,* and *car jack.* In none of these, so far as is known, does *jack* contain any particular significance. People clearly just liked the sound of it.

According to Dillard, *ace, deuce,* and *trey,* for *one, two,* and *three,* are also American, through the influence of French gamblers of New Orleans. He may be right in the case of *trey,* but the first two were in common use in Britain in the Middle Ages and may date from Norman times. *Ace* comes ultimately from the Latin *as,* a basic unit of currency, and *deuce* from the Latin *duos,* or *two.* The French gamblers of New Orleans did, however, give us another venerable gambling term: *to shoot craps.* In New Orleans the game the English called *hazard* became known as *crabs,* which mutated over time into *craps.* It has no etymological connection to the slang term for feces. The French were also ultimately responsible for *keno* (from *quine,* "a set of five"), an early form of bingo that was once very popular, though it left no linguistic legacy beyond its name.

More productive in terms of its linguistic impact was a much later introduction to America, *bridge,* which arrived from Russia and the Mideast in the early 1890s. The word is unrelated to the type of bridge that spans a river. It comes from the Russian *birich,* the title of a town crier. Among the expressions that have passed from the bridge table to the world at large are *bid, to follow suit, in spades, long suit,* and *to renege.*[16]

At about the time that bridge was establishing itself in America, a native-born gaming device was born: the *slot machine.* Slot machines of various types were produced in America as early as the 1890s, but they didn't come into their own until 1910, when an enterprising firm called the Mills Novelty Company introduced a vending machine for chewing gum, which dispensed gum in accordance with flavors depicted on three randomly spinning wheels. The flavors were cherry, orange, and plum—symbols that are used on slot machines to this day. Each wheel also contained a bar reading "1910 Fruit Gum," three of which in a row led to a particularly lavish payout, just as it does today. Also just as today a lemon in any row meant no payout at all—and from this comes *lemon* in the sense of something that is disappointing or inadequate. The potential of slot machines for higher stakes than pieces of chewing gum wasn't lost on the manufacturers, and soon, converted to monetary payouts, they were appearing everywhere that gambling was legal, though no one thought to call them *one-armed bandits* until the 1950s.[17]

Partly in response to the popularity of gambling, a pious young New Englander named Anne Abbott invented a wholesome alternative in 1843: the *board game*. Board games like chess and checkers had, of course, been around for centuries in almost all cultures, but never before had anyone devised a competitive entertainment in which players followed a path through a representation of the real world. Abbott intended the game not just as an amusement, but as an aid to upright living. Called *The Mansion of Happiness*, it required competitors to travel the board in pursuit of Eternal Salvation, avoiding such pitfalls along the way as Perjury, Robbery, Immodesty, Ingratitude, and Drunkenness. The idea of moving a playing piece along a route beset with hazards was hugely novel in 1843, and not only made Abbott a tidy sum but also inspired a flock of imitators.

One was a young man named Milton Bradley, who produced his first hit, *The Checkered Game of Life,* in 1860. Also morally uplifting, it was clearly inspired by, if not actually modeled on, Abbott's elevating divertissement. Bradley's most original stroke, however, came when he devised a way of packing eight separate games, among them checkers, chess, backgammon, and dominoes, into a small, easily portable box, which proved a hit with soldiers during the Civil War.

Rather more innovative was George Swinton Parker, founder of the second great name of the American games industry, Parker Brothers. Born into a venerable but declining family in Salem, Massachusetts, Parker loved the idea of board games, but hankered for a reward more immediately gratifying than future salvation. In 1883, aged just sixteen, he created a game called *Banking* in which the object was to speculate one's way to wealth. A new games-playing ethos was born, one that seized the imagination of Americans. This was more like it. As the writer Peter Andrews has put it: "Instead of the most pious player reaping the most joy in the next world, the smartest player got the most money in this one."[18]

With two of his brothers, Parker built the family firm into the biggest games company in the world. Parker himself invented more than a hundred games—or, more accurately, more than a hundred variations of essentially the same game. Almost always they were built around some world event or technological breakthrough that had recently seized the popular imagination. Among his more popular creations were *Klondike, Pike's Peak or Bust, The Motor Carriage Game, War in Cuba, The Siege of Havana,* and *The Philippine War* (death and destruction proving nearly as irresistible to games players as accumulating a pile of fantasy money).

However, the game that secured the company's fortunes was not invented by Parker or anyone else connected with the company. It was created during the early years of the Great Depression by one Charles Darrow, an unemployed salesman from Germantown, Pennsylvania, who sketched out the prototype on a piece of oilcloth spread out on his kitchen table and called it *Monopoly.* Darrow named the places on the Monopoly board after the streets of his favorite resort, Atlantic City, although one of the properties, *Marvin Gardens,* wasn't in Atlantic City but in the neighboring community of Margate, and was spelled *Marven.* The board also deviated from the truth with the name of one of the railroads, *Short Line,* which was actually a local bus company.

In 1934, Darrow submitted Monopoly to Parker Brothers. The company's executives dutifully tried the game but weren't impressed. They concluded that it had "fifty-two fundamental errors." For one thing, there was no finishing line, no visible ultimate goal. The idea of going around the board again and again struck them as faintly absurd. Then there was all this confusing business of mortgages and variable rents. All in all, the rules were too complicated and the game took too long to play. Clearly it would never sell, and they politely turned him down.

Undaunted, Darrow made up some games himself and took them to Wanamaker's Department Store in Philadelphia, where they became a local sensation. When Parker Brothers learned of this, it decided to give the game a try. In the first year, it sold a million Monopoly sets, a figure unknown in the world of games, and it has remained the best-selling board game in America ever since. His faith in the game vindicated, Darrow retired to an estate in the country, where he grew orchids and counted his money. He died in 1967.

Monopoly was the great craze of the early 1930s, but crazes had been a feature of American life since the 1820s, when the word unexpectedly took on the sense of a sudden widespread mania. (Previously it had signified something cracked or broken.) The curious thing about crazes is that they are usually invented elsewhere but taken up in America with such enthusiasm and panache as to make them seem native-born. Such was the case with one of the great nineteenth-century crazes, roller skating, a pastime invented in Holland and introduced to America in 1863.

While Europeans were juddering unsteadily along cobbled streets, Americans were building vast skating palaces like the Casino in Chicago and the Olympian Club Roller Skating Rink in San Francisco. Such places could accommodate up to a thousand skaters at a time on their polished ash and maple floors. Often they had their own orchestras, playing tunes to which the audience could perform the latest, American-invented steps like the *Philadelphia Twist,* the *Richmond Roll,* the *Picket Fence,* and the *Dude on Wheels.*

Much the same happened with the bicycle. Before an Englishman named J. I. Stassen coined the term *bicycle* in 1869, two-wheeled vehicles had gone by a variety of names: *velocipedes, dandy horses, draisines,* and *boneshakers. Boneshaker* was particularly apt. Early bikes ran on wooden wheels, had wooden saddles, and of course ran over much less smoothly paved surfaces. Early models were propelled either by pushing the feet along the ground or by means of a complicated treadle mechanism. Most came without brakes. They were, in short, neither safe nor comfortable. But they were hugely popular.

Soon people everywhere were getting in on the mania for *wheeling,* as it was known. Cycling quickly developed its own complex terminology. The more energetic adherents went in for *scorching* or *freewheeling* (sometimes shortened by the linguistically debonair to *freeling*). Scorchers who showed a selfish disregard of others were known as *road hogs.* Such was their capacity to startle or surprise other road users—one popular model was called the *Surprise*—that in some places laws were passed requiring cyclists not simply to slow down and dismount when approaching a horse, but to lead it to safety before continuing.[19]

As early as 1882, people were referring to them familiarly as *bikes.* Such was the popularity of the sport that in 1885 a playing card company in Cincinnati was inspired to try to cash in on the craze, which is how *Bicycle* brand playing cards came about. By the mid-1880s, cycling seemed to be as popular as a sport could get, but in 1888 came the invention of the pneumatic tire by the Scotsman John Dunlop, which, with other developments like lighter frames, handbrakes, gears, and safety chains, moved biking onto an even higher plane of popularity.

A large part of bicycling's popularity was that it was one of the few exhilarating enjoyments permitted to women, though some authorities worried that perhaps it was too exhilarating. The *Georgia Journal of Medicine and Surgery,* for one, believed that cycling was unsuitable for females because the movements of the legs and the pressure on the pelvis of the saddle were bound to arouse "feelings hitherto unrealized by the young maiden."[20] *Wheelman* magazine defended bicycling as a healthy pursuit for women, but added this ominous warning to its female readers: "Do not think of sitting down to table until you have changed your underclothing."

By 1895, ten million bicycles crowded U.S. roads, and manufacturers were producing a vast range of vehicles with jaunty, buy-me names like the *Sociable,* the *Quadrant,* the *Rudge Triplet Quadricycle,* and the *Coventry Convertible Four in Hand.* The craze looked set to run forever, but less than a decade later most people had packed up their bikes forever, having lost their hearts entirely to the greatest of all American passions, the automobile.

The first two decades of the twentieth century were a period of relative calm in the world of crazes, but in the 1920s, America made up for lost time. Among the phenomena that gripped the nation in that lively decade were dance marathons, flagpole-sitting competitions (the champion was an Alvin "Shipwreck" Kelly who maintained his perilous perch atop a Baltimore flagpole for twenty-three days and seven hours), beauty contests, coast-to-coast car races, coast-to-coast foot races known as *bunion derbies,* and miniature golf.

Miniature golf—at first called *dwarf golf*—was born in 1927 when a developer named Garnet Carter built a resort hotel called Fairyland on Lookout Mountain in Tennessee and added a miniature links complete with mechanical hazards. He intended it as a diversion for children, but to his astonishment the adults soon drove the mites off. Realizing that there must be something in this, Carter formed a company called Tom Thumb Golf and began producing factory-built courses. In just three years, 25,000 Tom Thumb courses were erected across America.[21]

At home, three other forms of amusement entered the American vocabulary in the period. One was *mahjong* (or *mah-jongg*), a game from China that swept the nation beginning in 1922. Mahjong—the name is Mandarin for "house sparrow," from a figure on the most important piece—was particularly fashionable among the *smart set* (a term roughly contemporaneous with the birth of the game in America). People paid up to $500 for their mahjong sets—more than the cost of a Model A Ford. Some even redecorated rooms of their houses in the Chinese style and invested in silk robes for themselves and their guests to help the mood along. For a decade or so, you couldn't hope to move in society if you didn't know the difference between a *South Wind* and a *Red Dragon,* or failed to comprehend cries of "Pung!" "Chow!" and "Broke the wall!"[22]

Rather less fashionable but no less influential was *ouija.* (The name is a portmanteau of the French and German words for "Yes.") Ouija, in which devotees place their hands on a small pointer that glides across the board picking out letters and numbers in response to questions, was invented sometime in the nineteenth century (accounts vary considerably both to year and place) but found a ready following in America in the 1920s, to such an extent that the *Baltimore Sun* appointed a Ouija Editor. As a widespread entertainment, ouija had faded by the 1940s, though occasionally it popped back into popularity and even sometimes into the news, as in 1956 when the descendants of an heiress named Helen

Dow Peck discovered to their horror that she had left her considerable fortune to a John Gale Forbes—a person of whom she apparently knew nothing—because his name had been revealed to her during a session with a ouija board almost forty years before. Fortunately for the descendants, no such person could be found and they got to keep the money.[23]

The final component of this home entertainment trio of the 1920s was the one that proved the most durable: the *crossword puzzle*. At first called a *word-cross,* the crossword puzzle was invented in 1913 by an Englishman employed by the *New York World* newspaper, but it didn't catch on in a big way until a small publishing company called Simon & Schuster published a crossword puzzle book in 1924. Like mahjong and ouija, it quickly became a national passion to such an extent that the Baltimore and Ohio Railroad put dictionaries in its passenger compartments for the benefit of crossword-addicted travelers—but unlike the first two it never faltered in popularity. Today, solving crossword puzzles remains the most popular sedentary amusement in America outside of watching television.

At about the same time that crossword puzzles, ouija boards, and mahjong were seizing America's attention, baseball became known as the *national pastime,* though it had effectively been that for the better part of a century. No one knows where or when baseball was first played. It has often been suggested that the game evolved from the English children's game *rounders.* Baseball and rounders do have unquestionable similarities—in both the batter hits a pitched ball and then sprints around a base path—but the difficulty is that the *Oxford English Dictionary* can find no citation for rounders before 1856, by which time baseball as both a sport and a name was firmly established in American life. (No one seems to have explored the possibility that rounders might in fact be derived from baseball.)

What is certain is that baseball's antecedents go back to well before the *Mayflower.* Cricket, played since the sixteenth century in England and commonly in America until the nineteenth, appears to be the grandfather of all bat-and-ball games, but many others followed in both Britain and America over the next two centuries—*tipcat* (or *kitcat*), *bittle-battle, stick ball, one old cat, two old cat, three old cat,* and *base* or *base-ball,* among others.* All involved the same principles of striking a ball with a stick or paddle and trying to traverse a defined path before being caught or thrown out by the fielding side. The first mention of baseball

*Cricket derives its curious name from an old French word, *criquet,* describing the sound made by a ball striking wood. The insect the cricket also comes from *criquet.*

is found not in America but in Britain, in a children's book called *A Pretty Little Pocket Book, Intended for the Amusement of Little Master Tommy and Pretty Miss Polly*, published in London in 1744.[24] But ball games by this time were already well rooted in America. The first mention of a bat in the context of American play is 1734, and there are many references throughout eighteenth-century America to ball games and their implements. The Boston Massacre, for instance, was provoked in part by someone waving a tipcat bat in a threatening manner at the British troops, and soldiers at Valley Forge are known to have passed the time in 1778 by "playing at base."[25]

By the early nineteenth century, ball games in America appear to have settled for the most part into a general form known as *town ball,* which came in two similar versions, the *Massachusetts game* and the *New York game.* The diverse etymologies of baseball terminology—*innings, shortstop, outfielder,* and so on—indicate that the modern game arose not as an outgrowth of any particular sport but by borrowing and absorbing elements from a variety of games. The question is, who was responsible for melding these disparate elements into a unified game?

The traditional answer is Abner Doubleday. According to David Hackett Fischer, "Doubleday appears to have codified one of many sets of rules before 1840." Fischer notes that Doubleday did not invent baseball, but, he adds, "neither was his association mythical, as some revisionists have suggested."[26]

In fact, it was entirely mythical. Responsibility for the Doubleday legend rests ultimately with Albert Goodwill Spalding, who was an outstanding ballplayer and an astute businessman but an undiscriminating historian. After a brief but distinguished baseball career—in just five seasons with the Boston Red Stockings and the Chicago White Stockings, he had a pitching record of 241–60, becoming baseball's first 200-game winner—Spalding opened a sporting goods store in Chicago, which grew into one of the world's largest manufacturers of sports equipment. By 1903, he was a seriously wealthy man and a figure of godlike authority among baseball followers.

In that same year—the year that also saw the first modern World Series, the Wright Brothers' first flight, and Henry Ford's first Model A—Henry Chadwick, editor of the respected *Baseball Guide*, wrote a short history of the game in which he traced its probable origins to rounders and cricket.* The patriotic Spalding was mortified at the

---

*Among his other accomplishments, Chadwick was responsible for baseball's system of scoring. It was he who bequeathed to us the mysterious practice of writing *K* for a strikeout. The explanation is that in the early days of baseball a person who

thought that baseball might not be an all-American invention. After stewing over the matter for two years, in 1905 he appointed a six-man commission to look into the question. The commission was guided by A. G. Mills, president of the National League and, it so happened, a friend for thirty years of the recently deceased Abner Doubleday. In 1907, the commission issued a report in which it stated without substantiation that the game was created by Doubleday at Cooperstown, New York, in 1839. When pressed for details, Mills revealed that he had heard the story from "a reputable gentleman" named Albert Graves, whose word he had accepted without question. (Graves would shortly end up in a lunatic asylum.)

To anyone who looked into the matter even slightly, it was obvious that the story didn't hold water. For one thing, Doubleday was not at Cooperstown in 1839, but at West Point, and in any case his family had left Cooperstown in 1837. At his death, Doubleday had left sixty-seven diaries, and not once in any of them did he mention baseball. Finally, if Mills's story is to be believed, not once in their thirty years of close friendship had Doubleday thought to mention to Mills that he had invented the game from which Mills was making his living. The matter was so preposterous that no one paid any attention to it until twenty-three years later when a Cooperstown businessman named Stephen C. Clark built a grand hotel to which few people came, partly because of the newly arrived Great Depression and partly because no one much went to Cooperstown anyway. Realizing that what Cooperstown needed was an attraction, Clark exhumed the Doubleday report and interested the major leagues in opening a Baseball Hall of Fame, and the rest is history. There is good reason to believe that the first Commissioner of Baseball, Kenesaw Mountain Landis, knew or at least strongly suspected that Doubleday never invented the game, but allowed the project to go ahead anyway.[27] Today even the Hall of Fame doesn't pretend that Doubleday has any connection with the birth of the game.

Insofar as baseball can be said to have a founder, it was Alexander Cartwright, a member of the New York Knickerbockers Club who in 1845 drew up a set of rules based on the form of town ball known as the New York game. In its rudiments, Cartwright's version of the game was very like that of today. It incorporated nine-player teams and an infield in the shape of a diamond with bases ninety feet apart. Three strikes made an out, and three outs concluded a team's at bat.

---

went down swinging was said to have *struck*. Because there was already a confusion of *S*'s scattered across his scoresheet, Chadwick decided to use the last letter of *struck: K*.

But in its details the game that Cartwright and his immediate successors played was replete with differences. For one thing, fielders could put out opponents by catching the ball on the first bounce as well as on the fly, or by hitting them with the ball as they ran (an option that no doubt brought fielders the most pleasure if not the most outs). They wouldn't wear protective gloves until the 1890s. Before that they caught balls barehanded or sometimes in their hats. The pitcher stood much closer to the batter than now, threw with an underhand delivery, and was required to keep offering pitches until the *batter* (an Americanism of 1824) found a pitch he liked. Until as late as 1887 he had to put the pitch where the batter instructed him to.[28] Pitchers stood not on a mound, but in a marked box (hence *to be knocked out of the box*), though they were allowed to take a small run and from quite early on they were able to throw curves, sinkers, and other such aerodynamic dazzlers. (The curveball appears to have been developed in the mid-1860s by W. A. "Candy" Cummings of the Brooklyn Excelsiors and Edmund Davis of Princeton.)

Batters were at first also known as *strikers,* and after 1856 as *batsmen.* The *catcher*—sometimes called a *catcher-out*—stood up to fifty feet behind home plate and would remain cautiously out of range of foul tips until the development of the catcher's mask in the 1890s. The *umpire,* a term first noted in a baseball context in 1856, also stood (or often sat) safely out of the way along the first-base line. In those days the umpire's judgment was trusted even less than now. Important matches also had a referee, whose job was simply to judge the umpire. (*Umpire,* incidentally, is one of those many words in which an initial *n* became attached, like a charged particle, to the preceding indefinite article. In Middle English, one was a *noumpere,* just as an apron was at first a *napron.*) Beginning in 1866 and for about ten years afterward, there was a tenth player, called the *right shortstop* or *right shortfielder,* who covered the shallow outfield between first and second base. *Baseball club* dates from 1855 and *baseball match* from 1856—though both concepts, and almost certainly the words themselves, were common much earlier. *Home run* (at first called a *home*) also dates from 1856. Early players were called *baseballists; baseballer* isn't found before 1886.

Uniforms were strikingly different, too. Cartwright's Knickerbocker Club, for example, wore uniforms of white shirts, blue trousers, and straw boaters, making them look more like the lounging aesthetes in Manet's *Déjeuner sur L'Herbe* than gutsy, knockabout athletes. In fact, they often were more like aesthetes than athletes. The early teams were intended as exclusive fraternal organizations for the upper crust, which is why to this day we call them *clubs.* Often the game was largely incidental to the social gathering afterward. Then two things happened: competition between clubs grew more prickly and intense, and the game spread to the masses, where it became evident that manual laborers often enjoyed certain advantages in terms of strength and endurance over stockbrokers and junior executives. At first, workingmen played in their own leagues—workingmen's matches on Boston Common often began at 5 A.M. so as not to interfere with the players' working day—but before long the gentlemen's teams began quietly recruiting them as paid ringers. Baseball began to lose its wholesome glow as words like *hippodroming* (throwing a game for a bribe) and *revolving* (jumping teams to secure better pay) entered the parlance of the game.

In 1859, when the National Association of Base Ball Players was formed (the *National* in the title was a trifle ambitious, since all the clubs were from greater New York), it insisted on amateurism and gentlemanly behavior. It got neither. As early as 1860, the Brooklyn Excelsiors were paying a salary to a fastball pitcher named Jim Creighton while the New York Mutuals were charging an admission of 10 cents to their matches and dividing the takings among themselves. Fair play was not always the rule of the day either. At least one crucial game was decided when the owner of one team had his dog frighten off an outfielder chasing a fly ball.

By 1869, America had its first forthrightly professional team, the Cincinnati Red Stockings, who racked up a record of fifty-seven wins, no losses, and one tie during the year, and played before crowds of as many as fifteen thousand people.[29] Two years later, after a dispute with the team's owner, the manager of the Red Stockings, Harry Wright, took his team and its name to Boston, which is why the major leagues have two teams with such similar names.

As baseball became increasingly professional, various leagues and alliances formed—including one called, a trifle redundantly, the League Alliance. In 1877 the National Baseball League, the first true major league, was formed.[30] The American League followed in 1901, though it had its roots in the old Western League. Among the early professional teams were the Philadelphia Athletics, Troy Haymakers, Brooklyn Atlantics, Detroit Wolverines, Fort Wayne Kekiongas (an Indian term of uncertain significance), Washington Olympics, Hartford Dark Blues, and Cleveland Spiders, who in 1899 earned the distinction of having the worst record ever recorded in the National League: 20–134. New York alone had the Mutuals, Highlanders, Harlems, Gothams, Putnams, and Eagles. Often the place-name meant little. Hartford played the 1877 season in Brooklyn. Often, too, if a team was out of a pennant race (so called because the competition was literally for a pennant), it didn't bother to make road trips toward the end of the season. Even when the opponent showed up, it wasn't always worth the bother. For their last game of the 1881 season, the Troy Haymakers had a paid attendance of just twelve.

Teams endlessly formed and reformed. Many faded away. Others evolved new identities—sometimes a series of new identities. The Chicago Cubs began life in 1876 as the White Stockings (the name was later appropriated by Charles Comiskey for a rival crosstown team) and between 1887 and 1905 went by a variety of official and unofficial nicknames—the Colts, Black Stockings, Orphans, Cowboys, Rough Riders, Recruits, Panamas, Zephyrs and Nationals—before finally settling down as the Cubs in 1905. A Brooklyn team began calling itself the Bridegrooms after four of its players were married in the same summer, but eventually metamorphosed into Dodgers—or, more specifically, Trolley Dodgers. The name referred not to the players, but to the intrepid fans who had to dodge across a series of trolley lines to reach the ballpark safely. The Pittsburgh Alleghenys became the more alliterative if not geographically apposite Pirates. The Boston Beaneaters became the Boston Braves. The Boston Red Stockings were known alternatively as the Pilgrims or Somersets before they returned to their roots as the Red Sox. The New York Mutuals were also known as the Green Stockings or Chocolate Stockings, depending on what uniforms they wore.

The first World Championship Series began in 1884 and was being shortened to World Series by 1889, though as we have already noted, the first real World Series dates only from 1903, when the upstart Boston Somersets of the newly created American League beat the Pittsburgh Pirates in a best-of-nine series. It was a ludicrously inflated title. Not only was the series not global, it wasn't even representative of the United States. In 1903, there was no team in the major leagues south of Washington, D.C., or west of St. Louis—a pattern that would remain unchanged until the 1950s, when the Athletics, Giants, and Dodgers began a western exodus.[31]

During the period between the 1880s and early 1900s, America's growing infatuation with baseball began to attract the attention of songwriters and other toilers in the popular arts. Most of these early creative efforts have been lost to us, but two have achieved a measure of immortality. The first was the poem "Casey at the Bat," written in 1888 as a trifle by a newspaperman named Ernest Lawrence Thayer. Thayer was an unlikely composer of popular verse. He came from a wealthy New England family and had enjoyed a dazzling career at Harvard, where he had edited the *Lampoon* and graduated *magna cum laude*. Great things were expected of him. Instead, to his parents' unending despair, he accepted a job from his friend William Randolph Hearst as resident hu-

morist on the *San Francisco Examiner.* "Casey at the Bat," a mock epic
poem of thirteen stanzas, famously records the failure of the Mudville
slugger Casey to fulfill his heroic destiny with runners on first and third
and his team down 4–2 in the bottom of the eighth.★ The poem ends
with the memorable lines

> *And somewhere men are laughing, and somewhere children shout;*
> *But there is no joy in Mudville—mighty Casey has struck out.*

It was published to no great acclaim on June 3, 1888. Thayer was paid
$5 for it, and that would very probably have been that except that a few
weeks later, at the other end of the country, an entertainer named William DeWolf Hopper found himself heading a bill for a performance to
which the New York Giants and Chicago White Stockings had been invited. Knowing of this, a friend of Hopper's pulled from his pocket a
poem that he had clipped from the *Examiner* on a recent trip west and
suggested that it would be just the thing for an audience that included
so many ballplayers. Hopper's recitation was a hit—such a hit that it became part of his standing repertoire. By the time he retired, Hopper calculated that he had recited the poem more than ten thousand times.[32]
Thayer never got an additional penny from his creation, and never wrote
another thing of note.

In 1908, a second creative composition became part of the American
cultural treasure chest when a pair of hack songwriters, Jack Norworth
and Albert von Tilzer, dashed off a tune and called it "Take Me Out to
the Ball Game." It was an instant success. Most people are unaware that
the singer of the song is a woman—a kind of early groupie—named
Katie Casey, and very few are familiar with the opening lines:

> *Katie Casey was baseball mad,*
> *Had the fever and had it bad;*
> *Just to root for the hometown crew,*
> *Ev'ry sou, Katie blew*
> *On a Saturday, her young beau*
> *Called to see if she'd like to go*
> *To see a show but Miss Kate said, "No.*
> *"I'll tell you what you can do:"*

★Nearly everyone (including evidently Thayer) assumes that Casey's strikeout
ended the game. In fact, since Mudville was the home team and there was "one
inning more to play," it would have had another at bat.

And then comes that oddly infectious chorus:

> *Take me out to the ball game*
> *Take me out with the crowd . . .*

The other oddity of the song is that neither of its writers had ever been to a ball game.

During its long adolescence in the nineteenth century, baseball generated a vast vocabulary. Among the terms that are still with us: *walk* for a base on balls and *goose egg* for a zero (1866), *fungo* and *double play* (1867), *bunt* (1872), *bullpen* (1877), *shutout* (1881), *bleachers* (1882), *raincheck* (1884), *southpaw* (1885), *charley horse* (1888), *fan* in the sense of supporter (1890s), *doubleheader* (1896), and *to play ball* in the sense of to cooperate (1901). But this is only the barest sampling. An exhaustive list would run to several pages.* For *hit* alone, more than a hundred terms had been recorded by 1938—*Texas Leaguer, squib, nubber, banjo, stinker, humpie, drooper,* and so on.[33]

Only sometimes do we know the derivation of these terms. *Southpaw* has been attributed to Charles Seymour of the *Chicago Times,* because pitchers at the city's old West Side ballpark faced west and thus a lefthander would face the batter with his throwing arm on his south side. *Bleachers* has been credited to another Chicago sportswriter, who applied it to those unfortunates who had to sit in an uncovered portion of grandstand and thus were "bleached" by the sun.[34] Mencken traces *charley horse* to a player named Charley Esper of the Baltimore Orioles, who "walked like a lame horse," but Flexner points out that the term was in use six years before Esper started playing.[35] *Banjo hit,* dating from 1925, was coined by the appealingly named Snooks Dowd of the Jersey City Giants, and evidently alludes to the plinking banjolike sound made by a poorly hit ball.

Other terms are much less certain. *Bullpen* is often said to have arisen because that is where ads for Bull Durham tobacco were placed, but the story owes more to folk mythology than to any documentary evidence. It is at least as likely to have been called the bullpen because of its similarity to the place where bulls were kept. At all events, the first reference to it, in the *Cincinnati Enquirer* in 1877, is not to an area where pitchers were confined, but to a place where fans were herded. Not un-

*One of the most complete was compiled by H. L. Mencken for his second supplement to *The American Language.* If you consult it, you may notice that one of Mencken's principal sources for the etymology of baseball terms was also named Bill Bryson: my father.

til 1910 did it come to signify a warm-up area for pitchers. *Fans* in the sense of enthusiasts is presumed to be a shortening of *fanatics,* but the conclusion is only speculative. Mencken suggests that it may come from *fancy,* as in *to fancy someone's chances.* In the early days, in any case, supporters weren't called fans but *cranks,* presumably because they cranked up the home team with their cheering. *Fungo* as a term for a warm-up or practice game is entirely mysterious. The earliest reference to it, in the 1867 edition of Chadwick's *Base Ball Reference,* gives no hint of its etymology. *Fungo bat* isn't recorded until 1938. Nor do we have any idea why ballplayers chasing after practice fly balls are said to be *shagging* them or why those engaged in an argument are said to be having a *rhubarb.* The latter term has been traced to 1946 and the Yankee broadcaster Red Barber but otherwise is unexplained.

Baseball remains one of the most fertile grounds for inventive wordplay in American life. Among the more notable—and on the face of it more bewildering—recent neologisms are *to dial 8* for a home run and *Linda Ronstadt* for a good fastball. *Dial 8* comes from the practice among hotels of requiring customers to dial 8 for a long-distance line. *Linda Ronstadt,* more complicatedly, is an allusion to her song "Blue Bayou," the significance of which becomes less puzzling when you reflect that a good fastball "blew by you."

Baseball terms presumed to be new often are not. *Cup of coffee* for a brief spell in the majors (so called because the named party had time for little else) and *can of corn* for a high fly ball were listed in *USA Today* in 1991 as "recent lingo," but in fact both were widely used in the 1920s.[36]

During the long period that baseball was developing from a gentleman's recreation to the national pastime, another sport was shaping up to challenge its unquestioned preeminence. I refer, of course, to football—or *American football,* as the rest of the world knows it. As a term, *football* has existed in English since 1486. In its early days it primarily signified an annual competition in which the inhabitants of neighboring English villages would try to kick or shove an inflated animal bladder between two distant points. Eventually, in a more organized form it evolved into two principal sports, *rugby* (after the English school of that name where it was first played in 1864) and *soccer* (from British university slang and current only since 1891). Outside North America, *soccer* is rarely heard.

In its earliest manifestations in America, football wasn't so much a sport as legalized mayhem, very like the village sport of medieval England. Beginning at Yale in about 1840, it became customary for freshmen to take on upperclassmen in a vast, disorderly shoving match at the epicenter of which was a makeshift ball. After one such match, the *New*

York Post fretted: "Boys and young men knocked each other down, tore off each other's clothing. Eyes were bunged, faces blacked and bloody, and shirts and coats torn to rags." Appalled at the injuries and disorder, Yale and Harvard banned the sport in the 1860s.

Students turned their attention away from annual brawls and took up rugby instead. At first, they used the English rules, but gradually they evolved forms of their own—even if they kept much of the terminology, like *offside, fair catch, halfback,* and *scrimmage* (or *scrummage,* from an English dialect word for a tussle, and now shortened in the rugby world to *scrum*). Even with the imposition of some sense of order, play remained undisciplined and dangerous. In 1878, Walter Camp, a Yale student who appears to have been regarded as something of a deity by both his peers and mentors (and not without reason; one of the Yale teams he led outscored its opponents 482 to 2 over the course of one season and 698 to 0 in another), proposed several rules to bring a greater maturity to the game. The principal ones were that teams be limited to eleven players and that each side be granted three chances—or *downs*—to advance the ball five yards. This led to the painting of white lines at five-yard intervals, which by 1897 had inspired the term *gridiron* for a football field.

By about 1880, football and rugby had permanently parted ways in America, and by 1890 Yale was regularly attracting crowds of forty thousand to its football games. Some things had still to change. The center didn't snap the ball with his hands, but kicked it back to the quarterback with his foot. Not until 1904 did a touchdown score more than a field goal. The forward pass wasn't written into the rules until 1906.[37] Even then, no one really understood its possibilities. When it was used, which was rarely, it involved a quarterback lobbing a short pass to a stationary receiver, who would then turn and run with the ball. Not until 1913 did Gus Dorais, the Notre Dame quarterback, and his teammate Knute Rockne come up with the idea of hitting a receiver on the run. In doing so, Notre Dame beat Army 35–13 and entered the realms of legend, at least on the sports pages.

Even with Camp's refinements, football remained violent and dangerous. In 1902, twelve American players died. In 1905, the number rose to seventy-one. To make matters worse, schools began to hire professional players. "One man played, under various pseudonyms, at nine schools over a period of thirteen years," Page Smith notes.[38]

Professional football grew up in mining and factory towns in the early 1900s, and the team names tended to reflect local industries, as with the Pittsburgh Steelers and Green Bay [Meat] Packers. Professional football was slow to establish itself. As late as 1925, the New York Giants franchise was purchased for just $500. Not until the 1950s and the age of television did professional football begin to attract a huge and devoted following.

Although football has spawned a vast internal vocabulary—*T-formation* (1931), *play-off* (1933), and *handoff* and *quarterback sneak* (early 1940s), to name just four—surprisingly few football terms have entered mainstream English. Among the few: *to blindside, cheap shot, game plan,* and *jock* for an athlete (from *jockstrap,* for protective wear, and ultimately from a sixteenth-century English slang term for the penis).[39]

At the time that football was rising to eminence in colleges, another perennially popular sport was taking shape. In the fall of 1891, a young Canadian named James Naismith had just joined the staff of the International YMCA Training School in Springfield, Massachusetts, where he was instructed to devise an indoor game that didn't involve bodily contact, that would not result in damage to the gym, and in which every player had a chance to get in on the action. The game he invented was basketball—or *basket ball,* as it was called until about 1912. Naismith hung peach baskets at either end of the gym and used a soccer ball for play. The first game, in December 1891, involved two teams of nine men each and was not exactly a barnburner. The final score was 1–0.[40]

As an off-season recreation, basketball took off in a big way, largely because it was so cheap and easy to set up. Within three years, a company was producing balls specifically for the sport and many of the nuances of play had already evolved. For instance, in 1893 came the free throw—or *free trial for goal,* as it was at first called. Five players to a side became standard in 1895, but the names of the positions—center, two forwards, and two guards—weren't fixed until the 1920s. By 1907, basketball was being called the *cage game. Cager,* whose continued currency is very largely the result of its convenience to writers of headlines, is first attested in 1922 in a newspaper in Ardmore, Oklahoma.

Oddly, although peach baskets were soon replaced by nets, until 1912 it didn't occur to anyone to cut a hole in the bottom of them. Until then it was necessary for someone to climb a ladder and retrieve the ball after each score. Scores remained low for years. During the first National Invitational Tournament at New York in 1934, for instance, New York University beat Notre Dame 25–18, and Westminster beat St. John's 37–33. Not until the evolution of the *jump shot* in the 1930s and *hook shot* in the 1940s and above all the *fast break* in the 1950s did the sport take on some real pace.

Many YMCA teams evolved into the first professional teams, notably the Celtics, who were formed in 1915 and came not from Boston but from New York. But financing was always a problem, and teams often had to resort to desperate expedients to keep from going under. One early team, to secure sponsorship, called itself the Fort Wayne Zollner Pistons. It was named for a Fred Zollner who, as you will have guessed, manufactured pistons. Professional basketball didn't really get going until the formation in 1949 of the National Basketball Association, created by the merger of two smaller leagues. Like football, professional basketball was essentially a child of television, and, like football, it has had surprisingly little influence on American English. In fact, if you discount occasional figurative applications for a few expressions like *slam dunk, air ball,* and *full-court press,* it has had none at all.

Of rather more interest linguistically is one of the more ancient of popular pastimes: golf. The game and many of the terms associated with it are of Scottish origin, among them *bunker, tee, divot, niblick, duffer, links,* and *golf* itself. The word, of uncertain origin though possibly from the Scottish dialect word *gouf,* meaning to strike or hit, was first recorded in 1457. Variant spellings suggest that until fairly recent times it was pronounced with the *l* silent.

Golf came to America surprisingly early. As far back as 1786, just ten years after the Declaration of Independence, Charleston had a place that styled itself a golf club, and Savannah got one in 1795, though there is no evidence that golf was actually ever played at either. Certainly neither had anything remotely describable as a course. In any case, both were defunct by the second decade of the nineteenth century. The first real golf course in North America was that of the Royal Montreal Golf Club, formed in 1873. The first in the United States was the Foxburg Golf Club, in Pennsylvania, founded in 1887.

Though the game is Scottish, many of the terms are American, notably *par,* which dates from 1898. *Par,* of course, signifies the score a good player should make on a given hole. Before *par* became current, the word used was *bogey,* an old Scottish word for a ghost or spirit. The notion was that each player was scoring against a hypothetical bogey man. However, in 1898, the rubber golf ball was invented and quickly displaced the old gutta-percha balls. (*Gutta-percha,* for the record, comes from a Malay word meaning "strip of cloth.") Because the new balls traveled farther, one stroke fewer was required on average on each hole. *Par* therefore came to signify the new notional number of strokes required, and *bogey* was preserved for the old number of strokes. Gradually, as gutta-percha balls disappeared altogether, *bogey* came simply to mean one stroke over par.[41]

Birdie, signifying one stroke under par, comes from a nineteenth-century American slang term meaning excellent. Both it and *eagle,* also an Americanism, meaning two strokes under par, became common in the 1920s, when golf really took off in the United States. In that decade the number of American courses went from fewer than five hundred to almost six thousand, a twelvefold increase.[42]

In the same period, golf became associated with two rather odd items of clothing. The first was *knickerbockers,* a nonce word coined by Washington Irving in 1809 for his *Knickerbocker's History of New York* (which wasn't actually called that; the formal title was *History of New York from the Beginning of the World to the End of the Dutch Dynasty by Diedrich Knickerbocker*). By means that escape rational explanation, the word attached itself first to women's underwear (panties are to this day called *knickers* almost everywhere in the English-speaking world but North America) and then, by a further dazzling flight, to the shortened trousers favored by golfers in the 1920s. Golf knickers further begat another short-lived item of apparel, the *plus fours,* so called because they were four inches longer than knickers.[43]

Finally, before we put the world of sports behind us, note must be taken of the recent controversy over the offensiveness of many team nicknames to Native Americans. In 1992, a movement called the National Coalition on Racism in Sports and the Media was formed, partly to protest against the use of nicknames like *Braves, Redskins,* and *Indians.* In the view of Clyde Bellecourt, director of the American Indian Movement, "calling the team the Washington Redskins is like calling them the Washington Negroes or the Washington Blackskins."[44]

In defense of *Cleveland Indians,* it has been noted that the team name actually commemorates a Native American, Louis F. "Alex" Sockalexis, a Penobscot Indian who had been one of the team's star players in the 1890s and in whose honor the Cleveland Indians were named in 1914, the year after his death. But the argument doesn't wash with some activists. As one put it, "In that case, they should call themselves the Cleveland Sockalexises."

A few colleges and high schools have changed their names from *Mohawks* or *Hurons* to something more innocuous and less emotive, and one newspaper, the *Oregonian* of Portland, announced in 1992 that it would no longer publish Indian-related nicknames, explaining that they tended to "perpetuate stereotypes that damage the dignity and self-respect of many people in our society."[45] But at the time of writing, no professional team was seriously contemplating a name change.

Chapter 17

OF BOMBS AND BUNKUM: POLITICS AND WAR

I

When, in about 1820, a congressman named Felix Walker was accused of speaking drivel—which, evidently, he was—he replied that he was speaking to the people of Buncombe County, North Carolina, his district. Almost immediately his congressional colleagues began referring to any political claptrap or bombast as *speaking to Buncombe.* Soon the phrase had spread beyond Washington and was being abbreviated to *buncombe,* often respelled *bunkum,* and eventually further contracted to *bunk. Debunk* did not come until 1927. *Bunkum* in turn begat *hokum*—a blend of *hocus* and *bunkum.* Thus with a single fatuous utterance, the forgotten Felix Walker managed to inspire half a page of dictionary entries.[1] In doing so, Walker touched on a central paradox of American political rhetoric—namely, that while politicians may mostly spout *hot air* (in its metaphorical sense, an Americanism of the 1840s), they also constantly refresh the language.

A few American political terms have considerable venerability. *Caucus,* from an Algonquian word for counselor, dates from the early seventeenth century, and as such is one of the oldest surviving Americanisms. *Mugwump* (at first often spelled *mugquomp*), another Algonquianism, followed soon after, making its first recorded appearance in 1643. For two hundred years it retained its original sense of a chief or leader before abruptly shifting in the 1880s to describe a political maverick. (The oft-quoted definition is that a *mugwump* is someone who sits with his *mug* on one side of the fence and his *wump* on the other.) *Favorite son* was first used of Washington as far back as 1789, and *administration* was coined by him soon after.

However, the golden age of American political terminology was the nineteenth century. Of the perhaps two hundred terms that gained some measure of currency in that tumultuous century, a good number were sufficiently useful to be still with us today, among them *spoils system, lobbyist, split ticket, party ticket, dyed-in-the-wool, office seeker, dark horse, lame duck, slate, standard-bearer, gag rule, straw vote, party machine, filibuster, slush fund, gubernatorial, junket* in the sense of a trip at government expense, *bandwagon* in the sense of a movement or fashion to climb aboard, *landslide* for an overwhelming victory, *to dodge the issue, to electioneer, to campaign, to gerrymander, to be in cahoots with, to logroll, to stump, to run, to muckrake, to mend fences, to whitewash,* and *to keep the ball rolling* (so said because in the 1840 presidential campaign a ten-foot leather ball bearing that slogan was rolled from town to town in support of William Henry Harrison).[2]

One of the first of these terms to enter common parlance was *gerrymander.* Meaning to redraw electoral boundaries to favor a particular party, it dates from 1812 and memorializes Massachusetts Governor Elbridge Gerry (shortly to become Vice-President under James Madison), whose party, the Jeffersonians, engaged in some audacious cartographic manipulations to preserve its grip on the state assembly. Noticing that one district in Essex County had a vaguely reptilian shape, the artist Gilbert Stuart sketched on a head and legs and called it a salamander. "No, a *gerrymander!*" cried an onlooker, and the term stuck. A small, overlooked aspect of the term is that we all mispronounce it. Gerry pronounced his name with the hard *g* of *Gertrude* rather than the soft *g* of *Gerald.*[3]

In the following decade, two other durable political terms arose, both in the New York state capital, Albany. One was *spoils system,* inspired by the expression "to the victor belong the spoils," which has a nice classical ring to it but in fact was first uttered by an otherwise forgotten New York legislator named William L. Marcy.[4] Also in Albany at about the same time arose the much-needed term *lobbyist* for someone who hung around the capitol lobby seeking favors of passing legislators. (They hung around the lobby because they weren't allowed into the legislative chambers.)

Several political terms were borrowed from abroad. The custom of describing politicians as belonging to the *left, right,* or *center* of prevailing political sentiment came into American usage in about 1840 from Britain, though the British had in turn borrowed it from France, where it originated in 1789 as a by-product of the Revolution. The terms reflect the seating arrangements of the French National Assembly, where it was customary for the more radical commoners to sit to the left of the president while the more conservative clergy and nobility filled the seats to the right. In neither Britain nor America did the terms reflect actual seating arrangements, but they proved convenient labels.[5]

From Britain as well came *dark horse* and *lame duck,* though neither had a political significance before America got its hands on them. *Dark horse* was coined by Benjamin Disraeli in his novel *The Young Duke* (1831). Though he was a politician himself, he meant it only in a horse-racing context. In America by the 1860s it was being extended to the political sphere. *Lame duck* was an eighteenth-century London stock market term for a defaulter. It reached America with that sense around 1800, but by mid-century had been usurped by politicians to describe someone serving out a term of office and awaiting the arrival of his successor. In its political sense the term was reintroduced to Britain from America, but there it took on, and has retained, the sense of a politician who is incompetent, powerless, or weak.

The oddest and certainly the most historically complicated foreign borrowing is *filibuster.* It began as the Dutch *vrijbuiter,* a pirate. To English speakers, *vrijbuiter* naturally yielded *freebooter.*★ But *vrijbuiter* was beyond the command of Spanish tongues. They converted the word to *filibustero.* The French then borrowed it as *filibustier.* From one of these, or both, the English reborrowed it as *filibuster.* Thus by 1585 *vrijbuiter* had given English two words with the same meaning. *Freebooter* went no further, but *filibuster* had a busy career ahead of it in American politics. First, still bearing something of its original sense, it came to describe Americans who formed private armies with a view to taking over Central American countries, for which there was a short but persistent fashion in the 1850s (the idea of manifest destiny rather going to some people's heads).

One of these hopeful militants was a character named William Walker. Born in 1824 in Tennessee, Walker was an extraordinary prodigy. He graduated *summa cum laude* from the University of Nashville at the age of just fourteen, and by the time he was twenty-five had qualified as both a doctor and a lawyer and somehow had also found time to edit a newspaper in New Orleans, take part in the California gold rush, and engage in three duels, which becomes slightly more remarkable when you realize that he was also exceedingly small—little larger than a modern jockey. Despite his diminutive stature, Walker was clearly a leader of men. In 1853, he raised and armed forty-five recruits and set off with them for Baja California with the aim of capturing its mineral resources and simultaneously endowing its peo-

---

★The *boot* in *freebooter* has nothing to do with footwear. It comes from an old German word, *būte,* "exchange," which also gave us *booty.*

ple with the benefits of American civilization, whether they wanted it
or not.

The enterprise failed, but Walker had found his calling. Over the next
seven years he divided his time between raising armies and finance and
sallying forth on a series of increasingly ambitious expeditions. Though
he had some successes—he took over Nicaragua for about a year—
ultimately each foray ended in defeat.

Finally in 1860, after his troops were routed in Honduras, Walker sur-
rendered to the British navy. To his astonishment, his captors did not
repatriate him to the United States as had always happened before, but
turned him over to the Honduran authorities, who promptly took him
and his coconspirators to a town square, lined them up before a firing
squad, and brought to a close their lives and the fashion for private revolutions.[6] But *filibuster* didn't die with them. By the mid-1850s, it was
being used in Congress to describe any vaguely disruptive debating tac-
tic, and by the 1880s had settled into its present sense of a willful delay-
ing action designed to thwart the passage of a bill.

Still other words might have filtered out into the world at large except
that Congress in its early days was remarkably unforthcoming about its
doings. Senate debates were kept secret until 1794, and were reported
only sketchily after that for several decades. The House attracted more
attention, partly because it was more open in its dealings but also because well into the nineteenth century it was regarded as the more pres-
tigious chamber. Not until well into the nineteenth century did the
Senate begin to take on an air of preeminence, for the simple reason that
the House, reflecting the growth of American population, began to
seem very crowded—by 1860 it had 243 members, by 1880 332—while
the Senate remained comparatively compact and thus more exclusive
and clubby. The men who made the Senate famous—Daniel Webster,
Henry Clay, and John C. Calhoun—would very probably have been in
the House had they been born a generation earlier.[7]

At all events, the public enjoyed no right of access to congressional
debates until as late as 1873, when the *Congressional Record* was at last
created. Contrary to common belief, the *Record* even now does not constitute a full, verbatim transcription of all the debates in Congress.
Speeches are frequently edited before being placed in the *Record*, and indeed the *Record* sometimes contains speeches that were never given at
all. It has, in the words of Daniel Boorstin, "no more than the faintest
resemblance to what is actually said" in Congress.[8]

The nineteenth century also marked a busy time for political parties
as alliances endlessly formed and reformed, often around a single issue
like slavery or immigration. Political parties in America effectively date

from the period immediately after the drafting of the Constitution, when the two main sides formed into loose associations. Those in favor of the Constitution pulled off something of a linguistic coup by dubbing themselves *Federalists*. In fact, the term would more accurately have described those who were against the Constitution and wished to revive or rejuvenate the Articles of Confederation. Deprived of the term, this faction became known by default as the *Anti-Federalists*, which was not only not accurate but had a negative ring to it that the more positive-sounding Federalists were delighted to exploit.[9] Saddled with a misleading name, the Anti-Federalists began, confusingly, sometimes to call themselves *Democrats*, sometimes *Republicans*, and sometimes *Democrat-Republicans*.[10]

A succession of party names briefly blazed and faded in the nineteenth century, like matches struck in a darkened auditorium—a not inapt metaphor, since that is how one of the more memorably known parties got its name. I refer to the *Equal Rights Democrats*, who were known to everyone as the *Loco-Focos*, and so called because when one of their meeting halls was plunged into darkness by saboteurs the adherents continued with the aid of the new sulfur matches called *locofocos*.[11] No less memorable were the *Know-Nothings*—not the sort of name that would seem to inspire confidence in their capacity to lead. Officially called the *American Party*, it was as much a secret society as a political body and got its name from the reply members were instructed to give when asked to elucidate the party's aims: "I know nothing." Despite the obvious shortcomings of trying to attract a national following when you won't tell the world what you are up to, the Know-Nothings proved immensely popular among anti-immigrant, anti-Irish, and anti-Catholic zealots, and for a time threatened to overtake the young Republican Party as a lasting political force in America.[12]

Among the other parties or subparties that passed through the busy scene that was the 1800s were the *Butt-enders, Roarers, Huge Paws, Copperheads, Ringtails, Featherheads, Ball-rollers, Barnburners, Anti-Masons, Free Soilers, Anti-Nebraskans, Anti-Renters, Pro-Bank Democrats, Hunkers, Constitutional Union Party,* and *People's Party*—though many of these appellations, it should be noted, were bestowed by antagonists and weren't necessarily used by the adherents themselves.

The watershed year for political parties was 1836, when two sides coalesced into pro- and anti–Andrew Jackson factions. The pro-Jacksonites styled themselves *Democrats*. On the anti side, *National Republicans, Anti-Masons,* and *Pro-Bank Democrats* rallied to the resuscitated name *Whigs*—a decidedly odd choice, since during the Revolutionary War, *Whig* had designated a person who had not supported the

British cause, and thus had long had a whiff of treachery about it. Despite its long-standing currency in both Britain and America, *Whig* is of mysterious origins. The *Oxford English Dictionary* says only that it "probably" comes from *Whiggamores,* a term applied to the members of a military expedition against Scottish insurgents in Edinburgh in 1648, but no explanation as to the source of *Whiggamores* is adduced.

The Jackson Democrats remained Democrats after 1836, but the Whigs had further turmoil, and eventual dissolution, to face. In the 1850s, the party splintered into an unhappy plethora of factions with names like the *Conscience Whigs* (those who were against slavery), the *Cotton Whigs* (those who were for), and the *Barnburners* (from a comic parable about an obstinate Dutch farmer who rid his barn of rats by burning it down). In 1855, the Whigs emerged from this internecine squabbling as *Republicans,* and thus have they remained. The symbols of the two main political parties—the elephant for the Republicans, the donkey for the Democrats—were the creation of Thomas Nast, the cartoonist who also gave human form to Uncle Sam.[13]

In this century, new political terms have been fewer in number, but no less resourceful. Among those that have arisen in the world of politics since 1900 and found a role in the wider world are *smoke-filled room, grass roots, pork barrel, square deal, new deal, keynote speech, off the record, egghead, brain trust,* and countless, mostly short-lived words ending in *-gate* (*Koreagate, Lancegate, nannygate, Quakergate, Hollywoodgate, cattlegate, Muldergate,* and *Irangate,* all, of course, inspired by *Watergate,* the illicit nocturnal fact-finding visit to the Democratic Party national headquarters in the Watergate complex in Washington in 1972).

Pork barrel had its roots in the 1800s. Throughout that century, *pork* was a common political shorthand term for any kind of dubious abundance (it evidently alluded to the fattiness of pork). Early in this century, for reasons unknown, the term grew into *pork barrel,* and became particularly associated with federal largess that a congressman managed to bring back to his home state.

Off the record was coined by the New York politician Al Smith in 1926. *Egghead* arose during the 1952 election campaign. It appears to have been inspired by Adlai Stevenson, or more precisely by Stevenson's domelike pate, and by late in the year was in common currency as a flip synonym for an intellectual.

The century has also seen any number of slogans and catchphrases emanate from political circles, from Teddy Roosevelt's *Speak softly and carry a big stick,* to Woodrow Wilson's *little group of willful men* and *to make the world safe for democracy,* to Coolidge's *The business of America is business,* to Truman's *The buck stops here,* to Kennedy's *Ask not what your country can do for you, but what you can do for your country.* Some much-quoted twentieth-century political phrases are actually mythical, however. Hoover never said *Prosperity is just around the corner,* and he never used the expression *a chicken in every pot*—though the Republican Party *almost* did in advertisements for him during the campaign of 1928. The words it headed its ads with were *A Chicken for Every Pot,* but even it acknowledged in the text that the expression was already old enough to be considered "proverbial."

One Washington term that has existed officially only since the early years of this century is, surprisingly, *White House.* On the original plans, the building was described only as "the Palace." No one knows when people started calling it the White House—but, oddly, it appears to have been before it was painted white. From 1800, when John Adams became its first resident, to 1814, when the British ransacked and partly burned it, the building was of unadorned gray Virginia freestone. Only after the British had vandalized it was it decided to paint it white to cover the smoke stains. So it is a little odd that people were calling it the White House as early as 1810. In any case, the name didn't become official until Theodore Roosevelt began printing it on the executive mansion stationery sometime after 1901.

Only in comparatively recent times, incidentally, has the White House become an unapproachable fortress. As late as the Harding era (1921–1923) the public was allowed to picnic on the White House lawn or even wander over and peer through the windows of the Oval Office.[14] Harding himself sometimes answered the White House front door.[15]

II

And so to military matters.

There is an old joke that goes: "Dear Diary: Today the Hundred Years War started." The fact is that most wars didn't get the name by which we know them until much later. The American Revolution wasn't normally called that before the nineteenth century. It was the *War for Independence,* or simply the *War with Britain.* The Civil War was at the time of its fighting more generally called the *War Between the States* by Southerners and the *War of the Rebellion* by Northerners. World War I for obvious reasons wasn't so called until there was a World War II. (It was the *Great War.*) *World War II,* although the term was commonly applied, didn't become official until the war was nearly over. Roosevelt didn't like either *World War II* or the *Second World War.* Throughout its early years, he called it—a trifle melodramatically—the *War for Survival,* then shortly before his death started referring to it as the *Tyrants' War.* Other names that were commonly attached to it were *War of World Freedom, War of Liberation,* and *Anti-Nazi War.* In 1945, the question of a formal name was put to Secretary of War Henry L. Stimson. His choice, *World War II,* was formally adopted by President Truman.[16]

Battles, too, often went by a variety of names, particularly those of the American Civil War. Ulysses S. Grant didn't refer to the *Battle of Shiloh* but of *Pittsburg Landing.* To the North it was the *Battle of Bull Run,* but to the South it was *Manassas.* The Northern *Antietam* was the Southern *Sharpsburg,* as the Southern *Murfreesboro, Perryville,* and *Boonsboro* were to Northerners respectively *Stone River, Chaplin Hills,* and *South Mountain.*[17]

Wars are always linguistically productive, though military slang and terminology, like soldiers themselves, tend to be continuously replaced with fresh recruits. In consequence, battlefield terms usually either survive more or less indefinitely—*bomb* dates from 1582, *grenade* (from *pomegranate* and ultimately from *Granada*) from 1532—or else fade from the vocabularies of all but military historians.

Almost all that survives from the period of the American Revolution, apart from the (mostly mythical) slogans and catchphrases discussed already in Chapter 3, is a single song: "Yankee Doodle Dandy." It was the most popular tune of the day, sung by both sides with lyrics that chided the other. No one knows who first sang it or when, though the mocking tone of the words in the best-known version suggests British authorship:

> *Yankee Doodle came to town,*
> *riding on a pony,*
> *stuck a feather in his cap,*
> *and called it macaroni.*

If you have ever wondered why Yankee Doodle called the feather in his cap *macaroni*—and I think there may be something wrong with you if you have not—the answer is that *macaroni* was a slang term of the day for a fop. The feather in his cap possibly alluded to the habit of colonial soldiers, who often had no uniforms, of sticking a feather or piece of paper in their caps as a means of distinguishing themselves during battle.

The War of 1812 gave us not only "The Star-Spangled Banner" and Uncle Sam, but also *conscript* as both a noun and a verb, and two catchphrases of some durability: *Don't give up the ship* and *We have met the enemy and they are ours.* Both belong to Admiral Oliver Hazard Perry and come from a naval engagement on Lake Erie. *Don't give up the ship* was the slogan emblazoned on a pennant flying from Perry's vessel (in point of fact, Perry *did* give up the ship, but accuracy seldom matters when a really good phrase is involved), and *We have met the enemy and they are ours* were the words with which he communicated his triumph to his commander in chief.[18]

Not until we get to the Civil War period do we at last begin to encounter strictly military terms that have passed into wider usage. Among the Civil War neologisms that are still with us are *K.P.* (for *kitchen police*), *AWOL* (*absent without leave*), *pup tents* (originally known as *dog tents*), and, rather surprisingly, *doughboy* and *grapevine* in the context of rumors. *Doughboy* appears to have been first applied to Union soldiers during the 1860s. (The earliest reference is found in the memoirs of George Armstrong Custer in 1867, but the context indicates that it was already widely known.) The origins are entirely mysterious. Since early colonial times, small fried cakes had been known as *doughboys,* and the word may betoken a similarity in appearance between these cakes and the buttons on cavalry soldiers' uniforms, but that is no more than a guess. At all events, the term faded from sight after about 1870 and didn't catch on again until the First World War.[19] *Grapevine,* or *grapevine telegraph,* as a notional medium for the transmission of rumors, is equally mysterious. It was widely used during the Civil War, usually with the sense of a wholly unreliable rumor, but what precisely inspired it is unknown.

We have been conditioned by Hollywood to think of Union soldiers dressed identically in blue and Confederate troops in gray. In fact, for the first year or so of the war, most soldiers wore the uniforms of their state militias, which came in any number of colors. Troops from Iowa and Wisconsin, for instance, wore gray uniforms that were very like the official Confederate outfits, leading to endless confusion on the battlefield. After the North lost the First Battle of Bull Run partly because Union troops failed to fire on an advancing contingent of Virginia militia, mistaking them for allies, the War Department rushed into production hundreds of thousands of standard uniforms. These were manufactured with an old process employing recycled woolen fibers known as *shoddy.* Because the uniforms were poorly made and easily came unstitched, *shoddy* came to denote any article of inferior quality. The system of producing uniforms en masse also led, incidentally, to the introduction of standard graduated sizes, a process that was carried over to civilian life after the war.[20]

One myth of the Civil War period is that *hooker* for a prostitute arose from the camp followers of Union General Joseph Hooker. It is true that the cadres of sexual entrepreneurs who followed Hooker's men from battlefield to battlefield were jocularly known as *Hooker's Division* or *Hooker's Reserves,* but *hooker* itself predates the Civil War. It was first noted in 1845 in reference to a section of New York, *Corlear's Hook,* also known as *the Hook,* where prostitutes congregated.[21]

One term that did spring to prominence during the Civil War, though again of greater antiquity, was the *Mason-Dixon line.* It had been laid out a century earlier by the English surveyors Charles Mason and Jeremiah Dixon, who were brought to America in 1763 to resolve a long-standing border dispute between Pennsylvania and Maryland. Though we tend to think of the Mason-Dixon line as a straight east-west demarcation, a good quarter of it ran north-south. It was only coincidentally that it delineated the boundary between slave and nonslave states. Had it not been for this, the line would doubtless have been forgotten, which would have been unfortunate, because it was one of the great scientific feats of its age. Mason and Dixon were not merely surveyors but accomplished astronomers and mathematicians, and their achievement in drawing an accurate line across 244 miles of wilderness had a measure of heroism and scientific scrutiny not easily appreciated today. To the dismay of historians, Mason's careful notes of his four years' work disappeared for almost a century. Then in 1860 they turned up—no one knows how or why—two thousand miles from where they had last been seen on a trash heap in Nova Scotia, where they were about to be burned.[22]

A final, incidental linguistic legacy of the War Between the States was the term *sideburns,* named for the Union commander Ambrose E. Burnside, whose distinctive muttonchop whiskers inspired a fashion and became known as *burnsides.* Within a decade the syllables had been transposed, but how or why is anyone's guess.

After its brief flurry of creativity during the Civil War, military terminology then grows quiet for nearly half a century. *Roughriders* from the Spanish-American War, *limey* for a British sailor, and *leathernecks* for Marines (so called because for a decade in the late nineteenth century they wore a uniform with a leather lining in the collar, said to be excruciatingly uncomfortable)[23] effectively exhaust the list of neologisms from the period of 1870–1917.

But the global hostilities of World War I prompted an outpouring of new terms, many of which are with us yet. Among the words or expressions that entered the language via military connections during the period are *dog tags, chowhound* and *chowtime, convoy, dawn patrol, dogfight, eyewash* in the sense of nonsense, *to go west* meaning to die, *stunt* in the sense of a bold or foolish act, *shellshock, gadget, to scrounge, booby trap, foxhole, brass hat, MP* for military police, *civvies* for civilian clothes, *draftee, pipe down* as a call for quiet (it originated in the nautical use of pipes to announce changes of watch and the like), and *to swing the lead*.[24] A few of these expressions predate the war—*stunt*, for instance, originated among U.S. college students in the 1870s, and *to go west* is even older—but didn't become part of the common argot until inducted into the military.

From the British came *bridgehead, ack-ack, blimp, tank,* and, somewhat unexpectedly, *basket case* for a severely wounded combatant. *Blimp* arose from its official designation, "Dirigible: Type B-Limp," and *ack-ack* was a slang shortening of *antiaircraft,* based on British telephonic code for the letters *AA.*

From the Germans came *zeppelin* (named for Count Ferdinand von Zeppelin, its designer), *black market* (from German *Schwarzmarkt*), and *Big Bertha* for an outsized gun. As was their custom, the Germans had named the gun after the wife of the head of Krupp Steel, the manufacturer, and with a certain lack of delicacy had called it not *Big Bertha* but *Fat Bertha.* Frau Krupp's response to this signal honor is not known.

From France, meanwhile, came *parachute, camouflage* (rather oddly from *camouflet,* meaning "to blow smoke up someone's nose," a pastime that appears on the linguistic evidence to be specific to the French), and *barrage* from *tir de barrage*) in the sense of concentrated artillery fire. *Barrage* already existed in English with the meaning of a barrier across a waterway, but previously had been pronounced to rhyme with *disparage.*[25]

World War II, as you might expect of a war involving millions of military people dispatched to almost every corner of the world, was wildly prolific of new terms, though the number shrinks appreciably once you strip out those words and expressions that are now used primarily in a historical context (*Lend Lease, V-E Day, Luftwaffe*) or not at all (*stupor juice* for strong liquor, *fringe merchants* for bombers who dropped their loads short, *repple-depple* for an overseas replacement depot).[26] Among the terms to come to prominence during the period and to live on after the war were *bazooka, blackout, GI, liberty* for shore leave, *pin-up girl, Dear John letter* (that is, one in which the recipient learns that his girl back home has fallen for another), *Mae West* for an inflatable jacket, *task force, crotch rot* for a fungal infection, *walkie-talkie, shit list, chickenshit, grabass, sucks* in the sense of being undesirable, *jeep, blitzkrieg, flak, fascism, gestapo, kamikaze, displaced person, blockbuster* (originally a bomb sufficiently powerful to destroy an entire city block, and later of course appropriated by the entertainment industry), the expression *the greatest thing since sliced bread,* and, not least, a robust and inventive use of *fuck.* One of the last named's offshoots is *snafu,* often said to be an abbreviation of "situation normal, all fouled up," but don't you believe it. Once there were many more in like vein—e.g., *tuifu* ("the ultimate in fuckups), *tarfu* ("things are really fucked up"), *fubar* ("fucked up beyond all recognition"), and *fubid* ("fuck you, buddy, I'm detached").[27] The use of *fucked* as a general descriptive ("this engine is completely fucked") appears also to be a legacy of the Second World War.

Several World War II words, it will be noted, were foreign creations. *Blitzkrieg* (literally "lightning war"), *flak* (a contraction of *Fliegerabwehrkanone,* "antiaircraft gun"), and *gestapo* (from *Geheime Staatspolizei,* "Secret State Police") are of obvious German derivation. Also from Nazi Germany came one of our more chilling phrases, *final solution* (German *Endlösung*), coined by Reinhard "the Hangman" Heydrich. *Fascism* dates from long before the war—from 1919, in fact, when Benito Mussolini launched the *Fascismo* movement in Italy—but came to prominence only in the period just before the war. It comes from the Latin *fasces,* "bundle," and alludes to a bundle of rods that was both a tool of execution and symbol of authority in imperial Rome.[28] *Kamikaze* is, of course, Japanese. It means "divine wind," and commemorates a timely typhoon that routed a Mongol seaborne attack early in Japan's history.

Among the nativeborn terms that are not self-evident, *bazooka* was called after a comical stage prop—a kind of homemade trombone—used by a popular comedian named Bob Burns, and *GI* stands for *general issue,* or possibly *garrison issue,* the idea of the latter being that soldiers in the 1940s were issued two sets of clothes, one marked "dress issue" and the other marked "garrison issue."[29] No one appears to have noted when *GI* was first applied to soldiers, but *GI Joe* can be dated with certainty. He first appeared in the June 17, 1942, issue of *Yank,* the armed forces newspaper, in a cartoon drawing by Dave Berger.[30]

Jeep, as a concept if not as a word, slightly predates America's involvement in the war. In 1941, just before Pearl Harbor, the army introduced a sturdy vehicle for negotiating rough terrain. The jeep was actually not a very good vehicle. It was heavy and difficult to maneuver, devoured oil, had a chronically leaky water pump and cylinder head, and could run continuously for no more than four hours. But something about its boxy shape and go-anywhere capabilities earned it instant and widespread affection. No one knows how it got its name. The most common, and seemingly most plausible, explanation is that it is taken from the letters *GP,* short for *General Purpose.* The problem is that *General Purpose* was never officially part of its title, and doesn't appear on any documents associated with it. The army, with its usual gift for clunky appellations, termed it a *truck, quarter-ton, four-by-four.* More puzzlingly, the prototype for the jeep was generally known—for reasons now lost—as a *peep.* Mencken stoutly maintains that *jeep* comes from the *Pop-*

eye the Sailor comic strip written by E. C. Segar.[31] It is true that a character named Eugene the Jeep appeared in the strip as early as March 1936, though no one has ever explained how, or more pertinently why, that character's name would have been applied to a vehicle. What is certain is that Segar did give the world another useful word at about the same time, *goon,* named for simian characters in the strip.

Toward the end of the war, a slogan, often accompanied by a cartoon drawing of the top half of a face peering over a fence or other barrier, mysteriously began appearing wherever the American army went. The slogan was *Kilroy was here.* No one has any idea who this Kilroy was. The figure at whom the finger is most often pointed is James J. Kilroy, an inspector of military equipment in Quincy, Massachusetts, who was said to have chalked the three famous words on crates of equipment that were then dispatched to the far corners of the world. Others attribute it with equal assurance to a Sergeant Francis Kilroy of the Army Air Transport Command, who also would have had the opportunity to place his name on boxes of supplies and munitions. But the theories are manifold. One desperately imaginative scholar has even interpreted it as an antiauthoritarian *Kill Roi,* or "Kill the King."★

One of the more striking fashions to grow out of World War II was a military affection for acronyms and other such shortenings. The practice had begun in earnest in civilian life during the New Deal years of the 1930s when combinations like *TVA, WPA, OPA,* and *PWA* (respectively, *Tennessee Valley Authority, Works Progress Administration, Office of Price Administration,* and *Public Works Authority*) became a part of everyday life. But the military took it up with a passion once the world went to war, and devised not only alphabet-soup acronyms like *OSRD-WD* (Office of Scientific Research and Development, Western Division), *ETOUSA* (European Theater of Operations, U.S. Army), and *JMUSDC* (Joint Mexican–U.S. Defense Commission), but also

---

★It is curious how often we have lost track of the inspiration behind our eponymous words. We have already seen that no one knows who the real McCoy was. Equally, most authorities agree that there must have been a Mr. Lynch who provided the inspiration for the word describing the abrupt termination of life without the inconvenience of a fair trial, and candidates almost without number have been suggested for this dubious honor. Indeed, it can appear that almost anyone named Lynch who had a position of authority anywhere in America between 1780 and 1850 has been mentioned as a candidate at one time or another. But in fact no one knows who he was or what he did to earn his morbid immortality. It has even been suggested that Lynch may not be a person at all, but a creek in South Carolina favored by locals for impromptu executions.

novel hybrids like *ComAirSoPa* (for Commander of Aircraft for the South Pacific) and *ComAmphibForSoPac* (Commander of Amphibious Forces in the South Pacific). Occasionally these things had to be rethought. When it was realized that nearly everyone was pronouncing the abbreviation for the Commander in Chief of the U.S. Fleet in the Pacific, *CinCUS,* as "sink us," it was hastily amended to the more buoyant-sounding *CominCh.*[32] Only rarely did the shortenings achieve a measure of catchiness, as with Seabees (out of *CBs,* from the navy's *Construction Battalion*), and *PLUTO* (for Pipe Line Under the Ocean).

Oddly, one of the things World War II didn't leave us with was a memorable song. Almost every other war had, from "Yankee Doodle" of the Revolution to "John Brown's Body" and "The Battle Hymn of the Republic" of the Civil War, to World War I's "Over There." Most World War II songs, by contrast, seemed to be begging for instant obscurity. Among the more notably forgettable titles to emerge in the early days of fighting were "They're Going to Be Playing Taps on the Japs," "Goodbye, Mama, I'm Off to Yokohama," "Let's Knock the Hit Out of Hitler," "Slap the Jap Right Off the Map," and "When Those Little Yellow Bellies Meet the Cohens and the Kellys." Only one achieved anything like permanence in the popular consciousness—and that as a catchphrase rather than a song. It was based on the supposedly real-life story of a naval chaplain, William A. McGuire, who reportedly climbed into the seat of an antiaircraft gun at Pearl Harbor after the gunner had been killed and began knocking Japanese planes from the sky as he cried the famous words: "Praise the Lord and pass the ammunition." In fact, as a bemused McGuire told the world after the song became a hit, he had never said any such thing, and indeed had never even fired a gun. All he had done was help lift some boxes of ammunition.[33]

On August 6, 1945, President Harry S Truman announced to the nation: "Sixteen hours ago an American airplane dropped one bomb on Hiroshima, an important Japanese army base. That bomb had more power than twenty thousand tons of TNT. It is an atomic bomb." It was the first time that most people had heard the term. In the following years, many other words connected with splitting the atom would become increasingly familiar to them: *nuclear, fission, fusion, radiation, reactor, mushroom cloud, fallout, fallout shelter, H-bomb, ground zero,* and, unexpectedly, *bikini* for a two-piece swimsuit designed by Louis Reard, a French couturier, in 1946, and named for Bikini Atoll in the Pacific, where America had just begun testing atomic bombs.

The dropping of atomic bombs on Hiroshima and Nagasaki marked the end of one war and the beginning of another: the cold war. The cold war may not have generated a lot of casualties, but it was nonetheless the longest and costliest war America has ever fought. War was unquestionably good for business—so good that in 1946 the president of General Electric went so far as to call for a "permanent war economy." He more or less got his wish. Throughout the 1950s, America spent more on defense than it did on anything else—indeed, almost as much as it did on all other things together. By 1960, military spending accounted for 49.7 percent of the federal budget—more than the combined national budgets of Britain, France, West Germany, and Italy.[34] Even America's foreign aid was overwhelmingly military. Of the $50 billion that America distributed in aid in the 1950s, 90 percent was for military purposes.

Cold war, the term that justified these gargantuan outlays, has often been attributed to the newspaper columnist Walter Lippmann. In fact, the expression was first used by the statesman Bernard Baruch in a speech in Columbia, South Carolina, in 1947, though credit for its coinage belongs to his speechwriter, Herbert Bayard Swope.[35] Out of the cold war came two other durable expressions—*iron curtain* and the *domino theory. Domino theory*—meaning the idea that if one nation fell to Communism, others would topple in its wake—was first used by the newspaper columnist Joseph Alsop in 1954, although it didn't become popular until the Vietnam War a decade later. *Iron curtain* is commonly attributed to Winston Churchill in an address he made in Fulton, Missouri, in 1946, but in fact the term had been in existence in the sense of an imaginary barrier since 1819, and had been used in political contexts since the 1920s.

The cold war, or more specifically the Cuban missile crisis, also brought to prominence *hawk* and *dove,* though again both had been around for some time. *Dove* had been the symbol of peace for centuries, and *hawk,* in the context of military belligerence, had been coined by Thomas Jefferson in 1798 in the expression *war hawk.* What was new was the conjoining of the terms to indicate a person's militaristic leanings.

On the field of battle, the Korean War pitched in with a number of terms, among them *demilitarized zone* and its abbreviated form, *DMZ* (originally signifying the disputed area along the 38th parallel dividing Korea into North and South), *brainwash* (a literal translation of the Mandarin *hsi nao), chopper* for a helicopter, *honcho* (from Japanese *hancho,* "squad leader"), and *hooch* (from Japanese *uchi,* "house"), which was at first used to describe the place where a soldier kept his mistress.

Several of these words were resurrected for the war in Vietnam a decade later, though that conflict also spawned many terms of its own, among them *free-fire zone; clicks* for kilometers; *grunt* for a soldier, first used dismissively by Marines, but taken on with affection by infantry-men; *search-and-destroy mission; to buy the farm,* meaning to die in combat; *to frag,* meaning to kill a fellow soldier, usually an officer, with a hand grenade or *fragmentation device,* hence the term; and a broad variety of telling expressions for the Vietnamese: *slope, gook, dink, zip, slant, slant-eye,* and *Charlie,* though many of these—like *slant-eye* and *gook*—were older terms recently revived. *Charlie* as an appellation for Viet Cong arose because *VC* in radio code was *Victor Charlie.*

Among the more sinister terms to catch the world's attention during the war in Vietnam were *Agent Blue, Agent Orange, Agent Purple,* and *Agent White,* for types of *defoliants*—another new word—used to clear fields, destroy crops, and generally demoralize and destabilize inhabitants of hostile territory, and *napalm,* from *naphthene palmitate,* which had much the same intent and effect. Though it first became widely known during the Vietnam War, *napalm* was in fact invented during the Second World War.

The military affection for clumsy acronyms found renewed inspira-tion in Vietnam with such concoctions as *FREARF* (for Forward Re-arm and Refuel Point), *SLAR* (Side-Looking Airborne Radar), *FLAR* (Forward-Looking Airborne Radar), and *ARVN,* pronounced "arvin" (Army of the Republic of South Vietnam). One of the more arresting, if least reported, of Vietnam-era acronyms was *TESTICLES,* a mne-monic for the qualities looked for in members of the 2nd Ranger Bat-talion, namely *teamwork, enthusiasm, stamina, tenacity, initiative, courage, loyalty, excellence,* and *sense of humor.*

But where the war in Vietnam really achieved semantic distinction was in the creation of a vast heap of euphemisms, oxymorons, and other verbal manipulations designed to create an impression of benignity and order, so that we got *pacification* for eradication, *strategic withdrawal* for re-treat, *sanitizing operation* for wholesale clearance, *accidental delivery of ar-maments* for bombing the wrong target, *to terminate with extreme prejudice* for a political assassination, and many, many others.

The Gulf War, despite its brevity, was also linguistically productive. The run-up to the war produced a number of interesting euphemisms for civilian hostages. The State Department referred to them variously as *restrictees* or *detainees,* while the Iraqi Foreign Office termed them *for-eign guests.* To President George Bush they were *inconvenienced people who want to get out.* Among the new formations to rise to prominence during the war itself were *clean bombing* (i.e., bombing with pinpoint precision), *headquarters puke* for a junior officer whose responsibilities keep him safely away from the front, *Nintendo effect* for the desensitizing effect of watching films of bombing raids that resemble video games of destruction, *Airwing Alpo* for in-flight rations on fighter aircraft, and *mother of all,* signifying ultimate, as in *mother of all tanks, mother of all wars,* etc.[36]

Finally, one of the most recent of military neologisms is also one of the most poignant: *ethnic cleansing,* signifying the removal or eradication of a portion of the indigenous population of an area. Apparently coined by Russian observers, it is a product of the war in the former Yugoslavia, and was first reported in English in the July 9, 1991, issue of *The Times* of London.

Chapter 18

SEX AND OTHER DISTRACTIONS

In 1951, the proprietor of the Hi Hat Lounge in Nashville, Tennessee, purchased a life-sized photograph of a naked young woman lying on a fluffy rug and proudly hung it behind his bar. Even by the relatively chaste standards of the day it was not a terribly revealing picture—only her posterior was exposed to view—and probably nothing more would have come of it except that one day an electrician arrived to do some work and recognized the woman in the photograph as his wife, which surprised him because she had never mentioned that she was doing nude modeling for a local photographer.

The electrician took the Hi Hat to court, and for a short while the matter became first a local and then a national sensation. With the eyes of America on him, Judge Andrew Doyle ruled that as art the photograph was perfectly acceptable, but that as a barroom decoration it was "unquestionably obscene." He suggested—apparently seriously—that one of the city's art galleries might like to take it over. In other words, if displayed in a darkened bar where it would be seen by no one but grown-up drinkers, the picture was held to be salacious and corrupting. But if placed in a public forum where anyone of any age could view it, it could be regarded as a local treasure.[1] And no one anywhere appears to have thought this odd.

I bring this up here to make the point that America's attitudes toward questions of public and private morality have long been a trifle confused. For this, as with so much else, we can thank the Puritans. As early as 1607, *puritanical* had come to mean *stern, rigid, narrowly moral,* and the view has been steadily reinforced ever since by history texts and literary works like Hawthorne's *Scarlet Letter* and Longfellow's *Courtship of Miles Standish.*

The Puritan age was, to be sure, one in which even the smallest transgressions—or even sometimes no transgression at all—could be met with the severest of penalties. Adultery, illegitimacy, and even masturbation were all at times capital offenses in New England. Almost any odd occurrence darkened Puritans' suspicions and fired their zeal for swift retribution. In 1651, when the wife of Hugh Parsons of Springfield, Massachusetts, complained that her husband sometimes threw "pease about the Howse and made me pick them up," and occasionally in his sleep made "a gablings Noyse,"[2] the town fathers concluded without hesitation that this was witchcraft and strung him up from the nearest gibbet.

Equally unlucky was George Spencer of New Haven, Connecticut. When a one-eyed pig was born in the town, the magistrates cast around for an explanation and lighted on the hapless Spencer, who also had but one eye. Questioned as to the possibility of bestiality, the frightened Spencer confessed, but then recanted. Under Connecticut law, to convict Spencer of bestiality required the testimony of two witnesses. So eager were the magistrates to hang him that they admitted the pig as one witness and his retracted confession as another.[3] And then they hanged him.

In many other ways, though, colonial New England was not as simon pure (the expression comes from a play of 1718 by Susanna Centlivre called *A Bold Stroke for a Wife*, and involving a character named Simon Pure) as we might think. Just half a century after the *Mayflower* Pilgrims landed on Massachusetts's shores, Boston was "filled with prostitutes," and other colonial centers were equally well equipped with opportunities for sexual license. Despite its modest size, Williamsburg, capital of Virginia from 1699 to 1779, contained three brothels (though curiously none of these has been incorporated into the sanitized replica community so popular with visitors today).[4]

Sex among the Puritans was considered as natural as eating, and was discussed about as casually, to the extent that, the historian David Fischer writes, "the writings of the Puritans required heavy editing before they were thought fit to print even in the mid-twentieth century."[5] Premarital intercourse was not just tolerated but effectively encouraged. Couples who intended to marry could take out something called a *precontract*—in effect, a license to have sex. It was the Puritans, too, who refined the intriguing custom of *bundling,* or *tarrying* as it was also often called, in which a courting pair were invited to climb into bed together. The practice appears to have originated in Wales, but was sufficiently little known in Britain to have become a source of perennial wonder to British visitors to New England up to the time of the American Revolution and somewhat beyond.

As one seventeenth-century observer explained it: "When a man is enamoured of a young woman, and wishes to marry her, he proposes the affair to her parents; if they have no objections they allow him to tarry the night with her, in order to make his court to her. After the young ones have sat up as long as they think proper, they get into bed together, also without pulling off their undergarments in order to prevent scandal. If the parties agree, it is all very well; the banns are published and they are married without delay. If not they part, and possibly never see each other again; unless, which is an accident that seldom happens, the forsaken fair proves pregnant, and then the man is obliged to marry her."[6]

In fact, more underclothes were yanked off than the chronicler dared imagine, and pregnancy was far more than "an accident that seldom happens." Up to a third of bundling couples found themselves presented with a permanent souvenir of the occasion. Nor did it necessarily mark the advent of a serious phase of a relationship. By 1782, bundling was so casually regarded, according to one account, that it was "but a courtesy" for a visitor to ask the young lady of the house if she cared to retire with him.

Although never expressly countenanced, fornication was so common in Puritan New England that at least one parish had forms printed up in which the guilty parties could confess by filling in their names and paying a small fine. By the 1770s, about half of all New England women were pregnant at marriage.[7] In Appalachia and other backcountry regions, according to one calculation, 94 percent of brides were pregnant when they went to the altar.[8]

Not until the closing quarter of the eighteenth century did official attitudes to sex begin to take on an actively repressive tinge with the appearance of the first *blue laws*. The term originated in Connecticut in 1781, because, it is often said, the state's laws concerning personal morality were printed on blue paper,[9] though other sources say that it was the church laws that were given the blue treatment.[10] Whichever, no one knows why blue was thought an apt color for such laws. It may simply be our curious tendency to equate blueness with extreme moral rectitude, as in the expressions *bluenose* and *bluestocking*. *Bluenose* is said to have begun as a jocular nineteenth-century New England term for the fishermen of Nova Scotia, whose lives on the frigid waters of the North Atlantic left them with permanently discolored hooters. More prosaically, it may simply refer to a type of potato associated with that maritime province. In either case, how the term then came to be attached to a person of puritanical bent is anyone's guess. Very possibly the two are not in fact connected.

Bluestocking, for a woman of pedantry and attendant lofty mien, is more easily explained. It comes from the *Blue Stocking Society*, a name derisively applied to a group of intellectuals who began meeting at Montagu House in London in about 1750. Although the congregation was mostly female, the inspiration for the pejorative name appears to have been a male member, one Benjamin Stillingfleet, who wore blue worsted stockings instead of the customary black silk hose, a mode of dress so novel as to be considered both comical and rather devilishly risqué. And speaking of risqué, why off-color jokes are called *blue* is another mystery, but it may be connected to the eighteenth-century slang use of *to blue* meaning to blush.

Seventeenth- and eighteenth-century users of English, Puritan and non-Puritan alike, had none of the problems with expressive terms like *belly, fart,* and, *to give titty* (for *to suckle*) that would so trouble their Victorian descendants. Even the King James Bible contained such later-indecorous terms as *piss, dung,* and *bowels.*[11] But as the eighteenth century gave way to the nineteenth, people suddenly became acutely—and eventually almost hysterically—sensitive about terms related to sex and the body.

No one knows exactly when or why this morbid delicacy erupted. Like most fashions, it just happened. In 1818, Thomas Bowdler, an Edinburgh physician, offered the world an expurgated version of Shakespeare's works suitable for the whole family, and in so doing gave the world the verb *to bowdlerize.* Bowdler's emendations were nothing if not thorough. Even the most glancing reminder of the human procreative capacity—King Lear's "every inch a king," for example—was ruthlessly struck out. His sanitized Shakespeare was such a success that he immediately embarked on a similar treatment of Gibbon's *Decline and Fall of the Roman Empire*, which had been completed only a quarter of a century before. But Bowdler's careful editing didn't inaugurate the change of mood, it merely reflected it.

Even before Bowdler began scratching away at the classics, people were carefully avoiding emotive terms like *legs, blouse,* and *thigh.* By the time Bowdler's *Family Shakespeare* appeared, *belly buttons* had become *tummy buttons, breast* had become *bosom,* and *underwear* had become *nether garments* or *small clothes* (and later *unmentionables*).

Though the practice began in Britain, it found its full flowering in America, where soon the list of proscribed words extended to the hundreds. Any word with an unseemly syllable like "cock" or "tit" in it became absolutely unutterable, so that words like *titter, titbit, cockerel, cockroach,* and *cockatoo* either disappeared from the American vocabulary or were altered to a more sanitized form like *tidbit, rooster,* or *roach.* There is at least one recorded instance of *coxswain* being changed to *roosterswain,* and bulls were sometimes called *male cows.* Before the century was half over, the list of unspeakable words in the United States had been extended to almost any anatomical feature or article of apparel associated with any part of the human form outside the head, hands, and ankles. *Stockings,* for instance, was deemed "extremely indelicate" by Bartlett in 1850; he suggested *long socks* or *hose* as more comely alternatives. Even *toes* became humiliating possessions, never to be mentioned in polite company. One simply spoke of *the feet.* After a time, *feet* too became unendurably shameful, so that people didn't mention anything below the ankles at all. It is a wonder that discourse didn't cease altogether.

Anxiety stalked every realm of life. Chamber pots, for instance, came with a crocheted cover to serve as a baffle so that anyone passing without would not hear the unseemly tinkle of the person passing within.[12] And it wasn't just the noise that was baffled. Visitors from abroad found the neurotic lengths to which euphemism was carried deeply mystifying. It was not enough merely to avoid mentioning an object. A word had to be found that would not even hint at its actual function. Unable to bring themselves to say *chamber pot* or even *commode,* Americans began to refer to the vessel as a *looking glass,* with obvious scope for confusion, not to say frustration, for anyone who sought the former and was given the latter.

Foreigners almost unfailingly ran aground in the shallow waters of American sensibilities. Frances Trollope noted the case of a German who stopped a roomful of conversation, and found himself being brusquely shown the door, for innocently pronouncing the word *corset* in mixed company. Elsewhere she discussed how a rakish young man tried to tease from a seamstress the name of the article of attire she was working on. Blushing hotly, the young lady announced that it was a frock. When the young man protested that there wasn't nearly enough material for a frock, she asserted it was an apron. Pressed further, she claimed it was a pillowcase. Eventually, she fled the room in shame and tears, unable to name the object. It was, in fact, a blouse, but to have uttered the word to a man would have been "a symptom of absolute depravity."

For women in particular, this rhetorical fastidiousness was not just absurd but dangerous. For much of the nineteenth century, *ankles* denoted the whole of a woman's body below the waist, while *stomach* did similar service for everything between the waist and head. It thus became impossible to inform a doctor of almost any serious medical complaint. Page Smith notes a typical case in which a young woman with a growth on her breast could only describe it to her physician as a pain in her stomach.[13]

Physical examinations were almost unknown. Gynecological investigations in particular were made only as a last resort, and then usually in a darkened room under a sheet. One doctor in Philadelphia boasted that "women prefer to suffer the extremity of danger and pain rather than waive those scruples of delicacy which prevent their maladies from being fully explored."[14] Death, in other words, was to be preferred to immodesty. But then given the depths of medical ignorance it was probably just as well that the medical men kept their hands to themselves. Such was the lack of knowledge in regard to female physiology that until the closing years of the nineteenth century it was widely believed that the touch of a menstruating woman could turn a ham rancid. (The *British Medical Journal* ran a lively correspondence on the matter in 1878.)[15] Nor was it just male doctors who were profoundly innocent. As late as 1901 in a book entitled *What a Young Wife Ought to Know*, Dr. Emma Drake was informing her readers that during pregnancy they might experience uncomfortable feelings of arousal. This, she explained frankly, was "due to some unnatural condition and should be considered a disease."[16]

Not surprisingly, sexual ignorance was appalling. On the eve of her wedding, the future novelist Edith Wharton asked her mother what would be expected of her in the bridal chamber. "You've seen enough pictures and statues in your life," her mother stammered. "Haven't you noticed that men are made differently from women?" And with that she closed the subject.[17]

Those who sought enlightenment from sex manuals were left little wiser. The two best-selling guides of the day were *What a Young Boy Ought to Know* and *What a Young Girl Ought to Know*, both written by a clergyman named Sylvanus Stall. Despite the books' titles, Stall was at pains to make sure that his young readers should in fact know nothing. To deal with the inevitable question of where babies come from, he suggested parents memorize the following roundabout answer:

> My dear child, the question you have asked is one that every man and woman, every intelligent boy or girl and even many very young children have asked themselves or others—whence and how they came to be in the world. If you were to ask where the locomotives and the steamship or the telegraph and the telephone came from, it would be wisest, in order that we might have the most satisfactory answer that we should go back to the beginning of these things, and consider what was done by George Stephenson and Robert Fulton, by Benjamin Franklin and Samuel Morse, by Graham Bell and Thomas Edison toward developing and perfecting these useful inventions.

So there you have it, my child—they come from eminent inventors. But no, Stall then abruptly switches tack and launches into a discussion of cornstalks and their tassels, with oblique references to Papa and Mama Shad, birds and eggs, oaks and acorns, and other such natural processes, but without so much as a hint as to how any of them manage to regenerate. Then, as a kind of cooling-down exercise after all this heady candor, he provides a brief sermon.

For young men, the great anxiety was *masturbation,* a term coined in a British medical journal in 1766 in an article entitled "Onanism: A Treatise on the Disorders Produced by Masturbation." The origins of the term are puzzling. The *Oxford English Dictionary* says that it comes from the Latin *masturbari,* but then calls that a term of "unkn. origin." The verb form *masturbate* didn't arise until 1857, but by that time the world had come up with any number of worrisome-sounding alternatives—*selfish celibacy, solitary licentiousness, solitary vice, self-abuse, personal uncleanliness, self-pollution,* and the thunderous *crime against nature.* By whatever name it went, there was no question that indulgence in it would leave you a juddering wreck. According to Dr. William Alcott's *A Young Man's Guide* (1840), those who succumbed to temptation could confidently expect to experience, in succession, epilepsy, St. Vitus' dance, palsy, blindness, consumption, apoplexy, "a sensation of ants crawling from the head down along the spine," and finally death.[18]

As late as 1913 the American Medical Association published a book that explained that *spermin,* a constituent of semen, was necessary for the building of strong muscles and a well-ordered brain, and that boys who wasted this precious biological elixir would turn from "hard-muscled, fiery-eyed, resourceful young men" into "narrow-chested, flabby-muscled mollycoddles."[19]

For women, ignorance was not just confined to matters sexual. Conventional wisdom had it that members of the fair sex should not be exposed to matters that might tax their fragile and flighty minds. Even as enlightened an observer as Thomas Jefferson believed that females should not "wrinkle their foreheads with politics" or excite their susceptible passions overmuch with books and poetry, but rather should confine themselves to "dancing, drawing, and music."[20]

Recounting the difficulties of trying to bring a liberal education to young women, Emma Willard, founder of the Troy Female Seminary, the first true American girls' school, noted how parents had covered their faces and fled a classroom "in shame and dismay" when they found one of the pupils drawing a picture of the human circulatory system on a blackboard.[21]

If by some miracle a woman managed to acquire a little learning, she was not expected to share it with the world. An influential manual, *A Father's Legacy to His Daughters*, cautioned its young readers, "If you happen to have any learning, keep it a profound secret, especially from the men."[22] When in 1828 Fannie Wright gave a series of public lectures, the nation's press was at first shocked and then outraged. A newspaper in Louisville accused her of committing "an act against nature." The *New York Free Enquirer* declared that she had "with ruthless violence broken loose from the restraints of decorum." The *New York American* decided that she had "ceased to be a woman" by her actions.[23] No one objected to the content of the lectures, you understand, merely that they were issuing from the mouth of a female.

The tiniest deviation from conventional behavior earned the rebuke of newspapers. In 1881, *The New York Times* editorialized against the growing use of slang by women, with the implication that it bespoke a dangerous moral laxity, and cited as an example the shocking expression *What a cunning hat.*[24]

Yet—and here is the great, confusing paradox of the age—at the very time that these repressive currents were swirling around, many women were stepping forward and demanding to be heard with a vigor and boldness that would not be repeated for a century. The women's movement of the nineteenth century grew out of a huge thrust for social change that gripped America like a fever between about 1830 and 1880. Scores of new ideas seized the popular consciousness and found huge, fanatical followings: *utopianism, spiritualism, populism, vegetarianism, socialism, women's suffrage, black emancipation, tax reform, food reform, communalism, mysticism, occultism, second adventism, temperance, transcendentalism.* People dipped into these social possibilities as if choosing from a bag of sweets. One group called for "free thought, free love, free land, free food, free drink, free medicine, free Sunday, free marriage, and free divorce." Another, styling itself the Nothingarians, rallied behind the cry "No God, no government, no marriage, no money, no meat, no tobacco, no sabbath, no skirts, no church, no war, and no slaves!" As Emerson wrote to Carlyle in 1840: "We are all a little wild here with numberless projects of social reform. Not a reading man but has a draft of a new Community in his waistcoat pocket."

Typical of this new spirit of experimentation was a commune called Fruitlands started in 1843 by A. Bronson Alcott and some followers. For various fashionable reasons, the members of the Fruitlands community rejected meat, cheese, tea, milk, coffee, rice, woolen clothing, leather shoes, and manure. One particularly zealous adherent refused to eat any root that pushed downward "instead of aspiring towards the sun." The colony lasted less than a year. Things went well enough during warm weather, but at the first sign of winter frost, it broke up and the members returned to their comfortable homes in Boston.

For women, the social ferment presented an opportunity to take part for the first time in public debate. It began with a few lectures, usually to other women in private homes, on subjects like abolition and education. But by mid-century, women were appearing on public platforms and speaking not just for abolition or vegetarianism or transcendentalism, but for their own interests.

Two of the most outspoken were the sisters Tennessee Claflin and Victoria Claflin Woodhull, who jointly ran a successful New York stockbroking firm and published a popular magazine, *Woodhull and Claflin's Weekly*, which espoused a variety of utopian schemes and engaged in an early form of "outing" when it exposed the affair of the preacher Henry Ward Beecher and Elizabeth Tilton, the wife of one of his parishioners. Curiously, they didn't attack Beecher for his reckless infidelity, but rather praised him for his "immense physical potency" and "amativeness."

Woodhull was particularly—and in the context of the times breathtakingly—forthright in her demands for free love. "If I want sexual intercourse with one or one hundred men I shall have it," she thundered. "And this sexual intercourse business may as well be discussed . . . until you are so familiar with your sexual organs that a reference to them will no longer make the blush mount to your face any more than a reference to any other part of your body."[25]

As a way of asserting their newfound sense of independence, many women took to wearing *bloomers,* an article of clothing named for Amelia Bloomer, a postmistress in upstate New York and a leading temperance lecturer. Bloomer did not invent bloomers but merely popularized them. Bloomers could hardly have been more modest. They were a sort of voluminous pants, not unlike modern baseball pants, worn under a short skirt or smock—"like a stratosphere balloon with two hot dogs peeping out at the bottom," as one historian has put it—and they freed women from the horrible constraints of corsets and bodices. They were decorous and they made eminent sense. But predictably they aroused enormous agitation, and from pulpits to newspaper editorial pages they were fulminated against as graceless at best, lascivious at worst. It was not until much later that *bloomers* came to signify a woman's underclothing.

Pressing the fight for woman's suffrage, Woodhull ran for President in 1872 as the candidate of the Equal Rights Party. (Her running mate was the freed slave Frederick Douglass.) Soon afterward, she moved to England, married an aristocrat, got religion, and recanted almost everything. She devoted much of the energies of her later years to trying to persuade newspapers to throw out their files of her earlier utterances.

By this time, however, others had rushed to fill the vacuum created by her departure. The forthrightness with which many of these early feminists put their views seems astonishingly out of keeping with our usual perception of the age. Angela Heywood launched a spirited campaign for free love in which she made the universal acceptance of *fuck* a central tenet. Why should she be compelled to use the term *generative sexual intercourse* in her lectures? she repeatedly asked. "Three words, twenty-seven letters, to define a given action . . . commonly spoken in one word of four letters that everybody knows the meaning of."[26]

No less unexpectedly, the most vociferous exponents of free love and other radical practices were to be found not in Boston or New York, but out on the prairies in places like Iowa, Kansas, and Illinois. The most radical freethinking newspaper, *Lucifer*, was based in Valley Falls, Kansas. It is worth noting, however, that even among the most committed bastions of libertarianism, sexual enlightenment was a sometimes elusive quality. Even there it was widely believed that masturbation dangerously "thinned the blood and destroyed vital energy." Many in the free love movement supported uninhibited sexual intercourse between men and women not because of its inherent liberating qualities, but simply because it displaced masturbation.[27]

Never before or since, in short, has there been a more confused and bewildering age. To read, on the one hand, the *New York Times* castigating women for saying *What a cunning hat,* and, on the other, Angela Heywood publicly arguing for the right to say *fuck* makes it all but impossible to believe that we are dealing with the same people in the same country in the same century.

Much the same paradox prevailed with sex itself. In perhaps no other time in history has sex been so rampantly suppressed or so widely available. In 1869, it was estimated that Philadelphia had twelve thousand prostitutes and Chicago seven thousand. No estimates appear to have been made for New York, but it is known that the city had over 620 brothels. For the less adventurous there was a huge stockpile of *pornography* (coined in England in 1854, from Greek elements meaning literally "harlot writing") in both words and pictures.

Many terms associated with illicit sex are very old. *Bordello* (from an Old French word for a small hut), *brothel* (from the Old English *brēothan,* meaning derelict), *whore* (another Old English word), *strumpet, harlot, bawdy house,* and *streetwalker* all comfortably predate the Pilgrims. Throughout the nineteenth century, prostitutes were also commonly known as *flappers,* a term resurrected for fast girls in the 1920s, and *gay women* or *gays.* How *gay* later became attached to homosexuals is a mystery. We know approximately when it happened—the late 1960s—but no one appears to know why or by what reasoning. No less mysterious is one of the more unattractive epithets for homosexuals, *faggot.* In its homophobic sense, the term is an Americanism first recorded in 1905, but beyond that almost nothing is known. In England, *faggot* and its diminutive, *fag,* have had a multiplicity of meanings, from a slang term for a cigarette to feeling fatigued to being burned at the stake. The American usage may come from the British schoolboy term *fag,* designating a boy who serves as a kind of slave for a more senior fellow, toasting his crumpets, fetching his slippers, and, in the right circumstances, assisting him through that sexual delirium known as puberty. Puzzlingly, though, there is no indication of *fag* ever having denoted a homosexual in Britain, and no one has ever posited a convincing explanation for the term's transmission to America.

Among other Americanisms connected with sex we find *red light district* from the 1890s (it comes, as you might guess, from the practice of burning a red light in the front window of a brothel); *hustler* from 1900; *floozie, trick, to be fast and loose,* and *cat house* from the early 1900s; and *John* for a prostitute's customer as well as *call girl* from the 1930s.[28]

Inevitably, all the loose talk of promiscuity and sexual assertiveness, and the growing availability of *smut* (an English dialect word related to *smudge,* and first recorded in 1722) in all its many forms, brought forth a violent reaction, which was personified most vigorously in the beefy shape of Anthony Comstock, one of the most relentless, unyielding, and proudly backward hunters-down of vice the United States or any nation has ever produced.

A former salesman and shipping-office clerk, Comstock had little education—he could barely read and write—but he knew what he didn't like, which was more or less everything, including athletic supporters. As founder and first secretary of the Society for the Suppression of Vice, he lobbied vigorously for a federal law against obscenity. The difficulty was that the Constitution reserved such matters for the states. The federal government could involve itself only in regard to interstate commerce, chiefly through the mail. In 1873, it passed what came immediately to be known as the Comstock Act. Described by a contemporary observer as "one of the most vicious and absurd measures ever to come before Congress," it was passed after just ten minutes of debate. In the same year, Comstock was appointed Special Agent for the U.S. Post Office to enforce the new law, and he went to work with a vengeance.

In a single year, Comstock and his deputies impounded 134,000 ·

pounds of books, 14,200 pounds of photographic plates, almost 200,000 photographs and drawings, 60,300 miscellaneous articles of rubber, 31,500 boxes of aphrodisiacal pills and potions, and 5,500 packs of playing cards.[29] Almost nothing escaped his ruthless quest to suppress vice wherever it arose. He even ordered the arrest of one woman for calling her husband a spitzbub, or rascal, on a postcard. By 1915 it had become Comstock's proud boast that his efforts had led to the imprisonment of 3,600 people and caused fifteen suicides. Among those trampled by his zeal was one Ida Craddock, whose book *The Wedding Night*, a work of serious fiction, had been found obscene by a jury that had not been allowed to read it.

Comstock's efforts were in the long run largely counterproductive. His merciless bullying earned sympathy for many of his victims, and his efforts at suppression had an almost guaranteed effect of publicizing the attacked object beyond the creator's wildest dream, most notably in 1913 when he turned his guns on a mediocre painting by Paul Chabas called *September Morn*—which featured a young woman bathing naked in a lake—and made it a national sensation. Before the year was out, practically every barbershop and gas station in the country boasted a print.

Strangely, the one thing the Comstock Act did not do was define what constituted lewd, obscene, or indecent material. Congress happily left such judgments to Comstock himself. Not until 1957 did the Supreme Court get around to considering the matter of obscenity, and then it was unable to make any more penetrating judgment than that it was material that appealed to "prurient interests" and inflamed "lustful thoughts." In effect it ruled that obscenity could be recognized but not defined—or as Justice Potter Stewart famously put it: "I know it when I see it."[30] In 1973, the court redefined obscene works as those that "appeal to the prurient interest, contain patently offensive conduct, and lack artistic, literary, political, or scientific value." But it left it to local communities to interpret those values as they wished.

Problems of definition with regard to obscenity are notoriously thorny. In 1989, following criticism of the National Endowment for the Arts for funding exhibitions of controversial works by Robert Mapplethorpe and Andre Serrano, U.S. Senator Jesse Helms produced a bill that would deny federal funding for programs deemed to be obscene or indecent. The bill was interesting for being a rare attempt to provide an omnibus definition of what constituted the obscene. Among the proscribed subjects were works of art "including but not limited to depictions of sadomasochism, homoeroticism, the exploitation of children, or individuals engaged in sex acts; or material which denigrates the objects or beliefs of the adherents of a particular religion or nonreligion; or material which denigrates, debases, or reviles a person, group, or class of citizens on the basis of race, creed, sex, handicap, age, or national origin." At last America had a bill that stated the precise boundaries of acceptability. Unfortunately, as critics pointed out, it was also full of holes.

Quite apart from the possibilities for abuse inherent in open-ended phrases like "including but not limited to" and "a particular religion or nonreligion," the law if followed to the letter would have made it illegal to provide funding for, among much else, Shakespeare's *Merchant of Venice*, *The Bacchae* by Euripides, *The Clouds* by Aristophanes, operas by Wagner and Verdi, and paintings by Rubens, Rembrandt, and Picasso. It would even have made it illegal to display the Constitution, since that document denigrates blacks by treating them as three-fifths human (for purposes of determining proportional representation). The bill was rejected and replaced by one prohibiting "obscene art," again leaving it to others to determine what precisely obscene might be, and trusting that they would know it when they saw it.

State laws regarding obscenity and morality have been equally—we might say ridiculously—prone to ambiguity. Two things are notable about such state laws: first, how intrusive they are, and second, how vague is the language in which they are couched. Many go so far as to proscribe certain acts (e.g., oral sex) even between consenting adults, even sometimes between husband and wife. Most states have laws against fornication and even masturbation lying somewhere on their books, though you would hardly know it, such is the evasive language with which the laws are phrased. One of the most popular phrases is *crime against nature* (though in California it is *the infamous crime against nature* and Indiana *the abominable and detestable crime against nature*), but almost never do they specify what a *crime against nature* is. An innocent observer could be excused for concluding that it means chopping down trees or walking on the grass.

Many others have laws against "self-pollution," but again without providing a definition of what is intended by the expression. Occasionally statutes include a more explicit term like *sodomy* or *masturbation,* but often this serves only to heighten the uncertainty. Indiana, for instance, has a law, passed in 1905, which reads in part: "Whoever entices, allures, instigates, or aids any person under the age of twenty-one (21) years to commit masturbation or self-pollution, shall be deemed guilty of sodomy."[31] If, as the law implies, masturbation and self-pollution are not the same thing, then what exactly *is* self-pollution? Smoking a cigarette? Failing to keep fingernails clean? Whatever it may be, in Indiana at least as late as the 1950s you could spend up to fourteen years in prison for it.

In those few instances where states have tried to be more carefully explicit in their statutes, they have usually ended up tying themselves in knots. Kansas, for instance, gave itself a law that made adultery in the form of vaginal intercourse illegal, but not when it involved deviate sex acts. What is certain is that most people have broken such a law at one time or another. The sex researcher Alfred Kinsey, not normally a man to make light of such matters, once remarked only half jokingly that with what he knew from his surveys, 85 percent of the people of Indiana should be in prison and the other 15 percent were anemic.

The difficulty, of course, is that acceptable behavior, not just in sex but in all things, is a constantly changing concept. Just consider the matter of beards. In 1840, Americans had been beardless for so long—about two hundred years—that when an eccentric character in Framingham, Massachusetts, grew a beard he was attacked by a crowd and dragged off to jail. Yet by the mid-1850s, just a decade and a half later, there was scarcely a beardless man in America. Or consider hemlines. In 1921, when hemlines began to climb to mid-calf, Utah considered imprisoning—not fining, but imprisoning—women who wore skirts more than three inches above the ankle. Virginia, alarmed by developments at the other end of the body, introduced a bill that would make it a criminal offense to wear a gown that displayed more than three inches of throat. Ohio decided to leave women unmolested, but to go to the heart of the matter and punish any retailer found selling a garment that "unduly displays or accentuates the female figure."[32] Such outrage wasn't reserved just for female attire. As late as 1935, any male venturing onto the beach of Atlantic City with a bare chest faced arrest for indecency.[33]

In short, standards of acceptability constantly change. A period of repression is almost always followed by a spell of license. The ferociously restrictive age of Anthony Comstock, which drew to a close with his death in 1915, was immediately followed by a period of relative abandon. Not only did hemlines climb to shocking heights, but young people, made suddenly mobile by the availability of cars, took to partying until all hours, drinking bathtub gin, and engaging in heavy sessions of *necking* and *petting*—activities that had always existed, of course, but had only recently acquired such explicit labels. Other newly minted terms of the period—*bedroom eyes; playboy; tall, dark, and handsome*—betray a frankness that could not have been expressed ten years earlier.

Nothing better captured the new spirit of sexual boldness, or the inevitable backlash against it, than the movies. After their cautious start, movies in the period 1915–1920 became wildly daring by the standards of the day. Studios cranked out a succession of pictures with provocatively enticing titles like *Virgin Paradise, Red Hot Romance, The Fourteenth*

Lover, Her Purchase Price, Flesh and the Devil, and *White Hot Stuff.*[34] One lurid poster promised viewers a motion picture featuring "neckers, pet-ters, white kisses, red kisses, pleasure-mad daughters, sensation-craving mothers . . . the truth—bold, naked, sensational."[35] Even historical epics got the treatment. *Helen of Troy* was advertised as "an A.D. Mamma in a B.C. town."[36] A very few, like the 1918 movie *A Man's World,* did con-tain brief nudity, and others certainly implied rampant sex, but for the most part the hottest thing was the poster.

In 1921, with Hollywood rocked by scandal—it was the year of the Fatty Arbuckle case and the death in sexually questionable circum-stances of a director named William Desmond Taylor—and with thirty-seven states and hundreds of municipalities threatening to come up with a confusion of censorship codes, Hollywood acted. It formed a body of-ficially called the Motion Picture Producers and Distributors of Amer-ica, Inc., but known to everyone as the Hays Office, after its first director, Will H. Hays. A former chairman of the Republican Party and Postmaster General under President Warren G. Harding, Hays was a nonsmoking, nondrinking Indiana Presbyterian whose pinched face had extreme moral rectitude written all over it. (But like many others in the Harding administration, his probity did not extend to financial deal-ings. He was happy to receive and adroitly launder hundreds of thou-sands of dollars in illegal campaign contributions.) At a salary of $100,000 a year, Hays became the moral watchdog of America's movies.

In 1927, the Hays Office issued a famous list of "Don'ts and Be Care-fuls." The list consisted of eleven proscribed acts, such as "excessive or lustful kissing," and twenty-six to be handled with extreme caution. In 1930 this was superseded by a much more comprehensive Production Code, which would remain the bible of film production for half a cen-tury. The code decreed several broad principles—that pictures should be wholesome, that the sympathies of the audience should never be "thrown to the side of crime, wrongdoing, evil, or sin"—and scores of specific strictures. It forbade the uttering on screen not just of every common swear word and racial epithet, but such dramatically useful terms as *eunuch, floozy, louse* (the Hays Office helpfully suggested *stinkbug* as an alternative), *guts, in your hat, nuts, nerts, cripes, hellcat, belch,* and even, remarkably, *virtuous* (on the presumption that it was a too explicit reminder that some people weren't). *Liar* was permitted in comedies but not dramas, and *traveling salesman* could be used but not in a context in-volving a farmer's daughter.[37] *Lord,* even in reverential contexts, had to be changed to *Lawsy.* One of the more indestructible myths concerning the code is that it decreed that when a man and woman were shown in bed together the man must always have at least one foot on the floor. It said no such thing. But it did touch on almost everything else. One movie historian commented that "it prohibited the showing or mentioning of almost everything germane to the situation of normal human adults."

Even *it* in the wrong context could be considered dangerously suggestive. In 1931, the Hays Office ordered Samuel Goldwyn to change the name of his comedy *The Greeks Had a Word for It* to *The Greeks Had a Word for Them*. In much the same spirit, the title of a Joan Crawford movie was changed from *Infidelity* to *Fidelity*. Three years later, when Goldwyn bought the rights to Lillian Hellman's play about lesbianism, *The Children's Hour*, Hays told him that he could by all means make it into a movie, as long as it didn't have anything to do with lesbians and he didn't call it *The Children's Hour*. The movie was made without lesbians and with the title *These Three*.[38]

Occasionally, producers could preserve a line through trade-offs. David O. Selznick managed to save Clark Gable's famous, and at the time shocking, "Frankly, my dear, I don't give a damn," in *Gone With the Wind*—a line not in the original script, incidentally—by sacrificing "May your mean little soul burn in hell for eternity."[39] But for the most part, films became sensationally cautious, and would remain so into the 1960s.

As late as 1953, the main character in *Gentlemen Prefer Blondes* was not permitted to say "Bottoms up" when quaffing a drink. In the Broadway production of *The Seven-Year Itch*, the main character committed adultery, but in the 1955 movie, Tom Ewell could only agonize over the dangerous temptation of it. *Captain's Paradise*, a 1952 British comedy in which Alec Guinness played a sea captain with wives in two ports, was allowed to be released in America only after the producers added an epilogue admonishing the audience not to try such a thing themselves.[40] Even Walt Disney was forbidden to show a cow with udders.[41]

Finally in 1968, with the Production Code almost universally ignored, it was abandoned and a new system of ratings was introduced. Originally films were rated, in order of descending explicitness, *X, R, M,* and *G*. *M* was later changed to *GP* and later still to *PG*. *XXX,* or *Triple-X,* though favored by owners of *porno theaters* (an Americanism of 1966), never had official standing.

Newspapers and magazines never had a regulatory body equivalent to the Hays Office. They just behaved as if they did. Well into the 1930s, the *New York Times* would not allow *syphilis* or *venereal disease* to besmirch its pages even in serious discussions.[42] In 1933, when there was a breakthrough in the treatment of syphilis, neither it nor most other papers could work out quite how to tell their readers. Most fell back on the conveniently vague term *social disease.* An innocent reader could well have concluded that it involved handshaking.

As late as 1943, when a husband's homosexuality was a factor in a sensational murder trial, few newspapers could bring themselves to name his affliction. One described the man as having "indications of an abnormal psychological nature."[43] *Rape* was commonly euphemized to *assault,* as in the famous—but probably apocryphal and certainly undocumented—story of an attacker who "repeatedly struck and kicked his victim, hurled her down a flight of stairs, and then assaulted her."

Because of social strictures against even the mildest swearing, America developed a particularly rich crop of euphemistic expletives—*darn, durn, goldurn, goshdad, goshdang, goshawful, blast, consarn, confound, by Jove, by jingo, great guns, by the great horn spoon* (a nonce term first cited in the *Biglow Papers*), *jo-fired, jumping Jehoshaphat,* and others almost without number—but even these cautious epithets could land people in trouble as late as the 1940s. Mencken notes how a federal judge in New York threatened a lawyer with contempt for having the impertinence to utter "darn" in his court. *Esquire* magazine found itself hauled into court by the Postmaster General in 1943 for daring to print *backside, behind,* and *bawdy house* in various issues. It wasn't even necessary to say a word to cause offense. During the Second World War, an anti-German song called "Der Fuehrer's Face" was banned from the nation's airwaves because it contained a Bronx cheer.

Television, too, had a self-imposed code of ethics. As early as 1944, when Norma Martin and Eddie Cantor sang a duet of the song "We're Having a Baby, My Baby and Me," and accompanied it with a little hula dance, the cameraman was ordered to blur the image.[44] On an early talk show when the English comedian Beatrice Lillie jokingly remarked of belly dances that she had "no stomach for that kind of thing," it caused a small scandal. In the early 1950s, after an Arkansas congressman with the God-fearing name Ezekiel C. Gothings held hearings on sex and violence on television (in which, *inter alia,* the young Paul Harvey expressed his profound shock at having seen one night "a grass-skirted young lady and a thinly clad young gentleman . . . dancing the hoochie-koochie to a lively tune and shaking the shimmy"), the networks adopted their own code, which essentially decreed that nothing that any person anywhere could possibly find immoral would ever appear on America's airwaves.[45]

Thus in 1952, when Lucille Ball became pregnant, the term wasn't permitted. She was *expecting.* Nor was it just sex that prompted censorship. In 1956, when Rod Serling wrote a script about a black youth in

Mississippi who is murdered after whistling at a white woman, the producers of *The U.S. Steel Hour* enthusiastically went along with the idea—so long as the victim wasn't black, wasn't murdered, and didn't live in the deep South.

Books, by comparison, showed much greater daring. *Fucking* appeared in a novel called *Strange Fruit* as early as 1945, and was banned in Massachusetts as a result. The publishers took the state to court, but the case fell apart when the defense attorney arguing for its sale was unable to bring himself to utter the objectionable word in court, in effect conceding that it was too filthy for public consumption.[46] In 1948, Norman Mailer caused a sensation by including *pissed off* in *The Naked and the Dead*. Three years later, America got its first novel to use four-letter words extensively when James Jones's *From Here to Eternity* was published. Even there the editors were at sixes and sevens over which words to allow. They allowed *fuck* and *shit* (though not without excising about half of such appearances from the original manuscript) but drew the line at *cunt* and *prick*.[47]

Against such a background, dictionary makers became seized with uncertainty. In the 1960s, the Merriam Webster *Third New International Dictionary* broke new ground by including a number of taboo words—*cunt, shit,* and *prick*—but lost its nerve when it came to *fuck*. Mario Pei protested the omission in *The New York Times*, but of course without being able to specifiy what the word was. To this day, America remains to an extraordinary degree a land of euphemism. Even now the U.S. State Department cannot bring itself to use the word *prostitute*. Instead it refers to "available casual indigenous female companions."[48] Producers of rapeseed are increasingly calling it *canola,* lest the first syllable offend any delicate sensibilities even though *rape* in the horticultural sense comes from *rapa,* Latin for turnip.[49]

Despite the growing explicitness of books and movies, in most other areas of public discourse—notably in newspapers, radio, and local and network television—America remains perhaps the most extraordinarily cautious nation in the developed world. Words, pictures, and concepts that elsewhere excite no comment or reaction remain informally banned from most American media.

In 1991 the *Columbia Journalism Review* ran a piece on the coverage of a briefly infamous argument between Pittsburgh Pirates Manager Jim Leyland and his star player Barry Bonds. It examined how thirteen newspapers from around the country had dealt with the livelier epithets the two men had hurled at each other. Without exception the papers had replaced the offending words with points of ellipsis or dashes, or else had changed them to something lighter—making *kissing your ass* into *kissing your butt,* for instance. To an outside observer, there are two immediately arresting points here: first, that *kissing your ass* is still deemed too distressingly graphic for modern American newspaper readers, and second, that *kissing your butt* is somehow thought more decorous. Even more arresting is that the *Columbia Journalism Review,* though happy to revel in the discomfort at which the papers had found themselves, could not bring itself to print the objectionable words either, relying instead on the coy designations "the F-word" and "the A-word."

Examples of such hyperprudence are not hard to find. In 1987, *New York Times* columnist William Safire wrote a column on the expression *cover your ass* without being able to bring himself to actually utter the dread phrase (though he had no hesitation in listing many expressive synonyms: *butt, keister, rear end, tail*). In the same year when a serious art-house movie called *Sammy and Rosie Get Laid* was released, Safire refused to name the film in his column. (The *Times* itself would not accept an ad with the full title.) Safire explained: "I will not print the title here because I deal with a family trade; besides, it is much more titillating to ostentatiously avoid the slang term."[50] Pardon me? On the one hand, he wishes to show an understandable consideration for our sense of delicacy; on the other, he is happy to titillate us—indeed, it appears to be his desire to *heighten* our titillation. Such selective self-censorship would seem to leave American papers open to charges of, at the very least, inconsistency.

In pursuit of edification, I asked Allan M. Siegal, assistant managing editor of the *Times,* what rules on bad language obtain at the paper. "I am happy to say we maintain *no* list of proscribed expressions," Siegal replied. "In theory, *any* expression could be printed if it were central to a reader's understanding of a hugely important news development." He noted that the *Times* had used *shit* in reports on the Watergate transcripts, and also *ass, crap,* and *dong* "in similarly serious contexts, like the Clarence Thomas sexual harassment hearings."

Such instances, it should be noted, are extremely exceptional. Between 1980 and July 1993, *shit* appeared in *The New York Times* just once (in a book review by Paul Theroux). To put that in context, during the period in review the *Times* published something on the order of 400 million to 500 million words of text. *Piss* appeared three times (twice in book reviews, once in an art review). *Laid* appeared thirty-two times, but each time in reference to the movie that Safire could not bring himself to name. *Butthead* or *butthole* appeared sixteen times, again almost always in reference to a particular proper noun, such as the interestingly named pop group *Butthole Surfers.*

As a rule, Siegal explained, "we wish not to shock or offend unless

there is an overweening reason to risk doing do. We are loath to con-
tribute to a softening of the society's barriers against harsh or profane
language. The issue is nothing so mundane as our welcome among paying customers, be they readers or advertisers. Our management truly
believes that civil public discourse is a cherished value of the democracy,
and that by our choices we can buttress or undermine that value."[51]

One consequence of the American approach to explicit language is
that we often have no idea when many of our most common expressions first saw light, since they so often go unrecorded. Even something
as innocuous as *to be caught with one's pants down* isn't found in print until
1946 (in the *Saturday Evening Post*), though it is likely that people were
using it at least a century earlier.[52] More robust expressions like *fucking-A*
and *shithead* are effectively untraceable.

Swearing, according to one study, accounts for no less than 13 percent of all adult conversation, yet it remains a neglected area of scholarship. One of the few studies in recent years is *Cursing in America*, but its
author, Timothy Jay of North Adams State College in Massachusetts,
had to postpone his research for five years when his dean forbade it. "I
was told I couldn't work on this and I couldn't teach courses on it, and
it wouldn't be a good area for tenure," Jay said in a newspaper interview.[53] "The minute I got tenure I went back to dirty words." And quite
right, too.

Chapter 19

FROM KITTY HAWK TO THE JUMBO JET

The story is a familiar one. On a cold day in December 1903, Orville and Wilbur Wright, assisted by five locals, lugged a flimsy-looking aircraft onto the beach at Kitty Hawk, North Carolina. As Wilbur steadied the wing, Orville prostrated himself at the controls and set the plane rolling along a wooden track. A few moments later, the plane rose hesitantly, climbed to about fifteen feet, and puttered along the beach for 120 feet before setting down on a dune. The flight lasted just twelve seconds and was shorter than the wingspan of a modern jumbo jet, but the airplane age had begun.

Everyone knows that this was one of the great events of modern technology, but there is still a feeling, I think, that the Wrights were essentially a pair of inspired tinkerers who knocked together a simple contraption and were lucky enough to get it airborne. We have all seen film of early aircraft tumbling off the end of piers or being catapulted into haystacks. Clearly the airplane was an invention waiting to happen. The Wrights were just lucky enough to get there first.

In fact, their achievement was much, much greater than that. To master powered flight, it was necessary to engineer a series of fundamental breakthroughs in the design of wings, engines, propellers, and control mechanisms. Every piece of the Wrights' plane was revolutionary, and every piece of it they designed and built themselves.

In just three years of feverish work, these two retiring bachelors from Dayton, Ohio, sons of a bishop of the United Brethren Church, made themselves the world's preeminent authorities on aerodynamics. Their homebuilt wind tunnel was years ahead of anything existing elsewhere. When they discovered that there was no formal theory of propeller dynamics, no formulae with which to make comparative studies of different propeller types, they devised their own. Because it is all so obvious to us now, we forget just how revolutionary their concept was. No one else was even within years of touching them in their mastery of the aerodynamic properties of wings. Their warping mechanism for controlling the wings was such a breakthrough that it is still "used on every fixed-wing aircraft that flies today."[1] As Orville noted years later in an uncharacteristically bold assertion, "I believe we possessed more data on cambered surfaces, a hundred times over, than all of our predecessors put together."[2]

Nothing in their background suggested that they would create a revolution. They ran a bicycle shop in Dayton. They had no scientific training. Indeed, neither had finished high school. Yet, working alone, they discovered or taught themselves more about both the mechanics and science of flight than anyone else had ever come close to knowing. As one of their biographers put it: "These two untrained, self-educated engineers demonstrated a gift for pure scientific research that made the more eminent scientists who had studied the problems of flight look almost like bumbling amateurs."[3]

They were distinctly odd. Pious and restrained (they celebrated their first successful flight with a brief handshake), they always dressed in business suits with ties and starched collars, even for their test flights. They never married, and always lived together. Often they argued ferociously. Once, according to a colleague, they went to bed heatedly at odds over some approach to a problem. In the morning, they each admitted that there was merit in the other's idea and began arguing again, but from the other side. However odd their relationship, clearly, it was fruitful.

They suffered many early setbacks, not least returning to Kitty Hawk one spring to find that a promising model they had left behind had been rendered useless when the local postmistress had stripped the French sateen wing coverings to make dresses for her daughters.[4] Kitty Hawk, off the North Carolina coast near the site of the first American colony on Roanoke Island, had many drawbacks—monster mosquitoes in summer, raw winds in winter, and an isolation that made the timely acquisition of materials and replacement parts all but impossible—but there were compensations. The winds were steady and generally favorable, the beaches spacious and free of obstructions, and above all the sand dunes were mercifully forgiving.

Samuel Pierpont Langley, the man everyone expected to make the first successful flight—he had the benefits of a solid scientific reputation, teams of assistants, and the backing of the Smithsonian Institution, Congress, and the U.S. Army—always launched his experimental planes from a platform on the Potomac River near Washington, which turned each test launch into a public spectacle, then a public embarrassment as his ungainly test craft unfailingly lumbered off the platform and fell nose first into the water. It appears never to have occurred to Langley that any plane launched over water would, if it failed to take wing, inevitably sink. Langley's devoted assistant and test pilot, Charles Manly, was repeatedly lucky to escape with his life.

The Wright brothers, by contrast, were spared the pestering attention of journalists and gawkers and the pressure of financial backers. They could get on with their research at their own pace without having to answer to anyone, and when their experimental launches failed, the plane would come to an undamaged rest on a soft dune. They called their craft the *Wright Flyer*—named, curiously enough, not for its aeronautical qualities but for one of their bicycles.

By the fall of 1903, the Wright brothers knew two things: that Samuel Langley's plane would never fly and that theirs would. They spent most of the autumn at Kitty Hawk—or more precisely at Kill Devil Hills, near Kitty Hawk—readying their craft, but ran into a series of teething problems, particularly with the propeller. The weather, too, proved persistently unfavorable. (On the one day when conditions were ideal they refused to fly, or do any work, because it was a Sunday.) By December 17, the day of their breakthrough, they had been at Kitty Hawk for eighty-four days, living mostly on beans. They made four successful flights that day, of 120, 175, 180, and 852 feet, lasting from twelve seconds to just under a minute. As they were standing around after the fourth flight, discussing whether to have another attempt, a gust of wind picked up the plane and sent it bouncing across the sand dunes, destroying the engine mountings and rear ribs. It never flew again.

Because it occurred so far from the public gaze, news of their historic achievement didn't so much burst onto the world as seep out. Several newspapers reported the event, but often with only the haziest idea of what had taken place. The *New York Herald* reported that the Wrights had flown three miles, and most other papers were similarly adrift in their details.

Many of those who had devoted their lives to achieving powered flight found it so unlikely that a pair of uneducated bicycle makers from Dayton, working from their own resources, had succeeded where they had repeatedly failed that they refused to entertain the idea. The Smithsonian remained loyal to Langley—he was a former assistant secretary of the institution—and refused to acknowledge the Wrights' accomplishment for almost forty years.

The Wrights' hometown, Dayton, was so unmoved by the news that it didn't get around to giving them a parade until six years later.

Unfazed, the brothers put further distance between themselves and their competitors. By 1905, in an improved plane, they were flying up to twenty-four miles, and executing complicated maneuvers, while staying aloft for almost forty minutes. Only the tiny capacity of the plane's fuel tank limited the duration of their flights.[5] The next year they received their patent, but even it was not the ringing endorsement they deserved. It credited them only with "certain new and useful improvements in Flying-machines."

The Wright brothers seemed unbothered by their lack of acclaim. Although they made no secret of their flying, they also offered no public demonstrations, and hence didn't attract the popular acclaim they might have. Indeed, in 1908, when the more publicity-conscious Glenn Curtiss flew over half a mile at Hammondsport, Connecticut, many assumed that that was the first flight.

In 1914, long after Langley himself was dead, the Smithsonian allowed Curtiss to exhume Langley's airplane, modify it significantly, and try to fly it in order to prove retroactively that the Wrights had not been the first to design a plane capable of flight. With modifications that Langley had never dreamed of, Curtiss managed to get the plane airborne for all of five seconds, and for the next twenty-eight years the Smithsonian, to its eternal shame, displayed the craft as "the first man-carrying aeroplane in the history of the world capable of sustained free-flight."[6]

The original Wright Flyer spent twenty-five years under dustcovers in a Dayton shed. When no institution in the United States wanted it, it was lent to the Science Museum in London and displayed there from 1928 to 1948. Not until 1942 did the Smithsonian at last accept that the Wrights were indeed the creators of powered flight, and not until forty-five years after their historic flight was the craft at last permanently displayed in America.

The Wright brothers never called their craft an *airplane*. The word had existed in America for almost thirty years and, as *aeroplane*, in Britain for even longer, having been coined in a British engineering magazine in 1869 to describe a kind of airfoil used in experiments. To the Wrights, *airplane* signified not the entire craft but only the wing. In the early days, there was no agreed term for an aircraft. Langley had called his contraption an *aerodrome*. Others had used *aerial ship* or *aerial machine*. The Wright brothers favored *flying machine*. Not until about 1910 did *airplane* become the standard word in America and *aeroplane* in Britain.

Flying and its attendant vocabulary took off with remarkable speed. By the second decade of the century, most people, whether they had been near an airplane or not, were familiar with terms like *pilot, hangar, airfield, night flying, cockpit, air pocket, ceiling, takeoff, nosedive, barnstorming, tailspin, crack-up* (the early term for a crash), *to bail out,* and *parachute.* Pilots were sometimes referred to as *aeronauts,* but generally called *aviators,* with the first syllable pronounced with the short ă of navigator until the 1930s.

In 1914, *airlines* entered the language. The first airlines were formed not to carry passengers but mail. Pan American Airways began by ferrying mail between Key West and Havana. Braniff, named for its founder, Tom Braniff, covered the Southwest. Other early participants were United Aircraft and Transport Corporation, which would eventually become United Airlines; Pitcairn Aviation, which would evolve into Eastern Air Lines; and Delta Air Lines, which had begun as a crop-dusting service in the South. *Airmail* was coined in 1917, and *airmail stamp* followed a year later.

Early planes were dangerous. In 1921, the average pilot had a life expectancy of nine hundred flying hours.[7] For airmail pilots, flying mostly at night without any proper navigational aids, it was even worse. While an airmail pilot on the St. Louis–Chicago run, Charles Lindbergh staked his life on a farmboy in Illinois remembering to put on a hundred-watt bulb in his backyard each night before he went to bed. It is little wonder that of the first forty pilots hired to carry airmail for the government, thirty-one died in crashes. Lindbergh himself crashed three planes in a year.

Largely because of the danger, flying took on a romance and excitement that are difficult to imagine now. By May 1927, when Lindbergh touched down at Curtiss Field on Long Island for his historic flight across the Atlantic, the world had become seized with a kind of mania about flying and was ready for a hero. Lindbergh was just the person to provide it.

In recent months, six aviators had died attempting to cross the Atlantic, and several other groups of pilots at or around Curtiss Field were preparing to risk their lives in pursuit of fame and a $25,000 payoff called the Oteig Prize. All the other enterprises involved teams of at least two men flying muscular, well-provisioned, three-engined planes. And here was a guy who had flown in from out of nowhere (and had incidentally set a coast-to-coast speed record in the process) and was aiming to fly the ocean alone in a frail, single-engined mosquito of a plane. That he had lanky boyish good looks and an aw-shucks air of innocence made him ideal, and within days, America and the world were gripped by a Lindy hysteria. On the Sunday after his arrival, thirty thousand people showed up at Curtiss Field hoping to get a glimpse of this untried twenty-five-year-old hero.

That Lindbergh was a one-man operation worked in his favor. Where others were fussing over logistics and stocking up on survival rations, he bought a bag of sandwiches at a nearby lunch counter, filled up his fuel tank, and quietly took off in the little plane named *The Spirit of St. Louis* (so called because his backers were from there). He departed at 7:52 A.M. on May 20, 1927, and was so loaded down with fuel that he flew most of the distance to Nova Scotia just fifty feet above the ocean.[8] Because a spare fuel tank had been bolted onto the nose, Lindbergh had no forward visibility. To see where he was going, he had to put his head out the side window. Thirty-four hours later, at 10:22 at night, he landed at Le Bourget Airport outside Paris. One hundred thousand people were there to greet him.

To the French he was *Le Boy.* To the rest of the world he was *Lucky Lindy*—and he was lucky indeed. Though he did not know it, the night before he had taken possession of the plane, one of the workmen fueling it had lost a piece of hose in the tank. Since a piece of hose could easily foul the fuel lines, there was no option but to take it out. The workman had cut a six-inch hole in the tank, retrieved the hose, and surreptitiously patched the hole with solder. It was a miracle that it held throughout the turbulent Atlantic crossing.

Lindbergh was by no means the first person to cross the Atlantic by air. In May 1919, eight years earlier, a U.S. Navy plane had crossed from Newfoundland to Lisbon, though it had stopped in the Azores en route. A little less than a month after that, John Alcock and Arthur Brown of Great Britain flew from Newfoundland to Ireland, the first nonstop flight. Lindbergh flew fifteen hundred miles farther, and he did it alone, and that was enough for most people. Indeed, most didn't want to be reminded that Lindbergh was not the first. When *Ripley's Believe It or Not,* a popular newspaper feature, noted that some twenty other people (including those in dirigibles) had crossed the Atlantic by air before Lindbergh, its offices were inundated with 250,000 letters attacking its unconscionable lack of patriotism.

Never before in modern history had anyone generated such instant and total adulation as Lindbergh. When he returned to America, the parade in his honor produced more confetti than had been thrown to greet the returning troops after the First World War. New York City gave him the largest dinner that had ever been put on for a private citizen. The New York Stock Exchange even closed for the day. Such was the hysteria that attached itself to Lindbergh that when his mother went to have her hair done in Washington, it took twenty-five policemen to control the mobs fighting to glimpse her.[9]

The immense excitement and sense of possibility that Lindbergh's solo flight generated helped to usher in the age of passenger travel. Within two years most of the airmail lines were carrying passengers, and others, like American Airways (later Airlines), National Airlines Taxi Service, and Northwest (later Northwest Orient) Airways Company, were rushing to join the market. Lindbergh himself helped to found what is generally credited as the first true passenger airline. Formed in 1929, it was called Transcontinental Air Transport, or TAT, but was commonly known as the Lindbergh Line. In July of that year, using Ford Trimotor planes, TAT began the first long-distance passenger services across America, and in so doing introduced concepts that are still with us: flight attendants (only men were employed at first), lavatories, meals on board, and individual reading lights. Three months later, the first in-flight movies were introduced. It also took the very bold—at the time almost unthinkable—decision not to carry parachutes.

Because of a paucity of suitable airports and certain vexing limitations of the Ford Trimotors, not least an inability to clear any but the smallest mountains, passengers flew only about two-thirds of the total distance across the country. Westward-bound travelers began with an overnight train ride from New York's Pennsylvania Station to Columbus, Ohio. There, safely past the Alleghenies, they boarded the first plane. It flew at about 2,500 feet and at a top speed of one hundred miles an hour, stopping in Indianapolis, St. Louis, Kansas City, Wichita, and Waynoka, Oklahoma. At Waynoka, passengers boarded yet another train to carry them past the Rockies to Clovis, New Mexico, where a plane was waiting to take them on to Los Angeles via Albuquerque, New Mexico, and Winslow and Kingman, Arizona. The whole undertaking was, by modern standards, drafty, uncomfortable, and slow. Altogether the trip took forty-eight hours—though that was twenty-four hours faster than the fastest train. As a reward for their bravery, and for paying an extravagant $351.94 for a one-way ticket, every passenger was given a solid-gold fountain pen from Tiffany's.[10]

Planes were unpressurized and unventilated. For many passengers, breathing at the higher altitudes was difficult. Often the rides were so rough that as many as three-quarters of the passengers became *airsick* (another new word of the age). Even the celebrated aviator Amelia Earhart was seen diving for the *airbag* (and another) on one early flight. For pilots there were additional difficulties. The Ford Trimotor, called with wary affection the *Tin Goose* by airline crews, was a challenging plane to fly. One of its more notable design quirks was that the instruments were mounted outside the cockpit, on one of the wing struts, and tended to became fogged once the plane was airborne.[11]

Almost from the start, TAT was dogged with misfortune. Six weeks after services began, a Los Angeles–bound plane crashed in bad weather in New Mexico, killing all eight passengers. Four months later, a second plane crashed in California, killing sixteen. People began to joke that *TAT* stood for "Take a Train." In between these two crashes came another—that of Wall Street, when shares plummeted on Black Monday, October 29, 1929, marking the start of the Great Depression. TAT's potential market all but dried up.

TAT lost almost $3 million in its first year and was taken over by Western Air Express, which itself evolved into Transcontinental and Western Air—TWA. (The name Trans World Airlines was the product of a later, more expansive age.) Within a year, it had slashed the one-way fare to just $160 (though there were no more free pens) and introduced the first *stewardess*. Her name was Ellen Church and she chose the job title herself.

On October 21, 1936, just nine years after Lindbergh's daring flight, Pan Am inaugurated regular passenger flights across the Pacific from San Francisco to Manila, with refueling stops at Honolulu, Midway, Wake, and Guam. Three years later, the airline also offered the first scheduled flights across the Atlantic, to Marseilles via the Azores and Lisbon, aboard its Flying Clippers, four-engine, twenty-two-passenger Boeing flying boats. Ocean flights inspired an ominous new term, *point of no return,* which first appeared in The *Journal of the Royal Aeronautics Society* in 1941 and quickly moved into the language in various figurative senses.

The logistics of Pan Am's Pacific operations were formidable. Wake and Midway were uninhabited, so everything needed on the islands, from pancake batter to spare engines, had to be shipped in. Three complete hotels were built in San Francisco, dismantled, shipped to Midway, Wake, and Guam, and there reassembled. By September 1940, Pan Am had extended its Pacific operations and was advertising flights to New Zealand in just four and a half days. If pressed for time, travelers could instead settle for two-day flight to Midway—"an ideal choice for those who seek a restful, carefree South Seas atmosphere," the ads boasted. What the ads didn't say was that Midway was a desolate heap of sand and that the few lonely people stationed there spent most of their time shooting rats. In any case, a little over two years later, Midway became a rather less desirable holiday spot when it found itself at the noisy epicenter of one of the greatest battles of the war in the Pacific.

Despite the risks and discomfort, the number of airline passengers soared. Between 1930 and 1940 the number of air travelers went from 417,000 to over three million.[12] World War II naturally acted as a brake on the growth of the airlines, but it also had the benefit of producing huge advances in long-distance aviation, which the airlines were quick to exploit with the return of peacetime. By 1947, Northwest Orient Airlines was boasting a flying time from Chicago to Shanghai of forty-one hours, and from New York to Tokyo of just thirty-nine, on its won-drous Stratocruisers, which offered every comfort. Because hotel stops were no longer necessary, they came equipped with beds known, almost inevitably, as *Skysleepers.* Six years later, Pan Am introduced transatlantic jet services, and beds became a thing of the past as the faithful Stratocruiser gave way to the Boeing 707. Instead of names, planes in-creasingly had numbers—a not insignificant loss to the romance of air travel.

Jet travel sprinkled the language with new words: *jet-hop* (1952), *jet-port* (1953), *jet set* (1960), *jet lag* (1966), and *jet fatigue* and *jet syndrome* (1968), alternative words for the more durable *jet lag.* Also in 1968 came an entirely new type of passenger plane named for, of all things, a cir-cus elephant that had lived a century earlier. I refer, of course, to the *jumbo jet.*

The jumbo became a feature of travel when introduced into service by Pan Am on January 21, 1970. (The first flight, from Kennedy Airport to Heathrow, took off seven and a half hours late because of an engine problem.) The plane's formal name was the Boeing 747, so called be-cause ever since the 707, Boeing's jetliners had been numbered in incre-ments of ten in the order in which they came off the drawing board. Interestingly, the feature that makes the jumbo instantly recognizable, its hump, came about because Boeing feared the plane would not be a suc-cess. The feeling in the early 1960s when the plane was being designed was that supersonic jets were just around the corner and that they would quickly render jumbos obsolescent as passenger carriers. The decision was therefore taken to design them so that they could easily be con-verted into freighters. Putting the cockpit out of the way up in a hump, made it possible to load freight through the aircraft's nose.[13]

That the most successful commercial aircraft in history should be called after a circus elephant is an obvious oddity. People are sometimes surprised to learn that Jumbo the elephant wasn't called that because he was big, but rather that big things are called *jumbo* because of him. In fact, when he was given his name—it is a shortening of *mumbo jumbo,* a term for a West African witch doctor, which found a separate usefulness in English as a synonym for *gibberish*—he was just a baby, only recently arrived at London Zoo. No one had any idea that he would grow to be-come the largest animal ever kept in captivity.

Most Americans became familiar with Jumbo when P. T. Barnum, the circus impresario, bought the elephant from London Zoo in 1884, a scandal that outraged millions of Britons, and began exhibiting him all over America. Barnum's handbills depicted Jumbo as absolutely enormous—one showed a coach and horses racing through his legs, with plenty of clearance. In fact, Jumbo was nothing like that tall. Though indisputably the largest elephant ever measured, he was no more than eleven feet seven inches in height. (Barnum was seldom troubled by considerations of accuracy. One of his other lasting creations, the "wild man from Borneo," was in fact a native of Paterson, New Jersey.)[14]

Nonetheless, thanks to Barnum's tireless and inventive promotion, the name *Jumbo* became associated with outsizedness, and before long people were buying jumbo cigars, jumbo suitcases, and jumbo portions of food and eventually traveling on jumbo jets. Jumbo's American career was unfortunately short-lived. One night in September 1885, after Jumbo had been on the road for only about a year, he was being led to his specially built boxcar after an evening performance in St. Thomas, Ontario, when an express train arrived unexpectedly and plowed into him, with irreversible consequences for both elephant and train. It took 160 men to haul Jumbo off the tracks. Never one to miss a chance, Barnum had Jumbo's skin and bones separately mounted, and thereafter was able to exhibit the world's largest elephant to two audiences at once, without any of the costs of care or feeding. He made far more money out of Jumbo dead than alive.[15]

Chapter 20

WELCOME TO THE SPACE AGE: THE 1950S AND BEYOND

In 1959, in one of those delvings into the future that magazines found so satisfying in the 1950s, *Newsweek* presented this confident scenario for the lucky housewife of 1979: "Waking to cool 1970-style music from a tiny phonograph built into her pillow, the housewife yawned, flicked a bedside switch to turn on the electronic recipe-maker, then rose and stepped into her ultrasonic shower."

Among the many things *Newsweek*'s soothsayer failed to foresee was that by 1979 the housewife would be an endangered species. What the world got instead were words like *workaholic, drive-by shootings, crack cocaine, AIDS, repetitive stress injury, gridlock,* and *serial killer.* We're still waiting for the ultrasonic shower.

If *Newsweek* surveyed the future in 1959 from a somewhat optimistic perspective, we can hardly blame it. In the 1950s, life in the United States was about as good as it gets. The Second World War had not only ended the Great Depression and decked the country with honor, but laid the groundwork for an economic boom almost beyond conceivable proportions. Where the war had reduced much of Europe and Asia to rubble, exhausted national treasuries, destroyed industries, and left millions homeless or even stateless, the United States was intact. Her twelve million returning servicemen and women came home to a country untouched by bombs. In 1945, the country had $26 billion worth of factories that had not existed when the war started, all but $6 billion of which could be converted more or less immediately to the production of nonmilitary goods: cars, televisions, refrigerators, tractors, processed foods, steel girders, you name it. And America, uniquely among nations in 1945, had money to spend—more than $143 billion in War and Savings Bonds alone.[1] The stage was set for the greatest consumer boom in history.

By the early 1950s, most American homes had a telephone, television, refrigerator, washing machine, and car—items that would not become standard possessions in Europe and Japan for years, and not always then. With just 6 percent of the earth's population and 7 percent of its land area, the United States by the mid-1950s was producing and consuming 40 percent of total global output—nearly as much as the rest of the world put together.[2] What is particularly notable is how self-contained America was in this period. Throughout the 1950s, imports amounted to no more than 3.2 percent of *gross national product* (an Americanism coined in 1946 by the economist Simon Kuznets, who won a Nobel Prize for his efforts) and direct exports to no more than 4.7 percent. The United States became the richest country in the world without particularly needing the rest of the world.

Partly it did so by being massively more efficient than its competitors. General Motors, with 730,000 employees, made a profit in 1966 of $2.25 billion. To equal this figure it would have been necessary to combine the total profits of the forty largest firms in France, Britain, and Germany, which together employed about 3.5 million people. American companies grew bigger than some countries. General Electric's sales in 1966 exceeded the gross national product of Greece. Ford was a bigger economic entity than Austria or Denmark. IBM generated more turnover than Sweden, Belgium, or Spain. And General Motors was bigger than them all.

In short, life in postwar America was bounteous, secure, and infinitely promising. The economy was running at full throttle, jobs and wages were plentiful, and stores bulged with consumer goods of a richness and diversity that other nations could simply gape at. America had truly become, in the words of John Kenneth Galbraith's 1958 book title, *The Affluent Society*. Only two things clouded the horizon. One was the omnipresent possibility of nuclear war. The other was a phenomenon much closer to home and nearly as alarming. I refer to teenagers.

Teenagers, it hardly needs saying, had always been around, but only recently had they become a recognized presence. So little had they been noticed in the past that *teenager* had entered the language only as recently as 1941. (As an adjective, *teenage* had been around since the 1920s, but it wasn't much used.) In the heady boom of the postwar years, however, America's teenagers made up for lost time. Between 1946 and 1960, when the population of the United States rose by about 40 percent, the number of teenagers grew by 110 percent as America underwent a massive *baby boom* (though that term would not be coined until 1978, in an article in the *New Yorker*).[3]

By the mid-1950s, teenagers were not just everywhere, but disturbingly so. To their elders they seemed almost another species. They dressed sloppily, monopolized the phone and bathroom, listened to strange music, and used perplexingly unfamiliar terms—*wheels* for a car, *square, daddyo, far out, beat, cool* and *coolsville, what a drag, bad news, big deal, chick, neat* and *neato, gone,* and *real gone*. They had a particularly rich supply of words for the culturally underendowed: *loser, creep, weirdo, square, drip,* and the much-missed *nosebleed*. Any stupid joke, particularly if voiced by one's immediate relatives, was met with a pained expression and a withering "hardeeharhar." They seemed to take pride in appearing demented and even created a word for the condition: *kooky* (probably modified from *cuckoo*). Movies like *Rebel Without a Cause* and *The Wild One* and books like *On the Road* and *The Catcher in the Rye* showed America's youth to be disaffected, willful, irrational, and possibly dangerous. One prominent psychologist, Robert Linder of Baltimore, gravely announced in a series of lectures that young people were "suffering from a form of collective mental illness,"[4] suggesting that he may have had a touch of it himself.

An ominous term, *juvenile delinquency,* began to fill news pages and excite comment. *The Blackboard Jungle,* a 1955 movie that dealt with delinquency and other manifestations of youthful angst, was thought so sensational that Clare Booth Luce, America's ambassador to Italy, led a campaign to forbid its being shown abroad lest people get the wrong impression about America. Apparently she was not worried that they might instead conclude that America no longer believed in freedom of expression. The movie's theme tune, "Rock Around the Clock," was for most nonteenagers their first experience of the music known as *rock 'n' roll,* a term popularized by a Cleveland disc jockey named Alan Freed, who had studied classical trombone before taking to the airwaves, where he introduced his listeners to the music of Chuck Berry, Fats Domino, and other such exotics. In 1951, he began referring to the music as *rock 'n' roll,* though among black Americans the expression was older, having originally been applied to sex and later to dancing.

Above all, what separated America's teens of the 1950s from previous generations was that they were rich. By mid-decade, one historian has noted, "America's 16.5 million teens were buying some 40 percent of all radios, records, and cameras, more than half the movie tickets, and even 9 percent of all new cars. Altogether they were worth over $10 billion a year to the economy."[5]

Much of their wealth came from, and often returned to, another phenomenon of the age, the hamburger joint, which provided employment for thousands of teenagers and a haunt for most of the rest. Though the hamburger had been part of the American diet for half a century, it underwent a kind of apotheosis in the 1950s. As late as 1950, pork was, by a considerable margin, still the most widely eaten meat in America, but two decades later Americans were eating twice as much beef as pork, nearly a hundred pounds of it a year, and half of that in the form of hamburgers. One company more than any other was responsible for this massive change in dietary habits: McDonald's.

The story as conveyed by the company is well known. A salesman of Multimixers named Ray Kroc became curious as to why a small hamburger stand on the edge of the desert in San Bernardino, California, would need eight Multimixers—enough to make forty milkshakes at a time, more than any other restaurant in America could possibly want to make—and decided to fly out to have a look. The restaurant he found, run by the brothers Maurice and Richard McDonald, was small, only six hundred square feet, but the burgers were tasty, the fries crisp, and the shakes unusually thick, and it was unquestionably popular with the locals. Kroc was fifty-two years old, an age when most men would be thinking of slowing down, but he saw an opportunity here. He bought the McDonald's name and began building an empire. The implication has always been that the original McDonald's was an obscure, rinky-dink operation in the middle of nowhere, and that it was only the towering genius of Ray Kroc that made it into the streamlined, efficient, golden-arched institution we know and love today. It wasn't entirely like that.

By 1954, when Kroc came along, the McDonald brothers were already legendary, at least in the trade. *American Restaurant* magazine had done a cover story on them in 1952, and they were constantly being visited by people who wanted to see how they generated so much turnover from so little space. With sales of over $350,000 a year (all of it going through one busy cash register) and profits above $100,000, McDonald's was one of the most successful restaurants in America. In his autobiography, Kroc makes it sound as if the McDonald brothers had never thought of franchising until he came along. In fact, by the time he visited them they had a dozen franchised operations going.

Almost everything later associated with the McDonald's chain was invented or perfected by the brothers, from the method of making French fries to the practice of trumpeting the number of hamburgers sold. As early as 1950, they had a sign out front announcing "Over 1 Million Sold." They even came up with the design of a sloping roof, red-and-white-tiled walls, and integral golden arches—not for the San Bernardino outlet but for their first franchise operation, which opened in Phoenix in 1952, two years before Kroc came along.

The McDonalds were, in short, the true heroes of the fast-food revolution, and by any measure they were remarkable men. They had moved to California from New Hampshire during the Depression years, and opened their first drive-in restaurant in 1937 near Pasadena. It didn't sell hamburgers. But in 1940, they opened a new establishment at 14th and E Streets, at the end of Route 66, in San Bernardino in a snug octagonal structure. It was a conventional hamburger stand, and it did reasonably well.

But in 1948 the brothers were seized with a strange vision. They closed the business for three months, fired the twenty carhops, got rid of all the china and silverware, and reopened with a new, entirely novel idea: that the customer would have to come to a window to collect the food rather than have it brought to the car. They cut the menu to just seven items—hamburgers, cheeseburgers, pie, potato chips, coffee, milk, and pop. Customers no longer specified what they wanted on their hamburgers but received them with ketchup, mustard, onions, and pickle. The hamburgers were made smaller—just ten to a pound—but the price was halved to 15 cents each.

The change was a flop. Business fell by 80 percent. The teenagers on whom they had relied went elsewhere. But gradually a new type of clientele developed, the family, particularly after they added French fries and milk shakes to the menu, and even more particularly when customers realized that the food was great and that you could feed a whole family for a couple of bucks. Before long, McDonald's had almost more business than it could handle.

As volume grew, the brothers constantly refined the process to make the production of food more streamlined and efficient. With a local machine shop owner named Ed Toman they invented almost everything connected with the production of fast food, from dispensers that pump out a precise dollop of ketchup or mustard to the lazy susans on which twenty-four hamburger buns can be speedily dressed. Toman even improved on Kroc's Multimixers, modifying the spindles so that shakes could be made in their paper cups rather than in tin canisters and then transferred. Above all, the McDonalds introduced the idea of specialization—one person who did nothing but cook hamburgers, another who made shakes, another to dress the buns, and so on—and developed the now universal practice of having the food prepared and waiting so that customers could place an order and immediately collect it.

The parallels between the McDonald brothers and Wright brothers are striking. Like the Wrights, the McDonald brothers never married and lived together in the same house. Like the Wrights, they had no special interest in wealth and fame. (The McDonalds' one indulgence was to buy a pair of new Cadillacs every year on the day that the new models came out.) Both sets of brothers were single-mindedly devoted to achieving perfection in their chosen sphere, and both sets created something from which others would derive greater credit and fame. The McDonald brothers had just one distinction that set them apart from the Wrights. They dreaded flying, which presented a problem in keeping tabs on their expanding empire. So when Ray Kroc came along and offered to form a partnership in which he would look after the franchising side of the operation, they jumped at his offer.

Kroc was, it must be said, a consummate seller of franchises. By 1961, the year he bought the brothers out for $2.7 million, there were two hundred McDonald's restaurants, and the company was on its way to becoming a national institution. Kroc achieved this success in large part by making sure that the formula of the original San Bernardino McDonald's was followed everywhere with the most exacting fidelity. His obsession with detail became legendary. He dictated that McDonald's burgers must be exactly 3.875 inches across, weigh 1.6 ounces, and contain precisely 19 percent fat. Big Mac buns should have an average of 178 sesame seeds. He even specified, after much experimentation, how much wax should be on the wax paper that separated one hamburger patty from another.

Such obsessiveness made McDonald's a success, but it also led to the creation of a culture that was dazzlingly unsympathetic to innovation. As he recounted in his autobiography, when a team of his most trusted executives suggested the idea of miniature outlets called MiniMacs, Kroc was "so damned mad I was ready to turn my office into a batting cage and let those three guys have it with my cane."[6] Their failing, he explained, was to think small. One could be excused for concluding that their failure was to think at all.

As an empire builder, Kroc had no peer, but as a dietary innovator, his gifts were modest. One of his biographers has noted: "Every food product he thought of introducing—and the list is long—bombed in the marketplace."[7] In consequence, the McDonald's menu is essentially a continuing testament to the catering skills of the founding brothers. The relatively few foods that have been added to the menu since 1954 have usually been invented by franchisees, not by headquarters staff, and often drew liberal inspiration from the creations of competing chains. The *Big Mac,* introduced nationwide in 1968, was invented and named by a franchisee in Pittsburgh named Jim Delligatti, though it was certainly similar to, if not actually modeled on, a two-patty, triple-deck sandwich created fourteen years earlier by the Big Boy chain in California. The *Filet-O-Fish* was thought up by a franchisee in a Catholic section of Cincinnati who wanted something to offer his customers on Fridays, but essentially it is just a large fishstick in a bun. The prototype for the *Egg McMuffin,* originally called the *Fast Break Breakfast,* came from a franchisee in Santa Barbara, but again it echoed a rival's product, an egg benedict breakfast roll from the Jack-in-the-Box chain.

Nonetheless, the McDonald's formula has clearly worked. In an average year, all but 4 percent of American consumers will visit a McDonald's at least once. McDonald's accounts for 32 percent of all hamburgers, 26 percent of all French fries, 5 percent of all Coca-Cola, and nearly a fifth of all meals taken in a public place. McDonald's buys more beef and potatoes and trains more people than any other organization, the U.S. Army included. It is the world's largest owner of real estate. In 1994, it had thirteen thousand restaurants in sixty-eight countries serving 25 million customers daily.[8] So international a commodity has the Big Mac become that since 1986, the *Economist* has used the cost of a Big Mac in various world cities as a more or less serious basis for an index comparing the relative value of their currencies.

McDonald's, like so much else of modern American life, from the supermarket to the shopping mall, was a creature of the two great phenomena of the postwar years: the car and the suburbs. Together they transformed they way we live.

Suburbs were hardly new in the 1950s. The word dates from as far back as 1325, and *suburbia* and *suburbanite* have been current since the 1890s. Before the American Revolution, most cities had their suburbs—places like Harlem, New York, and Medford, Massachusetts—but they weren't dormitory communities in the modern sense. Until about 1850, a suburb was defined as "an undifferentiated zone outside the city limits."[9] They were largely self-contained communities, and often the sites of noxious enterprises that were ill suited to the confined spaces of cities.

Of necessity, most people in colonial America lived densely packed together in cities—in 1715, Boston's fifteen thousand inhabitants shared just seven hundred acres of land—and went almost everywhere on foot. Walking was such an unquestioned feature of everyday life that until 1791, when William Wordsworth coined the term *pedestrian,* there was no special word to describe someone on foot. (Interestingly, *pedestrian* as an adjective meaning dull or unimaginative is significantly older, having been coined in 1716.)

Not until the development of the steam passenger ferry in the 1830s did the possibility of retiring at night to a home in a separate (if invari-ably close by) community begin to take root. The passenger ferry trans-formed a few places like Tarrytown, Stony Point, and Brooklyn, New York, but the expense, limited carrying capacity, and slow speed of fer-ries kept their overall effect slight. The history of suburban living in America really begins with the railroads. Starting with Naperville, Illi-nois, in 1857, railroad suburbs began to pop up all over. Orange and Secaucus, New Jersey; Oak Park, Lake Forest, and Evanston, Illinois; Scarsdale, New York; Darien and Fairfield, Connecticut; and hundreds of other communities were either created or wholly transformed by the railroads. Even California, a state not normally associated with railroads, spawned a number of such communities, notably San Rafael and Po-mona.[10] As railroad suburbs grew, two new words entered the language, *commute* and *commuter*, both Americanisms and both first recorded in 1865.[11]

The growing popularity of railroad suburbs inspired an entirely new type of community: the model suburb. As the name suggests, model suburbs were purpose-built communities, primarily for the well-to-do. Where railroad suburbs had grown willy-nilly, often absorbing existing communities, the model suburbs were built from scratch and offered not just handsome residential streets, but everything else their well-heeled citizens could require: parks, schools, shopping districts, and eventually country clubs. (The Country Club, built in the Boston suburb of Brookline in 1867, appears to have provided both the name and the model for this most suburban of social centers.) Among the more ven-erable of model suburbs are Beverly Hills, California; Shaker Heights, Ohio; and Forest Hills, New York.

The development of the streetcar in the closing years of the nine-teenth century provided a new boost and a measure of democratization to suburban living with the rise of streetcar suburbs, which pushed cities further into the countryside and offered the prospect of fresh air, space, and escape from the urban hurly-burly for millions of office and factory workers and their families.

Even taken together, all these early types of suburbs never added up to more than a peripheral feature of American life. Two factors con-spired in the 1940s to make the suburbanization of the country com-plete. The first was the need for cheap, instant housing immediately after the war. The second was the rise of the automobile in the early 1950s.

In 1945, America needed, more or less immediately, five million ad-ditional houses as war-deferred marriages were consummated and mil-lions of young couples settled down to start a family. The simplest and cheapest solution was for a developer to buy up a tract of countryside within commuting distance of a city and fill it with hundreds— sometimes thousands—of often identical starter homes. The master of the art was Abraham Levitt, who began scattering the eastern states with his Levittowns in 1947. By making every home identical and employing assembly-line construction techniques, Levitt could offer houses at re- markably low cost. At a time when the average house cost $10,000, Levitt homes sold for just $7,900, or $65 a month, with no down pay- ment, *and* they came equipped with all major appliances.

Soon housing developments were going up along the edges of every city. By 1950, a quarter of Americans lived in suburbs. Ten years later, the proportion had risen to one-third. Today, over half of Americans live in suburbs—more than in cities, farms, and rural communities combined.

As people flocked to the suburbs, jobs followed. Between 1960 and 1990, five of every six jobs created in America's thirty-five biggest met- ropolitan areas were in the suburbs. Instead of pouring into the cities by day to work, millions of Americans now seldom went into the cities at all. In the thirty years from 1960, the number of people who commuted across county lines—in effect, lived in one suburb and worked in another—tripled to over 27 million.[12] The suburbs had taken over.

As early as 1955, the phenomenon was noticed by the writer A. C. Spectorsky, who coined the term *exurbia* for this new kind of commu- nity that was emotionally and economically independent from the me- tropolis that had spawned it, but it was not until 1991, when a *Washington Post* reporter named Joel Garreau wrote a book titled *Edge City*, that this vast transition in living patterns gained widespread notice.

To qualify as an edge city by Garreau's definition, a community must have five million square feet of office space, 600,000 square feet of shop- ping space, and more people working there than living there. The United States now has more than two hundred edge cities. Los Angeles and New York have about two dozen each. Almost all have been created since 1960, and almost always they are soulless, impersonal places, unfo- cused collections of shopping malls and office complexes that are ruth- lessly unsympathetic to nonmotorists. Many have no sidewalks or pedestrian crossings, and only rarely do they offer any but the most skel- etal public transit links to the nearby metropolis, effectively denying job opportunities to many of those left behind in the declining inner cities. About a third of all Americans now live in edge cities, and up to two- thirds of Americans work in them.[13] They are substantial places, and yet most people outside their immediate area have never heard of them. How many Americans, I wonder, could go to a map and point to even the general location of Walnut Creek, Rancho Cucamonga, Glendale, Westport Plaza, Mesquite, or Plano? Anonymous or not, they are the wave of the future. In 1993, nineteen of the twenty-five fastest-growing communities in the United States were edge cities.

If affordable housing was the first thing most returning GIs wanted in 1945, then without question a car was the second. As late as 1950, some 40 percent of American households still did not have a car. That would change dramatically in the next decade as the automobile became not just a convenience of modern life but, for millions, a necessity. In the period 1950–1980, America's population rose by 50 percent, but the number of cars quadrupled, until the number of cars far exceeded the number of households (because of two-or-more-car families).[14]

In keeping with America's confident new age of materialism, cars grew bigger, flashier, and most powerful in the postwar years. The man at the forefront of the styling changes was one Harley J. Earl, a longtime General Motors designer whose fascination was the Lockheed P-38 Lightning fighter aircraft of World War II led him to put outsized tailfins on the 1948 Cadillac. The next year, racy portholes called *venti-ports* appeared on Buicks. The year after that, Studebaker produced the sleek, bullet-nosed Champion DXL, which actually *looked* like a plane, and the race was on. By the mid-1950s every carmaker was turning out huge, flashy, grinning-grilled, multitoned, chrome-heavy, monstrously tailfinned road beasts that were the hallmark of the decade—cars that looked, in the words of one observer, as if they should light up and play. The style was called the *Forward Look*.

Cars were given names suggesting that they were not just powerful, but barely under control—*Firedome V8, Thunderbird, Tempest, Comet, Fury, Charger*—and they came with features that promised a heady mix of elegance, comfort, and fingertip control. Impressive-sounding features had been part of the car salesman's armory for some time—as early as 1940, De Soto was boasting a model with *Fluid Drive Simplimatic Transmission*—but it was really the development of powerful V-8 engines, a direct spin-off of World War II technology, that allowed carmakers to provide lots of gadgetry and gave the marketing people the scope to scramble for technological hyperbole. Some actively suggested aeronautic qualities, like the 1955 Buick which came with *R.S.V.P.* (short for "Really Sensational Variable Pitch") *propeller blades*. As the ads explained, these changed their pitch "like the propellers on an air liner, and what that does to getaway from a standing start—or for a safety-surge when it's needed out on the highway—is something you can only believe from firsthand experience." Others, like the Thunderbird with its *Trigger-Torque Power* and *Speed-Trigger Fordomatic Transmission*, sounded as if they might have the capacity to shoot down rival motorists. The next year Thunderbird added *Cruise-O-Matic Transmission,* presumably so that the driver could keep both hands on the gun.

By 1956, cars had features that all but promised liftoff. Chryslers came with *PowerFlite Range-Selector, Torque-Flight Transmission, Torsion-Aire Suspension,* and *Super-Scenic Windshield.* The Packard offered *New Torsion-Level Ride* and *Twin Ultramatic Transmission,* while the Chevrolet Bel-Air had a hold-on-to-your-hats feature called a *Triple-Turbine TurboGlide.* Mercury, misreading the market, could offer nothing zippier than *Dream-Car Design* and a *Seat-O-Matic Dial* that remembered the driver's favored position, and paid heavily for its terminological timidity with lost sales.

The height of this techno-excess came in 1957 when Packard produced a 145-horsepower Super Eight model, which came equipped with everything but a stewardess. The vaunted features included *Prest-O-Justment Seats, Flite-Glo Dials, Comfort-Aire Ventilation, Console-Key Instrument Panel,* and *Push-Button Control Wrinkle-Resistant RoboTop Convertible Roof.* Unfortunately it drove like a tank. Five years later, Packard was out of business.

The irony in this is that virtually none of the modern improvements to cars, such as disk brakes, fuel injection, front-wheel drive, torsion bars, and the like, were invented in America. Detroit was more concerned with gloss and zip than with genuine research and development, and within twenty years it would be paying for this lapse dearly.[15]

In 1955, into the midst of this battlefield of technological hyperbole and aerodynamic styling came a car so ineptly named, so clumsily styled, so lacking in panache that it remains almost forty years later a synonym for commercial catastrophe. I refer, of course, to the wondrous Edsel.

It is hard to believe now what high hopes Ford, its dealers, and most of America had for this car when it was announced to the world. After the Ford Company's huge success during its first two decades, it began to falter dangerously, largely because of Henry Ford's extreme reluctance to offer six-cylinder engines or models with a few curves and a dash of styling. It fell behind not only General Motors, but even Walter Chrysler's Plymouth. By the 1950s, Ford desperately needed a success. A new midsized car seemed the best bet. General Motors had not introduced one since the La Salle in 1927 and Chrysler not since the Plymouth in 1928. Ford's most recent effort at a breakthrough vehicle had been the Mercury way back in 1938.[16] The time was right for a new, world-beating car. In 1952, Ford began work on a secret project it called the *E car.*

Huge care was taken with choosing a name. Ford's advertising agency,

Foote, Cone and Belding, drew up a list of 18,000 suggestions, and the Ford staff kicked in a further 2,500. The poet Marianne Moore was commissioned to come up with a list of names, and offered such memorable, if unusable, suggestions as the *Mongoose Civique,* the *Utopian Turtletop,* the *Pluma Piluma,* the *Pastelogram,* the *Resilient Bullet,* the *Varsity Stroke,* and the *Andante con Moto.*

All of these were carefully whittled down to a short list of sixteen names. On November 8, 1956, an executive committee met to make the final choice. After much discussion it reduced the list to four favored names: *Corsair, Citation, Ranger,* and *Pacer.* Then, for reasons that are much disputed (largely because no one wished afterward to be actively associated with the choice), the panel members opted for a name not on the list, *Edsel,* for Edsel Ford, Henry and Clara Ford's only child, who in turn had been named for Henry's best friend. The name had been considered once before, but had been discarded when consumer research showed that almost everyone thought it sounded like the name of a tractor or plow.

Having signally botched the name, the company went on to botch the design and production of the car. The chief stylist of the Edsel was Roy A. Brown, Jr. By all accounts, Brown's initial design was a winner.* But excessive tampering—in particular, the imposition of a grille that had been variously likened to a horse collar or toilet seat—doomed it. There was also the consideration that the Edsel was not well made. The publicity department's plan was to have seventy-five automotive writers drive identical green-and-turquoise Edsel Pacers from Detroit to their hometown dealers. But when the first Edsels rolled off the assembly line, they were so riddled with faults that Ford had to spend an average of $10,000 apiece—twice the cost of the car—making them roadworthy. Even then it managed to have just sixty-eight cars ready by launch day.[17] A further setback occurred when the Edsel made its public debut on a live national television special and wouldn't start. Edsel had the most expensive advertising promotion of any product up to that time, but the company could hardly give the cars away.[18] Two years, two months, $450 million, and 110,847 Edsels later, Ford pulled the plug, and the Edsel became part of history.

Despite these occasional setbacks, the automobile as a component of American life went from strength to strength. By 1963, one-sixth of all American businesses were directly involved with building, supplying,

---

*Brown had gained his reputation in the company by designing a stunning concept car called the Lincoln Futura. It never went into production, but it did eventually find greater glory—as television's Batmobile.

repairing, or selling cars or their components.[19] The production of cars consumed 20 percent of America's steel, 30 percent of its glass and over 60 percent of its rubber.[20] By the 1970s, 94.7 percent of American commuters traveled to work by car. About half had no access to any form of public transportation. They had to drive to work whether they wanted to or not. Most in fact wanted to. Today the car has become such an integral part of American life that the *maximum* distance the average American is prepared to walk without getting into a car is just six hundred feet.[21]

Despite the nation's attachment to the automobile, relatively few motoring terms have entered the general lexicon in the postwar years. Among the few: *gridlock,* coined in 1971, but not in general usage until about 1980; *fast lane* in a metaphorical sense ("life in the fast lane") in 1978; *drive-by shooting* in 1985; and *to jump-start* in a metaphorical sense ("jump-start the economy") as recently as 1988. And that's about it.

What increasingly changed were the types—or more particularly the pedigrees—of the cars Americans drove. Until the early 1970s, with the exception of the Volkswagen Beetle and a few incidental European sports cars, American cars were overwhelmingly American. (In 1954, of the 7.2 million new cars sold in America, only about 50,000, well under 1 percent, were imports.) But then Japanese manufacturers entered the market. *Made in Japan,* which in the 1950s had been a joke term synonymous with shoddiness, took on an ominous sense of reliability and efficiency. Japanese carmakers that few Americans had heard of in 1970 were, by 1975, household names.*

American carmakers, so invincible only a decade earlier, suddenly seemed worryingly inept. They continued churning out heavy, often unreliable *gas-guzzlers* (an Americanism of 1969) in overmanned factories that were massively uncompetitive compared with the lean-production techniques of the Japanese. By 1992, the American car industry was losing $700 million a month. Even those who patriotically tried to *buy American* (an expression that gained widespread currency in the late 1970s) often couldn't. Of the $20,000 purchase price of a Pontiac Le Mans in 1991, $6,000 went to South Korea, $3,500 to Japan,

---

*In case you have ever wondered, the following are the derivations of the more popular Japanese car names: *Honda,* named for the company's founder, Soichiro Honda; *Isuzu,* named for the Isuzu River; *Mitsubishi,* Japanese for "three stones," which feature on the family crest of the founder; *Nissan,* Japanese for "Japan Industry"; *Suzuki,* named for the founder, Michio Suzuki; *Toyota,* named for the founder, Sakichi Toyoda, and not, as many stories have it, because the early models looked like "toy autos."[22]

and between $100 and $1,500 each to suppliers in Germany, Taiwan, Singapore, Britain, Ireland, and Barbados.[23] By 1988, imports, primarily of cars but also of cameras, televisions, radios, and much else in which America had once been self-sufficient, were equivalent to over 13 percent of America's gross national product, and the country's annual trade deficit had grown to $150 billion—about $600 for every man, woman, and child in the country.

By 1990, America's sense of declining economic prowess generated a volume of disquiet that sometimes verged on the irrational. When a professor of economics at Yale polled his students as to which they would prefer, a situation in which America had 1 percent economic growth while Japan experienced 1.5 percent growth, or one in which America suffered a 1 percent downturn but Japan fell by even more, 1.5 percent, the majority voted for the latter. They preferred America to be poorer if Japan were poorer still, rather than a situation in which both became more prosperous.

Years before America suffered the indignity of watching its industrial advantage eroded, it experienced a no less alarming blow to its technological prestige. On October 5, 1957, the nation was shaken to the core to learn that the Soviet Union had successfully launched a satellite called *Sputnik* (meaning "fellow earth traveler"). Never mind that Sputnik was only the size of a beachball and couldn't do anything except reflect light. It was the first earthbound object hurled into space. Editorial writers, in a frenzy of anxiety, searched for a scapegoat and mostly blamed the education system (a plaint that would be continually refined and applied to other perceived national failings ever after). Four months later, America rushed to meet the challenge with the launch of its own Vanguard satellite.[24] Unfortunately, it rose only a few feet off the launchpad, tipped over, and burst into flames. It became known, almost inevitably, as the *Kaputnik*. A little over three years later, the United States suffered further humiliation when the Soviets launched a spaceship, *Vostok,* bearing the cosmonaut Yuri Gagarin, which made a single orbit of Earth and returned safely. A week later, Cuban exiles, with American backing, launched the disastrous Bay of Pigs invasion of Cuba, and were routed. Never had America's stock sunk so low in the world.

The country's response was not entirely unlike that of the Yale economics students mentioned above. Without any idea of what the payback might be other than in glory, the country embarked on the most expensive scientific enterprise ever undertaken on the planet with the single ultimate goal of landing a man on the moon before the Soviet Union did. On July 20, 1969, the goal was achieved when Neil Armstrong stepped from his Apollo II spacecraft and became the first person to set foot on an extraterrestrial landmass. America was back on top.

The heady first decade of the space program created, or significantly rejuvenated, a clutch of words, among them *reentry, liftoff, blastoff, mission control, A-OK, thrust, launchpad, orbit, gantry, glitch* (first recorded outside a Yiddish context when spoken by John Glenn in 1966), and *astronaut*. What is perhaps most interesting is how many space terms predate the space age, thanks for the most part to the world's abiding love for science fiction. Among the words that took flight long before any space traveler did we find *astronaut* (1880), *spaceship* (1894), *space suit* (1924), *rocket ship* (1928), *star ship* (1934), *space station* (1936), *blastoff* (1937), *spaceman* (1942), and *time warp* (1954).[25]

The space race did have many technological spin-offs, not least in the development of communications satellites and even more particularly in the advance of computing. So universal have computers become in offices, banks, stores, and homes that it is easy to forget just what a recent development they are. The word has existed in English since 1646, but originally meant only "one who computes." In 1872 the name was given to a type of adding machine, and in the 1940s *computer* at last took on its modern sense of a machine designed to perform complex and intricate electronic calculations. The first such machine to be called a computer was the *Electronic Numeral Integrator and Computer* (or *ENIAC*) built in 1945. Similar machines had been built earlier, but had been called *calculators* or *integrators*.

As late as 1956, no more than two dozen computers existed in the United States. In the following two decades, their numbers multiplied vastly, but even in 1976, the year Apple Computer was founded, there were still perhaps no more than fifty thousand computers in the world. A decade later, that many were being built every day.[26]

One of the first popular reports on the emergence of computers appeared in March 1961 in a *Life* magazine article, "The Machines Are Taking Over." In a tone of chirpy awe, the author noted how a room-sized "robot" (a word he used throughout the story) had transformed the efficiency of the Braun Brothers sausage factory in Troy, Ohio. When fed a stack of punch cards telling it what cuts of meat were available, this device "hummed softly, its lights flickered, and it riffled the deck of cards over and over again." After a mere thirty-six minutes of card-shuffling and cogitating, the Braun computer spewed out the optimum recipe for making bologna: "24 pounds of cow meat, 24 of beef, 103 of beef cheeks, 150 of beef plate, 30 of neck bone meat, 24 of picnics, 65 of neck trimmings, 10 of trim conversion, 20 of rework from previous batches." And that was *all* it did. It couldn't handle accounts or billing, or monitor the company's heating and electricity. Thirty-six minutes of intense thinking about beef cheek and neck trimmings, and the machine retired exhausted till the next day.

It doesn't seem a terribly impressive performance now, but just five years earlier, Braun Brothers would have needed several million dollars and a separate building to house the computer power necessary to calculate the best use of beef plate, trim conversion, and the other delectable constituents of a well-made bologna. At just $50,000, the Braun Brothers computer was a bargain.

The same article went on to note how a computer in Glendale, California, was programed with the five hundred words most frequently used by beatnik poets and told to create its own poems. Typical of the genre was "Auto-Beatnik Poem No. 41: Insects":

> *All children are small and crusty*
> *And all pale, blind, humble waters are cleaning,*
>
> *A insect, dumb and torrid, comes of the daddyo*
> *How is a insect into this fur?*

The reporter noted that when several of these poems were read to an unsuspecting audience at a Los Angeles coffeehouse, many listeners "became quite stirred up with admiration."[27]

Though the computer is a comparatively recent entrant into daily life, some of the terminology associated with it goes back half a century or so. *Computer bugs* dates from the 1940s. There is, it appears, a literal explanation behind the term. In 1945, an early U.S. Navy vacuum tube computer crashed. Its operators searched in mystification for a cause until they found a moth crushed between the contact points of an electrical relay switch. After that whenever a computer was down, it was said to need *debugging.*[28] *Bit* (a contraction of *binary digit*) was coined at about the same time, though its offspring, *byte* (eight bits, for the technically unaware), dates only from 1964, and was apparently chosen arbitrarily.[29] Equally arbitrary is the *Winchester disk drive* (first recorded in print in 1973). It doesn't commemorate any person or place, but simply was the code name under which IBM developed the technology.

Computers have spawned many technical languages—*Assembler, Pascal, C, C++, OLE, Lisp, Ada, Fortran, Cobol, Algol, Oberon,* and others almost without number—and these in turn have generated a huge vocabulary. But for the layperson searching for linguistic excitement, the computer world is pretty much a dead planet. Though computer terminology runs to many thousands of words, the great bulk coined in the past twenty years, probably more than half are merely elaborations on already existing words (*port, format, file, copy, array*), and those that are original to the field are almost always dully descriptive and self-evident of their function (*microprocessor, random access memory, disk drive, database*). A slight exception is the operating system known as *DOS*. It originated as *Q-DOS* (a play on *kudos*), and stood, rather daringly, for *Quick and Dirty Operating System*. When Microsoft bought the firm in 1981, it changed the name to the more staid *MS-DOS,* for *Microsoft Disk Operating System*.[30] That is about as lively a computer story as you will find.

Among the computer terms that have seeped into general usage are *hardware* and *software* (coined mid-1960s, in general usage by the mid-1970s), *microchip* (1965, and being reduced to plain *chip* by 1967), *computer dating* (1968), *word processor* and *word processing* (both 1970, but not current outside technical journals before 1977), *hacker* (presumably from the image of one hacking through a thicket of passwords, as with a machete) and *floppy disk* (both 1975), *user-friendly* (1981), and *computer virus* (coined by an American researcher named Fred Cohen in 1984).

Thanks largely to the computer and other new technologies, the English language is growing by up to twenty thousand words a year.[31] Though the bulk of these new terms are scientific, technical, or of otherwise specialized application, many hundreds of terms find their way into the main body of English each year. The third edition of the *American Heritage Dictionary,* published in 1992, contained ten thousand words, about 5 percent of the total, that had not existed in general American English twenty years before—words like *yuppie, sushi, sunblock,* and *sound bite*. The second edition of the *Random House* unabridged dictionary, published in 1987, underwent an even more extensive change, with fifty thousand new words and 210,000 of its 315,000 entries revised or updated. Such is the accumulation of new formations that "dictionaries are going to have to come out every six to eight years rather than every ten to keep up with the [new] vocabulary," an editor of the *AHD* said in an interview.[32]

Among the many hundreds of words that have entered English in the last decade or so one starkly stands out: *AIDS*. Short for *acquired immune deficiency syndrome,* it was coined in 1982, but didn't enter the general consciousness until about 1985. Previously it had been called *GRID,* for *gay-related immune deficiency,* but the name was changed—and, it must be said, the world's attention perked up—after it was found to be infecting heterosexuals, particularly hemophiliacs. The name for the active agent in AIDS, the *human immunodeficiency virus,* or *HIV,* was coined in May 1986 by a committee of virologists after a year in which the virus had gone by two names: *LAV* and *HTLV3*.

Before we leave the space age, one small rhetorical curiosity, which oddly failed to attract much attention at the time, needs mentioning. I refer to the utterance of Neil Armstrong when he became the first person to set foot on the moon. As millions of people watched, Armstrong somberly announced: "That's one small step for man, one giant leap for mankind." The sentence was reprinted in thousands of headlines the next morning, but in the excitement of his achievement no one seems to have noticed the tautology of it. According to the historian Richard Hanser, Armstrong was astonished and dismayed upon his return to his native planet to find that he had been misquoted everywhere. What he had said was "That's one small step for *a* man, one giant leap for mankind." The indefinite article had been lost in transmission.[33]

A more thorny issue is whether, in light of developments of recent years, he should have engaged in such manifestly gender-biased speech. But that is another chapter.

Chapter 21

AMERICAN ENGLISH TODAY

Early in 1993, Maryland discovered that it had a problem when someone noticed that the state motto, *Fatti maschii, parole femine* ("Manly deeds, womanly words"), was not only odd and fatuous, but also sexist. The difficulty was that it was embossed on a lot of expensive state stationery and engraved on buildings and monuments, and anyway it had been around for a long time. After much debate, the state's legislators hit on an ingenious compromise. Rather than change the motto, they decided to change the translation. Now when Marylanders see *Fatti maschii, parole femine,* they are to think, "Strong deeds, gentle words."[1] Everyone went to bed happy.

Would that all issues of sensitivity in language were so easily resolved. In fact, however, almost nothing in recent years has excited more debate or awakened a greater polarity of views than the vaguely all-embracing issue that has come to be known as *political correctness.* The term was coined in 1975 by Karen DeCrow, president of the National Organization for Women, but not until about 1990 did it begin to take on an inescapably pejorative tone.[2] Since that time, newspapers and journals have devoted acres of space to reports that have ranged, for the most part, from the mildly derisive to the openly antagonistic. Some treated the issue as a kind of joke (a typical example: a *Newsweek* report in 1991 that pondered whether restaurant customers could expect soon to be brought a *womenu* by a *waitron* or *waitperson*), while others saw it as something much graver. Under leading headlines like "The New Ayatollahs" (*U.S. News & World Report*), "Politically Correct Speech: An Oxymoron" (*Editor & Publisher*), and "The Word Police" (*Library Journal*), many publications have assayed the matter with a mixture of outrage and worry.

Most of the arguments distill down to two beliefs: that the English language is being shanghaied by people of linguistically narrow views, threatening one of our most valued constitutional freedoms, and that their verbal creations are burdening us with ludicrously sanitized neologisms that are an embarrassment to civilized discourse. Two authors, Henry Beard and Christopher Cerf, have made much capital (in the fullest sense of the word) out of these absurdities with their satirical and popular *Official Politically Correct Dictionary and Handbook*, which offers several hundred examples of absurd euphemisms designed to free the language of the slightest taint of bias. Among the examples they cite: *differently hirsute* for bald, *custody suite* for a prison cell, *chemically inconvenienced* for intoxicated, *alternative dentation* for false teeth, and *stolen nonhuman animal carrier* for milkman. What becomes evident only when the reader troubles to scan the notes on sources is that almost all of these excessively cautious terminologies, including those just listed, were made up by the authors themselves.

This might be excused as a bit of harmless, if fundamentally pointless, fun except that these entries have often been picked up by others and transmitted as gospel—for example, in a 1992 article in *The Nation*, which referred to the "grotesque neologisms" of the political correctness movement and included several examples—*involuntarily domiciled* for homeless, *vocally challenged* for mute—that never existed before Beard and Cerf concocted them as amusing padding for their curious book.[3]

Most of the genuine examples of contrived neologisms that the authors cite are in fact either justifiable on grounds of sensitivity (*developmentally challenged* for mentally retarded), widely accepted (*date rape, pro-choice*), never intended by the creator to be taken seriously (*terminological inexactitude* for *lie*), the creations of jargon-loving bodies like sociologists or the military (*temporary cessation of hostilities* for *truce*), drawn from secondary sources of uncertain reliability (*personipulate* for *manipulate*, taken from another book on political correctness, but not otherwise verified), or become ridiculous only when given a barbed definition (suggesting that *wildlife management* is a common euphemism for "killing, or permitting the hunting, of animals").

What is left after all this are no more than a few—a very few—scattered examples of genuine ridiculousness by extremist users of English, mostly from the women's movement and mostly involving the removal of "man" from a variety of common terms—turning *manhole* into *femhole, menstruate* into *femstruate,* and so on.

I don't deny that there is much that is worthy of ridicule in the PC movement—name me a sphere of human activity where there is not—and I shall cite some questionable uses presently, but it seems to me that this is a matter that deserves rather more in the way of thoughtful debate and less in the way of dismissive harrumphing or feeble jokes about waitrons and womenus. All too often overlooked in discussions of the matter is that at the root of the bias-free language movement lies a commendable sentiment: to make language less wounding or demeaning to those whose sex, race, physical condition, or circumstances leave them vulnerable to the raw power of words. No reasonable person argues for the general social acceptance of words like *nigger, chink, spazz,* or *fag.* But when the argument is carried to a more subtle level, where intolerance or contempt is merely implied, the consensus falls to pieces.

In 1992, *U.S. News & World Report* in an article headlined "A Political Correctness Roundup" noted that "an anti-PC backlash is underway, but there are still plenty of cases of institutionalized silliness." Among the "silliness" that attracted the magazine's attention was the case of students at the University of Wisconsin–Milwaukee being encouraged "to go to a toy store and investigate the availability of racially diverse dolls," and of a New York lawyer being censured for calling an adversary in court "a little lady" and "little mouse."[4]

That students should be encouraged to investigate the availability of racially diverse dolls in a racially diverse society seems to me not the least bit silly. Nor does it seem to me unreasonable that a lawyer should be compelled to treat his courtroom adversaries with a certain measure of respect. (I wonder whether the parties at *U.S. News & World Report* might have perceived a need for courtesy had the opposing counsel been a male and the words employed been "bub" or "dickhead.") But that, of course, is no more than my opinion, which is the overweening problem with any discussion of bias-free usage—it is fearfully subjective, a minefield of opinions. What follows are, necessarily and inescapably, mine.

That a subtle and pervasive sexual bias exists in English seems to me unarguable. Consider any number of paired sets of words—*master/mistress, bachelor/spinster, governor/governess, courtier/courtesan*—and you can see in an instant that male words generally denote power and eminence, and that their female counterparts just as generally convey a sense of submissiveness or inconsequence. That many of the conventions of English usage—referring to all humans as *mankind,* using a male pronoun in constructions like *to each his own* and *everyone has his own view on the matter*—show a similar tilt toward the male is also, I think, beyond question. The extent of this is not to be underestimated. As Rosalie Maggio points out in her thoughtful *Dictionary of Bias-Free Usage,* when Minnesota expunged gender-specific language from its lawbooks, it removed

301 feminine references from state statutes, but almost twenty thousand references to men.[5] There is no question that English is historically a male-oriented language.

The difficulty, as many critics of political correctness have pointed out, is that the avoidance of gender-specific constructions contorts the language, flouts historical precedent, and deprives us of terms of long-standing utility. People have been using *man, mankind, forefathers, founding fathers, a man's home is his castle,* and other such expressions for centuries. Why should we stop now?

For two reasons. First, because venerability is no defense. Ninety years ago, *moron* was an unexceptionable term—indeed, it was a medically precise designation for a particular level of mental acuity. Its loose, and eventually cruel, application banished it from polite society in respect for the subnormal. Dozens of other words that were once unselfconsciously bandied about—*piss, cretin, nigger*—no longer meet the measure of respectability. Just because a word or expression has an antiquity or was once widely used does not confer on it some special immunity.

Moreover, such words are often easily replaced. *People, humanity, human beings, society, civilization,* and many others provide the same service as *mankind* without ignoring half the populace. Since 1987, the Roman Catholic Church in the United States has used a text, the *Revised New Testament of the New American Bible,* that is entirely nonsexist. In it, Matthew 4:4 changes from "Not on bread alone is man to live" to "One does not live by bread alone." Matthew 16:23, "You are not judging by God's standards, but by man's," becomes instead "You are thinking not as God does, but as human beings do."[6] So seamlessly have these changes been incorporated that I daresay few people reading this version of the New Testament would even notice that it is scrupulously nonsexist. Certainly it has not been deprived of any of its beauty or power.

Unfortunately, there remains in English a large body of gender-specific terms—*gamesmanship, busman's holiday, manhole, freshman, fisherman, manslaughter, manmade, first baseman,* and others beyond counting—that are far less susceptible to modification. Maggio notes that many such "man" words are in fact unexceptionable because their etymology is unconnected to man the male. *Manacle, manicure,* and *manufacture,* for example, come from the Latin for *hand,* and thus are only coincidentally "sexist."[7] *Tallboy* similarly passes muster because the closing syllable comes from the French for wood, *bois.* But in many scores of others the link with gender is explicit and irrefutable.

This poses two problems. First there is the consideration that although many gender-based words do admit of alternatives—*mail carrier* for *mailman*, *flight attendant* for *stewardess*—for many others the suggested replacements are ambiguous, unfamiliar, or clumsy, and often all three. No matter how you approach them, *utility access hole* and *sewer hole* do not offer the immediacy of recognition that *manhole* does. *Gamestership* is not a comfortable replacement for *gamesmanship*. *Frosh, frosher, novice, newcomer, greenhorn, tenderfoot,* and the other many proposed variants for *freshman* suffer from either excessive coyness or uncertain comprehensibility.[8]

That is not to say that this must always be so. Twenty years ago, *chair* for *chairman* sounded laughable to most people. *Ms.,* if not absurd, was certainly contentious. Most newspapers adopted it only fitfully and over the protests of white-haired men in visors. Today, both appear routinely in publications throughout the English-speaking world and no one thinks anything of it. There is no reason that *gamestership* and *frosh* and *sewer hole* should not equally take up a neutral position in the language. But these things take time. *Ms.* was coined as far back as 1949, but most people had never heard of it, much less begun to use it, until some twenty years later. Even the seemingly innocuous *flight attendant,* coined in 1947, wasn't adopted by any airline until 1974 and didn't come into general usage until the late 1970s.

More pertinently, there is the question of whether such words can always be legitimately termed sexist. Surely the notion that one must investigate a word's etymology before deciding whether it is permissible suggests that there is something inadequate in this approach. I would submit (though I concede that I can sometimes feel the ice shifting beneath my feet) that just as *man* is not sexist in *manipulate* or *mandible* so it is not in any meaningful sense sexist in *manhole* or *Walkman* or *gamesmanship*.

A word that imparts no overt sense of gender—that doesn't say, "Look, this is a word for guys only"—is effectively neuter. Words, after all, have only the meanings we give them. *Piss* is infra dig in polite company not because there is something intrinsically shocking in that particular arrangement of letters but because of the associations with which we have endowed the word. Surely it is excessive to regard a word as *ipso facto* objectionable because of the historical background of a syllable embedded in it, particularly when that word does not fire gender-sensitive synapses in most people's minds.

My point becomes somewhat clearer, I hope, when we look at what I think is the greatest weakness of the bias-free usage movement—namely, that often it doesn't know where to stop. The admirable urge to rid the language of its capacity to harm can lead to a zealousness that is little short of patronizing. Maggio, for instance, cautions us not to "use *left-handed* metaphorically; it perpetuates subtle but age-old negative associations for those who are physically left-handed." I would submit that a left-handed person (and I speak as one myself) would have to be sensitive to the point of neurosis to feel personally demeaned by a term like *left-handed compliment.*

Similarly she cautions against using *black* in a general sense—*black humor, black eye, black mark, blacksmith* (though not, oddly, *blackout*)—on the grounds that most *black* words have a negative connotation that subtly reinforces prejudice. Or as she puts it: "Avoiding words that reinforce negative connotations of *black* will not do away with racism, but it can lessen the everyday pain these expressions cause readers." I cannot pretend to speak for black people, but it seems to me unlikely that many can have experienced much "everyday pain" from knowing that the person who shoes horses is called a blacksmith.

Even "violent expressions and metaphors"—*to kill two birds with one stone, how does that strike you, to knock someone dead, smash hit, one thing triggers another, to kick around an idea*—are to be excluded from our speech on the grounds that they help to perpetuate a culture sympathetic to violence.

Such assertions, I would submit, are not only an excessive distraction from the main issues, but dangerously counterproductive. They invite ridicule—and, as we have seen, there is no shortage of people who ache to provide it.

A final charge often laid against the bias-free speech movement—that it promotes a bias of its own—is also not always easy to refute. Maggio outlaws many expressions like *a man's home is his castle* (and rightly in my view) but defends *a woman's work is never done* on the grounds that "this is particularly true and usually more true than of a man with a paid job and a family." Just because a sentiment is true doesn't make it nonsexist. (And anyway it isn't true.) Others take matters much further. When the University of Hawaii proposed a speech code for students and staff, Mari Matsuda, a professor of law, endorsed the idea but added the truly arresting belief "Hateful verbal attacks upon dominant group members by victims is permissible."[9]

With respect, I would suggest that consideration, reasonableness, and a sense of fairness are qualities that apply to all members of a speech community, not just to those who hold the reins.

Only one other linguistic issue has soaked up more ink and excited more passion than political correctness in recent years, and that is the debate over education standards. Falling test scores, a decline in literacy, and the alarmingly poor performance of American students compared with those of other nations have all generated much journalistic hand-wringing. Troubling indicators of educational failure are not hard to find. Writing in *The Atlantic Monthly* in 1990, Michael J. Barrett noted that in a comparison of proficiency in mathematics among high school seniors from fifteen nations, the United States came twelfth in geometry and calculus and next to last in advanced algebra. (Hong Kong came first and Japan second in all three.) American eighth-graders did slightly better, though only slightly. In a comparison with students from nineteen other countries, the U.S. pupils came sixteenth in geometry, twelfth in algebra, and tenth in arithmetic.[10]

The inference we are encouraged to draw from this is that poor standards of education and economic decline go hand in hand. In 1992, Yoshio Sakurachi, the speaker of Japan's lower parliamentary house, stirred a brief but vocal controversy when he attributed America's poor economic performance to illiteracy among its workforce. One-third of American workers, Sakurachi declared, could not read. Many were outraged by his utterances, not so much because they were held to be inaccurate as because a Japanese had had the impertinence to express them.

In fact, no one knows how many Americans are illiterate. Defining literacy is a complicated matter. The Department of Education divides literacy into three categories—prose literacy (as in books and newspapers), document literacy (as on order forms and tax returns), and quantitative literacy (involving the sort of mathematical skills necessary to figure a 15 percent tip, say)—and further breaks down each category into four levels, thus giving us twelve quite distinct ways in which to be literate or not. At the simplest level of prose literacy, according to the department's criteria, a person should be able to write a simple declarative sentence describing the kind of job he or she wants. On this basis, the department believes that 96.1 percent of adult Americans are literate. But at the highest level of prose literacy—being able to read a newspaper editorial and briefly summarize its contents—the level of literacy falls to 78.9 percent. Put another way, slightly more than one American adult in five cannot read a newspaper effectively.[11] So although Mr. Sakurachi was incorrect in his assertion, he was not far off.

Even by the most conservative estimates, America has at least twenty million adults—equivalent to the populations of Illinois and Michigan—who cannot read well enough to understand the instructions on a medicine bottle or add and subtract with sufficient competence to tally a checkbook.[12] Probably the figure is much worse. Noting a "national tendency to graduate anyone who occupies a desk long enough," the journalist Jonathan Maslow quoted a woman in Jackson, Mississippi, who told him: "I went through twelve years of school and two years of community college without ever learning to read, and passed with flying colors."[13] Signs of national failure to educate students to even a basic level are not hard to find. In Mississippi, almost half of adults do not have a high school diploma. One-third of the people in Kentucky aged twenty-five or older are functionally illiterate.[14] Large employers like Ford, Motorola, and IBM routinely spend huge sums teaching their workers the basic skills that schools failed to impart. Just among private employers, the market for remedial reading textbooks runs to $750 million a year[15]—good news for publishers, but hardly a source of pride for the rest of us.

Any number of culprits have been cited for this national embarrassment. Many have blamed the shortness of American school days (six hours on average) and school years (175 to 180 days—60 days fewer than in some countries).[16] Others blame states, particularly in the South, for neglecting the central role of education. Until as recently as 1982, Mississippi did not even make school attendance mandatory. Previously up to six thousand Mississippi children a year didn't bother to start school.[17]

Still others attribute the decline in learning to a lack of encouragement and attention at home, as parents are increasingly absent through work or divorce. The economist Victor Fuchs has calculated that parents in white households spend on average ten fewer hours per week with their children than they did in 1960. In black homes the decline has been even greater at twelve hours.[18]

Almost everyone cites television as a primary or secondary factor. Without question, American children watch a lot of TV. The average child aged two or older spends four hours a day, about a quarter of his or her waking time, plugged to the box. By the time they are eighteen, American children have been exposed to no fewer than 350,000 commercials.[19]

Alarmed by such figures, Congress in 1990 introduced the Children's Television Act, mandating that stations show programs with some educational value. The result, alas, was not better programming but more creative program descriptions. One station described the cartoon series *GI Joe* as "a pedagogical tool" that "promoted social consciousness" and familiarized children with "the dangers of mass destruction." Another described *Chip 'n' Dale Rescue Rangers* as a valuable demonstration of "the rewards of team effort." *The Flintstones,* meanwhile, was found to promote initiative and family values. A few stations did provide some more demonstrably educational programs, but a survey found that the great bulk of these were shown before 7 A.M. "After that," as *The Economist* noted dryly, "the stations got down to the scholarly stuff."[20]

While there is no doubt something in such fears, it should also be noted that it is very easy to give a distorted impression of America's educational performance. Consider the matter of those high school seniors who did so poorly on math tests. What Barrett and other commentators fail to note is that in many foreign countries, education after the age of sixteen is a far more elitist undertaking than in the United States. Not only is high school in many places reserved for the brightest students, but coursework is frequently far more focused. In England and Wales, for instance, the relatively few young people who proceed to high school will study as few as three or four subjects in which they have already demonstrated considerable proficiency. That England and Wales came third or fourth in all the math tests is less a testament to the far-sightedness of the British education system than to the rigorousness with which the less apt are excluded. Yet it was against highfliers such as these that the American students were in most cases being compared.

Even when the comparison is not with foreign students but with other Americans, it is easy to draw misleading conclusions. This is particularly true with the Scholastic Assessment Test (formerly Scholastic Aptitude Test), the exam that millions of high school seniors take as part of the college admissions process.

Between 1964 and 1990, scores on the SAT declined in all categories, to the dismay of educators and commentators everywhere. On the verbal component of the test, mean scores declined from 468 to 419 for women, from 463 to 429 for men, and from 466 to 424 overall. On the math section, females dropped from 467 to 455, males from 514 to 499, and overall scores from 492 to 476 (in all cases out of a possible 800). "We may be seeing the erosion of reading skills in this information age where people are getting their information by means other than reading," observed one alarmed official of the College Board, the body that administers the tests.[21]

As Professor Harvey A. Daniels has put it, "More than any other single piece of apparent information about language, the fact that the SAT scores of college-bound high school seniors have been steadily dropping since 1964 has helped critics to persuade the general public that both American English and the public schools are in a bad way."[22] But, Daniels goes on to note, there may be other explanations beyond the possibility that students are dumber or their teachers less skilled than a quarter of a century ago.

For one thing, colleges are accepting more students. Eighty percent of American colleges now accept more than 70 percent of applications.[23] More people in consequence take the exams. It is self-evident that with more students taking the exams, scores will fall. If admission to college is less rigorous than it was twenty years ago, it may well also be that students are approaching the test less earnestly than in the past. A student who knows that his chosen university admits anyone with a high school diploma and a checkbook has little incentive to regard the test as anything but a formality.

Other complaints against the SAT are that it favors boys over girls because some of the questions assume a familiarity with sports—there is a correlation between the number of sports-based questions and the ten-point gap between male and female performance, which cannot be accounted for in terms of general mental capability—and that it favors the well-to-do over the less affluent because it assumes some knowledge of finance.[24] Above all, there is the distinct but little-considered possibility that the SAT has not kept pace with changes in school curriculums.

In short, falling SAT scores tell us nothing except that they have been falling. They don't even indicate how those who take the tests will perform at college. Daniels notes: "The correlation between SAT scores and freshman grade-point averages is about 0.43, a rate of prediction only about 12 percent better than rolling dice." He goes on: "At Bowdoin College, cum laude graduates were studied to see whether their SAT scores could have predicted their superior performance. Of these honors graduates, a plurality had average SATs, while 31 percent had scored significantly above the college averages and 24 percent below it."[25]

What is almost always overlooked in these debates is that people have been complaining about declining educational standards for about as long as there have been schools to complain about. "Bad spelling, incorrectness as well as inelegance of expression in writing, ignorance of the simplest rules of punctuation, and almost entire want of familiarity with English literature, are far from rare among young men of eighteen otherwise well prepared for college," lamented the president of Harvard in 1871.[26] A colleague of his despaired of "the tedious mediocrity" of compositions among students and the want of "fresh thought." Princeton University was so alarmed at the quality of its undergraduates that in the 1870s it established a remedial writing clinic. And these, as Daniels notes, were "the picked youth of the country," the lucky few who had been fortunate enough to get any kind of secondary education.

It comes as a surprise to many to learn that high school is effectively a twentieth-century development. For the great majority of Americans, free education beyond elementary school level scarcely existed before the closing years of the nineteenth century. As late as 1890 only 7 percent of fourteen-to-seventeen-year-olds were still in school. Levels of attendance improved dramatically after that, but even so, as late as 1930 barely half of that age group were still students—and there are grounds to suppose that even among the educated half, scholarly attainments were not all that sparkling.[27]

In 1935, Alice E. Watson, an educational expert, conducted a study of spelling proficiency among American high school students. She found that 80 percent could not spell *cuckoos,* and that over half could not spell *ancient, chemistry, bookkeeping, nursing, beautiful, forty, forcible, ceiling, neither, vegetable,* or *heroes.*[28]

Would high school students do better today? I suspect so. Certainly they would do no worse. Many studies clearly indicate that educational attainments are far higher now than they were forty or fifty years ago. For instance, modern sixth-graders in Indiana, administered a reading test that had been given statewide in 1944, were found to score significantly higher in every category measured. Other experimental comparisons in Iowa, Ohio, and California have produced similar results.

The fact is that by most measures the American educational system is not at all bad. Almost 90 percent of Americans finish high school, and a quarter earn a college diploma—proportions that put most other nations to shame. For minorities especially, improvements in recent years have been significant. Between 1970 and 1990 the proportion of black students who graduated from high school increased from 68 percent to 78 percent.[29] The United States is educating more of its young, to a higher level, than almost any other nation in the world. That is something to be proud of.

There is, of course, huge scope for improvement. Any nation where twenty million people can't read the back of a cornflakes box or where almost half of all adults believe that human beings were created sometime in the past ten thousand years[30] clearly has its educational workload cut out for it. But the conclusion that American education is on a steep downward slope is, at the very least, unproven.

Then how to account for our economic decline? In fact, we don't need to. America is richer today than ever before, and tomorrow it will be richer still. Consider the facts. Between 1980 and 1991, the American economy grew by almost a third. Between 1986 and 1991, American exports of iron and steel rose by 322 percent, of clothing by 260 percent, of pharmaceuticals by 126 percent, of electrical machinery and telecommunications equipment by 122 percent, and so on down the line. Altogether, between 1986 and 1991 the volume of American exports increased by 80 percent, and its share of world trade rose from 14 percent to 18 percent. And that is just visible trade. In almost every area of the service sector that is traded abroad—in fast food, entertainment, computer software, consultancy, construction, courier services, you name it—American supremacy is unchallenged.

At the time of writing, the United States was the world's largest exporter and, by almost any measure, its most productive country. Despite the rise of Japan as an economic power, the average American worker still produces almost twice as much per hour as the average worker in Japan.[31] Moreover, manufacturing productivity throughout the 1980s grew in America at a rate of 4.3 percent, well ahead of most other developed countries. The *average* American home has two telephones, two televisions (with cable hookup), a VCR, a microwave, and 1.4 cars. By almost any measure of wealth, America remains preeminent.

One important way it has maintained this preeminence is by remaining a melting pot. In the 1980s, the United States took in more immigrants than in any other period in its history apart from the peak first decade of this century. It has become truly a multiracial society. By 2000, only about half of Americans entering the workforce will be native-born and of European stock. By 2020, on present trends, the proportion of nonwhite and Hispanic Americans will have doubled, while the white population will have remained almost unchanged. By 2050, the number of Asian Americans will have quintupled.

Many see this as a threat. They note that already the most popular radio station in Los Angeles is a Spanish-language one, that Spanish is the mother tongue of half of the two million inhabitants of greater Miami, that 11 percent of Americans speak a language other than English at home. Some have even seen in this a kind of conspiracy. The late Senator S. I. Hayakawa expressed his belief in 1987 that "a very real move is afoot to split the U.S. into a bilingual and bicultural society."[32] Though he never explained what sinister parties were behind this move, or what they could possibly hope to gain by it, his views found widespread support and led to the formation of U.S. English, a pressure group dedicated to the notion that English should be the sole official language of the United States.

In fact, there is no reason to suppose that America is any more threatened by immigration today than it was a century ago. For one thing, only 6 percent of Americans are foreign-born, a far smaller proportion than in Britain, France, Germany, or most other developed countries. Immigration is for the most part concentrated in a few urban centers. Though some visitors to those cities may find it vexing that their waitress or cab driver does not always speak colloquial English with the assurance of a native-born American, it is also no accident that those cities where immigration is most profound—Miami, Seattle, Los Angeles, San

Francisco—are generally far more vibrant than those places like Detroit, St. Louis, and Philadelphia where it is not.

Nor is it any accident that immigrants are a disproportionate presence in many of those industries—pharmaceuticals, medical research, entertainment, and many others—that are most vital to America's continued prosperity. Up to one-third of the engineers in California's Silicon Valley, for instance, were born in Asia. As one observer has predicted: "America will win because our Asians will beat their Asians."[33]

Quite apart from the consideration that foreign cultures introduce a welcome measure of diversity into American life, no evidence has ever been adduced to show that immigrants today, any more than in the past, persist with their native tongues. A study by the Rand Corporation in 1985 found that 95 percent of the children of Mexican immigrants in America spoke English, and that half of these spoke *only* English. According to another survey, more than 90 percent of Hispanics, citizens and noncitizens alike, believe that residents of the United States should learn English.[34]

If history is anything to go by, then three things about America's immigrants are as certain today as they ever were: that they will learn English, that they will become Americans, and that the country will be stronger for it. And if that is not a good thing, I don't know what is.

NOTES ON SOURCES

CHAPTER 1 THE *MAYFLOWER* AND BEFORE

1. *American Heritage*, October 1962, pp. 49–55.
2. Flexner, *I Hear America Talking*, p. 271.
3. Heaton, *The Mayflower*, p. 80.
4. Wagenknecht, *Henry Wadsworth Longfellow: His Poetry and Prose*, p. 105.
5. Caffrey, *The Mayflower*, p. 141.
6. Blow, ed., *Abroad in America: Literary Discoverers of the New World from the Past 500 Years*, p. 79.
7. Morison, *Oxford History of the American People*, p. 19.
8. Enterline, *Viking America*, p. 10.
9. Morison, op. cit., p. 20.
10. *National Geographic*, November 1964, p. 721.
11. Enterline, op. cit., p. 136.
12. *Economist*, June 29, 1991, p. 100.
13. *Sydney Morning Herald*, September 16, 1992, p. 8.
14. *Economist*, October 24, 1992, p. 136.
15. *National Geographic*, June 1979, p. 744.
16. Stewart, *Names on the Land*, p. 23.
17. *American Heritage*, October 1962, p. 50.
18. Caffrey, op. cit., pp. 70–73.

CHAPTER 2 BECOMING AMERICANS

1. Mencken, *The American Language* (abridged), p. 434.
2. Ibid., p. 431.
3. Vallins, *Spelling*, pp. 79–85.
4. Krapp, *The English Language in America*, vol. 1, p. 201.
5. Baugh and Cable, *A History of the English Language*, p. 248.
6. Mencken, op. cit., p. 288.
7. Holt, *Phrase and Word Origins*, p. 55.
8. Fischer, *Albion's Seed*, p. 261.

9. Flexner, *I Hear America Talking*, p. 63, and Mencken, op. cit., p. 139.
10. *American Heritage*, February 1963, pp. 90–96.
11. Craigie, *The Growth of American English*, pp. 209–11.
12. Laird, *Language in America*, pp. 25–26.
13. Bailey, *Images of English*, pp. 68–69, and Mencken, op. cit., p. 111.
14. Stewart, *Names on the Land*, p. 63.
15. Holt, op. cit., pp. 49–50.
16. Carver, *A History of English in Its Own Words*, p. 182.
17. Bailey, op. cit., p. 67.
18. Cited by Marckwardt, *American English*, p. 28.
19. Krapp, op. cit., p. 175.
20. *American Heritage*, December 1983, p. 85.
21. Zinn, *A People's History of the United States*, p. 15.
22. *American Heritage*, April 1963, p. 69.
23. *National Geographic*, June 1979, p. 735.
24. Ibid., p. 764.
25. Morison, *Oxford History of the American People*, p. 41.
26. Lacey, *Sir Walter Raleigh*, p. 90.
27. Jones, *American Immigration*, p. 18.
28. Ibid., p. 22.
29. Morison, op. cit., p. 82.
30. Takaki, *A Different Mirror*, p. 57.
31. Ibid., p. 60.

CHAPTER 3 A "DEMOCRATICAL PHRENZY": AMERICA IN THE AGE OF REVOLUTION

1. Morison, *Oxford History of the American People*, p. 172.
2. Fischer, *Albion's Seed*, p. 30.
3. *American Heritage*, June 1970, pp. 54–59.
4. Stephen T. Olsen, "Patrick Henry's 'Liberty or Death' Speech: A Study in Disputed Authorship," in *American Rhetoric: Context and Criticism*, Benson, ed., pp. 19–27.
5. Quoted in Cmiel, *Democratic Eloquence: The Fight over Popular Speech in Nineteenth-Century America*, p. 56.
6. *American Heritage*, December 1973, p. 37.
7. Quoted in Cmiel, op. cit., p. 54.
8. Page Smith, *A People's History of the United States*, vol. 1, p. 271.
9. Letter to William Randolph, June 1776, in Boyd, ed., *The Papers of Thomas Jefferson*, vol. 1, p. 409.
10. Page Smith, op. cit., p. 223.
11. Wills, *Inventing America*, p. 45.
12. Ibid., p. 35.
13. Brodie, *Thomas Jefferson: An Intimate History*, p. 103.
14. Fischer, op. cit., p. 6.
15. Ibid., p. 471.
16. Ibid., p. 259.

17. Dillard, *All-American English*, p. 55.
18. Wills, op. cit., p. 36.
19. Quoted in Krapp, *The English Language in America*, vol. 1, p. 46.
20. Flexner, *I Hear America Talking*, p. 7.
21. Cmiel, op. cit., p. 45.
22. Krapp, op. cit., p. 44.
23. Mencken, *The American Language* (abridged), p. 539.
24. Dillard, op. cit., p. 53.
25. Hibbert, *Redcoats and Rebels: The War for America, 1770–1781*, pp. 31–35.
26. Stephen E. Lucas, "Justifying America: The Declaration of Independence as a Rhetorical Document," Benson, op. cit., p. 71.
27. Letter to Henry Lee, May 8, 1825, in Boyd, op. cit.
28. Wills, op. cit., p. xxi.
29. Cmiel, op. cit., p. 83.
30. Boyd, op. cit., vol. 1, p. 423.
31. Lucas, op. cit., pp. 67–119.
32. Hibbert, op. cit., p. 117.
33. Ibid., p. 117.
34. Safire, *Coming to Terms*, p. 140.
35. Simpson, *The Politics of American English, 1776–1850*, p. 23.
36. Boyd, op. cit., vol. 1, p. 404.
37. Mencken, op. cit., p. 502.
38. Flexner, op. cit., p. 7.
39. Flexner, *Listening to America*, p. 328.
40. Boorstin, op. cit., p. 381.

CHAPTER 4   MAKING A NATION

1. Mee, *The Genius of the People*, p. 30.
2. Page Smith, *A People's History of the United States*, vol. 3, p. ix.
3. Schwarz, *George Washington: The Making of an American Symbol*, p. 47.
4. Mee, op. cit., p. 143.
5. Flexner, *Listening to America*, p. 281.
6. Page Smith, op. cit., vol. 1, p. 78.
7. Aldridge, *Benjamin Franklin and Nature's God*, p. 22.
8. Page Smith, op. cit., vol. 3, p. 397.
9. Morison, *Oxford History of the American People*, pp. 308–9.
10. Seavey, *Becoming Benjamin Franklin: The Autobiography and the Life*, p. 150.
11. Wright, *Franklin of Philadelphia*, p. 53.
12. Ibid., p. 54.
13. Granger, *Benjamin Franklin: An American Man of Letters*, p. 66.
14. Wilcox, ed., *The Papers of Benjamin Franklin*, vol. 15, p. 174.
15. Carr, *The Oldest Delegate: Franklin in the Constitutional Convention*, p. 16.
16. Boorstin, *The Americans: The National Experience*, p. 357.
17. Mee, op. cit., p. 90.
18. Page Smith, op. cit., vol. 6, p. 376.
19. Cooke, *Alistair Cooke's America*, p. 140.

20. Mee, op. cit., p. 120.
21. Ibid., p. 237.
22. Boorstin, *Hidden History*, p. 187.
23. Boorstin, *The Americans: The National Experience*, p. 402.
24. Mee, op. cit., pp. 248–49.
25. Boorstin, *The Americans: The National Experience*, p. 415.
26. Ernst and Schwartz, *Censorship: The Search for the Obscene*, p. 8.
27. Morison, op. cit., p. 311.
28. Page Smith, op. cit., vol. 3, pp. 122–23.
29. *American Heritage*, October 1969, pp. 84–85.
30. *Verbatim*, Summer 1991, p. 6.
31. Flexner, *I Hear America Talking*, p. 9.
32. Simpson, *The Politics of American English, 1776–1850*, p. 41.
33. *Journal of American History*, December 1992, pp. 939–40.
34. *American Heritage*, December 1963, p. 27.
35. Quoted in Boorstin, *The Americans: The National Experience*, p. 344.
36. *National Geographic*, July 1976, pp. 92–93.
37. Ibid., p. 97.
38. Mee, op. cit., pp. 33–40.

CHAPTER 5 BY THE DAWN'S EARLY LIGHT: FORGING A NATIONAL IDENTITY

1. Holt, *Phrase and Word Origins*, p. 243.
2. *American Heritage*, October/November 1983, p. 104.
3. Page Smith, *A People's History of the United States*, vol. 3, p. 757.
4. Flexner, *I Hear America Talking*, p. 124.
5. Morison, *Oxford History of the American People*, pp. 283–84.
6. Craigie and Hulbert, *A Dictionary of American English on Historical Principles*, vol. 2, p. 397.
7. Carver, *A History of English in Its Own Words*, p. 9.
8. *New Yorker*, September 4, 1989, p. 11.
9. Boorstin, *The Americans: The National Experience*, p. 280.
10. Mencken, *The American Language* (abridged), p. 236.
11. Ibid., p. 135.
12. Page Smith, op. cit., vol. 4, p. 252.
13. Ibid., vol. 3, p. 47.
14. Commager, *The American Mind: An Interpretation of American Thought and Character Since the 1880's*, p. 16.
15. Cmiel, *Democratic Eloquence: The Fight over Popular Speech in Nineteenth-Century America*, p. 159.
16. Dillard, *American Talk*, p. xiii.
17. Quoted in Mencken, op. cit., p. 29.
18. Ibid., p. 267.
19. Daniels, *Famous Last Words: The American Language Crisis Reconsidered*, p. 43.
20. Mencken, op. cit., p. 77.

21. *Journal of American History*, December 1992, p. 913.
22. Quoted in Mencken, op. cit., p. 87.
23. Marckwardt, *American English*, p. 70.
24. *Journal of American History*, December 1992, p. 928.
25. Quoted in Wortham, *James Russell Lowell's "The Biglow Papers": A Critical Edition*, p. xxii.
26. Quoted in Boorstin, *The Americans: The Democratic Experience*, p. 293.
27. Cmiel, op. cit., p. 66.
28. Letter to Lincoln, November 25, 1860, in *Harper Book of American Quotations*, p. 121.
29. Wills, *Lincoln at Gettysburg*, p. 90.
30. Cmiel, op. cit., p. 137.
31. Ibid., p. 144.
32. Wills, *Inventing America*, p. xiv.

CHAPTER 6 WE'RE IN THE MONEY: THE AGE OF INVENTION

1. *American Heritage*, August 1964, p. 93.
2. Ibid., August/September 1984, p. 20.
3. Brogan, *The Penguin History of the United States of America*, p. 274.
4. Bursk, Clark, and Hidy, eds., *The World of Business*, vol. 2, p. 1251.
5. Commager, *The American Mind*, p. 5.
6. Daniels, *Famous Last Words: The American Language Crisis Reconsidered*, p. 41.
7. Wylie, *The Self-Made Man in America: The Myth of Rags to Riches*, p. 10.
8. Boorstin, *The Americans: The National Experience*, p. 115.
9. Flexner, *Listening to America*, pp. 365–66.
10. *American Heritage*, December 1989, p. 108.
11. Holt, *Phrase and Word Origins*, p. 5.
12. Flexner, op. cit., p. 364.
13. Root and de Rochement, *Eating in America*, p. 321.
14. Zinn, *A People's History of the United States*, p. 316.
15. *American Heritage*, October 1959, p. 38.
16. Zinn, op. cit., p. 327.
17. Flexner, op. cit., p. 452.
18. Burnam, *The Dictionary of Misinformation*, p. 37.
19. Keeley, *Making Inventions Pay*, p. 10.
20. Gies and Gies, *The Ingenious Yankees*, pp. 208–10.
21. Barach, *Famous American Trademarks*, p. 75.
22. Page Smith, *A People's History of the United States*, vol. 4, pp. 822–23.
23. Ibid., pp. 813–17.
24. Carver, *A History of English in Its Own Words*, p. 245.
25. *American Heritage*, September/October 1990, p. 58.
26. Ibid., April 1965, p. 95.
27. Ibid., p. 96.
28. Barnhart, ed., *Barnhart Dictionary of Etymology*, p. 1121.
29. *Economist*, April 13, 1991, p. 83.

30. *American Heritage*, September/October 1990, p. 48.
31. Carver, op. cit., p. 242.
32. Gies and Gies, op. cit., p. 368.
33. Ibid., p. 311.
34. *American Heritage*, September/October 1990, pp. 48–59.
35. Page Smith, op. cit., vol. 7, p. 858.
36. Ibid.
37. Zinn, op. cit., p. 248.
38. Collins, *The Story of Kodak*, p. 72.
39. Flatow, *They All Laughed* . . . , p. 31.
40. *American Heritage*, November 1979, p. 76.
41. Page Smith, op. cit., vol. 7, p. 858.
42. *American Heritage*, August/September 1978, p. 42.
43. Goldberger, *The Skyscraper*, p. 83.
44. *American Heritage*, August/September 1978, p. 44.

CHAPTER 7   NAMES

1. Boorstin, *The Americans: The National Experience*, p. 305.
2. Flexner, *I Hear American Talking*, p. 312.
3. Krapp, *The English Language in America*, vol. 1, p. 175.
4. Stewart, *Names on the Land*, p. 64.
5. Ibid., p. 33.
6. Ibid., p. 258.
7. Fischer, *Albion's Seed*, p. 420.
8. Stewart, op. cit., p. 58.
9. Ibid., p. 10.
10. *American Demographics*, February 1992, p. 21.
11. Stewart, op. cit., p. 70.
12. Ibid., p. 223.
13. *Atlantic Monthly*, November 1992, p. 149.
14. Mencken, *The American Language* (abridged), p. 649.
15. Dillard, *American Talk*, p. 59.
16. Mencken, *The American Language*, Supplement II, p. 533.
17. Stewart, op. cit., p. 327.
18. Page Smith, *A People's History of the United States*, vol. 4, pp. 473–74.
19. Fischer, op. cit., p. 654.
20. Rodgers, *Chagrin . . . Whence the Name?*, pp. 1–13.
21. *New Republic*, July 29, 1991, p. 8.
22. Mencken, *The American Language*, (abridged), p. 656.
23. *Atlantic Monthly*, September 1990, p. 20.
24. Stewart, op. cit., p. 344.
25. Ibid., pp. 166–67.
26. Ibid., p. 189.
27. Mencken, *The American Language* (abridged), p. 686.
28. Lacey, *Sir Walter Raleigh*, p. 11.
29. Fischer, op. cit., p. 59.

30. Ibid., p. 94.
31. Ibid.
32. Levin, *Cotton Mather*, p. 1.
33. Mencken, *The American Language* (abridged), pp. 577–78.
34. Forbes, *Paul Revere and the World He Lived In*, p. 5.
35. Mencken, *The American Language* (abridged), pp. 579–81.
36. Ibid., p. 585.
37. Sullivan, *Our Times: The United States 1900–1925*, vol. 1, p. 250.
38. Mencken, *The American Language* (abridged), p. 597.

CHAPTER 8   "MANIFEST DESTINY": TAMING THE WEST

1. Goetzmann, *Exploration and Empire*, p. 5.
2. Dillon, *Meriwether Lewis: A Biography*, p. 336.
3. Hart, *The Story of American Roads*, p. 24.
4. Root and de Rochement, *Eating in America*, pp. 110–11.
5. Page Smith, *A People's History of the United States*, vol. 3, p. 534.
6. Moulton, *The Journals of the Lewis and Clark Expedition*, p. 181.
7. Ibid., p 181.
8. Cutright, *Lewis and Clark: Pioneering Naturalists*, pp. viii–ix.
9. Brogan, *The Penguin History of the United States of America*, p. 263.
10. De Tocqueville, *Journey to America*, p. 185.
11. Boorstin, *The Americans: The National Experience*, pp. 91–93.
12. Ibid., p. 93.
13. Boorstin, *Hidden History*, p. 200.
14. Boorstin, *The Americans: The National Experience*, p. 121.
15. Gies and Gies, *The Ingenious Yankees*, p. 255.
16. Zinn, *A People's History of the United States*, p. 149.
17. *American Heritage*, February 1962, p. 5.
18. *Atlantic Monthly*, November 1992, p. 152.
19. Dillard, *American Talk*, p. xix.
20. Takaki, *A Different Mirror*, p. 192.
21. Fischer, *Albion's Seed*, p. 62.
22. Boorstin, *The Americans: The Democratic Experience*, pp. 22–23.
23. Ibid., p. 24.
24. Weston, *The Real American Cowboy*, p. 136.
25. Dillard, *American Talk*, p. 114.
26. Weston, *The Real American Cowboy*, p. 210.
27. Savage, *Cowboy Life: Reconstructing an American Myth*, p. 6.
28. *American Heritage*, February 1971, p. 68.
29. Boorstin, *The Americans: The National Experience*, p. 83.
30. Holt, *Phrase and Word Origins*, p. 80.
31. *Washington Post*, December 8, 1989, p. C5.
32. Boorstin, op. cit., p. 288, and Flexner, *I Hear America Talking*, pp. 111–12.
33. Carver, *A History of English in Its Own Words*, p. 199.
34. Harris, *Good to Eat: Riddles of Food and Culture*, p. 117.
35. Zinn, *A People's History of the United States*, p. 515.

36. *Economist*, June 8, 1991, p. 49.
37. Quoted in *Atlanta Journal*, March 17, 1991, p. A12.

CHAPTER 9   THE MELTING POT: IMMIGRATION IN AMERICA

1. Jones, *American Immigration*, pp. 104–5.
2. Ibid., pp. 114, 290.
3. Ibid., p. 107.
4. Ibid., p. 124.
5. Zinn, *A People's History of the United States*, p. 317.
6. Boorstin, *The Americans: The Democratic Experience*, p. 249.
7. Page Smith, *A People's History of the United States*, vol. 6, p. 344.
8. Grosvenor (ed.), *Those Inventive Americans*, p. 146.
9. *New Yorker*, April 9, 1990, p. 30.
10. *American Heritage*, April 1992, p. 58.
11. Ibid., p. 62.
12. Page Smith, op. cit., vol. 6, p. 366.
13. *New York Times*, August 26, 1990, p. 6E.
14. Zinn, op. cit., p. 341, and Brogan, *The Penguin History of the United States of America*, p. 413.
15. Jones, op. cit., pp. 140–41.
16. Dillard, *American Talk*, p. 30.
17. Mencken, *The American Language* (abridged), p. 90.
18. Dillard, op. cit., p. 82.
19. Marckwardt, *American English*, p. 57, and Boorstin, *The Americans: The National Experience*, p. 287.
20. Carver, *A History of English in Its Own Words*, p. 242.
21. Fischer, *Albion's Seed*, p. 431.
22. Jones, op. cit., pp. 270–71.
23. *American Heritage*, April 1992, p. 62.
24. Ibid., p. 62.
25. Mencken, op. cit., p. 251.
26. *Time*, June 13, 1927, p. 12.
27. Mencken, op. cit., p. 254.
28. *American Heritage*, April 1992, p. 70.
29. Jones, op. cit., p. 298.
30. Mencken, op. cit., p. 253.
31. Beam, *Abridged Pennsylvania German Dictionary*, p. iv.
32. Ibid., pp. viii–ix.
33. Beam, *Pennsylvania German Dictionary*, p. v.
34. Marckwardt, op. cit., p. 59.
35. Page Smith, op. cit., vol. 4, p. 741.
36. Jones, op. cit., pp. 264–65.
37. Quoted in *New York Times*, October 14, 1990, p. 4E.
38. Boorstin, *Hidden History*, pp. 214–15.
39. Jones, op. cit., p. 39.

40. Zinn, op. cit., p. 293.
41. Tannahill, *Sex in History*, p. 400.
42. Jones, op. cit., p. 133.
43. Ibid., p. 312.
44. Johnson, *Modern Times: The World from the Twenties to the Eighties*, p. 204.
45. Quoted in Wills, *Inventing America*, p. xx.
46. *Time*, June 13, 1927, p. 12.
47. *National Geographic*, September 1992, pp. 66–67.
48. Jones, op. cit., pp. 32–35.
49. Fischer, op. cit., p. 305.
50. McPherson, *Battle Cry of Freedom: The American Civil War*, p. 18.
51. Zinn, op. cit., pp. 174–75.
52. Ibid., p. 203.
53. Page Smith, op. cit., vol. 4, p. 586.
54. Zinn, op. cit., pp. 183–84.
55. Quoted in McDavid, *Varieties of American English*, p. 78.
56. Krapp, *The English Language in America*, vol. 1, pp. 161–62.
57. Dohan, *Our Own Words*, p. 241.
58. Marckwardt, op. cit., p. 66.
59. Ibid., p. 65.
60. Dillard, op. cit., p. 22.
61. Mencken, op. cit., p. 743.
62. Smitherman, *Black Talk*, p. 14.
63. Ibid., p. 10.

CHAPTER 10   WHEN THE GOING WAS GOOD: TRAVEL IN AMERICA

1. Boorstin, *Hidden History*, p. 60.
2. Hibbert, *Redcoats and Rebels: The War for America, 1770–1781*, p. 335.
3. Root and de Rochement, *Eating in America*, p. 42.
4. Morison, *Oxford History of the American People*, p. 141.
5. Carver, *A History of English in Its Own Words*, pp. 147–48.
6. Cooke, *Alistair Cooke's America*, p. 77.
7. Boorstin, *The Americans: The National Experience*, p. 394.
8. Boyd, ed., *The Papers of Thomas Jefferson*, vol. 1, p. 408.
9. Wills, *Inventing America*, p. 43.
10. Rae, *The Road and the Car in American Life*, p. 15.
11. Page Smith, *A People's History of the United States*, vol. 3, p. 74.
12. *American Heritage*, December 1983, p. 91.
13. Davidson, *Life in America*, vol. 1, p. 199.
14. Flexner, *Listening to America*, p. 144.
15. Johnson, *The Birth of the Modern: World Society, 1815–1830*, p. 171.
16. *American Heritage*, February 1977, p. 16.
17. McPherson, *Battle Cry of Freedom: The American Civil War*, p. 12.
18. Patton, *Open Road: A Celebration of the American Highway*, p. 37.
19. Ciardi, *Good Words to You*, pp. 233–34.

20. Barnhart, ed., *Barnhart Dictionary of Etymology*, p. 1086.
21. Jackson, *Crabgrass Frontier: The Suburbanization of the United States*, pp. 106–7.
22. Ibid., p. 105.
23. *Economist*, October 26, 1991.
24. Nye, *Electrifying America: Social Meanings of a New Technology*, p. 93.
25. Jackson, op. cit., p. 158.
26. Carver, op. cit., p. 243.
27. Page Smith, op. cit., vol. 7, p. 865.
28. Beebe, *Big Spenders*, p. 184.
29. Page Smith, op. cit., vol. 7, p. 866.
30. Flexner, *I Hear America Talking*, p. 330.
31. Dohan, *Our Own Words*, p. 266.
32. Flexner, *I Hear America Talking*, p. 333.
33. Hokanson, *The Lincoln Highway: Main Street Across America*, pp. 6–10, and *American Heritage*, June 1974, pp. 32–37 and 89.
34. Strasser, *Satisfaction Guaranteed: The Making of the American Mass Market*, p. 6.
35. Page Smith, op. cit., p. 868.
36. *American Heritage*, August 1973, p. 11.
37. Ibid., December 1975, p. 66.
38. Liebs, *Main Street to Miracle Mile: American Roadside Architecture*, p. 208.
39. Finch, *Highways to Heaven*, p. 162.
40. Liebs, op. cit., p. 177.
41. Barnhart, op. cit., p. 680.
42. Patton, op. cit., p. 199.
43. Rowsome, *The Verse by the Side of the Road: The Story of the Burma-Shave Signs*, p. 18.
44. Jackson, op. cit., p. 249.
45. *Economist*, August 10, 1991, p. 28.
46. Patton, op. cit., p. 85.

CHAPTER 11   WHAT'S COOKING?: EATING IN AMERICA

1. Caffrey, *The Mayflower*, p. 166.
2. Root and de Rochement, *Eating in America*, p. 54.
3. William and Mary Morris, *Morris Dictionary of Phrase and Word Origins*, p. 231.
4. Root and de Rochement, op. cit., p. 29.
5. Ciardi, *A Browser's Dictionary*, p. 212.
6. Mee, *The Genius of the People*, p. 91.
7. Root and de Rochement, op. cit., pp. 94–95.
8. Ibid., p. 162.
9. Boorstin, *The Americans: The Democratic Experience*, p. 324.
10. Carver, *A History of English in Its Own Words*, p. 146.
11. Funk, *Word Origins and Their Romantic Stories*, p. 170.

12. *American Heritage*, December 1989, pp. 123–31.
13. Ibid.
14. Mencken, *The American Language* (abridged), p. 264.
15. Ibid., p. 225.
16. Liebs, *Main Street to Miracle Mile: American Roadside Architecture*, p. 196.
17. Levenstein, *Revolution at the Table: The Transformation of the American Diet*, p. 189.
18. Ibid., p. 92.
19. Bursk, Clark, and Hidy, eds., *The World of Business*, vol. 1, pp. 426–27.
20. Levenstein, op. cit., pp. 198–99.
21. Funk, op. cit., p. 186.
22. Smelser, *The Life That Ruth Built*, pp. 207–8, and *American Speech*, Fall 1984, p. 213.
23. Barnhart, Steinmetz, and Barnhart, *Third Barnhart Dictionary of New English*, p. 497.
24. Allen, *Only Yesterday: An Informal History of the 1920s*, p. 68.
25. Holt, *Phrase and Word Origins*, p. 59.
26. Boorstin, *The Americans: The National Experience*, p. 287.
27. Dillard, *American Talk*, p. 85.
28. Ibid., p. 84.
29. Ibid., p. 88.
30. Allen, op. cit., p. 205.
31. Root and de Rochement, op. cit., p. 389.
32. Allen, op. cit., p. 209.
33. Bursk, Clark, and Hidy, op. cit., pp. 345–47.
34. Dohan, *Our Own Words*, p. 270.

CHAPTER 12 DEMOCRATIZING LUXURY: SHOPPING IN AMERICA

1. Craigie and Hulbert, *A Dictionary of American English on Historical Principles*, vol. 1, p. 748.
2. Frieden and Sagalyn, *Downtown, Inc.: How America Rebuilds Cities*, p. 8.
3. Pound, *Selfridge: A Biography*, pp. 34–55 and 112–187.
4. Goldberger, *The Skyscraper*, p. 42.
5. Boorstin, *The Americans: The Democratic Experience*, p. 122.
6. Strasser, *Satisfaction Guaranteed: The Making of the American Mass Market*, p. 213.
7. Information provided to the author of Nabisco.
8. Boorstin, *The Americans: A Democratic Experience*, p. 126.
9. *American Heritage*, October/November 1985, pp. 24–28.
10. Flexner, *Listening to America*, p. 494, and Liebs, *Main Street to Miracle Mile: American Roadside Architecture*, pp. 119–26.
11. Liebs, *Main Street to Miracle Mile*, p. 125.
12. *Atlantic Monthly*, June 1992, p. 31.
13. Schrank, *Snap, Crackle, and Popular Taste: The Illusion of Free Choice in America*, p. 111.

14. Strasser, *Never Done: A History of American Housework*, p. 276.
15. Kowinski, *The Malling of America: An Inside Look at the Great Consumer Paradise*, pp. 104–5.
16. *Business Week*, November 17, 1957, p. 137.
17. Gruen and Smit, *Shopping Town USA: The Planning of Shopping Centers*, p. 20.
18. *Atlantic Monthly*, May 1993, p. 132.
19. Kowinski, *The Malling of America*, p. 112.
20. Frieden and Sagalyn, *Downtown, Inc.*, p. 13.
21. Jackson, *Crabgrass Frontier: The Suburbanization of the United States*, p. 261.
22. *American Demographics*, April 1990, p. 38.
23. Schor, *The Overworked American: The Unexpected Decline of Leisure*, p. 107.
24. *Atlantic Monthly*, May 1993, p. 102.
25. *Economist*, August 29, 1992, p. 37.

CHAPTER 13   MANNERS AND OTHER MATTERS

1. Blow, ed., *Abroad in America: Literary Discoverers of the New World from the Past 500 Years*, p. 149.
2. Ibid., p. 139.
3. Ibid., p. 215.
4. Garrett, *At Home: The American Family: 1750–1870*, p. 155.
5. Deetz, *In Small Things Forgotten: The Archaeology of Early American Life*, p. 123.
6. Elias, *The History of Manners*, vol. 1, p. 127.
7. *American Heritage*, December 1989, p. 106.
8. Flexner, *I Hear America Talking*, p. 19.
9. Boorstin, *The Americans: The National Experience*, p. 135.
10. *American Heritage*, August/September 1978, p. 41.
11. Boorstin, op. cit., p. 141.
12. *American Heritage*, December 1989, p. 111.
13. Blow, op. cit., p. 159.
14. Rybczynski, *Home: A Short History of an Idea*, p. 139.
15. Ibid., p. 142.
16. Ibid., pp. 148–49.
17. Nye, *Electrifying America: Social Meanings of a New Technology*, p. 242.
18. Strasser, *Never Done: A History of American Housework*, p. 76.
19. Nye, op. cit., p. 52.
20. *American Heritage*, November 1979, p. 78.
21. Page Smith, *A People's History of the United States*, vol. 7, p. 856.
22. Johnson, *Modern Times: The World from the Twenties to the Eighties*, p. 224.
23. *American Heritage*, September/October 1990, p. 58.
24. Barnhart, ed., *The Barnhart Dictionary of Etymology*, p. 902.
25. Boorstin, *The Americans: The Democratic Experience*, p. 330.
26. *New York Times*, July 1–3, 1921.
27. Allen, *Only Yesterday: An Informal History of the 1920s*, p. 137.
28. *Economist*, August 28, 1993, p. 57.

29. Sterling and Kittross, *Stay Tuned: A Concise History of American Broadcasting*, pp. 61–63.
30. Ibid., p. 60.
31. Schiller, *Mass Communications and American Empire*, p. 25.
32. Udelson, *The Great Television Race: A History of the American Television Industry 1925–1941*, p. 12.
33. *New York Times*, April 8, 1927.
34. Quoted in Schrank, *Snap, Crackle, and Popular Taste: The Illusion of Free Choice in America*, p. 17.
35. Castleman and Podrazik, *Watching TV: Four Decades of American Television*, p. 16.
36. Ibid., p. 45.
37. Safire, *Coming to Terms*, p. 47.
38. Castleman and Podrazik, op. cit., p. v.
39. *American Heritage*, August/September 1984, p. 25.
40. Flatow, *They All Laughed . . .* , p. 61.
41. Strasser, *Never Done: A History of American Housework*, p. 289.
42. Schor, *The Overworked American: The Unexpected Decline of Leisure*, p. 8.
43. Rybczynski, *Waiting for the Weekend*, pp. 142–43.
44. Schor, op. cit., p. 22.
45. *Utica* (N.Y.) *Observer*, March 4, 1991.
46. Schor, op. cit., p. 29.
47. Ibid., p. 2.
48. Ibid.

CHAPTER 14   THE HARD SELL: ADVERTISING IN AMERICA

1. Collins, *The Story of Kodak*, p. 49.
2. Boorstin, *The Americans: The Democratic Experience*, p. 374.
3. Collins, op. cit., pp. 54–55.
4. Ibid., p. 72.
5. Strasser, *Satisfaction Guaranteed: The Making of the American Mass Market*, pp. 46–47.
6. Flexner, *Listening to America*, p. 17.
7. Ibid., p. 20.
8. Strasser, op. cit., p. 97.
9. *Time*, June 13, 1927, p. 12.
10. *American Heritage*, October 1977, p. 67.
11. Mencken, *The American Language* (abridged), 218.
12. *American Heritage*, October 1977, pp. 64–69.
13. Ibid., September/October 1990, p. 56.
14. *Economist*, September 7, 1991, p. 89.
15. Ibid., August 14, 1993, p. 7.
16. *New York Times Magazine*, July 7, 1957, p. 14.
17. Diamond, *Trademark Problems and How to Avoid Them*, pp. 188–195.
18. Sterling and Kittross, *Stay Tuned: A Concise History of American Broadcasting*, p. 71.

19. Castleman and Podrazik, *Watching TV: Four Decades of American Television*, p. 70.
20. *New York Times Magazine*, September 30, 1990, p. 76.
21. Schrank, *Snap, Crackle, and Popular Taste: The Illusion of Free Choice in America*, p. 101.
22. Lutz, *Doublespeak*, p. 82.
23. Ibid., pp. 16–17.
24. Hendon, *Classic Failures in Product Marketing*, p. 169.
25. Ibid., p. 168.

CHAPTER 15   THE MOVIES

1. Flexner, *Listening to America*, pp. 374–75.
2. Cook, *A History of Narrative Film*, p. 7.
3. Jowett, *Film: The Democratic Art*, p. 27.
4. Cook, op. cit., pp. 10–11.
5. Flexner, op. cit., p. 378.
6. Cook, op. cit., p. 12.
7. Ibid., p. 24.
8. Rybczynski, *Waiting for the Weekend*, p. 137.
9. Mencken, *The American Language* (abridged), p. 738.
10. Flexner, op. cit., pp. 382–83, and *American Speech*, Fall 1983, pp. 216–24.
11. Page Smith, *A People's History of the United States*, vol. 7, p. 880.
12. *American Heritage*, December 1983, p. 24, and *New Republic*, July 29, 1991, p. 7.
13. Berg, *Goldwyn: A Biography*, pp. 140, 214–19, 238, 248–55, 380.
14. *New York Times*, March 28, 1993, p. 15H.
15. *Economist*, October 2, 1993, p. 108.
16. Berg, op. cit., p. 262.
17. Jowett, op. cit., p. 357.
18. Ibid.

CHAPTER 16   THE PURSUIT OF PLEASURE: SPORT AND PLAY

1. Krout, *Annals of American Sport*, p. 11.
2. Fischer, *Albion's Seed*, pp. 146–47.
3. Ibid., p. 6.
4. Ibid., p. 8.
5. Ibid., p. 16.
6. Flexner, *Listening to America*, pp. 504–6.
7. *American Heritage*, December 1967, p. 107.
8. Boorstin, *The Americans: The Democratic Experience*, p. 158.
9. Morison, *Oxford History of the American People*, p. 88.
10. *American Heritage Dictionary*, 2nd ed., p. xxiii.
11. Fischer, op. cit., p. 737.
12. Dillard, *American Talk*, p. 65.
13. Adams, *Western Words: A Dictionary of the American West*, p. 109.

14. Dillard, op. cit., pp. 65–71.
15. Holt, *Phrase and Word Origins*, p. 200.
16. Dillard, op. cit., p. 74.
17. Boorstin, op. cit., p. 73.
18. *American Heritage*, June 1972, p. 67.
19. Rae, *The Road and the Car in American Life*, p. 29.
20. Atwan, McQuade, and Wright, *Edsels, Luckies and Frigidaires: Advertising the American Way*, pp. 151–52.
21. Liebs, *Main Street to Miracle Mile: American Roadside Architecture*, pp. 138–42.
22. Allen, *Only Yesterday: An Informal History of the 1920s*, p. 68, and *American Heritage*, June 1972, p. 68.
23. *American Heritage*, February/March 1983, pp. 24–27.
24. Dulles, *America Learns to Play: A History of Popular Recreation, 1607–1940*, p. 185.
25. Flexner, op. cit., p. 33.
26. Fischer, op. cit., p. 151.
27. *American Heritage*, June/July 1983, pp. 65–67.
28. Will, *Men at Work: The Craft of Baseball*, p. 102.
29. Voigt, *American Baseball: From Gentleman's Sport to the Commissioner System*, p. 30.
30. Ibid., p. 135.
31. *American Heritage*, June/July 1983, p. 74.
32. Ibid., October 1967, pp. 64–68.
33. Mencken, *The American Language, Supplement II*, p. 737.
34. Krout, op. cit., p. 142.
35. Mencken, op. cit., p. 735, and Flexner, op. cit., p. 39.
36. *USA Today*, February 28, 1992, p. 18.
37. *Time*, September 23, 1940, and *American Speech*, Summer 1988, p. 116.
38. Page Smith, *A People's History of the United States*, vol. 6, p. 848.
39. Safire, *On Language*, p. 289.
40. Flexner, op. cit., pp. 48–49.
41. Ibid., pp. 261–80.
42. Jackson, *Crabgrass Frontier: The Suburbanization of the United States*, p. 99.
43. Holt, op. cit., p. 154.
44. *Washington Post*, January 21, 1992, p. D5.
45. *New York Times*, February 16, 1992, p. 1.

CHAPTER 17   OF BOMBS AND BUNKUM: POLITICS AND WAR

1. Holt, *Phrase and Word Origins*, pp. 42, 129.
2. Mencken, *The American Language, Supplement I*, pp. 280–83.
3. Mencken, *The American Language* (abridged), p. 179.
4. Brogan, *The Penguin History of the United States of America*, p. 274.
5. Carver, *A History of English in Its Own Words*, p. 165.
6. McPherson, *Battle Cry of Freedom: The American Civil War*, pp. 111–15.
7. *American Heritage*, December 1975, p. 13.

8. Boorstin, *Hidden History*, p. 263.
9. Mee, *The Genius of the People*, p. 285.
10. Page Smith, *A People's History of the United States*, vol. 3, p. 145.
11. Ibid., vol. 4, p. 126.
12. Brogan, op. cit., p. 312.
13. Flexner, *I Hear America Talking*, p. 161.
14. Allen, *Only Yesterday: An Informal History of the 1920s*, p. 104.
15. Johnson, *Modern Times: The World from the Twenties to the Eighties*, p. 214.
16. *American Heritage*, December 1991.
17. Mencken, *The American Language, Supplement II*, p. 590.
18. Page Smith, op. cit., vol. 3, pp. 608–9.
19. Flexner, op. cit., p. 405.
20. McPherson, op. cit., pp. 323–25.
21. Flexner, op. cit., p. 450.
22. *American Heritage*, February 1964, pp. 23–96.
23. Ciardi, *A Browser's Dictionary*, p. 227.
24. Barfield, *History in English Words*, p. 76.
25. Holt, op. cit., p. 16.
26. Fussell, *Wartime: Understanding and Behavior in the Second World War*, pp. 255–56.
27. Ibid., p. 259.
28. Carver, op. cit., p. 252.
29. William and Mary Morris, *Morris Dictionary of Phrase and Word Origins*, p. 246.
30. Flexner, *Listening to America*, p. 330.
31. Mencken, *The American Language* (abridged), p. 759.
32. Ibid., p. 508.
33. Lingeman, *Don't You Know There's a War On?: The American Home Front 1941–1945*, pp. 219–21.
34. *Economist*, February 27, 1993, p. 108.
35. *New York Times*, February 2, 1992, p. 17.
36. *American Speech*, Spring 1992, pp. 86–89.

CHAPTER 18   SEX AND OTHER DISTRACTIONS

1. *Life*, October 8, 1951, pp. 61–62.
2. *American Heritage*, December 1983, p. 86.
3. Fischer, *Albion's Seed*, p. 92.
4. Flexner, *Listening to America*, p. 449.
5. Fischer, op. cit., p. 87.
6. Page Smith, *A People's History of the United States*, vol. 1, p. 69.
7. Hibbert, *Redcoats and Rebels, The War for America, 1770–1781*, p. 7.
8. Fischer, op. cit., p. 681.
9. Flexner, op. cit., p. 492.
10. Ciardi, *Good Words to You*, p. 42.
11. Cmiel, *Democratic Eloquence: The Fight over Popular Speech in Nineteenth-Century America*, p. 117.

12. Garrett, *At Home: The American Family: 1750–1870*, p. 136.
13. Page Smith, op. cit., vol. 6, p. 264.
14. Tannahill, *Sex in History*, p. 336.
15. Ibid.
16. *American Heritage*, October 1974, p. 74.
17. *Observer*, November 14, 1993, Books section, p. 20.
18. *American Heritage*, October 1974, p. 73.
19. Ibid., p. 94.
20. Zinn, *A People's History of the United States*, pp. 109–16.
21. Ibid., pp. 116–17.
22. *American Heritage*, October 1974, p. 43.
23. Cmiel, op. cit., p. 81.
24. Ibid., p. 162.
25. Page Smith, op. cit., vol. 6, p. 264.
26. Ibid., vol. 6, p. 271.
27. Ibid., vol. 6, p. 273.
28. Flexner, op. cit., pp. 452–55.
29. *American Heritage*, October 1973, p. 86.
30. *Economist*, March 14, 1992, p. 51.
31. Barnett, *Sexual Freedom and the Constitution: An Inquiry into the Constitutionality of Repressive Sex Laws*, p. 33.
32. Allen, *Only Yesterday: An Informal History of the 1920s*, p. 77.
33. Flexner, op. cit., p. 62.
34. Schumach, *The Face on the Cutting Room Floor: The Story of Movie and Television Censorship*, p. 18.
35. Allen, op. cit., p. 84.
36. *American Heritage*, February/March 1980, p. 17.
37. Mencken, *The American Language* (abridged), pp. 360–61.
38. Berg, *Goldwyn: A Biography*, pp. 266–67.
39. Schumach, op. cit., p. 216.
40. Ibid., p. 222.
41. *American Heritage*, February/March 1980, p. 20.
42. Mencken, *The American Language, Supplement I*, p. 647.
43. Ibid., p. 646.
44. Castleman and Podrazik, *Watching TV: Four Decades of American Television*, p. 14.
45. Ibid., p. 71.
46. Ernst and Schwarz, *Censorship: The Search for the Obscene*, p. 95.
47. Sagarin, *The Anatomy of Dirty Words*, p. 167.
48. Safire, *Coming to Terms*, p. 51.
49. *Economist*, November 28, 1992, p. 35.
50. Safire, op. cit., p. 100.
51. Letter from Allan M. Siegal, July 23, 1993.
52. Funk, *A Hog on Ice and Other Curious Expressions*, p. 88.
53. *Buffalo News*, September 20, 1992.

CHAPTER 19 FROM KITTY HAWK TO THE JUMBO JET

1. *American Heritage*, June 1970, pp. 61–69.
2. Moolman, *The Road to Kitty Hawk*, p. 124.
3. *American Heritage*, June 1970, pp. 61–69.
4. Moolman, *The Road to Kitty Hawk*, p. 117.
5. Ibid., p. 158.
6. *American Heritage*, April 1975, pp. 94–95.
7. Milton, *Loss of Eden: A Biography of Charles and Anne Morrow Lindbergh*, p. 42.
8. Ibid., p. 116, and *American Heritage*, April 1971, pp. 43–47, 81–84.
9. Ibid., p. 127.
10. *American Heritage*, December 1975, pp. 23–28.
11. Milton, *Loss of Eden*, p. 166.
12. Johnson, *Modern Times: The World from the Twenties to the Eighties*, p. 224.
13. *Condé Nast Traveler*, December 1989, pp. 135–78.
14. Page Smith, *A People's History of the United States*, vol. 4, p. 780.
15. *American Heritage*, August 1973, pp. 63–85.

CHAPTER 20 WELCOME TO THE SPACE AGE: THE 1950S AND BEYOND

1. Lingeman, *Don't You Know There's a War On?: The American Home Front 1941–1945*, p. 374.
2. *Atlantic Monthly*, January 1990, p. 48.
3. *Economist*, December 21, 1991, p. 72.
4. Oakley, *God's Country: America in the Fifties*, p. 270.
5. Ibid., pp. 285–86.
6. Kroc, *Grinding It Out: The Making of McDonald's*, p. 162.
7. Love, *McDonald's: Behind the Arches*, p. 5.
8. *Guardian*, May 10, 1993.
9. Binford, *The First Suburbs: Residential Communities on the Boston Periphery*, p. 1.
10. *American Heritage*, February/March 1984, pp. 21–37.
11. Mencken, *The American Language* (abridged), p. 245.
12. *American Demographics*, May 1993, p. 44.
13. *Independent on Sunday*, November 15, 1992, p. 8.
14. Jackson, *Crabgrass Frontier: The Suburbanization of the United States*, p. 246.
15. Ibid., p. 247, and Schrank, *Snap, Crackle, and Popular Taste: The Illusion of Free Choice in America*, p. 65.
16. Brooks, *Business Adventures*, p. 35.
17. Lacey, *Ford: The Men and the Machines*, p. 489.
18. Brooks, op. cit., p. 31.
19. Rae, *The Road and the Car in American Life*, p. 48.
20. Schrank, op. cit., p. 64.
21. *Economist*, August 29, 1992, p. 37.
22. *American Speech* 66:1 (1991), pp. 105–6.
23. *Economist*, October 26, 1991, America Survey, pp. 11–12.

24. Boorstin, *The Americans: The Democratic Experience*, pp. 591–92.
25. Bailey, *Images of English: A Cultural History of the Language*, p. 221.
26. Tedlow, *New and Improved: The Story of Mass Marketing in America*, p. 348.
27. *Life*, March 3, 1961, pp. 109–17.
28. Flatow, *They All Laughed . . .* , p. 181.
29. Carver, *A History of English in Its Own Words*, p. 263.
30. *Economist*, January 9, 1993, p. 62.
31. *New York Times*, April 3, 1989, p. 1.
32. *Atlanta Journal and Constitution*, August 2, 1992, p. M1.
33. *American Heritage*, June 1970, p. 59.

CHAPTER 21   AMERICAN ENGLISH TODAY

1. *Washington Post*, March 28, 1993, p. A15.
2. Safire, *Safire's New Political Dictionary*, p. 590.
3. *Nation*, October 12, 1992, p. 405.
4. *U.S. News & World Report*, June 22, 1992, pp. 29–31.
5. Maggio, *The Dictionary of Bias-Free Usage: A Guide to Nondiscriminatory Language*, p. 17.
6. *New York Times*, April 5, 1987, p. 1.
7. Maggio, op. cit., p. 173.
8. Ibid., p. 112.
9. *Editor & Publisher*, March 6, 1993, p. 48.
10. *Atlantic Monthly*, November 1990, p. 84.
11. *New York Times*, January 21, 1992, p. C6.
12. *Atlantic Monthly*, August 1990, pp. 28–33.
13. Ibid., p. 28.
14. *Economist*, August 8, 1992, p. 41.
15. Ibid., January 18, 1992, p. 80.
16. *Atlantic Monthly*, November 1990, p. 87, and *Economist*, November 21, 1992, Education Survey, p. 7.
17. *Atlantic Monthly*, August 1990, p. 30.
18. Schor, *The Overworked American: The Unexpected Decline of Leisure*, p. 13.
19. *American Heritage*, May/June 1988, p. 10.
20. *Economist*, October 10, 1992, p. 63.
21. *New York Times*, August 28, 1990.
22. Daniels, *Famous Last Words: The American Language Crisis Reconsidered*, p. 118.
23. Ibid., p. 118.
24. *New York Times*, October 28, 1990.
25. Daniels, op. cit., pp. 123–24.
26. Quoted in Daniels, op. cit., p. 51.
27. Boorstin, *The Americans: The Democratic Experience*, pp. 454, 500.
28. Watson, *Experimental Studies in the Psychology and Pedagogy of Spelling*, pp. 25–26.
29. *Economist*, July 18, 1992, p. 49.

30. *New York Times*, July 26, 1992, p. E5.
31. *Economist*, January 18, 1992, p. 80.
32. *Education Digest*, May 1987.
33. *Economist*, January 18, 1992, p. 80.
34. Ibid., December 26, 1992, p. 58.

SELECT BIBLIOGRAPHY

Adams, Ramon F. *Western Words: A Dictionary of the American West.* Norman: University of Oklahoma Press, 1968.

Aldridge, Alfred Owen. *Benjamin Franklin and Nature's God.* Durham, N.C.: Duke University Press, 1967.

Allen, Frederick Lewis. *Only Yesterday: An Informal History of the 1920s.* New York: Perennial/Harper & Row, 1964.

————. *The Big Change: America Transforms Itself 1900–1950.* New York: Harper & Brothers, 1950.

Amis, Kingsley. *The Amis Collection: Selected Non-Fiction, 1954–1990.* London: Penguin, 1991.

Atwan, Robert, Donald McQuade, and John W. Wright. *Edsels, Luckies and Frigidaires: Advertising the American Way.* New York: Dell, 1979.

Bailey, Richard W. *Images of English: A Cultural History of the Language.* Ann Arbor: University of Michigan Press, 1991.

Bailey, Thomas A. *Voices of America: The Nation's Story in Slogans, Sayings and Songs.* New York: Free Press, 1976.

Balio, Tino, ed. *Hollywood in the Age of Television.* Boston: Unwin Hyman, 1990.

Barach, Arnold B. *Famous American Trademarks.* Washington: Public Affairs Press, 1971.

Barbour, Philip L., ed. *The Complete Works of Captain John Smith (1580–1631).* 3 vols. Chapel Hill: University of North Carolina Press, 1986.

Barfield, Owen. *History in English Words.* London: Faber & Faber, 1953.

Barnett, Walter. *Sexual Freedom and the Constitution: An Inquiry into the Constitutionality of Repressive Sex Laws.* Albuquerque: University of New Mexico Press, 1973.

Barnhart, David K. *New-Words: A Dictionary of the Newest and Most Unusual Words of Our Times.* New York: Collier Books/Macmillan, 1991.

Barnhart, Robert K., ed. *The Barnhart Dictionary of Etymology.* New York: H. W. Wilson, 1988.

————, Sol Steinmetz, Clarence L. Barnhart. *The Second Barnhart Dictionary of New English.* Bronxville, N.Y.: Barnhart/Harper & Row, 1980.

————, Sol Steinmetz, and Clarence L. Barnhart. *Third Barnhart Dictionary of New English*. New York: H. W. Wilson Co., 1989.

Bartlett, John Russell. *Dictionary of Americanisms: A Glossary of Words and Phrases Usually Regarded as Peculiar to the United States*. Boston: Little, Brown, 1859.

Baugh, Albert C., and Thomas Cable. *A History of the English Language*. 3rd ed. London: Routledge & Kegan Paul, 1978.

Beam, C. Richard. *Abridged Pennsylvania German Dictionary*. Kaiserslautern, Germany: Heimatstelle Pfalz, 1970.

————. *Pennsylvania German Dictionary: English to Pennsylvania Dutch*. Lancaster, Pa.: Brookshire Publications, 1985.

Beard, Henry, and Christopher Cerf. *The Official Politically Correct Dictionary and Handbook*. New York: Villard, 1993.

Beebe, Lucius. *The Big Spenders*. London: Hutchinson, 1966.

Benson, Thomas W., ed. *American Rhetoric: Context and Criticism*. Carbondale: Southern Illinois University Press, 1989.

Berg, A. Scott. *Goldwyn: A Biography*. New York: Ballantine, 1989.

Binford, Henry C. *The First Suburbs: Residential Communities on the Boston Periphery, 1815–1860*. Chicago: University of Chicago Press, 1985.

Blow, Robert, ed. *Abroad in America: Literary Discoverers of the New World from the Past 500 Years*. Oxford: Lennard Publishing, 1989.

Boorstin, Daniel. *The Americans: The Colonial Experience*. New York: Vintage/Random House, 1974.

————. *The Americans: The Democratic Experience*. New York: Vintage/Random House, 1974.

————. *The Americans: The National Experience*. New York: Vintage/Random House, 1974.

————. *Hidden History: Exploring Our Secret Past*. New York: Vintage/Random House, 1989.

Boyd, Julian P., ed. *The Papers of Thomas Jefferson*. 26 vols. Princeton, N.J.: Princeton University Press, 1950.

Brodie, Fawn M. *Thomas Jefferson: An Intimate History*. New York: W. W. Norton, 1974.

Brogan, Hugh. *The Penguin History of the United States of America*. London: Penguin, 1990.

Brooks, John. *Business Adventures*. London: Penguin, 1959.

Burnam, Tom. *The Dictionary of Misinformation*. New York: Ballantine, 1975.

Bursk, Edward C., Donald T. Clark, and Ralph W. Hidy, eds. *The World of Business*. 2 vols. New York: Simon & Schuster, 1962.

Caffrey, Kate. *The Mayflower*. London: Andre Deutsch, 1975.

Calder, Jenni. *There Must Be a Lone Ranger: The American West in Film and Reality*. New York: Taplinger, 1974.

Carr, William G. *The Oldest Delegate: Franklin in the Constitutional Convention*. Newark, Del.: University of Delaware Press, 1990.

Carruth, Gorton, and Eugene Ehrlich. *The Harper Book of American Quotations*. New York: Harper & Row, 1988.

Carver, Craig M. *A History of English in Its Own Words*. New York: HarperCollins, 1991.

Castleman, Harry, and Walter J. Podrazik. *Watching TV: Four Decades of American Television.* New York: McGraw-Hill, 1982.

Chubb, Michael, and Holly R. Chubb. *One Third of Our Time?: An Introduction to Recreation Behavior and Resources.* New York: Wiley, 1981.

Ciardi, John. *A Browser's Dictionary: A Compendium of Curious Expressions & Intriguing Facts.* New York: Harper & Row, 1980.

———. *Good Words to You: An All-New Dictionary and Native's Guide to the Unknown American Language.* New York: Harper & Row, 1987.

Clark, Gregory R. *Words of the Vietnam War.* Jefferson, N.C.: McFarland, 1990.

Clark, Ronald W. *Benjamin Franklin: A Biography.* New York: Random House, 1983.

Clark, Thomas D. *Frontier America.* New York: Scribner's, 1959.

Cleary, David Powers. *Great American Brands: The Success Formulas That Made Them Famous.* New York: Fairchild, 1981.

Cmiel, Kenneth. *Democratic Eloquence: The Fight over Popular Speech in Nineteenth-Century America.* New York: Morrow, 1990.

Cobbett, William. *A Years [sic] Residence in the United States of America.* New York: Augustus M. Kelley, 1969.

Collins, Douglas. *The Story of Kodak.* New York: Abrams, 1990.

Commager, Henry Steele. *The American Mind: An Interpretation of American Thought and Character Since the 1880s.* New Haven, Conn.: Yale University Press, 1950.

Cook, David A. *A History of Narrative Film.* New York: W.W. Norton, 1981.

Cooke, Alistair. *Alistair Cooke's America.* New York: Alfred A. Knopf, 1987.

Cottle, Basil. *Names.* London: Thames & Hudson, 1983.

Cowan, Ruth Schwartz. *More Work for Mother: The Ironies of Household Technology from the Open Hearth to the Microwave.* New York: Basic Books, 1983.

Craigie, Sir William A. *The Growth of American English.* Oxford: Oxford University Press, 1940.

———, and James R. Hulbert. *A Dictionary of American English on Historical Principles.* 4 vols. Chicago: University of Chicago Press, 1940.

Crane, Verner W. *Benjamin Franklin and a Rising People.* Boston: Little, Brown, 1954.

Cummings, Richard Osborn. *The American and His Food.* New York: Arno, 1974.

Cutright, Paul Russell. *Lewis and Clark: Pioneering Naturalists.* Urbana: University of Illinois Press, 1969.

Daniels, Harvey A. *Famous Last Words: The American Language Crisis Reconsidered.* Carbondale: Southern Illinois University Press, 1983.

Davidson, Marshall B. *Life in America.* 2 vols. Boston: Houghton Mifflin, 1974.

Deetz, James. *In Small Things Forgotten: The Archaeology of Early American Life.* New York: Anchor/Doubleday, 1977.

Deighton, Lee C. *A Comparative Study of Spellings in Four Major Collegiate Dictionaries.* Pleasantville, N.Y.: Hardscrabble Press, 1972.

Diamond, Sidney A. *Trademark Problems and How to Avoid Them.* Chicago: Crain Communications, 1973.

Dillard, J. L. *All-American English*. New York: Random House, 1975.

———. *American Talk: Where Our Words Come From*. New York: Vintage/ Random House, 1977.

Dillon, Richard. *Meriwether Lewis: A Biography.* New York: Coward-McCann, 1965.

Dohan, Mary Helen. *Our Own Words*. Baltimore: Penguin, 1974.

Dulles, Foster Rhea. *America Learns to Play: A History of Popular Recreation 1607–1940*. New York: Peter Smith, 1952.

Elias, Norbert. *The History of Manners*. 2 vols. New York: Pantheon, 1978.

Enterline, James Robert. *Viking America: The Norse Crossings and Their Legacy*. Garden City, N.Y.: Doubleday, 1972.

Erens, Patricia. *The Jew in American Cinema*. Bloomington: Indiana University Press, 1984.

Ernst, Morris L., and Alan U. Schwartz. *Censorship: The Search for the Obscene*. London: Collier-Macmillan, 1964.

Finch, Christopher. *Highways to Heaven: The Auto Biography of America*. New York: HarperCollins, 1992.

Fischer, David Hackett. *Albion's Seed: Four British Folkways in America*. New York: Oxford University Press, 1989.

Flatow, Ira. *They All Laughed . . . : From Light Bulbs to Lasers: The Fascinating Stories Behind the Great Inventions That Have Changed Our Lives*. HarperPerennial, New York, 1992.

Flexner, Stuart Berg. *I Hear America Talking: An Illustrated Treasury of American Words and Phrases*. New York: Van Nostrand Reinhold, 1976.

———. *Listening to America: An Illustrated History of Words and Phrases from Our Lively and Splendid Past*. New York: Simon & Schuster, 1982.

Foner, Eric. *Tom Paine and Revolutionary America*. New York: Oxford University Press, 1982.

Forbes, Esther. *Paul Revere and the World He Lived In*. Boston: Houghton Mifflin, 1942.

Friedel, Robert, and Paul Israel. *Edison's Electric Light: Biography of an Invention*. New Brunswick, N.J.: Rutgers University Press, 1986.

Frieden, Bernard J., and Lynne B. Sagalyn. *Downtown, Inc.: How America Rebuilds Cities*. Cambridge, Mass.: MIT Press, 1989.

Funk, Charles Earle. *A Hog on Ice and Other Curious Expressions*. New York: Harper & Brothers, 1948.

Funk, Wilfred. *Word Origins and Their Romantic Stories*. New York: Grosset & Dunlap, 1950.

Fussell, Paul. *Wartime: Understanding and Behavior in the Second World War*. New York: Oxford University Press, 1989.

Garrett, Elisabeth Donaghy. *At Home: The American Family: 1750–1870*. New York: Abrams, 1990.

Garrison, Webb B. *Why You Say It*. New York: Abingdon, 1955.

Gies, Joseph, and Frances Gies. *The Ingenious Yankees*. New York: Thomas Y. Crowell, 1976.

Glenn, Robert B., Stewart A. Kingsbury, and Zacharias P. Thundyil. *Language and Culture: A Book of Readings.* Marquette: Northern Michigan University Press, 1974.

Goetzmann, William H. *Exploration and Empire: The Explorer and the Scientist in the Winning of the American West.* New York: Norton, 1978.

Goldberger, Paul. *The Skyscraper.* New York: Knopf, 1981.

Gorn, Elliott J., and Warren Goldstein. *A Brief History of American Sports.* New York: Hill & Wang/Farrar, Straus & Giroux, 1993.

Gould, Stephen Jay. *Bully for Brontosaurus: Reflections in Natural History.* London: Hutchinson Radius, 1991.

Granger, Bruce Ingham. *Benjamin Franklin: An American Man of Letters.* Norman: University of Oklahoma Press, 1976.

Griffin, Bulkley S., ed. *Offbeat History: A Compendium of Lively Americana.* Cleveland: World Publishing, 1967.

Grosvenor, Melville Bell, ed.-in-chief. *Those Inventive Americans.* Washington, D.C.: National Geographic Society, 1971.

Grover, Kathryn, ed. *Dining in America: 1850–1900.* Amherst: University of Massachusetts Press, 1987.

Gruen, Victor, and Larry Smit. *Shopping Town USA: The Planning of Shopping Centers.* New York: Reinhold, 1960.

Harder, Kelsie B., ed. *Illustrated Dictionary of Place Names: United States and Canada.* New York: Van Nostrand Reinhold, 1976.

Harris, Marvin. *Good to Eat: Riddles of Food and Culture.* New York: Simon & Schuster, 1985.

Hart, Val. *The Story of American Roads.* New York: William Sloane Associates, 1950.

Hawke, David Freeman. *Paine.* New York: Harper & Row, 1974.

Heaton, Vernon. *The Mayflower.* Exeter, England: Webb & Bower, 1980.

Hemans, Felicia. *The Poetical Works of Mrs. Felicia Hemans.* Boston: Phillips, Sampson, 1857.

Hendon, Donald W. *Classic Failures in Product Marketing.* New York: Quorum Books, 1989.

Hendrickson, Robert. *The Facts on File Encyclopedia of Word and Phrase Origins.* New York: Facts on File, 1980.

Hibbert, Christopher. *The Court at Windsor: A Domestic History.* London: Penguin, 1982.

————. *Redcoats and Rebels: The War for America, 1770–1781.* London: Grafton, 1990.

Hokanson, Drake. *The Lincoln Highway: Main Street Across America.* Iowa City: University of Iowa Press, 1988.

Holt, Alfred H. *Phrase and Word Origins.* New York: Dover, 1961.

Hume, Ivor Noël. *Here Lies Virginia: An Archaeologist's View of Colonial Life and History.* New York: Knopf, 1963.

Hynd, Noel. *The Giants of the Polo Grounds: The Glorious Times of Baseball's New York Giants.* New York: Doubleday, 1988.

Ingstad, Helge. *The Norse Discovery of America.* 2 vols. Oslo: Norwegian University Press, 1985.

Jackson, Donald. *Among the Sleeping Giants: Occasional Pieces on Lewis and Clark.* Urbana: University of Illinois Press, 1987.

Jackson, Kenneth T. *Crabgrass Frontier: The Suburbanization of the United States.* New York: Oxford University Press, 1985.

James, Sydney V. *Colonial Rhode Island: A History.* New York: Scribner's, 1975.

Johnson, Paul. *Modern Times: The World from the Twenties to the Eighties.* New York: Harper & Row, 1983.

————. *The Birth of the Modern: World Society 1815–1830.* New York: HarperCollins, 1991.

Jones, Maldwyn Allen. *American Immigration.* Chicago: University of Chicago Press, 1960.

Jordan, Phillip D. *The National Road.* Indianapolis: Bobbs-Merril, 1948.

Josephy, Alvin M., Jr., ed.-in-charge. *The American Heritage Book of Indians.* Boston: American Heritage, 1961.

Jowett, Garth. *Film: The Democratic Art.* Boston: Little, Brown, 1976.

Keeley, Joseph C. *Making Inventions Pay: A Practical Guide to Selling, Protecting, Manufacturing, and Marketing Your Inventions.* New York: McGraw-Hill, 1950.

Kowinski, William Severini. *The Malling of America: An Inside Look at the Great Consumer Paradise.* New York: Morrow, 1985.

Krapp, George Philip. *The English Language in America.* 2 vols. New York: Century, 1925.

Kroc, Ray, with Robert Anderson. *Grinding It Out: The Making of McDonald's.* Chicago: Contemporary Books, 1977.

Krout, John Allen. *Annals of American Sport.* New Haven: Yale University Press, 1929.

Lacey, Robert. *Sir Walter Raleigh.* London: Weidenfeld & Nicolson, 1973.

————. *Ford: The Men and the Machine.* Boston: Little, Brown, 1986.

Laird, Charlton. *Language in America.* New York: World, 1970.

Levenstein, Harvey A. *Revolution at the Table: The Transformation of the American Diet.* New York: Oxford University Press, 1988.

Levin, David. *Cotton Mather: The Young Life of the Lord's Remembrancer, 1663–1703.* Cambridge, Mass.: Harvard University Press, 1978.

Liebs, Chester H. *Main Street to Miracle Mile: American Roadside Architecture.* Boston: New York Graphic Society/Little, Brown, 1985.

Lingeman, Richard R. *Don't You Know There's a War On?: The American Home Front 1941–45.* New York: Putnam's, 1970.

Love, John F. *McDonald's: Behind the Arches.* Toronto: Bantam, 1986.

Lowance, Mason I., Jr. *Increase Mather.* New York: Twayne, 1974.

Lutz, William. *Doublespeak.* New York: Harper & Row, 1989.

Luxenberg, Stan. *Roadside Empires: How the Chains Franchised America.* New York: Viking, 1985.

Madison, James, Alexander Hamilton, and John Jay. *The Federalist Papers.* Ed. Isaac Kramnick. London: Penguin, 1987.

Maggio, Rosalie. *The Dictionary of Bias-Free Usage: A Guide to Nondiscriminatory Language.* Phoenix: Oryx Press, 1991.

Marckwardt, Albert H. *American English*. Rev. by J. L. Dillard. 2nd ed. New York: Oxford University Press, 1980.

Martineau, Harriet. *Society in America*. 3 vols. London: Saunders & Otley, 1837.

Mathews, Mitford M., ed. *A Dictionary of Americanisms on Historical Principles*. 4 vols. Chicago: University of Chicago Press, 1951.

McAlister, Lyle N. *Spain and Portugal in the New World, 1492–1700*. Minneapolis: University of Minnesota Press, 1984.

McDavid, Raven I., Jr. *Varieties of American English*. Stanford: Stanford University Press, 1980.

McPherson, James M. *Battle Cry of Freedom: The American Civil War*. London: Penguin/Oxford University Press, 1990.

Mee, Charles L., Jr. *The Genius of the People*. New York: Perennial Library/ Harper & Row, 1988.

Mencken, H. L. *The American Language: An Inquiry into the Development of English in the United States*. 4th ed. New York: A. Knopf, 1937.

————. *The American Language: An Inquiry into the Development of English in the United States, Supplement I*. New York: Knopf, 1945.

————. *The American Language: An Inquiry into the Development of English in the United States, Supplement II*. New York: Knopf, 1948.

————. *The American Language: An Inquiry into the Development of English in the United States*. The Fourth Edition and the Two Supplements, Abridged. Ed. and with new material by Raven I. McDavid, Jr. New York: Knopf, 1989.

Meyer, Jerome S. *World Book of Great Inventions*. Cleveland: World, 1956.

Milton, Joyce. *Loss of Eden: A Biography of Charles and Anne Morrow Lindbergh*. New York: HarperCollins, 1993.

Moolman, Valerie. *The Road to Kitty Hawk*. Alexandria, Va.: Time-Life Books, 1980.

Morison, Samuel Eliot. *The Oxford History of the American People*, New York: Oxford University Press, 1965.

————. *The European Discovery of America*. 2 vols. New York: Oxford University Press, 1971.

Morris, William, and Mary Morris. *Morris Dictionary of Word and Phrase Origins*. 2nd ed. New York: Harper & Row, 1971,

Moulton, Gary E., ed. *Atlas of the Lewis and Clark Expedition*. Lincoln: University of Nebraska Press, 1983.

————, ed. *The Journals of the Lewis & Clark Expedition: August 30, 1803–August 24, 1804*. Lincoln: University of Nebraska Press, 1986.

Nye, David E. *Electrifying America: Social Meanings of a New Technology, 1880–1940*. Cambridge, Mass.: MIT Press, 1990.

Oakley, J. Ronald. *God's Country: America in the Fifties*. New York: Dembner, 1986.

O'Malley, Michael. *Keeping Watch: A History of American Time*. New York: Viking Penguin, 1990.

Opie, Iona, and Peter Opie. *The Oxford Dictionary of Nursery Rhymes*. Oxford: Clarendon Press, 1951.

Partridge, Eric, and John W. Clark. *British and American English Since 1900*. London: Andrew Dakers, 1951.

Patton, Phil. *Open Road: A Celebration of the American Highway*. New York: Simon & Schuster, 1986.

Peirce, Neal R. *The New England States*. New York: W. W. Norton, 1976.

Petroski, Henry. *The Evolution of Useful Things*. New York: Vintage/Random House, 1994.

Pound, Reginald. *Selfridge: A Biography*. London: Heinemann, 1960.

Pyles, Thomas. *Words and Ways of American English*. New York: Random House, 1952.

————. *Selected Essays on English Usage*. Gainesville: University Presses of Florida, 1979.

Quinn, David Beers. *Set Fair for Roanoke: Voyages and Colonies, 1584–1606*. Chapel Hill: University of North Carolina Press, 1984.

————. *North American from Earliest Discovery to First Settlements*. New York: Harper & Row, 1985.

Rae, John B. *The Road and the Car in American Life*. Cambridge, Mass.: MIT Press, 1971.

Rodgers, Elizabeth G. *Chagrin . . . Whence the Name?* Chagrin Falls, Ohio: published privately, 1988.

Root, Waverley, and Richard de Rochement. *Eating in America: A History*. New York: Morrow, 1976.

Rosenberg, Bernard, and David Manning White, eds. *Mass Culture: The Popular Arts in America*. Glencoe, Ill.: Free Press, 1957.

Rowsome, Frank, Jr. *The Verse by the Side of the Road: The Story of the Burma-Shave Signs*. Brattleboro, Vt.: Stephen Greene, 1965.

Rybczynski, Witold. *Home: A Short History of an Idea*. New York: Penguin, 1987.

————. *Waiting for the Weekend*. New York: Viking, 1991.

Safire, William. *On Language*. New York: Avon, 1980.

————. *What's the Good Word?* New York: Times Books, 1982.

————. *Take My Word for It*. New York: Times Books, 1986.

————. *Coming to Terms*. New York: Doubleday, 1991.

————. *Safire's New Political Dictionary: The Definitive Guide to the New Language of Politics*. New York: Random House, 1993.

Sagarin, Edward. *The Anatomy of Dirty Words*. New York: Lyle Stuart, 1968.

Savage, William W., Jr., ed. *Cowboy Life: Reconstructing an American Myth*. Norman: University of Oklahoma Press, 1975.

Schiller, Herbert I. *Mass Communications and American Empire*. New York: Augustus M. Kelley, 1969.

Schor, Juliet B. *The Overworked American: The Unexpected Decline of Leisure*. New York: Basic Books, 1991.

Schrank, Jeffrey. *Snap, Crackle, and Popular Taste: The Illusion of Free Choice in America*. New York: Delacorte, 1977.

Schumach, Murray. *The Face on the Cutting Room Floor: The Story of Movie and Television Censorship*. New York: Morrow, 1964.

Schwarz, Barry. *George Washington: The Making of an American Symbol*. Ithaca, N.Y.: Cornell University Press, 1987.

Seavey, Ormond. *Becoming Benjamin Franklin: The Autobiography and the Life*. University Park: Pennsylvania State University Press, 1988.

Shearer, Benjamin F., and Barbara S. Shearer. *State Names, Seals, Flags, and Symbols: A Historical Guide*. New York: Greenwood, 1987.

Simpson, David. *The Politics of American English, 1776–1850*. New York: Oxford University Press, 1986.

Small, Herbert. *The Library of Congress: Its Architecture and Decoration*. New York: Arthur Ross/W. W. Norton, 1982.

Smelser, Marshall. *The Life That Ruth Built: A Biography*. Lincoln: University of Nebraska Press, 1975.

Smith, Elsdon C. *The Story of Our Names*. New York: Harper & Brothers, 1950.

Smith, Page. *A People's History of the United States*. 8 vols. New York: McGraw-Hill, 1984.

Smitherman, Geneva. *Black Talk: Words and Phrases from the Hood to the Amen Corner*. Boston: Houghton Mifflin, 1994.

Sperber, Hans, and Travis Trittschuh. *American Political Terms: An Historical Dictionary*. Detroit: Wayne State University Press, 1962.

Stedman, Raymond William. *Shadows of the Indian: Stereotypes in American Culture*. Norman: University of Oklahoma Press, 1982.

Sterling, Christopher H., and Jon M. Kittross. *Stay Tuned: A Concise History of American Broadcasting*. Belmont, Calif.: Wadsworth, 1978.

Stewart, George R. *Names on the Land: A Historical Account of Place-Naming in the United States*. New York: Random House, 1945.

———. *American Place-Names: A Concise and Selective Dictionary for the Continental United States of America*. New York: Oxford University Press, 1970.

Story, G. M., W. J. Kirwin, and J.D.A. Widdowson, eds. *Dictionary of Newfoundland English*. 2nd ed. Toronto: University of Toronto Press, 1990.

Strasser, Susan. *Never Done: A History of American Housework*. New York: Pantheon, 1982.

———. *Satisfaction Guaranteed: The Making of the American Mass Market*. New York: Pantheon, 1989.

Sullivan, Mark. *Our Times: The United States 1900–1925*. 2 vols. New York: Scribner's, 1926.

Takaki, Ronald. *A Different Mirror: A History of Multicultural America*. Boston: Back Bay Books/Little, Brown, 1993.

Tannahill, Reay. *Sex in History*. London: Abacus/Sphere, 1981.

Tedlow, Richard S. *New and Improved: The Story of Mass Marketing in America*. New York: Basic Books, 1990.

Terrace, Vincent. *The Complete Encyclopedia of Television Programs 1947–1976*. 2 vols. South Brunswick, N.J.: Barnes, 1976.

Thomas, Benjamin P. *Abraham Lincoln: A Biography*. New York: Modern Library, 1968.

Thomas, Charles Kenneth. *An Introduction to the Phonetics of American English*. New York: Ronald, 1947.

Thornton, Willis. *History: Fact and Fable*. New York: Barnes & Noble, 1993.

Tocqueville, Alexis de. *Journey to America*. Trans. George Lawrence. Garden City, N.Y.: Anchor/Doubleday, 1971.

Trollope, Frances. *Domestic Manners of the Americans*. New York: Knopf, 1949.

Tulloch, Sarah. *The Oxford Dictionary of New Words: A Popular Guide to Words in the News*. Oxford: Oxford University Press, 1991.

Udelson, Joseph H. *The Great Television Race: A History of the American Television Industry 1925–1941*. University: University of Alabama Press, 1982.

Vallins, G. H. *Spelling*. London: Andre Deutsch, 1954.

Van Doren, Carl. *Benjamin Franklin*. New York: Viking, 1938.

———. *The Great Rehearsal: The Story of the Making and Ratifying of the Constitution of the United States*. New York: Viking, 1948.

Vieyra, Daniel I. *Fill 'er Up: An Architectural History of America's Gas Stations*. New York: Macmillan, 1979.

Voigt, David Quentin. *American Baseball: From Gentleman's Sport to the Commissioner System*. University Park: Pennsylvania State University Press, 1983.

Wagenknecht, Edward. *Henry Wadsworth Longfellow: His Poetry and Prose*. New York: Ungar, 1986.

Ward, Sir A. W., ed. *The Cambridge History of English Literature*, Vol. 14. New York: Macmillan, 1931.

Warren, Louis A. *Lincoln's Gettysburg Declaration*. Fort Wayne, Ind.: Lincoln National Life Foundation, 1964.

Watson, Alice E. *Experimental Studies in the Psychology and Pedagogy of Spelling*. New York: Teachers College/Columbia University, 1935.

Well, J. C., *Accents of English: Beyond the British Isles*. Cambridge: Cambridge University Press, 1982.

Weston, Jack. *The Real American Cowboy*. New York: Schocken, 1985.

Will, George F. *Men at Work: The Craft of Baseball*. New York: HarperPerennial, 1991.

Willcox, William B., ed. *The Papers of Benjamin Franklin*. New Haven, Conn.: Yale University Press, 1972.

Wills, Garry. *Inventing America: Jefferson's Declaration of Independence*. Garden City, N.Y.: Doubleday, 1978.

———. *Lincoln at Gettysburg: The Words That Remade America*. New York: Touchstone/Simon & Schuster, 1992.

Wortham, Thomas. *James Russell Lowell's "The Biglow Papers": A Critical Edition*. DeKalb: Northern Illinois University Press, 1977.

Wright, Esmond. *Franklin of Philadelphia*. Cambridge, Mass.: Belknap Press/Harvard University Press, 1986.

Wright, Frances. *Views of Society and Manners in America*. Cambridge, Mass.: Belknap Press/Harvard University Press, 1963.

Wyllie Irvin G. *The Self-Made Man in America: The Myth of Rags of Riches*. New York: Free Press, 1954.

Zinn, Howard. *A People's History of the United States*. New York: HarperPerennial, 1990.

INDEX

A&P, 211–212
Abbott, Anne, 270
ABC of Nutrition, The (Fletcher), 192
Absorbine Jr., 240
acronyms, military, 299–300, 302
Adams, Abigail, 127
Adams, John, 33, 34, 35, 45, 53
  in Continental Congress, 44
  Declaration of Independence and, 40, 46
  as Vice-President, 59
  in White House, 293
Adams, John Quincy, 77, 221
Adams, Samuel, 33, 158
Adventures of Robin Hood, The, 256
advertise, to, 237
advertiser, 237
advertising, 235–247
  anxiety and, 239–240
  on billboards, 237
  electric signs in, 224–225
  giveaways in, 238
  illiteracy in, 241, 246
  to mass markets, 236–237
  of miracle cures, 240
  multicultural, 247
  product names and, 241–245
  on radio, 245
  slogans in, 237–238, 240
  on television, 229, 230, 244–247
  truth in, 246–247
advertising agency, 237
Affluent Society, The (Galbraith), 335
Africa, expressions from, 153–155
African-Americans, *see* blacks

Africanisms in the Gullah Dialect (Turner), 153
AIDS, 350
air brakes, 96*n*
air conditioner, 232
air conditioners, 83, 94–95, 231–232
airplanes, *see* aviation
air shafts, 137
Albion's Seed (Fischer), 36–37
Alcock, John, 329
Alcott, A. Bronson, 311–312
Alcott, William, 310
Algonquian, 4, 22
Allen, Frederick Lewis, 202
alligator, 132
almighty dollar, 85
Alsop, Joseph, 301
alternating current, 95–96
America:
  colonists in, 1–5
  as eastern states only, 124–125
  European explorers in, 5–12
  naming of, 9
  regional identities in, 36–37
  see also New World; United States
American, Americans, 29, 35
American Cookery (Simmons), 184
American Democrat, The (Cooper), 75
Americanisms, 75–76, 84
American Language, The (Mencken), 281*n*
American Notes (Dickens), 74, 75, 219, 220
American Restaurant, 337
American Telephone and Telegraph, 92
amusement parks, 163

★ 395 ★

420   4/97

Bryson, Bill

Made in America

DATE DUE

DEMCO